910.452 Rousmaniere, John.
ROU
After the storm.

10/02

AFTER THE STORM

Also by John Rousmaniere

The Annapolis Book of Seamanship
Desirable and Undesirable Characteristics of Offshore Yachts (editor)
Fastnet, Force 10
The Golden Pastime: A New History of Yachting
The Low Black Schooner: Yacht America, 1851–1945

AFTER THE STORM

TRUE STORIES OF DISASTER AND RECOVERY AT SEA

JOHN ROUSMANIERE

International Marine / McGraw-Hill

Camden, Maine · New York · Chicago · San Francisco · Lisbon
London · Madrid · Mexico City · Milan · New Delhi · San Juan
Seoul · Singapore · Sydney · Toronto

International Marine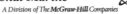
A Division of The McGraw-Hill Companies

2 4 6 8 10 9 7 5 3 1
First Edition
Copyright © 2002 John Rousmaniere
All rights reserved. The name "International Marine" and the International
Marine logo are trademarks of The McGraw-Hill Companies.
Printed in the United States of America.

Library of Congress Cataloging-in-Publication Data

Rousmaniere, John.
    After the storm : true stories of disaster and recovery at sea /
    John Rousmaniere.
        p.   cm.
    Includes bibliographical references (p.   ) and index.
    ISBN 0-07-137795-6 (hardcover : alk. paper)
        1. Shipwrecks. I. Title.
G525 .R779 2002
910.4′52—dc21   2001008576

This book is printed on 55# Sebago by R. R. Donnelley
Design by Dennis Anderson
Page layout by Shannon Swanson, Olive Juice Designs
Map illustrations by Susan Carlson
Chapter opening photo by Getty Images/Stone
Production management by Janet Robbins
Edited by Jonathan Eaton and Alice M. Bennett

Revised Standard Version of the Bible, copyright © 1952 (2nd ed., 1971) by the Division of
Christian Education of the National Council of the Churches of Christ in the United
States of America. Used by permission. All rights reserved.

To Leah
"Let me now go to the field"

Contents

INTRODUCTION

FEW EVENTS CAN THRASH A LIFE—or glorify it—as effectively as a storm at sea. It is a chaotic thing, as indifferent to normal order as a war. A few extraordinary souls like it that way. Beryl Smeeton, one of the storm warriors who appear in these pages, was twice almost killed near Cape Horn, yet welcomed "a feeling of exhilaration, a feeling of battle" that came upon her during a fight for survival. Most people, however, are less enchanted by terrible weather. We will meet both types in these linked stories of the timeless human struggle with storms and their consequences, as gale forces explode out many miles and down many years to alter lives and communities. The storms that arise here range through much of human history, from Mediterranean gales of biblical times to recent Cape Horn blows reported via e-mail by awestruck racing sailors. Twelve storms are described at length—eight gales, two hurricanes, one waterspout, and the black squall that ended a poet's romance with the sea.

While some of these storms are connected by history or geography, all dozen share three features. First, each makes clear that storms are equal-opportunity oppressors that do not care at all whether a mariner goes to sea to catch fish or search for God, carry cargo or seek adventure, win a war or win a race. Whether their interest is in striving against the sea for financial gain, or in floating upon it sweetly, all may go out there as long as they are properly respectful of its powers and prepared for its whims. Just as no one is privileged, no one is invulnerable.

Second, storms change lives, reputations, and history, sometimes with brutal directness but often slowly and paradoxically. A blizzard on Massachusetts Bay makes an instant villain of a steamboat captain but instant heroes of the weathermen who failed to forecast it. A hurricane in the Western Pacific stops a war but triggers an arms race that leads to a greater conflict. An accident in the North Atlantic wipes out most of a family in twenty minutes but inspires its only survivor to publish a book that consoles other mourners. One storm off Newfoundland causes a survivor to write the soulful hymn "Amazing Grace"; almost two hundred years later, another turns a self-described "tough kid" into a teacher of tolerance.

A storm's story, therefore, is more than a simple thrilling account of heroism or tragedy in a hard blow. A storm at sea cannot be defined by any single measure, if it can be defined at all. These chapters tell of the forces that propelled the sailors into the storm's path. They lay out the sailors' qualities, the ship's vulnerabilities, and the spar- and soul-rattling stresses imposed by weather and seas. There is the looming power of accident, for at sea, contingency shoots random holes into the best-laid plans. A storm's story does not end as the blow itself moves on. Every storm has elements that scar sailors, their families, their communities, and history. "There are more consequences to a shipwreck than the underwriters notice," mused Henry David Thoreau as he paced the wreck-strewn beaches of Cape Cod. If the narrow dollars-and-cents calculations of insurance adjustors tell only a small part about a storm, so also does a narrow narrative.

I can testify that storms change lives because one changed mine. When a gale of wintry power assaulted our boat (and three hundred competitors) while we were racing near England in August 1979, I experienced the same wild mix of contradictory emotions that prevailed in the crew of the *Pollux* in chapter 7. There was the same messy mix of giddy exhilaration, placid spiritual contentment, cold can-do purposefulness, and a conviction that this sixty-knot gale with its forty-foot waves imposed no threat whatso-ever to my life. A different perspective on the Fastnet storm appeared when we reached the harbor. On a wharf jutting out from the shore, a crowd of agitated, grim-faced women and men stared out to sea, much like the des-perate wives and fathers in chapter 3. Not having been out in the storm, these shore people were not inclined to romanticize it. All they knew was that it had sunk five boats and killed fifteen sailors.

Though profoundly moving, their fear seemed remote. Like many sur-vivors of disasters, I felt privy to special knowledge. In Rafael Yglesias's novel *Fearless*, a survivor of a plane crash feels like a different order of human than his friends and family. He is, he decides, "no longer like them." When I told the woman I was seeing at the time how enthralling the storm experience had been, her reaction was abrupt and puzzling. "I hung around the telephone for three days with tears in my eyes worrying that you were dead, *and you were out there having a good time?*" My denial—my sedative against anger and fear—wore off as I wrote a book about the storm, and my repressed vulnerability surfaced as I interviewed survivors of appalling incidents. I survived the ensuing feelings of chaos thanks to the love of my family, a caring therapist, and the regimen of raising my two boys as a single father while earning a living. In time there bubbled up a new religious life, which I grounded in four years of study at a theological seminary where I earned a divinity degree and met my wife.

Every storm story here, therefore, blows across a broad natural and human canvas. Each also nurtures or challenges belief. The natural human quest for meaning burrows deep into any storm. Many characters in these pages believe in God, and in many forms. "Old sailors may have odd ways of showing their religious feelings," Joshua Slocum observed, "but there are no infidels at sea." Many storm survivors call on their faith. Others create myths that help them through chaos with a sense of order and pride. Although some of those myths (like the many explanations for the abandonment of the ghost ship *Mary Celeste*) are bizarre, even hilarious, they make sense in their own way in the moment. With some mariners, these myths take the form of strange superstitions that seem like a laundry list of flakiness: rabbits encountered on footpaths or black bears seen dancing in the rigging foretell disaster; ships must not sail on Friday; sailors must not whistle for wind or eat bananas. But faith also can be mundane, and even like idolatry. In chapter 2, the captain of the *Elizabeth*, carrying home the gifted Margaret Fuller, stakes all on a lighthouse and is proved disastrously wrong.

And then there are the human beliefs about the sea itself. No physical entity has inspired such hate, and such love. While the wind has usually been considered good—in the Bible, the same Hebrew and Greek words mean both "wind" and "divine spirit"—for millennia the sea was feared as the home of chaos, evil, and despair. At the far other end of belief stands the modern notion that the sea is an enchanted preserver of life. One enthusiastic romantic went so far as to call it "our great green mother." In fact, a healthy relationship with the sea moves between the extremes of floating gently upon it and striving fiercely against it. In any case it must never be taken for granted. In every storm I have sailed through, there was at least one moment when I took a break from the ruthless disciplines of seamanship, looked around, and reflected, "How lovely!" In one gale in the Gulf Stream, rows of crisp white-crowned waves formed a picturesque seascape of dynamic beauty, until one of those lovelies threw the boat over on her side and hurled a shipmate across the cabin, smashing his ribs.

Of all the beliefs of the men and women in these pages, not the least important is faith in the power of personal connection to steer people through disaster. In the chaos of any storm (whether at sea or on land), the norm at first seems to be alienation, not human contact. "This is the disintegrating power of a great wind: it isolates one from one's kind," Joseph Conrad observed in *Typhoon*. Conrad's long experience at sea also taught him that most men and women struggle against this alienating power. "It is, after all, the human voice that stamps the mark of human consciousness upon the character of a gale."

When I began work on this book in August 2000, that voice was well known to me through my experience in storms and other crises. Sampling the literature of post-traumatic stress disorder, I found that psychologists also see the desire for social connection as a sign of mental health in crisis, even when that crisis involves a struggle for personal survival. The surprise for me, as I wrote these chapters, was the diverse ways in which most people on the tiny island of a vessel at sea affirm their humanity despite appalling conditions. This is so even among the fabled "iron men in wooden ships" aboard fishing and trading ships. A word said or a hand reaching out at the right moment may make all the difference.

Repeatedly in these stories, people caught in the most desperate moments search for human connection—in a heroic attempt at rescue, a show of sympathy, a timely command, a symbolic act of good cheer, or in an event as simple as the offer of a cigarette.

In September 2001, as I was writing the last two chapters, the most terrible storm came upon us in acts of fascistic terrorism that killed thousands, including a former shipmate of mine. The human connection briefly seemed remote, but after that dreadful tempest the familiar struggle for connection stirred and asserted itself. There is no reason to doubt the fundamental belief that a good life is connected not only to God and nature and the sea, but also to other lives.

A PROCEDURAL NOTE: No quote in this book is invented, but a few storm narratives are necessarily conjectural (and clearly identified as such). Although this is not a manual on seamanship, some technical material is included to lay out the crew's options and place the stories in historical context. Storm seamanship is covered in more detail in the appendix, where there is also a short glossary. I have tried to keep technical terminology to a minimum, for example, by using "storm," "gale," and "hard blow" synonymously, not according to their definitions in the Beaufort Scale of Wind Forces. (The 1889 storm at Samoa is described as a "hurricane" because that was what it was called at the time.) I follow the convention of placing "the" before the names of commercial and naval vessels and withholding the article in the names of pleasure boats. Quotes from the Bible are from the Revised Standard Version.

JOHN ROUSMANIERE
MARCH 2002

1

Ariel and Percy Bysshe Shelley

Italy, 1822

"We drive along this delightful bay in the evening wind under the summer moon until earth appears another world."

—Percy Bysshe Shelley

"THE DEVIL IS BREWING MISCHIEF," muttered a sailor, staring out at the sea from his safe perch on a boat moored in the harbor. Out there, over the Mediterranean, layers of black clouds poured across the sky. As the fishermen felt the first blasts of the storm and scrambled to reef their sails, a sailor glanced up and watched in amazement as a strange little schooner—part yacht, part miniature warship—smashed wildly through the waves. The heavy spray flying out from her plunging bow glowed orange in the late afternoon sunlight that reflected off the tumid under-bodies of the thunderheads.

This odd boat was sailing far too fast. The fisherman shouted to the yachtsmen to shorten sail. Somebody shinnied up the schooner's main-mast and clawed at the topsail, while on deck two men gestured uselessly as the boat, barely in control, continued to charge north into the rain squalls and lightning.

Muttering about crazy yachtsmen, the fisherman turned his boat's stern to the gale and scudded south toward Leghorn, keeping his eye on the schooner. Her hull disappeared in the trough of a wave, bobbed up, disappeared again, rose lethargically—and vanished. Days later, after her poet-owner's body was recovered on a beach, his friends did what they could to give him a Homeric cremation.

Percy Bysshe Shelley had built his dream boat in his dream country and sailed her into a storm whose violence far outmatched not only his limited seamanship but his lifelong romance with what he called the "eloquence in the tongueless wind." The young English exile with eyes described as "large and animated, with a dash of wildness" is best known for his romantic poetry. "Ozymandias" is a democrat's vision of the "colossal wreck" of empires, "To a Skylark" ("Hail to thee, blithe Spirit! / Bird thou never wert") is a favorite of lovers and schoolteachers, and in other poems he appealed to a nature far more gentle and protective in abstract theory than the real, violent nature he encountered on that fierce July day in 1822. Shelley is the archetypal sweet-tempered rebel against all conventions hinting of violence. As a lively, tender-hearted boy, he protested against his ferocious father, against schoolboy bullying, against authoritarian institutions of every shape and size, and against every traditional belief and superstition he could confront, including the ancient fear of the sea. Before he turned twenty he proclaimed himself a "democrat, great lover of mankind, and atheist." To that list he later added political radical, visionary, vegetarian, linguist, moody genius, and utopian. "The good time will come," read the inscription on his ring. Shelley was convinced that because "poetry turns all things to loveliness," poets should be made kings and rule the world.

He also advocated free love, which was why he was an exile in Italy. He first eloped with a sixteen-year-old girl, then abandoned her before running off with another teenager, Mary Godwin, whom he eventually married after his first wife's death. Mary was the illegitimate daughter of one of the first feminists, Mary Wollstonecraft, and the idealist William Godwin, whose optimism matched his son-in-law's. "What the heart of man is able to conceive," Godwin declared, "the hand of man is strong enough to perform." No less brilliant than her husband, Mary Wollstonecraft Shelley at nineteen responded to a challenge to write a ghost story by turning out a tale about a utopian scientist named Frankenstein and the creature he constructs, who is destroyed in large part by loneliness. Perhaps that was a parable for her relationship with Shelley, who scorched his candle at both ends as they and his friend and fellow poet George Gordon, Lord Byron, drifted around Europe in a movable commune. Mary suffered through it all, enduring six pregnancies, all but one of them ending in a miscarriage or the baby's death.

In the spring of 1822 she was pregnant again. Shelley was exhausted, cynical, and interested only in escaping to the seaside. He took her and their young son, their only surviving child, to Spezia, a fishing village on Italy's Bay of Lerici. With their friends Edward and Jane Williams and their children, they squeezed into a damp boathouse with salt-speckled windows and a ground floor that was flooded at high tide. Mary was furious. She later complained, "Had we been wrecked on an island in the South Seas, we could scarcely have felt ourselves farther from civilization and comfort." It did not help that her husband was depressed and also flirting with Jane Williams. The one solace was his love of the sea and his strange little schooner, *Ariel*, in which he and Mary drifted about the bay in the light winds that usually prevailed that summer.

"I WOULD RETIRE with you and our child to a solitary island in the sea," Shelley told Mary, "would build a boat, and shut upon my retreat the floodgates of the world." His vision of the sea as a benign region in which to float safely ran contrary to the usual apprehension of a fearsome place populated by monsters poised to strike men and women who ventured out from orderly land. Such fears seemed to him irrational. For Shelley, salt water and boats offered sanctuary from the worst monsters of them all— the family and institutions that oppressed him on shore. Although he sometimes expressed a mystical, part suicidal desire to merge with the ocean, his passion was to sail upon it. His obsession with the sea began

His eyes "large and animated, with a dash of wildness," Percy Bysshe Shelley was twenty-seven when he sat for this portrait by Amelia Curran. (Courtesy National Portrait Gallery, London)

during his unhappy childhood, when he sought in boats an escape from a miserable life on land. From sketching sailboats and making paper models, he graduated to being taken out in them. Boats were a true passion for him. Concerned with his emotional connection and the picturesque views that sailing offered, he made little effort to master the rudimentary arts and technology of seamanship, or even to learn how to swim. Inland in Italy, Williams built a small boat in which the two friends sailed the river Arno, Williams at the helm and Shelley as passenger. One day the boat capsized and Shelley sank to the river bottom. Williams had to haul him up by his hair.

That experience did not deter Shelley. Early in 1822, at one of their riotous parties, Shelley and Byron were persuaded by the writer Edward John Trelawny, a disreputable character, that what they needed and deserved were yachts. The wealthier Byron commissioned a large three-masted square-rigger that he named *Bolivar* after the Latin American revolutionary. Shelley ordered a smaller, two-masted, fore-and-aft rigged schooner that he planned to call *Ariel*, honoring Shakespeare's sprite. Trelawny, at the remote shipyard where the vessel was under construction, took it upon himself to name the boat *Don Juan* after the cynical seducer in one of Byron's poems. When Shelley saw this name and not his own choice painted in large letters across the mainsail, he cursed "my poor boat's infamy" and spent days trying to remove it with turpentine. He finally had the whole panel of cloth cut out and replaced. Then Shelley went sailing.

By June he and Mary were regularly on the Bay of Lerici. Although she complained of that "night of gaiety and thoughtlessness" when he impulsively committed much needed household funds to buy the yacht, she delighted in sailing with him. They went along on a wavering course, he steering absentmindedly, with one hand on the tiller and the other holding the book he was reading. Mary would remember in her mourning how, "lying down with my head on his knee, I shut my eyes and felt the wind and our swift motion alone."

I

"WE DRIVE ALONG this delightful bay in the evening wind under the summer moon until earth appears another world," Shelley wrote of a day on the Bay of Lerici. In that lyrical sentence lies the essence of the romantic escape to that old terror, salt water.

Of the first English yachtsman, King Charles II, his friend Samuel Pepys said that "two leagues travel at sea was more pleasure to him than twenty by land." The king had fled in a boat from the Puritan Roundheads who overthrew his father in 1644 and later beheaded him. After his restoration to the throne in 1660, Charles found escape from troublesome court and religious disputes (of the sort that had cost his father his head) in the yacht the Dutch gave him as a blatant bribe to forestall war. The vessel so delighted Charles that he built more than twenty yachts for himself, his mistresses, and his family. (The word "yacht," a handsome pleasure vessel, is derived from the Dutch adjective *jaght*, meaning "quick." A *jaght schippe* was a fast, smallish ship.) Also fleeing sectarian battles on a yacht's deck was Charles's contemporary Roger North, who wrote lyrically of a rewarding sailing day when he "sat out eight whole hours and scarce knew what time it was. For the day proved cool, the gale brisk, the air clear, and no inconvenience to molest us, nor wants to trouble our thoughts, neither business to importune, nor formalities to tease us; so that we came nearer perfection of life than I ever was sensible of otherwise."

Shelley might have written something like that, but unlike North and King Charles he had no interest in seamanship. Whereas Charles, as Pepys observed, "possessed a transcendent mastery of all maritime knowledge," Shelley was pleased to be ignorant of sailing skills. "Shelley enjoyed nothing better than simply drifting wherever the boat would take him," writes one of his biographers, A. B. C. Whipple, himself a sailor. "He hated the interruption of having to handle oars or sails." When at the helm, he pulled a book from the small cabin, whose sole purpose seems to have been to protect a bulging bookcase from the elements, and became so distracted that the sails were left to luff as *Ariel* yawed about. Shelley's relationship with the water was founded wholly on an enchanted identification with nature, which he believed to be generally nurturing. He began his poem "Alastor, or The Spirit of Solitude" with a greeting to the children of nature, whom he called Mother: "Earth, ocean, air, belovèd brotherhood!" He knew nature could be destructive. In his "Ode to the West Wind" he wrote: "Wild Spirit, which art moving everywhere; / Destroyer and preserver; hear, oh, hear!" Yet Shelley placed most of his bets on the preserving aspect and ended on an optimistic note, "If winter comes, can spring be far behind?" As the critic Lionel Trilling summarized "Ode to the West Wind," "The cycle of the seasons must always have its import of despair, but its import of hope seems to be more insistent."

For Shelley the sea, like the wind, was not a challenge but a tame, enchanting friend. One day on the water in *Ariel*, Shelley and Williams were moved by an approaching storm—not by its threats and challenges, but by its picturesqueness. What Williams wrote of the experience in his journal speaks for a particular temperament: "Thursday, May 2. Cloudy, with intervals of rain. Went out with Shelley in the boat—fish on the rocks—bad sport. Went in the evening after some wild ducks—saw nothing but sublime scenery, to which the grandeur of a storm greatly contributed."

While most of us would be awed by that example of what was called the romantic sublime, mariners long ago learned to temper their awe with distrust. "Trace the sky the painter's brush, the winds around you soon will rush," goes the old weather saying, and it is no harmless nursery rhyme. A black cloud may be sublimely beautiful, yes; but it may also drop a gale upon a careless crew, capsize their ship, and hurl them headlong into the deep.

ROMANTIC OBSESSION goes only so far, and the storm is the hurdle at which it becomes self-destructive. "He who will learn to pray, let him go to sea," says an old proverb reflecting the ancient conviction that the deep is the ultimate locus of both remote awe and terror. That the sea carries a vast range of meaning—often preserving and merciful, often destructive and terrifying—is hardly a novel idea, of course. From the ancient storm stories of the all too human adventurer Odysseus and the prophet Jonah to recent accounts of heroism and fallibility aboard yachts racing at high speeds in the Southern Ocean, the sea has usually been described in terms of absolutes—the preserver *or* the destroyer, not a bit of each. The seafarer, meanwhile, has been portrayed as a romantic hero awed by the sea *or* the spineless coward who experiences it in terror.

So we appear to cope with the sea by making it an ongoing morality play. But as students of disasters, storms, and human stress tell us, events and the people caught up in them are more complex, unpredictable, and interesting than that. Of every ten people in a crisis, psychologists report, one or two behave heroically, another one or two are helpless, and the rest muddle along, trying to do their decent best. Who will be in those groups is not easy to predict, except that well-trained people who know basic skills and have been through simulated disasters generally fall into the first group. Yet it is not unknown for the most capable crew members in a gale to be those so young that they do not realize their peril.

Otherwise the storm at sea is not so simple that it samples only one of the extremes of awe and horror. We may simultaneously feel heroic and helpless, awestruck and terrified, enchanted and insane. Likewise, recovery from such an experience is neither instantaneous nor sure. The thought of "closure" is a fantasy as the storm experience ripples out—like the great cresting waves that storms create in the sea—over many miles and down through many generations.

THIS AMBIVALENCE HELPS EXPLAIN why mariners are famous believers. If survival were either sure or impossible, there would be no nautical superstitions or myths. But nothing is certain upon the sea except that it is uncertain and unique. "Sailors are friends with the supernatural," the maritime folklorist Horace Beck has observed. "Fog, ice, mirage, exhaustion, bad food, and isolation from normal living enable a man to see, to hear, and to feel things not ordinarily experienced by other mortals." As Beck suggests in the phrase "isolation from normal living," mariners do inhabit another world from that of land. Attempting to gain a sense of comfort in this Other World, mariners throughout history have believed in higher forces, if somewhat strangely. "Old sailors may have odd ways of showing their religious feelings, but there are no infidels at sea," Joshua Slocum remarked after his solitary voyage around the world in a small boat. He confessed his own "longing to call on a Father."

Other seamen have nurtured less traditional beliefs that would strike a modern, self-conscious rationalist like Percy Bysshe Shelley as perversely irrational. As if to stress that the sea is the Other World where contrariness reigns, many sailors believe that black cats are lucky to have aboard a ship but that rabbits belong nowhere near a vessel. (Should a rabbit hop across a sailor's path while he is headed to the wharf, he must immediately turn around and go home.) At one time or another it has been believed that for a vessel to survive a voyage, she must never be boarded by a woman, a red-haired virgin, a solitary bird, any land bird except the dove, a citizen of Finland, or an ordained minister; and if anybody comes on board carrying a banana or an umbrella, woe betide that ship and her crew. This list is only a tiny sampling of the thousands of maritime superstitions, many of them so weirdly microscopic in their specificity that they seem less like expressions of the heartfelt fears of all terrified seamen than like the malicious gossip of the neglected, the oppressed, and the insane.

The Bible, the most thorough written expression of and influence on traditional Western beliefs, pictures the sea as evil from almost its first to its last words. In the third verse of Genesis, God creates order and the earth out of the dark primordial waters. Over a thousand pages later (in the Christian Bible), in the second to last chapter of the Book of Revelation, we are told that, come the Apocalypse, the drowned will be found and the sea will be "no more." In between, the sea is the setting for the worst destruction—and therefore also for the Bible's greatest miracles. Noah's ark rises above the flood, the waters are held back to allow the Jews to escape from Egypt, Jonah is rescued from "the heart of the seas" by a great fish, and Jesus' divinity is finally made obvious when he walks on the water (Genesis 1, Revelation 21, Genesis 7–8, Exodus 14, Jonah, Mark 6). The destructive power of the sea is a crucial metaphor through the Book of Psalms, where the Hebrew word for "despair" is derived from the word "deep sea"—for example, "Out of the depths I cry to thee, O Lord!" (Psalm 130) and, in Psalm 42:

> Deep calls to deep at the thunder of thy cataracts;
> All thy waves and thy billows have gone over me. . . .
> I say to God, my rock: "Why has thou forgotten me?"

Church tradition carried on the theme of an evil sea, subject only to divine control, in several miraculous maritime stories. Saint Andrew, the first disciple Jesus called, brought back to life forty young men whose ship was sunk in a storm whipped up by the devil. Saint Nicholas stilled raging seas, saved drowning sailors, and was the patron saint of sailors long before his name became associated with Christmas. In one of the few legends in which the sea preserves life, Saint Ursula and her eleven thousand virgins delayed their forced marriage with pagans by sailing for years until they were martyred, still (happily) virgins.

This idea of the sea as a malicious primal force that plays casually with men's lives is not solely ancient or biblical. Sir Francis Drake, after one particularly fierce storm, likened the ocean to a tennis player because its "rowling seas" tossed his ship "like a ball in a racket." Likewise his contemporary,

Shakespeare, in *Pericles*, compared the sea to a "vast tennis court" on which the winds and the waters bat about both ships and sailors. When the modern American writer William Styron recently sought a vivid metaphor for clinical depression in his memoir, *Darkness Visible*, he looked to the Other World and found a storm at sea. Depression, he wrote, is "a howling tempest in the brain."

Shelley and other romantics turned this image on its head. To them nature and the sea are other to normal human existence, yes, but that makes them *safe*. True chaos occurs among humans on shore. Nature begets order. In his essay "On Love," Shelley wrote of nature as a friend who will "awaken the spirits to a dance of breathless rapture, and bring tears of mysterious tenderness to the eyes." As alluring as that "dance of breathless rapture" is, to think of the sea only as a playmate is risky business. Those who know the sea's capabilities, even if they cannot go so far as to assign evil to the oceans, will probably find Shelley's friend Byron more in tune with reality as he observes, "Man marks the earth with ruin, his control stops with the shore." That is because those who know the sea best know its ambivalence. Joseph Conrad, an experienced seaman, turned the old tennis image in a tragic direction in his memoir, *The Mirror of the Sea*: "I looked upon the true sea," Conrad wrote, "—the sea that plays with men until their hearts are broken, and wears stout ships to death. Nothing can touch the brooding bitterness of its soul." The sea can preserve and it can destroy, and it can do much else between those extremes. Psalm 107 has often been appropriated by mariners because it appears so joyful, with what at first seems to be a celebration of those who "went down to the sea in ships." Yet three verses later it says that the sailors' "courage melted away in their evil plight." *Here* in our land world there is order. *Out there* in the Other World of the sea, there is havoc beneath the order that we attempt to impose through the skills of careful seamanship. Even the most skilled professional mariners are respectful, and they go down to the sea cautiously, even fearfully.

II

THE BEST EVIDENCE that Shelley did not take the sea seriously was his boat. The strange *Ariel* was so poorly planned and had so many bizarre features that the shipyard almost refused the commission to build her. She was all but wide-open to the sea, with little or no decking and, for shelter,

Edward Williams's sketches of Shelley's *Ariel (top)* and Byron's larger *Bolivar* do not indicate that *Ariel* had almost no deck and so was exposed to filling up. Williams died with Shelley in the squall. (© Copyright The British Museum)

only the small cabin that protected the large library Shelley carried along. If the rig and sails were disproportionately large for her hull, it was because of Shelley's ego. When *Ariel* first lay side by side with Byron's *Bolivar*, he complained that she looked tiny, so Williams piled on towering topmasts and a false bow and stern that stretched her original length, which was probably about thirty-five feet, disproportionately. "Rigged like a frigate though extremely small," was how Thomas Medwin, a navy captain and Shelley's cousin, contemptuously described her. She also was extremely unstable. One of a naval architect's most important duties is to provide a properly shaped and ballasted hull to resist the side forces of the wind and waves so the vessel will not capsize. After *Ariel* was launched she was so tippy that another two tons of pig iron and sand were dumped into her bilge.

Open to spray, top-heavy with her overly large rig, and probably still underballasted, *Ariel* was an accident waiting to happen. So long as the wind remained light and the sea flat, she was safe. In the bay's prevailing calms she was "fast as a witch," as Williams confidently reported, without risking her crew's lives. But a friend reported that when the afternoon sea breeze came up as thermal air rose over Italy and the hot land sucked cool air from the Mediterranean, the pretentious miniature ship was "very crank," or hard to steer.

Eventually a storm would come. A storm always comes. "A settled summer where thermal winds predominate does not mean a summer without strong winds," writes Rod Heikell, an authority on sailing in the Mediterranean. "The blue sea can be quickly covered with white caps and steep seas whipped up by a wind blowing out of a clear azure sky." On especially hot summer days, a *tempoale*, or thunder squall, can arise in a few minutes when a little cool, dry air mixes with the hot humid air. The squall will churn dangerously for a few minutes to an hour. Worse yet is the *provenza*, or cold front. Cold, dry air sweeps down from the Alps into the blanket of moist, warm air over the Mediterranean. As this volatile mix seethes, a wall of cold air forms and advances. It is heralded by a fog bank in a calm. Then comes a line of black squalls bringing a gusty wind and rain and, sometimes, waterspouts. Occasionally a summer northerly gale sweeps in behind the cold front to blow for two or three days and turn the shallow coastal waters into steep, confused seas.

∾

"I STILL INHABIT THIS DIVINE BAY," Shelley wrote a friend in late June, "reading Spanish dramas & sailing & listening to the most enchanting music." Although Mary hated Spezia, he hoped to spend the rest of his life there. "My only regret is that the summer must pass." With characteristic self-absorption, Shelley did not mention that Mary's pregnancy, the most difficult of her seven, had ended very recently not only in yet another miscarriage but almost in her death. Shelley had nursed her for days, but when the crisis ended he was away on his first long sail in *Ariel*. He headed out into the Mediterranean July, bound for the harbor town of Livorno (Leghorn), forty-five miles to the south. With him were Edward Williams, an Englishman named Roberts who had helped design *Ariel*, and the boat's caretaker, eighteen-year-old Charles Vivian. The weather cooperated, and they reached their destination without trouble.

Shelley and Williams traveled inland to Pisa to see Byron and Leigh Hunt, another romantic poet, about a new political magazine they hoped to publish. Byron's household was in its usual state of chaos, with a brawl going on in one corner and a furious argument being waged with the Vatican about his living arrangements with his current mistress. The discussions about the magazine were productive, and Hunt lent Shelley a copy of a collection of the last poems by their recently deceased friend John Keats.

As they left the house on the morning of July 8, Hunt looked to the north and noted a sky of thunderheads. He made Shelley and Williams promise they would not try to sail home to Spezia if the weather was poor and the sea rough.

HUNT PROBABLY KNEW his friend well enough to predict that he might well ignore the warning. Most people feel, in an abstract way, as challenged by the prospect of engaging with stormy weather as they might be by the opportunity to climb Mount Everest. In the end the question is whether they take the bait and actually risk what sailors call a "hard chance."

To appreciate the conditions Shelley would face in his small boat in a hard squall, consider the storm experience almost sixty years later of a more energetic and capable individual in a boat even smaller and less seaworthy than *Ariel*. Theodore Roosevelt was a paragon of the striver philosophy that he called "the strenuous life" and that (as we will see in chapter 6) profoundly influenced amateur outdoorsmen in the twentieth century. In the winter of 1880, when Roosevelt was twenty-two, he and his brother Elliott were shooting birds on Long Island Sound when a sharp northwest gale blew in. As Roosevelt made clear in an account of his battle for survival, he found it a "bully" experience. Here are excerpts from his crisply told story, which was not published for more than a century:

> The tide had turned and was coming in against the wind so there was a very heavy sea running; the little boat staggered bravely on through the great billows, her bow now almost out of the water, and now burying herself so that the seas came in over the lee coamings; and heeling over now and then till we had to start the sheets. As the great waves struck her, sending clouds of white foam over us, she would stand almost still, and then, rushing forward, bury herself in the greenish masses of water. Under the rough touch of the wind the ice-covered shrouds sang like the chords of an Aeolian harp, a fitting accompaniment to the angry roar of the waves. . . .

Danger appeared ahead:

> We were beating out on the port tack, everything shrouded from sight by the clouds of flying scud, when I heard a peculiar washing sound in the waves ahead, as if they were striking round something; I knew it could not be land and it did not sound like ice. Peering ahead as well as I could in another moment I saw the gloom of a large coasting schooner dead ahead; "helm-a-lee, helm-a-lee," I sung out, and as the boat ran up in the wind the coaster passed us but a few feet distant going wing and wing, everything reefed down tight as could be. Her long black hull was whitened with ice and only two men were on deck, one motionless at the wheel and the other tapping some of the running rigging with a marlin spike to free it from ice; a moment afterwards she had wallowed by us, and disappeared in the gloom.

The Roosevelts safely reached their home port of Oyster Bay, "so stiff with cold and fatigue that it was hard work even to let down the sails." That they were invigorated by their struggle with the storm is obvious from Roosevelt's narrative. Its driving, unsentimental, yet emotive style handsomely satisfies the rule of concise writing, laid down by the modern-day composer and lyricist Stephen Sondheim, that "reduction releases power."

III

WHEN SHELLEY MET HIS STORM, he was less confident, less well prepared, and in the end less fortunate than Roosevelt. Enough is known
about that day to allow us to surmise a narrative:

It is the steamy afternoon of July 8, 1822. Percy Bysshe Shelley and
Edward Williams board *Ariel* in the anchorage at Leghorn with Charles
Vivian, the young deckhand, and they make ready to weigh anchor. Thun-
derstorms swing by overhead, but the sky briefly clears, and the little
schooner ghosts out of the harbor through a light breeze and oily water.
Edward John Trelawny is meant to follow them in Byron's *Bolivar*, but
lacking the necessary paperwork to clear port, he is detained by officials. A
sailor tells Trelawny that *Ariel* should not have sailed. He points to the
scuddy black clouds and, under them, a layer of fog indicating that a cold
front is imminent. "Look at those black lines and the dirty rags hanging on
them out of the sky," the seaman says, "—they are a warning. Look at the
smoke on the water. The devil is brewing mischief." Roberts, who sailed
down with Shelley but has remained behind, climbs to the top of a tower
with a spyglass and finds *Ariel* several miles out, sailing toward what is
obviously is a *tempoale*.

A hundred miles to the north, Shelley's cousin, Royal Navy captain
Thomas Medwin, looks aloft and sees clouds flying south toward Leghorn
in "masses on masses up-piled." The sight is so violent that it reminds him
of the aftereffects of an explosion of a mine. Then comes the storm. "Neither in the Bay of Biscay, or Bengal, nor between the Tropics, nor on the
Line, did I ever witness a severer one," Medwin will say.

Ariel drifts northward in the light westerly wind through a fleet of fishing boats, whose fishermen are too occupied with their lines and nets to
pay much attention to the little yacht. Soon they are in a bank of fog that
obscures everything in the pulsing wisps of gray. Moisture falls out of the
air like drops from a squeezed sponge. Shelley, at the helm, is enthralled by
this womblike experience until a chill wind pulls him out of his reverie.
Cold, dry air from the approaching front moves in, and the fog vanishes.
Above are rows and layers of black thunderheads, with bulging, poxlike
mammatus underbellies, some glowing an eerie orange in the afternoon
sun. Shelley, with his literary mind, might well have recalled the sky that

Shelley's voyage along the Italian coast was between his summer home at Spezia and Leghorn. The accident occurred on the return trip, about ten miles north of Leghorn.

foretold Julius Caesar's assassination in Shakespeare's play, when the watch saw the "horrid sights" of red squall clouds:

> Fierce fiery warriors fought upon the clouds
> In ranks and squadrons in right form for war,
> Which drizzled blood upon the Capitol.

All is darkness or light—white darts of rain pouring down from the thick sky onto white sails, while a sheet of white-capped waves rushes toward them over the black sea. The chiaroscuro of the seascape charms Shelley, but it frightens the fishermen, who tie in reefs and turn their bows toward Leghorn so they can scud under some control before the gusting north wind. The first squall roars down, with shots of cold air and hail dropping from above as the new weather bursts down onto the sea. *Ariel* accelerates and heels far over, her rail digging into the confused waves and scooping up water. Shelley fights the helm, Williams is agitated, the boy stands alert at the mast, awaiting the order to climb aloft and take in the topsail. The rail dips again, and with water shin deep and sloshing from side to side, the little schooner settles deeper into the sea.

A fishing boat under shortened sail appears alongside, her crew shouting inaudibly in the roar of wind and sea. Shelley waves them away. He has no idea what to do except to hang on to his bare control. On his own initiative the boy shinnies up the mainmast and claws down the topsail.

Williams grapples with the halyards, but Shelley drops the tiller and drags him away.

The wind eases briefly, and then another, even more vicious squall roars down, followed by the cold *provenza*. Caught broadside in the trough of the sea, half-filled with water, *Ariel* has lost all defenses. The next wave falls upon her and she capsizes, throwing the three men into the water as the boat spirals down through the Mediterranean. It has taken only a few minutes for the romance to become a shipwreck.

IV

RIPPLING OUT FROM THE SQUALL came the questions, the mourning, and the mythmaking. Mary Shelley waited at Spezia, her eye to a telescope and the house filled with gloomy speculation. "Prognostics hovered around us," she remembered. Ever the romantic, she would describe this time of the most intense anxiety in the coldly clinical language of the picturesque that her husband always favored:

> The beauty of the sea seemed unearthly in its excess: the distance we were at from all signs of civilization, the sea at our feet, its murmurs or its roaring for ever in our ears—all these things led the mind to brood over strange thoughts, and, lifting it from everyday life, caused it to be familiar with the unreal. A sort of spell surrounded us, and each day, as the voyagers did not return, we grew restless and disquieted.

She and Jane Williams finally ran to Byron's palazzo demanding, "Where *is* he?" No news there, and they returned "to wait ten days for the confirmation of our sentence of a life of eternal pain." The silence ended when Trelawny identified a water keg and some bottles that washed up on the shore as the schooner's. The corpses were found on the beach several miles apart, their faces and eyes so eaten away by the fishes that they were unrecognizable until the volume of Keats's poems was found in a coat pocket.

Italian law required that, out of concern for diseases, victims of wrecks be buried or cremated where they were washed ashore. Byron, Leigh Hunt, and Trelawny decided the occasion called for a hero's funeral, with sprinklings of oblations and odes sung to the literary gods. In another of those maddeningly impersonal expressions of the romantic sublime, Leigh Hunt remembered, "the Mediterranean, now soft and lucid, kissed the shore as if to make peace with it." The day of his friend's funeral of course must be picturesque. Byron was just as cool. "We have been burning the bodies of Shelley and Williams on the seashore, to render them fit for removal and regular interment," he wrote a friend. "You can have no idea what an extraordinary effect such a funeral pile has, on a desolate shore, with mountains in the background and the sea before, and the singular appearance the salt and frankincense gave to the flame."

For all their talk, neither Hunt nor Byron could bring himself to watch the cremation up close. Hunt remained in his carriage. Byron, who had been prepared to recite Greek odes to the memory of "the best and least selfish man I ever knew," swam out to sea, suffering a blistering sunburn. Only Trelawny remained at the pyre for the completion of the somber ceremony. Remarkably, Shelley's heart was not burned (possibly because it remained engorged with blood), and Trelawny snatched it from the fire. The ashes were eventually buried in the Protestant cemetery at Rome, while control of the heart was bitterly disputed by Shelley's family and friends until, reduced to dust, it was eventually buried with Shelley's son.

Byron gave up his yacht—he had "taken a disgust to sailing"—and fled to Greece to fight in the revolution against the Turks. At the age of thirty-six he was bitterly disillusioned and, he said, "literally speaking, a young old man." He became ill, and incompetent doctors accidentally bled him to death.

MARY SHELLEY, who did not observe the cremation, was left all but destitute financially and emotionally by the sudden end of a marriage that she called "romantic beyond romance." Twenty-five years old, alone, physically weak, she lacked all reserves. "And so here I am!" she wrote a friend in late August. "I continue to exist—to see one day succeed the other; to dread night; but more to dread morning & hail another cheerless day. . . . At times I feel an energy within me to combat with my destiny—but again I sink—I have but one hope for which I live—to render myself worthy to join him."

Her father would have none of this. "If you cannot be independent, who should be?" William Godwin demanded. A challenge to affirm her own identity was just the thing. Advice to pull up one's socks may sound like a cliché, but students of the psychological consequences of disaster have learned that finding a purpose in life while recovering one's core beliefs,

In keeping with the "James Dean effect" that attaches itself to youthful deaths, Shelley's passing was highly romanticized. Louis-Edouard Fournier's 1889 painting of his waterside cremation is almost entirely inaccurate. Mary Shelley was not present, and most of his few friends on hand could not bear to watch. (Board of Trustees of the National Museums and Galleries on Merseyside, Walker Art Gallery, Liverpool)

"Sailors are friends with the supernatural." The sea has long been regarded as the Other World where chaos, monsters, and occasional miracles reign. (Author's collection)

identity, and relationships are the best first steps toward recovery from the emotional numbness that follows a traumatic event. Mary Shelley promptly set about reinvigorating her old high standards, the foremost being, as she told her journal, "Seek to know your own heart & learning what it loves best—try to enjoy that." Returning to England, she devoted her remaining twenty-nine years to writing, raising their son, and defending and enhancing Shelley's reputation. She deeply resented the belief held by many people that Shelley had committed suicide. After *Ariel* was raised with a large hole in her side, Mary found temporary solace in an unsubstantiated rumor that pirates in two boats had run him down and murdered him. In 1826 two sailors reported with far more convincing detail that they had sailed by a schooner yacht in the squall, had done what they could to persuade her crew to shorten sail, and then had helplessly watched her sink. *Ariel*'s crew, they implied, did not do themselves in and were not murdered. They died because they handled their inept boat ineptly.

Mary Shelley knew already what her husband had learned too late: that nature is not always a friend, and least of all the sea. She did not mind going out on the water, but whenever her son Percy was with her they remained ashore, refusing to board even large ferryboats.

ANOTHER WOUNDED SURVIVOR of Shelley's death was his reputation, which was reshaped over time as his admirers found comfort in highly dramatized, even mythological explanations of his life and death. In the end he became a canonized rebel.

To anyone with a romantic turn of mind, his death seemed a tragedy so fated and brilliant that the chief victim himself might have scripted it. Even the location in passionate Italy was apt. "Where should a poet fall asleep, but at Spezia? Where should he continue to slumber but at Rome?" one of his friends asked rhetorically, without appearing to consider Shelley's personal stake in the matter. In artistic collective memory, Shelley was the archetype of the brilliant young idealist ascending gloriously to immortality at the very peak of his powers. To the many who have cared far more about abstract symbolism than about the tangible human tragedy of the sinking of the *Ariel*, it seemed poetic justice that he died at the helm of his "perfidious bark." That her capsize might have been accidental or the result of his own incompetence was dismissed because such conclusions lent support to criticisms of his careless life, including his radical politics. "Viewed cynically," observes a student of his reputation, "Shelley's death and cremation could be said to be the best thing that ever happened to him because they provided a focal point for critics and biographers defending Shelley against the scathing criticism that shaped his reputation during his life time." In short, he became everything he had wanted *not* to be, which was an institution. Young visitors to the Temple of Poseidon at Cape Sounion, in Greece, carved his name next to that of another sailing romantic hero, his friend Byron, who also died young in circumstances that were romanticized (Byron was killed by incompetent doctors, not, as many wanted to believe, by a royalist's bullet or by drowning in the Hellespont).

Of course an apparently fated, dramatic, and romantic death was not Shelley's alone. He was not the only person whose reputation was shaped without his approval by an early, violent demise. Psychologists have recently described what they call the "James Dean effect" in popular feelings about death. In experiments, when people are presented with an invented character for whom they may choose a life story, they prefer to grant the person an early death—a "peak end" when life seems thrilling—rather than a longer, blander life that runs a full course and ends in illness. This romantic editing device seems to shorten Shakespeare's seven ages of man by at least two. The James Dean effect is named for the charismatic young actor who is said to have declared, "Dream as if you'll live forever, live as if you'll die today," and who fulfilled his promise by dying in an automobile smashup at age twenty-four after making only three films. "Live fast, die young," is another version of this slogan, as is the rock and roll musician Billy Joel's "Only the good die young." Poets somehow seem to be the best examples, from Keats, Shelley, and Byron to Rupert Brooke and Joyce Kilmer, both of whom died in the First World War. The actor Rudolph Valentino filled the bill in the 1920s, as did Dean, Buddy Holly, John F. Kennedy, and Marilyn Monroe three or four decades later. In all these cases an early death effectively shackled their reputations. One irony of Shelley's death is that its nature left him exactly in the position he had long despised—in a niche not of his own making, defined by values he had not chosen. Percy Bysshe Shelley was never tamed until after his storm.

Did Shelley commit nautical suicide? Any life that is studied minutely reveals a few hints of a death wish. The life of a moody, edgy, poet whose subject matter is the ambiguous boundary between the extremes of

Clouds in "masses on masses up-piled," with poxlike *mammatus* underbellies, loom over a violent sea. This photograph, taken near Australia during the 2001 race from Sydney to Hobart, Tasmania, shows something like what Shelley saw in his storm. (Illbruck Challenge/Ray Davies) preservation and destruction is bound to provide more than enough hints to fuel the star-seeking retroactive suicide watch. He spoke of suicide often enough, and in the summer of 1822 he had acquired some drugs that could have caused his death. Yet he did not use them, and when he died it was on the sailboat he loved and where he spent his happiest moments— without, nevertheless, having the slightest idea what he was doing. Shelley was so incompetent a sailor that he would not even have known how to engineer his destruction in a sailboat. As energetically as this fascinating and in many ways lovable man worked to assign meaning to every corner of life and nature, he died in an accident for which he was sublimely unprepared.

THIS STORY INTRODUCES the five elements of a broad understanding of a storm: its demanding weather; the seamanship needed to cope with it; the trauma and stress for survivors; the search for meaning at every stage; and finally, the complex, often surprising consequences for the victim's reputation and community. As we will see throughout this book, a sailor need not be a landlubber and a heretic to get into serious trouble at sea. Seamen more experienced and competent than Shelley, who have handled vessels far more seaworthy than *Ariel*, are also vulnerable. Even when business, not fantasy, inspires people to brave the Other World of the sea, there are storms to struggle with both physically and in other ways.

2

The *Elizabeth* and Margaret Fuller

New York, 1850

*"There are more consequences to a shipwreck
than the underwriters notice."*

—Henry David Thoreau

IN MAY 1850, twenty-eight years after Percy Bysshe Shelley
sailed out from Leghorn and into a squall, another gifted writer
was in the same Italian port, nervously preparing to board a
much larger vessel for a longer passage that she feared she would
not survive. So well known was Margaret Fuller for her courage
that the hint that she was frightened by the prospect of a voyage
in a big full-rigged ship would have astonished her many admirers, who believed she was above fear. An early champion of
women's rights, the first female American journalist, and a war

correspondent and nurse during the recent revolution in Rome, she seemed beyond restriction. "By birth a child of New England, by adoption a citizen of Rome, by genius belonging to the world"—so read the inscription on the memorial stone created for her after her death. But what shaped her reputation for years afterward was an image of the end of that voyage, one not of triumph but of passivity: a woman in a white nightgown slumped on a wrecked ship's deck "with her hands upon her knees and tempestuous waves breaking over her."

Two months before her helpless end, well before temporary captain Henry Bangs bet his ship on a lighthouse, Margaret Fuller was in Leghorn looking for a ship to carry her, with her Italian common-law husband and their toddler son, back to New England. Reports of her new family had caused scandal. Despite warnings from friends that she should not return, she insisted on carrying on with her mission. Still, the longer she read the shipping news, the greater cause she found to be anxious about taking her new family on this voyage. She had come to Europe without such deep worry, but then she had not been a mother. "Thus it seems safety is not [to] be found in the wisest calculation," she gloomily noted on learning that a well-respected vessel had run up on the beach along the south shore of Long Island within a few hours of New York harbor. She filed that report in her memory alongside accounts of other wrecks, of shipboard fires, of captains and crews abandoning leaking ships and leaving passengers to fend for themselves, and of rampant disease. If tales of contagious illness frightened her and other passengers, they terrified mariners even more than the thought of storms. On runs to New York in the early 1850s, during one four-month period one out of every seven ships contained cholera, and 1,933 men, women, and children—2 percent of all passengers—were buried at sea. When a tough captain who had gotten his passenger ship through a gale was informed of a single case of smallpox, an observer recalled that "the tempest had not shaken the firm nerves of the captain, but he quailed at the hideous name of this scourge of God."

Margaret Fuller's fears of the sea and ships were typical of most people of her century. When the Reverend William Whiting, head of the Choristers' School at Winchester College in England, learned in 1860 that one of his students would soon board a ship bound for America, he wrote a poem asking divine protection "for those in peril on the sea." The hymn began,

"Eternal Father, strong to save." One of its original stanzas (later deleted) expressed the ancient wariness of the sea with far more power than any deckhand's foolish superstition about sailing with a clergyman or a red-haired woman:

Most Holy Spirit! Who didst brood
Upon the chaos dark and rude,
And bid its angry tumult cease,
And give, for wild confusion, peace;
O hear us when we cry to Thee,
For those in peril on the sea!

FACING THOSE PERILS in the spring of 1850, Margaret Fuller labored over the choice of a vessel. When she finally chose a ship, she characteristically made her decision for personal reasons: she liked the people. Captain Seth L. Hasty of the *Elizabeth* and his wife, Catherine, from Scarborough, Maine, were on a delayed honeymoon two years after their marriage. Margaret liked them immediately, and not only because she shared the widespread belief that, despite occasional bad apples, masters of sailing vessels were models of bravery. (Sea captains were the heroes of the mid-nineteenth century that cowboys would be in the twentieth and firemen would become in the early years of the twenty-first.) She also found the Hastys to be kind and cultured. They reciprocated her admiration. As she showed them around Florence, like many people who met Margaret Fuller they came to admire her energy, knowledge, and generosity. "We owed her half our pleasure," Catherine Hasty reported. "She knew everything about everything." On their assurances that the voyage would be safe, she purchased three tickets for the *Elizabeth*'s passage from Leghorn to New York and got busy putting together a medicine chest and purchasing fruit, chickens, and a goat (to provide fresh milk for her eighteen-month-old Angelino). She hired another passenger, a young Italian woman named Celeste Pardena, to help care for the boy.

In mid-May they came aboard the *Elizabeth* in Leghorn with the ship's fifth passenger, Horace Sumner. His brother, the prominent New England abolitionist Charles Sumner, would have been horrified had he known that in the cargo, amid tons of fine Italian marble, lay an immense statue by Hiram Porter of the recently deceased Southern apologist for slavery, John C. Calhoun. That the *Elizabeth* was carrying such valuable cargo spoke well of her and Captain Hasty. In her seventh year, the ship was in early middle age at a time when most ships fell apart or were wrecked within twenty years of their launching. No quick clipper ship, she was a sturdy load-carrying nautical dray about 130 feet long, with a capacious hold, seventeen crew members, and cabins for several passengers. A cosmopolitan entity, like many ships of that time, she had been built in Maine, was managed by a New York shipper, and hailed from Philadelphia, the hometown of her first mate, Henry P. Bangs.

As secure as the *Elizabeth* and her officers seemed, on the eve of her departure Margaret Fuller wrote her mother a letter that reads like the parting words of a soldier heading into battle. "There seems somewhat more of danger on sea than on land," she noted before sending her love to her family and ending, "I hope we shall be able to pass some time together yet in this world; but if God decrees otherwise—here and hereafter, My dearest Mother."

Her fears were all too quickly realized. First came the scourge of God. Exhausted by weeks of supervising the complicated stowage of the marble so it would not shift in the hold and capsize the ship, Captain Hasty became ill two days out of Leghorn and soon showed the pustules of small-pox. His wife and Margaret nursed him constantly. Margaret (who had been a nurse during the Italian revolution) confessed that never had she seen such suffering. After ten wretched days, he died at Gibraltar like "a lit-tle infant," she said. The frightened port authorities would not permit a doctor to board the *Elizabeth* or allow Hasty's body to be brought ashore, so he was buried at sea in an impressive ceremony.

The first mate, Henry Bangs, took command, and the ship sailed on June 8. Smallpox next struck Margaret Fuller's son Angelino, swelling his eyes shut and scarring his body. She nursed him through the crisis until the boy recovered on the eighth day out, and soon enough "Nino" was wrestling with the sailors, as the adults in the ship's company recovered from the double shock of plague and loss of their captain.

I

ONCE HER BOY WAS OUT OF DANGER, Margaret returned to her normal state of buoyant optimism. At age forty, she had done better than merely survive a life of unusual struggle. "On the 23rd of May 1810 was born one who had *feeling*, which is the source of sorrow," said her father of Sarah Margaret Fuller, and Timothy Fuller did his best to guarantee that sorrow would be her constant acquaintance. A brilliant, demanding congressman, lawyer, and writer whose motto was "mediocrity is obscurity," he expected miracles of the oldest of his eight children. As a young woman in Cambridge and western Massachusetts, she inhabited a one-child intellectual workhouse of his creation. At age three she was reading English; at eight, Latin; at fifteen, Italian and German—the latter so well that she translated Goethe into English while also serving as schoolmistress to her brothers and sisters.

Against this relentless pressure, she defended herself with relentless, contrived cheerfulness. She once acknowledged her powerful will in an aphorism of her own invention, "If all the shipwrecked submitted to be drowned, the world would be a desert"—words that would come to be tragically ironic. She paid a price. By day an obedient prodigy, at night she was haunted by nightmares in which horses stampeded over her, loathsome faces stared at her, and her dead sister lay in an open grave. So she refused to sleep. "No one understood this subject of health then," she later wrote in an autobiographical fragment that she titled "Overwork." "No one knew why this child, already kept up so late, was still unwilling to retire. Poor child! Far remote in time, in thought, from that period, I look back on these glooms and terrors, wherein I was enveloped, and perceive that I had no natural childhood!"

After her father died of cholera in 1835, when she was twenty-five, she scraped out a living as a schoolteacher, translator, editor, and writer, all while caring for the family and suffering debilitating bouts of depression and migraine. Always ambitious, she sought and won the attention of Ralph Waldo Emerson, America's philosopher of individualism and self-reliance. He thought well enough of her to choose her to edit his magazine the *Dial*, where she edited the writings of Henry David Thoreau, Nathaniel Hawthorne, and other writers in the literary movement known as the American Renaissance. These relationships had their intense moments, yet they were worked out as friendships in the traditional meaning of the word. Her first consummated love affair apparently did not come until she moved to New York in the 1840s.

She blossomed in her thirties through willful self-renewal. At heart an outsider (as she put it, "a pilgrim and sojourner on earth"), she was incapable of obeying her world's narrow expectations of a woman, summarized in the ideal of "true womanhood." Rejecting the dogma that women must stay home, provide nurture, and think pure thoughts, she also rebelled against her father's model of an intellectual machine. Like Shelley, she made an enemy of restriction of any kind. "Very early," she once said, "I knew the only object in life was to grow." By growth she meant accepting change and complexity. "Nature seems to delight in varying the arrangements, as if to show that she will be fettered by no rule; and we must admit the same varieties that she admits." Guided by her romantic connection with nature and feelings, and by her keen intellect and strong will, Margaret Fuller worked through her anger at her father and succeeded in rising above sullen victimhood to become a separate person. Although she continued to pay a price with deep depressions, she figured out how to use them creatively. "From the darkest comes my brightness, from Chaos depths my love."

In the early 1840s she assumed the mantle of prophet for women. In her book *Woman in the Nineteenth Century* and other energetic writings (including an essay provocatively titled "The Great Lawsuit: Man vs. Men, Woman vs. Women"), she watered the seeds of feminism planted by Mary Shelley's mother, Mary Wollstonecraft. Margaret Fuller counseled women inmates in prisons, supported economic reforms, vigorously protested the "separate spheres" in life assigned to women and children, and hosted educational forums for women that she called "conversations." In these forums she told her audience to leap over "the fences of society as easily as over the fences of the field." Women, she said, must feel free to take on any work, no matter how risky or traditionally masculine. "Let them be sea captains if you will." Among her students were Elizabeth Cady Stanton, Julia Ward Howe, and other leaders of the nascent women's rights movement. Howe, author of the lyrics of "The Battle Hymn of the Republic," later wrote a biography of her mentor. (In chapter 6 we will see how her daughter helped change the life of another Margaret Fuller.)

Margaret Fuller's most memorable appeal to women (and men) of her time and ours is that of visionary for a richer, more integrated life in which the feelings and the intellect engage each other. Emerson understood this and said, "She excels other intellectual persons in this, that her sentiments are more blended with her life." She, as usual, said it more colorfully: "To me it seems that it is madder never to abandon oneself than often to be infatuated, better to be wounded, a captive, a slave, than always to walk in armor." That suggests her flair. The editor of her letters, Robert N. Hudspeth, has written: "Margaret Fuller is our Romantic critic: devoted to the self, to quests, to transcendence. Her natural gesture was one of extravagance." Red-haired, florid-faced, confrontational, and proud, she expressed her thoughts and pronouncements in a manner that irritated or intimidated austere "cold roast" Yankees but delighted the less repressed. "Her eye pierced through your disguises," said a woman friend. Not everybody enjoyed the assault. After she advised Emerson, "You are intellect. I am life," and told Henry David Thoreau, the hermit of Walden Pond, that he was a bare hill needing to be warmed by spring, the two men backed away from her.

In 1844 she left Boston for New York, whose rambunctious nature better suited her. After two years of writing for Horace Greeley's reform-minded *New York Tribune*, he sent her to Italy to cover the nationalist revolution known as the *Risorgimento*, on which she, like many liberal Americans, placed great hopes. There she met Giovanni Angelo, the Marchese d'Ossoli, of whom little is known except that he was ten years younger than she was, poorly educated, kind, and as devoted to her as she was to him. They had a child together. (No wedding record has been found, and historians regard their relationship as a common-law marriage.) Ossoli served in the republican army and Fuller worked as a nurse in a Roman hospital. The collapse of the revolution and the Roman republic left her deeply discouraged:

> I am tired out. I am tired of thinking and hoping. Tired of seeing men err and bleed. I take interest in some plans—in Socialism, for instance—but the interest is as shallow as the plans. These are needed, even good, but men will still blunder and weep as men have blundered and wept so many thousands of years. Gladly would I creep into some green recess where I might see a few not unfriendly faces and where not more wretches would come than I could relieve. Yes, I am weary and faith sings and soars no more.

She added, "I have seen too much sorrow. I grow sick as I think of the past." Yet she turned to the past to renew herself again. In Florence during the winter of 1849–50, she wrote a history of the failed revolution while keeping company with the English poets Robert Browning and Elizabeth Barrett Browning, in involuntary exile in Italy after eloping against the wishes of Elizabeth's father. When the manuscript was finished, Margaret

Margaret Fuller was in a contemplative mood as she sat for this daguerrotype in 1846. She usually was all energy, welcoming change and inviting challenges. "To me it seems that it is madder never to abandon oneself than often to be infatuated, better to be wounded, a captive, a slave, than always to walk in armor." (Courtesy Museum of Fine Arts, Boston. Reproduced with permission. © 2000 Museum of Fine Arts, Boston. All rights reserved.)

Fuller was determined to return home to Boston with Ossoli and their son.

She was appalled to learn that she would not be widely welcomed. Except for Emerson and a few other old friends, people made it clear in their letters that they wanted her to stay in Europe. "We, as well as all your friends who have spoken to us about it, believe it will be undesirable for you to return at present," sniffed one woman, who hinted at widespread dismay because she had a sexual relationship with an unknown, impecunious Italian. Margaret, not one to shrink from a personal challenge, refused to change her plans.

II

BEATING INTO THE PREVAILING WESTERLY WINDS, the square-rigged *Elizabeth* was unable to hold anywhere near far enough north to follow the 3,300-mile Great Circle track that, arcing across the map of the Atlantic, provides the shortest distance to New York. After over a month of slow sailing, she finally neared Bermuda, where the breeze faired and gave her a fast reach over the last eight hundred miles to New York.

Margaret Fuller, who loved motion, travel, nature, and complexity in equal measure, undoubtedly was entranced by the voyage once her boy was out of danger. Like Shelley, with whose life and poems she felt a deep connection ("Shelley was all eros," she said—a compliment), she enjoyed boats and the encounters with nature that they provided. As a young woman she had come back from an evening sail and joyfully written about it to a friend:

> We went out in the boat, a poor leaky nutshell but we were all *delighted*. . . .
> a radiant sunset, the river perfectly still, we glided down so gently, the girls
> singing sweet songs and when night came on the perfect harmony of blue
> black and french gray the reflection of the shrubs and the thinly veiled stars
> conveying the feeling of purity and fixedness—The eye was filled, the mind
> gently stirred, the heart calmed.

Not entirely satisfied by the romantic sublime's abstract interest in the picturesque, Margaret would have delighted in the real life of a rolling ship at sea, surrounded only by the broad horizon and the blue, green, and white of the water. With her romantic's love of nature and the pleasure she took in raw energy, Margaret surely was thrilled by the ship's two-day crossing of the voluptuous Gulf Stream. Under a rich blue sky by day and towering thunderheads by night, the swirling river of heated water overflows with tropical

weeds housing colonies of tiny crabs, and offers porpoises, the occasional
whale, and fleets of Portuguese men-of-war tacking back and forth under
their dainty, translucent sails, trailing lethal tendrils to entrap and poison
prey. In the warm evenings she and Ossoli would have delighted in the sight
of the phosphorescent trails of porpoises torpedoing through the sea. After
dawn, they would have led Angelino on hunts along the *Elizabeth*'s deck for
flying fish that had been stranded aboard during the night.

As enchanting as nature is on a long ocean cruise, she also would have
been taken by shipboard life—the humor and charm of the enveloping
human connections aboard a vessel sailing twenty-four hours a day, seven
days a week. There were her man and her boy, of course, and also Catherine Hasty, whom she sustained through weeks of mourning. And as a
reader of the works of her former Cambridge neighbor and schoolmate
Richard Henry Dana Jr., and as a woman who had experienced her own
severe trials and exuberant joys, she understood the lives of seamen. "A
sailor's life is at best but a mixture of a little good with much evil and a little pleasure with much pain," Dana had written ten years earlier in *Two
Years before the Mast*. "The beautiful is linked with the revolting, the sublime with the commonplace, and the solemn with the ludicrous." Knowing
that, Margaret would have poured out her generous font of sympathy on
the steward, George Bates, the cook, Joseph McGil, and the other sailors
who played on deck with Nino.

AS AN ADMIRER OF SEA CAPTAINS, she would have trusted Henry P.
Bangs as implicitly as she had trusted her late friend Seth Hasty. One worry
of Bangs's that she did not share, because it was beyond even her broad
range of expertise, was the ship's last hundred miles of sailing down the
dangerous shallow, tide-swept, and narrowing funnel between the New
Jersey and Long Island shores, leading to the channel snaking around
Sandy Hook, New Jersey, into New York harbor.

Little is known about the man who had to navigate these hazards except
a few facts in census records, ship's articles, and family records. Thirty-
seven years old in 1850, Henry Bangs was small, a little over five feet six,
with dark hair and complexion. He divided his time ashore between the
major port of Philadelphia and the smaller one of Trenton, New Jersey, farther up the Delaware River. He came from a seafaring family. His father,
Captain Elijah Keeler Bangs, had commanded merchant ships for many

years with the mixed success and stubborn resourcefulness typical of career sea captains. During the Napoleonic Wars he suffered three substantial setbacks. He was twice arrested for trading with the enemy (first by the French, then by the English), and later he was shipwrecked off Holland, "each time losing all his possessions," according to a family historian, and each time saving his life and ultimately returning to sea with another ship.

Resilient old Elijah Bangs opened a door for his son, but Henry had to walk through it on his own. The road to a command was a long one. In the words of another captain, Charles E. Ranlett, the typical ambitious young mariner endured "a long, hard apprenticeship, with slow promotions from the galley to the forecastle, from forecastle to the berth of second and first officer, and finally, if the boy was of the right stuff, to the quarterdeck." Even a good fellow with the right stuff had no guarantee. "There would still be labor and hardship and anxiety; there would still be discomfitures and reverses," Ranlett warned, but young men enjoyed plenty of opportunities: "There was a boundless field for his ambition, and he entered upon it, rejoicing 'as a strong man to run a race.'"

Henry Bangs obviously had convinced himself and others that he had the right stuff, because the 1850 census listed him as a "Ship Master." He had commanded a few vessels, and Captain Hasty had named him first mate of the *Elizabeth* as she delivered a valuable cargo. Bangs appeared to be closing in on the high position of full-time sea captain that his father had held before him. It meant nothing that he owed his new command to Hasty's death; sudden death was a fact of life at sea. The question now was whether he could make good on his luck.

Now, on the afternoon of July 18, 1850, with the *Elizabeth* about a hundred miles out, Henry Bangs would have looked ahead to the landfall at New York with the same mixed feelings that his passenger Margaret Fuller had about her return to Boston. In his case the worry was more immediate, for he faced a shipmaster's most demanding task—making a safe landfall on a difficult shore.

III

NO PART OF A VOYAGE promotes more anxiety than the approach to its end. Joseph Conrad wrote of "the Landfall's vigilant look" that came across a ship captain's face within a day of land. That worry may well be too much to bear. In *The Mirror of the Sea*, his memoir of twenty years at sea, Conrad described an otherwise capable shipmaster who suffered such debilitating tension headaches when approaching coastlines that he gave up the sea altogether. Just why captains could be so undone is seen in two short accounts of landfalls that went bad in storms—one involving the disastrous attempt of a big square-rigger to enter San Francisco Bay in 1891, the other a small yawl along the New Jersey coast in 1992.

The square-rigger was another, larger *Elizabeth*, a 231-foot three-masted "Down-Easter" out of Searsport, Maine, commanded by Captain John Herbert Colcord. Those were names to conjure with in 1891. The Down-Easters were the best big sailing vessels at the end of the great age of sail; the Colcord family produced several distinguished shipmasters; and the small town on Penobscot Bay, besides being wealthy enough to finance this *Elizabeth* and other ships, was to sea captains what Annapolis is to admirals—one out of ten American merchant captains of the 1870s and 1880s hailed from Searsport, population 1,700.

When the *Elizabeth* doused most of her sails and stopped off the entrance to San Francisco just after noon on February 21, 1891, she was partway into her seventh circumnavigation of the globe in nine years, the fourth under Colcord's command, carrying general cargo from New York to San Francisco, then wheat to Liverpool, then coal back to New York. Proven as they were, Colcord and his ship were destroyed in less than ten hours by a cascading series of accidents centering on a storm that interrupted a landfall. Even smallpox works more slowly than a landfall gone bad.

After a 133-day voyage from New York, Colcord sought a tow through the Golden Gate into the harbor. Unable to strike a deal with the captain of the tugboat on station, Colcord sailed up the channel and was almost through when the wind shifted ahead at gale force and pressed the ship toward the rocky Marin County shore. For a fifty-dollar fee another tug passed him a towline, but it snapped several times, and with her captain probably distracted by this contagion of local incompetence, the *Elizabeth* drifted back out the channel and onto a dangerous shoal known as "the Potato Patch." She struck so hard that part of her keel broke off and floated to the surface in front of her thoroughly alarmed crew. Colcord put his wife and children into a small boat to get them to safety, but the ship rode over the boat and capsized it, throwing them into the water (a second boat eventually retrieved them and carried them to one of the tugs that were impotently drifting around). That night the gale built to force 10 (sixty knots), and the ship's destruction on the shoal was accompanied by numerous other tragedies. A sea swept the deck and killed Colcord, most of the crew mutinied and abandoned ship, and the remaining nine men clung to the bowsprit in the black of night until another breaker got all but one of them. Of the vessel's twenty-nine crew and passengers, only eleven survived. The San Francisco shipmasters took up a collection so that Colcord's corpse and family could be sent back to Searsport on the train.

OVER A CENTURY LATER, another flawed, tragic landfall destroyed a much smaller sailing vessel in the funnel into New York. In September 1992 the thirty-five-foot yawl *Katsura* headed out in a strong northeast wind from Edgartown, on Martha's Vineyard, toward Delaware Bay and a canal leading into Chesapeake Bay. Although the nor'easter seemed like a sailor's dream, there was a lot more in it than a good breeze. Tropical storm Danielle was creeping up the Middle Atlantic coast off Delaware and New Jersey, and newspapers and television stations from Washington to Massachusetts predicted easterly gales in the waters *Katsura* would sail through.

When clear of the island, the boat's owner, Myron Mintz, and his crew of three steered *Katsura* southwest toward their destination on a long leg across the funnel, miles from land. That night the wind fulfilled the predictions, strengthening to forty knots. Sea height averaged fifteen feet, and the biggest waves were much higher. She moved along rapidly under mainsail and engine, rolling her rails under. Her owner became seasick and went below, where he conducted the navigation. At about 9:30 P.M. the yawl's mizzenmast snapped. This eliminated the boat's two electronic navigation aids, the Loran-C and radar devices, whose antenna and scanner were secured halfway up the mast. In his years of owning the yawl, Mintz had prepared *Katsura* well for this passage, which he made frequently between the Chesapeake and his summer home on Martha's Vineyard. The crew salvaged the mast and laid it across the deck a few feet behind the steering wheel and compass.

At the time of this accident, according to a reliable position taken just before the mast went over the side, *Katsura* was thirty miles due east of the nearest New Jersey shore and, sailing a course of 240 degrees, was headed straight for the entrance to Delaware Bay, ninety miles ahead, off Cape May, New Jersey. But over the next three and a half hours, something interfered with those navigational certainties to set up a catastrophe almost as bad as the one that had destroyed Captain Colcord and the *Elizabeth* in the mouth of San Francisco Bay in 1891. At about 2:00 A.M. *Katsura*'s crew on deck were surprised to see lights looming ahead and also to feel the water become extremely rough, with breaking waves. Lights should not have appeared on the bow for several hours more, and the water should have been deep enough that the waves, while steep, were rollers with occasional spray, not breakers.

Soon the keel bounced off the bottom once or twice, and then the boat was hard aground in plunging seas that took out the rig, holed the hull, and swept two crew members overboard to their deaths. Mintz and the other survivor waded ashore through the surf and called the police from a pay telephone. They were in a state park near Barnegat Light, seventy miles north of Cape May. Somehow, instead of sailing a course of 240 degrees (about southwest) after losing her mizzen, *Katsura* had sailed 270 degrees (west). The causes of this large anomaly became the subject of litigation brought by the estates of the dead men. Among the claims was that the men on deck had made a thirty-degree steering error for almost four hours.

In such seas, some sloppy steering is to be expected, but a course error so large and for so long is highly improbable. A more likely explanation for the tragic accident was that the magnetic compass the helmsmen were steering by had developed an error of thirty degrees. Such an error is usually caused by deviation, or the influence on a magnetic compass of another magnetic force. Since the error apparently began at the time of the dismasting, it probably had to do with the broken mast and its equipment being placed near the compass. That equipment included a radar scanner and possibly a horn, each containing large magnets (the main element of a radar scanner, in fact, is called a magnetron). Subsequent experiments proved that when a scanner is within three feet of a compass, a large deviation results.

Therefore *Katsura* was done in by the unintended consequences of good seamanship. Had the yawl's crew simply cast the broken mast and its gear overboard and allowed it to drift as a hazard to navigation, she and they might still be sailing today.

IV

ALTHOUGH THOSE FATAL WRECKS and radar magnetrons were far in the future as Henry Bangs commanded the *Elizabeth* up the funnel-shaped approach to New York on July 17, 1850, he knew that every landfall is risky. Some are more dangerous than others, and New York has always been one of the more dangerous ones. Among all ports on the American East Coast, only Cape Hatteras has had more shipwrecks than New York. Robert Greenhalgh Albion noted in his history of New York harbor, "Year after year vessels by the dozen would pile up on the sands of that desolate angle, uninhabited at that time save for a few scattered fishing villages." These waters between the New Jersey and Long Island shores led to the country's busiest port. In July 1850 more than three dozen ships a day entered or cleared New York; 110 wharves handled half the country's imports and a third of its exports, as well as the great wave of immigrants from the Irish potato famine and the failed European revolutions of 1848. In 1850 alone the city received almost 213,000 immigrants, a number approximating half its population.

The problem for an incoming shipmaster like Henry Bangs was safely navigating the funnel to the harbor's mouth. Poorly marked by lighthouses, the New Jersey and Long Island shores could be unforgiving to ships grounded in strong winds and steep waves. Within six hours after the *John Milton* struck the south shore of Long Island in a strong onshore wind in February 1858, she lost her entire crew of twenty-seven and all her structure above the waterline except for two deck beams and the ship's bell. Said a witness, "She melted like a lump of sugar."

Shipwrecks then were as routine as automobile accidents are today. The shipping news sections of daily newspapers ran columns with titles like "Gales, Disasters, Etc." and "Missing Vessels." A typical column, which appeared in the *New York Tribune* on July 15, 1850, reported the disappearance of a captain from a ship in Charleston, South Carolina; the death of another captain off Key West, Florida; and the loss off Cape Race, North Carolina, of a ship named the *Corsair*, with the subsequent rescue of her 230 crew and passengers. The *Tribune*'s Missing Vessels column for July 17 included the following notice from Baltimore: "Fears are entertained for the safety of the bark *Abby Baker* and the schooner *Flight*, which sailed from this port for California eight months ago. The former was spoken about four months ago, and has not been heard from since." Wrecks and disappearances were so frequent that in 1852 a marine insurer, the Atlantic Mutual Insurance Company, began keeping "Vessel Disasters" scrapbooks of news clippings. Within ten years the company compiled twenty-five of these volumes.

Regular destruction prevailed even among New York's most skilled sailors in the area's toughest vessels. These were the harbor pilots who, in their weatherly schooners, sailed out from the protection of Sandy Hook to go aboard arriving ships and navigate them through the winding channel to the city. Eighteen pilot schooners were lost before 1858—some run down by other vessels, others wrecked on the shore. The risk may have been the inspiration for the swaggering of the typical Sandy Hook pilot who, got up in a top hat and frock coat, climbed ships' ladders with the dignity of an admiral and was greeted with commensurate respect.

Such pride would have been felt also by Henry Bangs as the *Elizabeth* sailed fast up the funnel on July 18 in a rising southeast wind. Yet his ego should have been tempered by anxiety. A careful captain devoted hours to reviewing local charts (the detailed maps of waterways, including their sea bottom), and also *The American Coast Pilot*, a sailing guide known as Blunt's in honor of the family that had been publishing it since 1796. The charts would have encouraged him with their clear delineation of the many shoals and the few lighthouses. Blunt's, moreover, would have warned him not to put too much trust in charts but to take into account all factors, including the depth of the water measured by frequent soundings. Edmund March Blunt, the Jeremiah of seafaring, warned, "Mariners who have escaped all former dangers of the voyage are often shipwrecked upon some sudden rock or shoal at the entrance of their destined port." He strongly urged captains approaching New York to double-check their positions and the weather at every possible opportunity by taking soundings and checking the barometer.

Blunt's caution was well placed. With few exceptions, aids to navigation were none too dependable before the federal government began to assert its authority over coastal navigation later in the 1850s. There was no coast guard, and lighthouses were few and unreliable. The early history of lighthouses in America and Britain is less a story of technological advance than one of a long conflict among wary sea captains, stingy governments, and greedy local citizens who made their living by looting wrecks. An aspiring English lighthouse builder reported that his wrecker neighbors objected to his plans to build a light on the grounds that "I take away God's grace from them." Many of the lights that were built were shoddy and poorly equipped. Towers blew down, and the cheap lard that was issued to fuel the lamps solidified in cold weather. The lights themselves usually had the same characteristics and so were indistinguishable one from another. New York seamen sardonically joked that it was easy to pick out the white rotating light on Fire Island beach from the neighboring white rotating lights: all a sailor had to do was peer through the dark and spot the small grove of trees surrounding the Fire Island tower.

Even if the structure and the light were reliable, the keepers often were anything but. Some were too depressed, lazy, or drunk to trim the light's wick and wind its rotating mechanism. One moody keeper complained, "I have known the distracted feeling of leaving a loving wife and romping child behind . . . , have been closed up for weeks hearing nothing but the Atlantic's mighty waves crash against and over our bottle-like edifice, and the screams of the sea gulls, as if taunting us in our lonely plight." One student of the psychology of lightkeepers was Robert Stevenson, a famous Scottish lighthouse builder. His views on keepers were summarized by his grandson, the novelist Robert Louis Stevenson: "They usually pass their time by the pleasant human expedient of quarreling; and sometimes, I am assured, not one of the three is on speaking terms with any other." Three was a healthy number because it led to constant bickering and so "the lightkeepers, agreeing ill, keep one another to their duty." In America, even long after the federal government developed a professional lighthouse service, there remained serious concerns about keepers' reliability. In the 1902 edition of the government's *Instructions to Light-Keepers*, two of the first ten rules banned liquor, two barred keepers from engaging in private business, another two required them to keep the light clean, and the remaining four insisted on basic competence.

As sorry as many lighthouses and their keepers were, the United States did have one lighthouse in 1850 that was considered absolutely dependable, and that was the one Henry Bangs attended to. The Navesink Highlands lighthouse stood over 250 feet above the water, and its two rotating lights reached out as far as twenty miles. The key was the light's revolutionary Fresnel lenses, the only ones in America. Beehive-shaped glass caps with the surface made up of many prisms were placed over the flames and produced a light eight times brighter than the ones sent out by the usual polished reflectors. With so few trustworthy aids to navigation in the funnel, it was natural for Bangs to place his hopes on this unusually effective one—so long, of course, as he heeded old Edmund March Blunt's warning not to trust it only.

AS BANGS PLANNED HIS COURSE to pass within range of the Navesink lights, the *Elizabeth* raced north toward New York in a pounding rain and the enveloping roar of her bow wave. Bangs should have been able to draw some conclusions about the weather he would face as he dove deeper into the funnel. Meteorology was becoming a science during his lifetime, and an alert master could cobble together an accurate forecast using four modern tools.

The first of the four was the experienced seaman's "weather eye" or (because weather changes are not always seen) "weather sense." It is a combination of observation and comparison with past events. A simple rule is that white clouds indicate fair weather, black clouds bad. Anyone who goes outdoors learns that as a child. A sharp weather eye also takes mental snapshots of clouds, the flight paths of birds, and the direction of waves and compares present images with recent ones to identify trends. Other senses can tell more. Sweat may mean the high humidity of an approaching nor'easter (usually the most vicious of all storms, with northeast winds), whereas dry nostrils alert you to a clearing sky and dry northwesterlies. Many people become exhausted and careless in hot weather, depressed in rain, and slow thinking in the cold. Old injuries begin to hurt a day or two before a nor'easter (Jonathan Swift was sure that aching corns and teeth were reliable predictors of storms). "Wind is like massage stimulating ten million nerve ends on the surface of our skin," Lyall Watson observed in *Heaven's Breath*, his natural history of wind. When a pathologist measured the responses of triplets to changeable weather, he found that his three subjects had the same measurable physiological responses to each passing cold front. Blood pressure dropped, and body weight, blood acidity, and white blood cell count increased.

Waves are especially valuable because, since they respond to wind and carry long distances, they recount the recent history of weather. Waves that look and feel too big for the local wind may be from a storm over the horizon. "The sleeping giant" (as the ocean sailor William Albert Robinson called this effect) yawns and stretches itself into full consciousness in the waves sent by distant storms. A small storm may send out rollers more than five hundred miles, or a day and a half, from its center—about the distance from Cape Hatteras to New York.

The weather sense was the first of the four tools that Henry Bangs could have relied on as he sailed into the New York funnel. The new rain and freshening wind should have told him that the weather was changing rapidly. Besides his senses and experience, he should have consulted three other resources. One was a growing database of historical weather behavior and seasonal patterns that was published in two volumes—the Blunt family's *American Coast Pilot* and, for the ocean, Matthew Fontaine Maury's newly published (in 1847) *Wind and Current Chart of the North Atlantic*. They would provide him with average weather conditions for times of the year as well as warnings on how to anticipate storms.

The third and fourth weather tools were more analytical. One was a new way to exploit the barometer developed by Robert Fitzroy, a descendant of King Charles II by one of his mistresses, who was captain of the *Beagle* during Darwin's voyage to the Pacific. Fitzroy determined that what was most important was not the atmospheric pressure as shown by the barometer at any moment but the direction and rate of change: the faster the change, the greater the wind and (often) the worse the weather.

The fourth tool was the theory of circulation around weather systems developed by the American William Redfield. Observing that trees fell in different directions on different sides of a storm, he concluded that the wind does not blow straight from high atmospheric pressure to low pressure but forms a vortex rotating counterclockwise around a low, aiming fifteen degrees in, and clockwise around a high-pressure system, aiming out. (The patterns are opposite in the Southern Hemisphere.) According to this "law of storms," therefore, wind direction indicates the location of the center of a low or storm. According to Buys Ballot's law, which a Dutch meteorologist derived from Redfield's theory, when observers in the Northern Hemisphere stand with their backs to the wind, they can locate the low's center by pointing to their left. As Henry Bangs sailed north up the funnel in the strong southeast wind, therefore, he should have known that the sleeping giant of bad weather was stretching astern and off to his left. He might have had a barometer (not all ships did), but it would only have confirmed what the deteriorating weather was already telling him: a storm was overtaking the *Elizabeth*.

His predicament was later described perfectly by Redfield in *The American Coast Pilot*. When a ship sails northwest near New York in a "very considerably and rapidly" rising southeast wind, Redfield wrote, "the projection of this will give us a Cyclone coming up from the S. Westward, as usual thereabouts, and we are thus right in its track." The question was what strategy to adopt to minimize time spent in the storm. Redfield warned that carrying on by continuing to scud (run before the wind) would only carry the ship along the route of the storm, which would overtake and possibly overwhelm her. Heaving-to (almost stopping) was no better because it stopped the ship in the storm's path. The best strategy was to turn hard to starboard and reach to the east, away from the advancing storm. That, insisted Redfield, is the only way to "get *out* of the cyclone circle." To stay in the circle invited catastrophe.

Henry Bangs did not change course. If he believed that the strengthening southeast wind and growing seas were the harbingers of a storm he was racing to New York, he said nothing to his passengers to show he was concerned about a giant, sleeping or awake. His interest lay less in weather than in lighthouses. He was looking for the Navesink Highlands light to guide him down the last miles of the funnel to the New York harbor entrance. That bright light was his Torah, his Cross, his total and ultimate guide to his destination.

WHILE BANGS SHOULD HAVE SENSED that something was awry to the south, he could not know the full extent of his predicament. The day before, on July 17, a hurricane had come ashore near Cape Race, North Carolina, wrecked dozens of ships, and whirled north through bays and rivers. According to one report, "Everywhere, so far as heard from outside the Capes and in the Chesapeake Bay, the wind blew with great fury, producing an almost unprecedented heavy sea." The storm capsized a ferryboat in Philadelphia, killing twenty people, and dense rains caused serious flooding that eventually would reach to northern Vermont. In the hurricane's dangerous right-hand sector lay the approaches to New York harbor and other waters around Long Island that Walt Whitman would call the "Sea of the brine of life and of unshovell'd yet always-ready graves / Howler and scooper of storms, capricious and dainty sea."

The first signs of this unusually dangerous storm reached New York on the evening of the eighteenth, when the *Elizabeth* was about halfway into the funnel and approximately fifty miles south of New York harbor. That was when an amateur weather watcher in Newark, William Whitehead, noted that his rain gauge, four and three-quarters inches deep, had overflowed and that the wind was blowing up into "the fitful gusts of a hurricane, more violent than experienced in July for 30 years." Within a few hours thousands of roofs were blowing off houses, hundreds of ships were dragging anchor or snapping their cables, and vessels were grounding or sinking up and down both sides of the great funnel.

V

THE *ELIZABETH* RACES DOWN the funnel at eight or, on the faces of waves, ten knots. The southeast wind that has been on her stern for several days has increased to almost gale force. If it were on her bow, she would be heeled far over, deluged with spray, her crew and passengers barely hanging on. But such a wind from astern is a comfort to a captain eager to make port. Surge, climb up the back of the next wave, surge again, climb again—the day runs on.

On the afternoon of the eighteenth Henry Bangs announces that the *Elizabeth* is off the New Jersey shore, somewhere below Barnegat Inlet, and that tomorrow morning they will breakfast at New York City. Catherine Hasty will look back on this news and recall, "All were in ecstasy"—a generous memory considering that her own joy was tempered by her mourning. Her new friend, Margaret Fuller, comforts her: "I shut myself away with my sorrow but Margaret came and kissed me."

At 2:30 in the morning, Bangs checks his position by taking a sounding, as Blunt's urged. A sailor goes forward and heaves the lead (pronounced *led*) line, a long rope marked at every fathom, or six feet, and weighted down by a bit of lead with some tallow to pick up a sample from the sea bottom to check against the notes on the charts. The man reports twenty-one fathoms. (Whether the tallow was inspected we do not know.) Although that depth would put the ship toward the middle of the funnel, Bangs is sure that he sees the rotating Navesink light dead ahead, which means the *Elizabeth* is a bit close to the New Jersey shore. Only one of the twin lights is shining, but that does not concern him. He orders the helmsman to alter course a few degrees to starboard to put the light on the port bow.

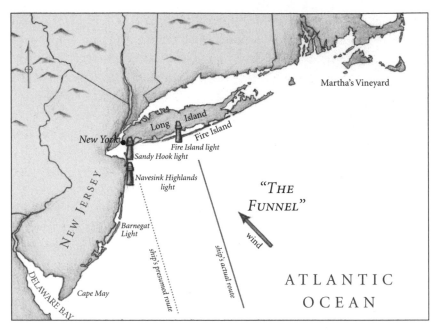

Of the dangerous funnel into New York between New Jersey and Long Island, historian Robert Greenhalgh Albion wrote, "Year after year vessels by the dozen would pile up on the sands of that desolate angle, uninhabited at that time save for a few scattered fishing villages." The most important lighthouses, at Navesink Highlands and Fire Island, had similar light characteristics.

Morally sure that in a couple of hours the light will be abeam and the *Elizabeth* can soon after turn west around Sandy Hook, where she will pick up a pilot and sail into the harbor he has been hunting down for six difficult weeks, Henry Bangs feels satisfied. He is living out every navigator's dream—a nighttime landfall on the brightest of all lights, with the promise of entering the harbor in the light of day. Feeling the wind and sea rise, he orders a reef taken in, and with that Captain Bangs leaves the deck, walks down to his cabin, throws himself down on his bunk, and falls fast asleep.

A LITTLE OVER AN HOUR LATER, just after 4:00 A.M., the lookout is horrified to see the rollers ahead rise up into huge, vertical walls of white water exploding in thick spray. He cries out, but nobody hears him as the ship careers through these immense piles of foam on the bare edge of control. The steersman throws his weight into the wheel to resist her skidding into a wild broach that would leave the 130-foot ship lying beam-to in the trough of the breaking seas with her sails aback, flopped on her side near capsize. The *Elizabeth* sluices wildly through the plunging breakers until with a hard *whack* she comes to a dead, shuddering stop. The next wave pries up her stern and hurls her forward and onto her side with a great cracking of wood, as the marble blocks and statues fly through her planking. The waves plunge down upon the helpless grounded ship like wolves on a wounded deer, shattering spars and lifeboats and driving sand-filled water through every companionway and port. The crew and passengers stagger on deck in their nightclothes.

As dawn comes over the already half-destroyed ship, Bangs sees that the ship has struck at high tide on a bar less than a quarter mile off a flat beach stretching from the rising sun to a single rotating light on the top of a lighthouse about two miles to the west. He realizes he has deceived himself. The rotating light he saw before dawn was not Navesink Highlands. He is more than fifty miles east of there. The *Elizabeth* has run up on Fire Island beach. Adding to his horror is the awareness, now that his ship is no longer running with the wind but stopped dead, that the *Elizabeth* is in the midst of a great storm.

He does not have to be told that the ship is doomed, and very likely his people with her. On a normal, placid July morning, his crew and passengers could easily paddle the quarter mile from the bar to the beach in dories or improvised rafts. But not this day, in a falling tide under the jackhammer of a hurricane's jetting waves. With tons of water crashing on the ship, the seamen escort the passengers forward on the steeply tilting deck to the forecastle, where they should be safe until the tide rises in midafternoon. Catherine Hasty slips and falls into a hatch, and a sailor pulls her back by her hair. Another seaman carries Nino in a bag tied around his neck.

When the sailors talk of swimming ashore for assistance, Margaret Fuller gives one her life jacket, and he and some others improvise rafts. Not all survive—Horace Sumner's body will never be found—but Bangs, Catherine Hasty, and others are washed onto the beach, badly bruised and stripped almost naked by the waves before fishermen drag them out of the sea.

A fisherman runs to the lifesaving station that was established at the lighthouse only two years ago, even though ships have been wrecking on the long, narrow Fire Island beach for two centuries. (The name was inspired either by a typographical error—there are five small islands nearby—or by a fire in colonial days.) When the lifesaving crew finally drags the boat to the wreck site, the sea is far too high for them to row out. An effort to lob life-lines to Margaret and the others using a mortar gun fails, and the crew, fishermen, and surviving sailors and passengers helplessly watch the battering of the ship.

Margaret, her husband, their little boy, and the young Italian woman, Celeste Pardena, wait in the forecastle with some crew members. Celeste is in hysterics; Ossoli calms her with prayers. In early afternoon the high water returns and, enhanced by the storm surge, floods the forecastle. The mate and steward help the exhausted, soaking family up to the deck. In her white nightgown, under the plunging waves, Margaret sits quietly next to the foremast in full view of the people on the beach only a few hundred feet away. The mate, Davis, crawls aft to their cabin and retrieves food and personal items that he ties around Margaret with kerchiefs. He tells her they must try to swim to shore before the ship falls apart. She refuses to go without her son and husband. From on shore, people squinting through the heavy spray see (as a journalist records) a hopeless women in a white night-gown, "with her hands upon her knees and tempestuous waves breaking over her."

At 2:30 P.M. the rising tide under the storm surge lifts the *Elizabeth*, and as the ship rises she twists, implodes, and melts into pieces, leaving only a shred of deck. As the sailors dive overboard, the steward, George Bates, orders Margaret to come with him. "I see nothing but death before me," she tells him. "I shall never reach the shore." Bates grabs the boy and a broken spar and leaps into the water. A breaker rips out the masts; the deck follows. Ossoli and Celeste fly into the surf, and when the next wave retreats, not even Margaret is left.

Her body and Ossoli's are not found. After Nino's corpse appears in the surf, Catherine Hasty and the sailors take him to a nearby house where, as though expecting a miracle, they keep watch over him all night. In the morning they bury him in a sailor's sea chest.

VI

WHEN THE NEWS of the *Elizabeth* and her well-known passenger reached the mainland, hundreds made their way to the wreck site to mourn, gawk, search for valuables or bodies, or salvage the cargo (the statue of John C.

Calhoun, its left arm broken off, was shipped to Charleston). The newspapers expressed outrage that although every passenger died, including two women and a child, almost all the crew members were saved. Ralph Waldo Emerson, furiously wrote to the English writer Thomas Carlyle, "She was drowned with her husband and child on the wreck of the ship *Elizabeth* on the 19 July, at 3 in the P.M. after sitting all day, from morning, in plain sight of the shore." Despairing, "I have lost my audience," he sent Henry David Thoreau to find her corpse and history of the Italian revolution.

Then thirty-three and polishing up *Walden*, his rumination on solitude in nature, Thoreau had some experience in this grim exercise. A year before, on a beach on Cape Cod, he had watched somber clusters of families searching the sands for the remains of loved ones. Then he chose to reflect not on the hard reality of the searchers' dignified patience but on the more abstract factor of chance. How was it that some bodies were recovered and others were lost forever? Not even the insurance companies had a clue. "There are more consequences to a shipwreck than the underwriters notice," he remarked in *Cape Cod*. "The Gulf Stream may return some to their native shores, or drop them in some out-of-the-way cave of Ocean, where time and the elements will write new riddles with their bones."

Now, on Fire Island beach, Thoreau was not an observer of searchers but himself paced the beach for days and made inquiries of local land pirates who claimed to be able to help but turned out to be frauds. Unable to find Margaret or her manuscript, he at least found her portable writing desk, some of her letters, and one of Ossoli's shoes and his coat, from which he removed a button as a remembrance. One morning, while walking a few miles west of the wreck, Thoreau was shocked to discover bones with tooth marks and a few shreds of flesh left by the fish. These bones were human, he decided, but whether they were male or female he was unable to say. He paid the lighthouse keeper to bury them in the sand. After writing to Charles Sumner to report this find and his failure to locate Sumner's brother, Thoreau went home to Concord, where the wanderer in nature had unpleasant dreams of buttons and the clothes of dead men.

A year later, on a beach at Cape Cod, he was moved to ruminate on how "it was my business to go in search of the relics of a human body" and how he had come upon those bones and believed himself to be witnessing a momentous event, but from a great emotional distance. These bones "were alone with the beach and the sea, whose hollow roar seemed addressed to them, and I was impressed as if there was an understanding between them and the ocean which necessarily left me out, with my sniveling sympathies. That dead body had taken possession of the shore, and reigned over it as no living one could, in the name of a certain majesty which belonged to it." As Thoreau struggled to gain a connection with this moment, Margaret Fuller might have been satisfied to learn that she had indirectly brought a little warmth to his chilly hill.

LIKE SHELLEY, Margaret Fuller became a character in the melodrama of the "James Dean effect," which requires that a good life terminate early, before the passage of time brings disintegration. In the legend-making time after her death, people seized on the last helpless image of Margaret and used it to reshape the world's most willful woman, until then gossiped about as the paragon of sin, into a paragon of true womanhood. She became another helpless female wrecked upon the sea, like the young captain's daughter in Henry Wadsworth Longfellow's wildly popular ballad of 1839, "The Wreck of the *Hesperus*":

> The salt sea was frozen on her breast,
> The salt tears in her eyes;
> And he saw her hair, like the brown sea-weed,
> On the billows fall and rise.

The New England literary lion Bronson Alcott decided that the image of the passive woman in white suited Margaret as she should have been, as Saint Margaret. "We have none so near our concept of the ideal woman as the noble lady gone down into the sea." Emerson was at first appalled. He had believed that the only thing fated about her return was the inevitable triumph of her genius. Now all was hypocrisy, he told his journal:

> It is a bitter satire on our social order, just at present, the number of bad cases. Margaret Fuller having attained the highest & broadest culture than any American woman has possessed, came home with an Italian gentleman who she had married, & their infant son, & perished by shipwreck on the rocks of Fire Island, New York. . . . And her friends said, "Well, on the whole, it was not so lamentable, & perhaps was the best thing that could happen to her. For, had she lived, what could she have done?"

Margaret Fuller once advised Henry David Thoreau, the hermit of Walden Pond, that he was like a bare, chilly hill that needed to be warmed. He searched the beach for her remains and belongings. (Courtesy Thoreau Society, Lincoln, Massachusetts)

Henry Bangs placed all his hopes in the Navesink Highlands light, which with its Fresnel lens was America's brightest aid to navigation in 1850. (U.S. Coast Guard)

Cap Cook Cast a Way on Cape Cod 1802

"She melted like a lump of sugar," said a witness to the destruction of a ship grounded in breakers. The forces involved are obvious in this painting of a wreck on Cape Cod, *Capt. Cook Cast a Way on Cape Cod 1802*, attributed to M. F. Cornè. (Courtesy Peabody Essex Museum, Salem, Massachusetts)

The top inscription on the Margaret Fuller memorial in Mt. Auburn Cemetery, Cambridge, Massachusetts, reads, "By birth a child of New England, by adoption a citizen of Rome, by genius belonging to the world." (John Rousmaniere)

Emerson nevertheless helped assemble a sanitized biography of a new Saint Margaret who lacked a challenging personality, radical politics, and a common-law marriage. This and other prettified simplifications of a complex woman's life irritated a number of her friends, one of whom accused the typical martyrologist of turning Margaret "round and round until he gets her in certain lights familiar or propitious to himself, and then blows a succession of brilliant bubbles."

Misleading as it was, the image of Saint Margaret was unbreakable. When a plaque honoring her was placed on Fire Island beach near where the *Elizabeth* grounded, the inscription set her on a pedestal as "noble in thought and in character, eloquent of tongue and pen, an inspiration to many of her own time, and her uplifting influence abides with us." (The plaque was lost in the sands by the early twentieth century.) On the legally unsupported but socially approved assumption that she was safely married, librarians cataloged her books under the name Ossoli, which also is the family name ascribed to her on the memorial stone in Mount Auburn Cemetery, under which her son's ashes are buried. The inscription describes her accurately as "by genius belonging to the world" and also, just as accurately, draws attention to her intense loyalty to Ossoli and their son in their last hours: "United in life the merciful Father took them together and in death they were not divided." (The last clause quotes a verse from the Old Testament [2 Sam. 1:23]: "They were lovely and pleasant in their lives, and in their death they were not divided.")

THE PRICKLY FULLER did survive in some circles (and not only in her great-nephew Buckminster Fuller, the iconoclastic designer and futurist). Nathaniel Hawthorne probably drew on her for the doomed heroine in *The Blithdale Romance* and the independent Hester Prynne in *The Scarlet Letter*. Many hopeful New England parents named their daughters for her (one was Margaret Fuller Glover Ames, another remarkable woman who, as we will see in chapter 6, suffered a triple loss in a storm at sea in 1935). Away from her canonization, her old friends affectionately remembered her feisty personality. "Gray-headed men of today, the happy companions of her youth, grow young again while they speak of her," Julia Ward Howe noted in her biography of Fuller, published in 1883. But as those who had known her left the scene, she became forgotten. It took the rise of another women's movement in the 1960s to bring her back in all her complexity and forcefulness. Margaret Fuller's writings are now part of the canon of American literature.

VII

BESIDES A FAIRER APPRECIATION of Fuller's life and work, the modern era also brought new ways to understand the wreck of the *Elizabeth*.

An understanding of the medical situation of the soaking wet woman in white suggests that her passivity had less to do with the triumph of true womanhood than with hypothermia. The storm and wreck left her exposed for several hours to cool water and a hurricane-force wind without any waterproof or insulating clothing to protect her against the chill. It is also likely that there was little food for the people waiting on the wrecked ship. In such circumstances, as a person's trunk temperature drops from the normal 98.6 degrees into the mid- or even low nineties, the body goes into self-preservation mode. As blood circulation to the extremities slows, agility and physical strength quickly decline, as does thinking. Victims of hypothermia usually become disoriented, incoherent, and unable to care for themselves. As the body is chilled to about ninety-four degrees, muscle rigidity may set in and the victim may become semiconscious. Under the stress of the environment as well as of the dashing of her hopes, even Margaret's extraordinary internal resources could not resist melting away with the ship beneath her.

WHAT OF THE CAUSES of the wreck itself? The *Elizabeth* was lost because her captain, Henry Bangs, believed she was almost fifty miles west of her actual position. He was certain the ship was off the New Jersey shore, when in fact she was off Fire Island.

Although large (almost one degree of longitude at that latitude), this navigational error was not uncommon. An inaccurate chronometer, a slip of the hand on the sextant or the pen, a small lapse while making navigational calculations, an error in estimating speed or current—any or some or all of those might have added up to a fifty-mile error. The issue is not so much that Bangs *made* the error. Rather, it is that he failed to check for it. Navigation offers numerous opportunities for errors, and it also contains more than enough redundancies and procedures for identifying mistakes. The carpenter's rule of "measure twice, cut once" is standard operating procedure among experienced navigators and ship's officers. Today, for example, a good navigator never relies entirely on global positioning system (GPS) satellite data but regularly checks those positions against ones derived from compass bearings on charted objects or dead reckoning navigation (based on speed and course).

In 1850 a captain or navigator would have been expected to sail slowly and cautiously toward a landfall, feeling his way according to the rule of "log, lead, and lookout." While repeatedly checking the distance sailed on the log (a primitive odometer), he would take many depth soundings and bottom samples to compare with the chart, and also assign one or more alert sailors to keep a lookout. The lead line was the key to double-checking a vessel's position in the New York approaches because it provided information about the changing nature of the sea bottom. In *The American Coast Pilot* the Blunts likened marine navigation to travel by foot, horse, or carriage: "If you wish to navigate with thc lead, in addition to having a good chart, you must watch the changes as you would the aspect of a country over which you are traveling." That is as true today, when electronic sounding devices are used, as it was in the day of the lead line. The 1998 edition of the *United States Coast Pilot*, the modern successor to Blunt's, advises that in the funnel leading to New York, "many vessels have been wrecked on the coast of New Jersey and Long Island through failure to take frequent soundings when the position was uncertain."

Such disciplines have been so forcibly imposed over the centuries that it is incredible that Bangs took only one sounding that night. No less incredibly, only a dozen or so miles from what he believed was his goal, he went to his bunk and fell asleep.

We are left groping for an explanation. Perhaps Bangs's mistake was overconfidence. There are occasions when even the most cautious navigators in their eagerness for certitude are as vulnerable as teenagers at a prom. But at his age and experience, Bangs should long before have had Pollyannaism flushed from his system. That leaves only one plausible explanation for the wreck of the *Elizabeth*: her acting captain was so exhausted that he lost touch with his situation.

The telltale evidence is that *he fell asleep*. If Bangs was exhausted—and the evidence points that way—it does not demand too great a swing of the imagination to speculate on why. He was the emergency captain of a ship that had been harboring smallpox (and for all everybody knew was still harboring it). The crew was one man short and may have had an inexperienced new mate. The transatlantic voyage had been long and monotonously easy until the southeast gale arose just as the *Elizabeth* entered the hazardous funnel. And perhaps, like Joseph Conrad's captain who suffered migraines when approaching shore, Henry Bangs could not adapt his self-confidence and his brain to the steps needed to make a successful landfall. Under these many pressures, Bangs could well have pushed himself to exhaustion.

SLEEP DEPRIVATION has attracted considerable attention in studies of human errors in the military and in civilian life. In extremely dangerous situations, exhausted people may be caught up in wild fantasies, or they may forget all their training and normal caution. Tired sailors have imagined that hostile strangers have sneaked aboard; tired soldiers have been known to throw themselves down in exposed roadside ditches to snatch a few minutes of sleep.

The lack of self-care by commanders is a constant problem in ships at sea, military units, and other hierarchical organizations where leaders are like gods. Richard Henry Dana Jr. described the duty of a shipmaster to care for himself in his manual *The Seaman's Friend*: "Upon his character, and upon the course of conduct he pursues, depend in a great measure the character of the ship and the conduct of both officers and men. He has a power and influence, both direct and indirect, which may be the means of much good or much evil." Commanders may make their subordinates rest, but nobody polices the commander's own self-care. Ellen MacArthur, a single-handed offshore sailor, in 2001 described her situation like this: "One person in isolation suffering from days too hot to sleep, too rough to sleep, too noisy, violent and fast to sleep. Too nervous to sleep, no rules to sleep to, no-one to tell you to go to sleep, too many repairs to sleep."

THE HIGH COST OF EXHAUSTED LEADERS has been demonstrated in research done by and for the military into military situations where alertness is proved to be crucial. Jonathan Shay, a psychiatrist, has written of the risks to military leaders: "Sleep deprivation, in particular, promotes: catastrophic operational failure; fratricide and other accidental deaths; otherwise preventable noncombatant casualties; loss of emotional control; and failure of complex social judgment."

Shay cites as an example the First Battle of Savo Island in the Second

World War, one of the worst naval disasters in American history (I will discuss another in chapter 7). After the successful Allied invasion of Guadalcanal in 1942, eight Japanese ships made a daring, successful night raid in a rainstorm on a much larger fleet of American and Australian ships. Within forty minutes enemy gunfire tore apart five heavy cruisers, sinking four of them with a loss of 1,000 dead and 709 wounded. (Fortunately, the raiders did not attack the many supply ships that the warships were guarding.) Subsequent investigations concluded that what was missing at Savo was not hardware but an alert, aggressive, and flexible state of mind called "battle mindedness." The culprit was the careless brain brought about by long-term sleep deprivation. According to the navy report, "Fatigue was a contributing factor in the degree of alertness maintained." This fatigue fed mistakes, and also overconfidence. Like navigators who are sure they have sighted the light they need to make a perfect landfall, all expected everything to go exactly according to their own best wishes. The Allies had made several wrong assumptions, including believing that each ship's squads of well-trained human lookouts would be alert.

"Oh the stupendous optimism of that night!" Samuel Eliot Morison wrote of Savo in his history of the American navy in the war. He could have added, "Oh the stupendous exhaustion." The lookouts were so tired after almost two days of continuous combat duty that, in a state of bare consciousness, they stared low for submarines and high for airplanes and so were oblivious to the Japanese surface ships until they started firing. The ships' bridges were not much better prepared. When hostile gunfire was first exchanged, the worn-out commanders of two American heavy cruisers—one of whom had not been to bed for almost two days—convinced themselves that they were firing on friendly ships and attempted to countermand the orders of their gunnery officers.

Experiment as well as history has proved that exhausted people may be no better at recognizing the danger of their situation than alcoholics and drug addicts. Denying their vulnerability, they become high on sleep deprivation and the invulnerability it seems to promise. As psychologist John Leach describes the overarching problem, "Man is notoriously inept at monitoring his own condition." The dangers of sleep loss are regularly underestimated because some functions are not impaired. In tests on firing ranges, for instance, sleep-deprived soldiers fired their weapons just as accurately as rested soldiers, but their judgment was poor; when "friendly" figures appeared, the well-rested soldiers held their fire, but the exhausted riflemen fired on. They become captives of "droning"—a passive, reactive, lockstep state of mind exemplified by the phrase "one foot in front of the other." Because drones may be able to function in a simple way but are incapable of making sound judgments, we insist that our doctors get their sleep and that airline pilots and truck drivers are on duty for only a pre-scribed number of hours.

But not nineteenth-century sea captains. The *Elizabeth* ran aground because Henry Bangs—unlike his alert and sensitive passenger Margaret Fuller—had ceased paying attention to himself and his duties.

AFTER THE WRECK, while the storm was still blowing, Bangs spent much of the day attempting to rescue the men, women, and child still aboard his disintegrating ship. He then slipped away, leaving Catherine Hasty—his former captain's widow—to relate the ship's story to newspaper reporters.

The destruction of the *Elizabeth* appears to have wrecked Bangs's ambi-tions. On his next (and last) known voyage, in February 1852, instead of commanding another respected merchant vessel carrying valuable works of art and genteel passengers, Henry Bangs sailed as mate aboard a trading schooner bound from Philadelphia for Cuba. He died sometime later, leav-ing his wife so destitute that in 1860 the census—which ten years earlier had ascribed to him the elevated position of "Ship Master"—listed her occupation as "Servant." Her name, incidentally, was Elizabeth.

3

The Yankee Gale

Gulf of St. Lawrence, 1851

*"Then, too, at sea—to use a homely but expressive
phrase—you miss a man so much."*
—Richard Henry Dana Jr.

A STROLL THROUGH the burial ground in an old American
waterfront town usually leads to at least one monument to a seaman or ship that did not return home. In Scarborough, Maine,
for example, an obelisk was put up in memory of Seth Hasty,
who died of smallpox aboard the *Elizabeth* while being nursed
by Margaret Fuller. Our reaction to such a shrine may depend
on its size or beauty, but mostly we are moved by the number of
people mentioned. A memorial to an individual seems dignified
and orderly. It inspires satisfying thoughts about the nobility of

a life cut short and the sweet devotion of the friends and family who subscribed to build the monument.

Seamen's group memorials, however, are not so easily absorbed because they invariably involve terrible accidents. They may leave us stunned and anxious to walk on. At Truro, near the tip of Cape Cod, there is a towering monument to fifty-seven men and boys lost in seven vessels in the same storm on the same day in October 1841. Across Massachusetts Bay, a bronze sailor at a steering wheel looks out from Gloucester's waterfront over ten plaques inscribed with the names of more than 5,300 seamen lost at sea. Such numbers suggest that the mortality rate of fishermen at sea was like that of soldiers in combat (which, in fact, it often was). We find ourselves wondering about the fabled romance of "iron men in wooden ships" whose courage and muscle gave no quarter either to the sea or to deep feeling—or so we have been told.

Sometimes a single storm is memorialized in more than one place. In Boothbay, Maine, a monument honors the memory of the thirteen men and boys who died in a storm in October 1851 aboard a schooner called the *C. G. Matthews*—one of the five local fishing schooners that went down in that same gale with a total loss of twenty-three. Four hundred miles east of Boothbay, in Kildare Capes, Prince Edward Island, a stone in an Anglican churchyard is dedicated to the memory of many more victims of that same October storm, "the 160 American sailors who lost their lives during the 'Yankee Gale' of 1851."

Because it was so destructive, the 1851 gale in the Gulf of St. Lawrence was granted the rare privilege of a unique name. Until hurricanes were first named in 1951, few storms were given an identity other than the month or year when they blew through. Storms could be memorialized in a general way, however. Up and down the American East Coast there are many Hurricane Creeks that were redirected by heavy blows, Hurricane Hills that were stripped of hardwoods in a storm, and Hurricane Holes where boats found protection from a blast. When storms were named, it often was for their victims. The *Portland* storm of November 26, 1898, the subject of a later chapter, is called after its most prominent victim, the sidewheeler *Portland*. The Yankee Gale of October 3–5, 1851, off the Canadian maritime province of Prince Edward Island, was named for its hundreds of victims who had sailed up from the United States and were therefore known as Yankees.

I

AMERICAN FISHERMEN had been going to the rich waters of the Gulf of St. Lawrence since before the Revolution, more recently to catch mackerel. Searching for cool water, the fish swam north in the spring from the Carolina coast in schools so large and active that when they passed by, even experienced seamen mistook them for a new breeze filling in. Their hunters were equally noticeable. Pacing the beach at the tip of Cape Cod one spring, Henry David Thoreau saw a solid white wall of mackerel boats apparently suspended above the horizon "in countless numbers, schooner after schooner, till they made a city on the water. They were so thick that many appeared to be afoul of one another; now all standing on this tack, now on that." When the mackerel left the cape's warming waters and swam north and east, the city of fishing schooners broke up, went home to unload their catches, and provisioned for the summer and fall fishing season on the Gulf of St. Lawrence, which the fishermen called the Bay.

In June 1851, in fishing villages from Cape Cod to far Down East Maine, masters and their crews feverishly prepared their vessels for the familiar passage east to the Bay. Among the several dozen schooners that sailed out of Southport, Maine, an island town near Boothbay, was the *C. G. Matthews*, a typical mackerel boat of her time. Her captain was thirty-one-year-old Joseph P. Harris, who owned her and several other boats with his brother Paul. Joseph sailed them, and Paul ran the business ashore. Under Joseph was a crew of twelve men and boys, most in their twenties but one only sixteen. This crew had originally planned to ship out in another schooner, the new *G. W. Reed* (like the *Matthews*, probably named for an investor). When the *Reed* was launched, while they were "rolling" her—racing from one side to the other to rock her hull and thereby shake off debris that had adhered to the bottom during construction—she suddenly capsized. Understandably concerned about their safety, not to speak of their shares in her success, the crew members rebelled and signed on with Harris and the *Matthews*. The *Reed*, meanwhile, was worked over, a new crew was hired, and she sailed east in the wake of the mackerel.

Arriving in July, the *Matthews* and the *Reed* joined a crowd even larger than the one that amazed Thoreau at Cape Cod. A Prince Edward Island newspaper described it this way: "Here the fleet of vessels congregated at one time will often amount to 2,000 sail, although as a general thing not more than 200 to 400 vessels sail in company. At night when the fleet is safely anchored, the lanterns lighted on each vessel and hanging from the shrouds, one may fancy himself looking upon some huge city lying in repose, with its lamps all trimmed and burning." As this immense fleet gathered in the Bay, the crews readied their "jigs" (handlines) for the great mackerel kill. Built specifically for jigging, most of the schooners were fifty-footers called "pinkies"—derived from "pink," which meant "drawn in." Their sterns were not square like those on most schooners but were pinched to a high, rising point.

This arrangement protected the helmsman from waves. It also provided a hull that allowed these little ships to easily heave-to—jog along slowly under shortened sail with the helm lashed with lines so there was no need for a steerer. Heaving-to was favored for surviving storms and also for the unique requirements of fishing in the Bay. When going after cod on the shallow waters of the Grand Banks and Georges Bank, schooners stopped and anchored, but anchors would not dig into the Bay's deep, rocky bottom, so the pinky captains preferred to heave-to. As the schooner slowly worked her way along, sliding sideways to leeward about as fast she progressed ahead, the crew stood in their assigned places along the rail (the cook forward, then the captain, and finally the novices way aft so their lines would not tangle the others), and "jigged" their handlines, twitching them up and down. When they got a bite they snapped the lines up and overhead to land the fish in barrels on the deck behind them. A visitor to a mackerel boat remarked on the frenetic activity:

> There are few things more exciting than catching mackerel where the fish are biting fast. Everyone moving his hands and arms as if his life depended upon his exerting himself to the utmost, the constant flip, flip of the fish, as they fly from the water into the strike-barrels, and the short, quick, impatient cries—"keep lines clear," "whose lines are these in my berth?," "there's a bloater [extra large fish]," "more bait here, skipper"—with now and then a strong expletive, indicating the breaking of a jig, or the parting of a line. The whole attention is absorbed in the business, and I have stood for nearly an hour, without stirring my feet or changing my position in the least; for any movement, or shifting our feet or body, will almost certainly embarrass the proceedings of our next neighbor.

After catching fish all day, they cleaned fish all night. To the disapproval of devout folk, they even worked on Sunday. When all the barrels were packed after two or three months, a schooner hoisted flags in her rigging, collected letters home from other crews, and sailed back home to Southport, Newburyport, Gloucester, Cape Cod, or wherever to collect $2.25 a barrel of fish and pay the crew's shares.

SUCH WAS IDEAL MACKEREL FISHING—a team enterprise, a full hold, a safe return. If almost all these schooners were Yankee vessels, it was because many Canadians knew too well how rare such perfection was and were more interested in the safer option of farming. (Prince Edward Island is the setting for *Anne of Green Gables* and other rural novels by Lucy Maud Montgomery.) For all the fish that swam in the Bay, the island was a trap for careless or unlucky seamen. A recent pilot book lays out the problems clearly:

> The harbors are small and shallow, with narrow entrances through sand bars, which become impassable in a heavy sea. All harbor entrances break in a moderate sea and in some areas it becomes impossible to locate the best channel. *Caution:* The channels through the bars are liable to be blocked or shifted by storms. . . . *Anchorage:* With few exceptions, the anchorage is poor along this coast. The bottom is of red sandstone, thinly covered in places with sand and gravel, making for poor holding ground.

Blowing across the two-hundred-mile bay near the St. Lawrence River's mouth, the gales could be vicious, even in summer. "The river was lashed to fury by the wind and threw its boiling spray far up the shore," said George Hepworth, a cruising sailor, of one summer storm. "It resembled in its windings and its agonies an immense serpent in its death agony, writhing, tossing, tumbling, and moaning in its fury." Aware that such storms were possible, though hoping they were not likely, Yankee fishermen trusted in their weather eye. Should they be wrong, they had confidence that their years of experience on the Bay would lead them to safety on the open sea. Should they not escape the Bay, they placed their faith in their pinkies, which, they were certain, would heave-to and hold their ground against any northerly gale that threatened to blast them down onto the island. They had survived such storms before, and they would again if luck went their way.

∽

EVEN EXPERIENCED NEW ENGLAND shipmasters (one of them noted) had "hard-lined, parchment-looking faces, deeply scored with anxiety and dread." The depth of concern among seamen and, even more, among their people ashore was revealed in the 1850s to a young journalist who, on a lark, went out from Gloucester for some winter cod fishing on Georges Bank.

All seemed pleasant until there came a night spent anchored in a gale, surrounded by other schooners. When the captain placed a hatchet near the bow cleat so the anchor rode could be quickly cut if another vessel dragged down, the writer was suddenly overwhelmed by a longing for his sweetheart back home. "Not that I was afraid of death—no, that was not the feeling; but there was one at home whom I wanted to see, and, holding her hand on mine, I should have been better reconciled." Another schooner did go adrift that night. Missing the writer's ship, she rammed and sank a third pinky, taking down both crews. To the writer's amazement, after the storm passed the next morning his shipmates went right back to fishing without a comment on the tragedy. When the hold was filled, the schooner sailed home to Gloucester.

As the ship neared port, the writer discovered that his own fears were small compared with those of the townspeople. The shoreline was covered with men and women shouting questions about other ships still out on the banks. A few were so desperate to hear about their loved ones that they rowed out to the schooner and demanded information about one crew or another. "The town was in commotion. Such anxiety I hope never again to witness. When the vessel came alongside the wharf I put my luggage out, and concluded not to repeat the experiment of making a trip to Georges in midwinter. When I got home they told me that I had grown much older in the few weeks of my absence."

HENRY DAVID THOREAU, walking on Cape Cod, also was struck by community concerns, but as much by their ambivalence and variety as by their occasional intensity. "The inhabitants hear the crash of vessels going to pieces as they sit round their hearths," Thoreau noted about Truro, near Highland Light lighthouse. Down on the rocky beach, life went on: among the anxious families searching for their dead he discovered wreckers looking for treasure and farmers calmly harvesting seaweed to fertilize their crops. He innocently inquired of an elderly man if he liked the sound of the surf. The fellow grimly replied that he certainly did not. "He had lost at least one son in 'the memorable gale,' and could tell many a tale of the shipwrecks which he had witnessed there."

Such a gritty relationship with the sea was new to Thoreau, who had been raised far inland with a cool, abstract Shelleyan appreciation of the romantic sublime seascape. "The stranger and the inhabitant view the shore with very different eyes," he mused. "The former may have come to see and admire the ocean in a storm; but the latter looks on it as the scene where his nearest relatives were wrecked."

Back up the hill in Truro, Thoreau learned another lesson of coastal life, that for every grieving man there was at least one grieving woman: "I found it would not do to speak of shipwrecks here, for almost every family has lost some of its members at sea. 'Who lives in that house?' I inquired. 'Three widows,' was the reply."

Mortality Rates, Fishing and War

Place or Event	Mortality Rate	Time (years)
Southport, Maine, 1851	54 per 1,000 fishermen	1
Civil War battles, 1861–65	40.1 per 1,000 Union troops	4
Gloucester, Mass., 1830–97	30 per 1,000 fishermen	67
World War I combat, 1917–18	17.1 per 1,000 U.S. troops	2
World War II combat, 1941–45	8.6 per 1,000 U.S. troops	5

A SEAMAN IN THE DAYS OF SAIL—and especially a fisherman—was engaged in one of history's most dangerous trades. A nineteenth-century seaman was four times more likely to suffer an accident than a miner. Sometimes fishing was more dangerous than going to war. Gloucester lost a total of 668 schooners and 3,755 men between 1830 and 1897, meaning that throughout most of the nineteenth century, year in and year out, this town with an average population of about 8,000 could count on losing ten boats and 56 men. The mortality rate among fishermen was about 30 per 1,000—a rate well above that of United States armed forces in the two world wars. For every two American soldiers or sailors who died in combat in the Second World War, seven men or boys of Gloucester died on the fishing grounds. These devastating figures actually understate the risk to seamen compared with those of men in uniform, for whereas only a few

THEY THAT GO
DOWN TO THE SEA
IN SHIPS
1623 — 1923

Familiar as a symbol of Yankee enterprise, this statue on the Gloucester waterfront with its quotation from Psalm 107 is in fact part of a memorial. The names of more than 5,300 fishermen lost at sea are inscribed on nearby plaques. The mortality rate of nineteenth-century Gloucester fishermen approximated that of soldiers in combat. (John Rousmaniere) soldiers were in combat units, every fisherman was on the front lines. ("Fisherman" was a flexible term. At a time when school attendance was poorly enforced, boys as young as nine shipped out as cooks, and many teenagers handled fishing lines.)

Why did they keep going out? Economics played a powerful role. What historian Stephan Thernstrom said of Newburyport, Massachusetts, applies to the other fishing towns: "the relentless pressure of poverty." In towns that offered few if any employment alternatives, almost every able-bodied man and teenager—approximately half the town's males—went to sea in fishing schooners or merchant vessels. Even if there were alternatives, they paid poorly. Workers in the textile mills made about sixty cents a day, which fishermen usually could match even in bad years. Nine months of fishing brought $150 to $800 ($2,500 to $13,000 today) in shares of a schooner's catch.

Even when fishing paid poorly, men in rural coastal villages were pushed out to sea by a number of forces. One was custom. Youngsters who did not eagerly anticipate the adventure of experiencing the mystery of the awesome deep went to sea, for while they may have dreamed of better lives inland, the only life they knew was seafaring. The spray speckling a town's windows also salted its rituals, economy, vocabulary, diet, identity, social structure, and mythology. When Margaret Fuller insisted of women, "Let them be sea captains if you will," she restated the national conviction that even commanders of pinkies ruled the world.

Seafaring also offered freedoms and opportunities that could not be matched by farming or a job on an assembly line. Boys wanting to see something of the world instinctively went to sea. Assuming that they survived, they usually were satisfied, and their communities profited by their experience. In Sarah Orne Jewett's 1896 novel *The Country of the Pointed Firs*, which she based on years of living among seamen in coastal Maine, an old sea captain looks back from the end of the age of sail to a better time, when the maritime trades educated young men: "They may not have had the best of knowledge to carry with 'em sight-seein', but they were some acquainted with foreign lands an' their laws, an' could see outside the battle for town clerk here in Dunnet; they got some sense o' proportion. Yes, they lived more dignified, and their houses were better within an' without. Shipping's a terrible loss to this part o' New England from a social point o' view, ma'am."

That "social point o' view" included other forms of independence. Coastal villages were nurseries for entrepreneurs. From the day they first signed on to a vessel for a microscopic share of her profits, young seamen believed, rightly or wrongly, that they were in control of their destiny. Before Joshua Slocum took the ultimate independent step of sailing alone around the world, he spent three decades as a fisherman, commercial seaman, and boatbuilder. One of his sons succinctly summarized his view of life in these words: "Anything to make a dollar, danger or no. Father was a trader in any line." Such an outlook cannot be easily discarded, regardless of the risks that surround it.

WHEN JOSEPH HARRIS, in Southport, Maine, prepared the *C. G. Matthews* to head up to the Gulf of St. Lawrence in 1851, Southport and its neighboring villages of Boothbay and Boothbay Harbor had a combined population of 2,800 and sent out approximately seventy fishing schooners crewed by about 700 men and boys. Every eight or nine years, the towns lost at least two schooners and 20 to 30 sailors. Southport alone lost 38 men and boys from a population of 543 in 1851. Even before the *Matthews* headed east to the Bay, the area had already lost 15 men and boys, including a pair of brothers and a father and his two sons. Losing one seaman was bad enough for a family, but losing two would be disastrous, and Harris made it a policy not to sign on brothers or other close relatives.

The risk was also the community's. Not only did fishing towns send almost all their able-bodied men and boys out to sea, but everybody ashore was connected to seafaring by blood, friendship, and economic dependence. Many people ashore were shipbuilders, sailmakers, suppliers, or investors; almost a fifth of the men of Boothbay owned shares in fishing boats or other commercial vessels. As one indication of how a single stormy day could devastate a town, Marblehead, Massachusetts, dominated the fisheries until a gale on September 19, 1846, destroyed eleven of its schooners and killed sixty-five of its men and boys. The next year Marblehead sent out only fifteen schooners instead of the usual dozens and thereby ceded leadership to Gloucester.

These risks to family and town were not denied. When the Boothbay-Southport history was published in 1906, amid the many genealogies, stories of land disputes, and generous profiles of local businessmen, the author, a local merchant named Francis B. Greene, included a stark chapter simply titled "Casualties." Looking back from the dawn of the automobile and telephone era, Greene traced the long, sad history of accidents under sail all the way back to 1624, when two men were lost in the wreck of a fishing boat that had come up from Plymouth Colony (the vessel was raised and went back into service). In the intervening years Greene found so many hundreds of deaths at sea that he summarized the chapter as a history of "the many broken homes consequent upon a seagoing life." As a less explicit reflection of the carnage that swept through fishing towns, Greene also provided a long chapter on the many institutions that served as that era's community mental health centers—the region's many churches.

In even more poignant language, at Gloucester's 250th anniversary celebration in 1892, the clergyman who presented the upbeat historical address paused in the middle of his roster of local triumphs to acknowledge the darker side of the town's commercial success: "The shadow of this picture of enterprise," he said somberly, "is that cast by the weeds of the widow, and the picture itself is marred by the tears of the fatherless. . . . The ocean is our mausoleum, and few are the hearts here which look upon its floods without a shudder."

II

ON THE WARM, CALM AFTERNOON of October 3, 1851, fishing, not mourning, is on the minds of the thousands of Yankees drifting in their pinkies on the Gulf of St. Lawrence. Late in the day flocks of seabirds are seen flying ashore, and to the northwest there is what one sailor calls "a lurid brassy appearance" that reminds some well-traveled sailors of a West Indies sky on the eve of a hurricane. A long, rolling swell gradually swings in from the ocean, and as it rises so does the southeast breeze, at first gently and then with force.

The wind backs into the northeast and by dark is blowing at near gale force, directly down on Prince Edward Island. Barometers fall precipitously; one on nearby Nova Scotia drops 31 millibars (almost one inch) in twenty-three hours. At an average of 1.4 millibars an hour, that is well above the one millibar-an-hour rate that today places a depression in the category of a highly explosive meteorological "bomb." Recognizing that a large storm is racing toward them, many captains try to sail east beyond the island's last bit of land, East Point, to get into open water. But the light headwinds and then the northeast gale block them. Unable to make their way to windward into the blow, they attempt to hold their position by heaving-to, but the wind tears away their sails, leaving them drifting help-lessly down on the island. They hope the storm will die before they fetch up on the rocks, but it refuses to quit. One captain's log entries comprise a long column of the words, "Fresh gales and cloudy," "Fresh gales and cloudy," "Fresh gales and cloudy"—hour by hour for almost two days.

FEW YANKEES WIN THE FIGHT to keep off the island. One of those who does is Henry Bray, of the schooner *Harvest Home* out of Southport, and he barely makes it, as he describes in his story as transcribed by a friend, thick Down East dialect and all:

> We had been jiggin' mack'rel fer several days in th' bend o' th' island, an' long 'bout th' fust o' October we had caught 150 bar'els that wuz stowed in 'er hold below, when one night, just at dark, er leetle air o' wind cum out o' th' east'ard. It wuz thick er dungeon o' fog, an' ca'm es er mill-pond, an' had ben thick es mud fer two or three days, sort o' mullin' an' fixin' up fer sumthin'. . . .
>
> It soon begun to breeze up, an' pretty soon it wuz er blowin' er good stiff breeze, an' we wuz headin' 'er off to th' south'ard. I knowed well 'nough th' Old Man wuz plannin' to git 'er out by East Pint, afore we had to heave 'er to under 'er two-reefed fores'l. 'Long 'bout ten o'clock that night she had all she could carry under 'er three lowers [mainsail, foresail, and forestaysail], an' it er breezin' on all th' time. Pretty soon she rolled down 'til 'er sheer poles [rods just above the deck] wuz under water, an' then th' Old Man says: "Boys, stand by to take in th' mains'l, an' we'll tuck two reefs in it." By th' time we had it reefed an' set ag'in, we had to scratch th' fores'l down an' put two reefs in that; an' by th' time we had it swayed up, th' Old Man told us to haul th' jib down. Sumbudy cast off th' halyards an' she fetched er slat an' parted th' jib sheet, an' that sail ripped open an' slat to pieces afore we could git it down.
>
> It wuz er screechin' rite out loud by that time, I tell yer, an' er haulin' out to th' [northeast] all th' time, an' er headin' o' us off an' drivin' us inshore. It wuz er pipin' on harder all th' time an' th' old gal wuz er makin' bad weather o' it. Sometimes she would fetch er dive an' go under chock to 'er fore m'st an' every thin' loose on deck wuz washed overboard.

They take the mainsail off her ("it wuz sum job, I tell yer") and under severely shortened sail heave-to in a powerful wind and immense sea. The challenge is to keep her bow at least partially aimed into the seas; if caught broadside to a breaking wave, she will be swamped:

> When she would rise on er sea she would lay over on 'er side, 'til th' water wuz up eround 'er hatches on deck. Her whole lee side wuz under water, an'

New England fishermen in the nineteenth century worked Georges Bank for cod in the winter and "the Bay"—the Gulf of St. Lawrence north of Prince Edward Island—for mackerel in the summer and fall. The Yankee Gale was a nor'easter blowing across the bay onto the island.

we wuz er hangin' onto er lifeline, what wuz made fast to wind'ard 'long 'er weather rail, an' we wondered if she wuz ever goin' to cum up ag'in a'tall.

By an' by, 'way went th' fores'l, th' foregaff snapped off like er pipe stem, an' that last sail slat to pieces quicker'n you could say Jack Robinson. When she fell off in th' trough o' th' sea, er comber broke onto 'er weather quarter, washed two men overboard, smashed our yawl boat to pieces, hangin' to th' davits, an' broke th' main boom short off th' slings. Arter erwhile we got th' storm trys'l bent on to try an' hold 'er up, but in erbout ten minutes arter we had 'er set, she busted clean open an' slat to pieces. Then she fell off ag'in, an' th' Old Man scud 'er under bare poles, 'bout all we could do now enyway. In erbout an hour it wuz daylight, an' we wuz watchin' fer er chanct to beach 'er.

Twelve hours into the gale, with the storm sails shredded, the captain's only hope is to await daylight, turn the stern into wind and sea, scud before the blow, and by some miracle find an opening through which to run her onto the shore.

We knowed, well 'nough, that we had but one chanct in er thousand fer 'er to go over th' bar on er sea. When we reached th' shoal, she fell in th' trough o' er heavy sea an' struck th' bar, an' both 'er masts went over th' bow broken off short. She then swung eround side to, an' th' next heavy comber rolled 'er over on 'er beam ends, in th' breakers, on th' beach.

The *Harvest Home* spills her crew into the breakers. Henry Bray grabs a floating hatch cover that eventually is heaved ashore, where a man hauls him to dry land. Another Ishmael, he discovers that he alone is left to tell the story. "I wuz th' only one saved o' all our crew. All th' rest o' my poor shipmates wuz lost."

THE *HARVEST HOME* was only one of many wrecks in the Yankee Gale, and Henry Bray one of just a few survivors. The lowest estimate was that 74 ships were destroyed and 150 men were lost, although the numbers probably were closer to 100 and 200. Some schooners that also attempted to run the bar became piles of oak, pine, and corpses. (All that was found of the *Mary Moulton* of Castine, Maine, was a box containing the ship's papers.) Other ships sank at anchor or were rammed or capsized. Ironically, the *G. W. Reed*, which had frightened her crew off to the *C. G. Matthews* when she rolled over at her launching, rode out most of the gale alongside the *Matthews* until the *Matthews* disappeared. The *Reed*'s crew sailed home, carrying the bad news to Joseph Harris's widow, three young children, and brother and partner, as well as to the twelve families of his crew. The gale killed another 11 Southport men and boys, making a total of 38 maritime deaths that year. More than half a century later Francis B. Greene, the local historian, observed of 1851: "For fatalities to our town that year has eclipsed all others."

III

As often occurs after disasters, a spate of scapegoating and finger-pointing followed the gale. Some Prince Edward Islanders faulted the fishermen themselves either for their irreligious fishing on Sunday or for their seamanship. A newspaper editor who argued against all evidence that the gale was nothing much ("Not a rickety outhouse has been injured that we have heard of") claimed that the damage was due to "bad ships, badly managed." Other witnesses who were inclined to take the storm's force and longevity more seriously put the editor's antagonism down to self-interest, for he was a fevered opponent of spending money on improving harbors and building lighthouses.

There could be no disagreement about the heroism of the islanders who risked their own necks to rescue sailors whom they took into their homes or to recover bodies that they buried (many in sailcloth) in their own church burial grounds or in improvised cemeteries near the sea. In 2001, the 150th anniversary of the Yankee Gale, Dave Hunter, a Prince Edward Island historian, described this behavior as a natural outpouring of concern on the part of islanders:

> In a maritime region everyone understood how it felt to lose loved ones to a wreck, and I believe this is what governed their reactions. Those who survived were quickly taken into Island homes, and treated as their own. . . . The whole community pitched in to help, not because they had to but more, I think, because that is what they would have wanted others to do for them. It is shocking to see the numbers that died while plying their trade.

Seafarers living hundreds of miles away in isolated coastal or island towns did not have to be told that the islanders would help. A man in Maine asked one of the Prince Edward Island newspapers for assistance in finding the remains of his son, who was aboard a schooner. "All hands on board perished. Myself and family have been extremely anxious to obtain his poor body. . . . If you can hear of any body come on shore, and been buried answering this description, do my good sir write me, and you will get the prayers of an afflicted family for your health and prosperity in this life and a blest immortality beyond the grave." The editor replied that his son's body had been located and its distinguishing features noted before he was given a proper burial, and now the grave would be marked. More than

Most vessels caught in the gale were sharp-sterned pinkies, like this one just stemming the tide under jib as her crew takes a breather from their labors. It was hard, risky work. When a landsman who had gone out in a pinky returned home, "they told me that I had grown much older in the few weeks of my absence." (Courtesy Boothbay Region Historical Society)

The Gloucester Fishermen's Wives Memorial, sculpted by Morgan Faulds Pike and installed on the town's waterfront in 2001, honors the remote, often forgotten victims of the fishing wars. When Thoreau visited a coastal town, "I found it would not do to speak of shipwrecks here, for almost every family has lost some of its members at sea. 'Who lives in that house?' I inquired. 'Three widows,' was the reply." (John Rousmaniere)

65 American sailors were buried in six island cemeteries, including the one at Kildare Capes, where a memorial stone was later placed. In Boothbay the operator of a local ferry service donated a monument to the 13 men lost on the *C. G. Matthews*.

Other Americans made pilgrimages to the island that fall and winter. Some were shipowners or insurance adjusters sorting out their losses, but many were relatives of seamen looking for remains. According to one heartrending story, a seventy-year-old retired ship captain named James Wixon went up from Maine in search of his four sons and nephew, all lost with the *Franklin Dexter*. The sight of familiar clothing drying on a fence led him to inquire further. Coffins were disinterred, and as they were opened, revealing his nephew and three of his sons, poor old Captain Wixon fainted dead away. Islanders helped the captain find the fourth son's corpse on the rocks. The five coffins were placed aboard a schooner bound for America, the *Seth Hall*, and Wixon took a steamship home.

Up to this point, Wixon's story is straightforward, if somewhat amazing (although its details have been confirmed by Edward MacDonald, a Prince Edward Island historian). From there it assumes the mystical proportions that often adhere to tales of storms at sea when people are attempting to deal with catastrophe. It seems that the ship's youthful captain, Seth Hall (for whom the vessel was named), was warned by older sailors that bad weather was approaching, but he laughed at them and headed out anyway. The outcome of his blasphemy became well known on the island. As Lucy Maud Montgomery summarized the story in her novel *The Golden Road*, "He did sail out of the harbor; and the storm did catch him, and the *Seth Hall* went down with all hands, the dead and the living finding a watery grave together. So the poor old mother up in Maine never had her boys brought back to her after all. Mr. Coles says it seems as if it were foreordained that they should not rest in a grave, but should lie beneath the waves until the day when the sea gives up its dead."

The belief that storms come from higher powers seems to be behind another tale that arose from the Prince Edward Island gale: a wind gust spun a church ninety degrees so that its altar faced east, as it should have been built, instead of its original north.

~

BOOTHBAY, SOUTHPORT, AND GLOUCESTER continued to send fishing boats up to the Bay. Handlines gave way to nets, which depleted the mackerel stock, and many fishermen shifted over to sardines to feed the canneries built in the old fishing towns or went ashore to work in factories. In the early twentieth century the catch of choice became lobsters, which until then were used mainly as fertilizer but had come to be considered a delicacy by "cottagers," "rusticators," and other summer people who ventured up from Boston and New York on the *Portland* and other big sidewheelers.

IV

GIVEN THAT LONG STORY of destruction, it is reasonable to ask how it affected the men and their communities. Sailors are often spoken of as though they are warriors not only impervious to emotional pain but beneficiaries of it. "It was a dog's life but it made men of those who followed it," the retired shipmaster says in Sarah Orne Jewett's *The Country of the Pointed Firs*. All the same, there is little reason to believe that fishermen and fishing towns were any more callous toward anguish than the families of firemen, soldiers, or policemen, all of whom may be victims, survivors, or rescuers.

Nobody lacks an emotional threshold. The British Army discovered in the Second World War that even its toughest sergeants had feelings. After a number of battles in which a great many of their men were lost, sergeants who had been the backbone of fighting units suddenly became helplessly anxious. "I can't put any definite time on when I felt myself slipping," said one sergeant; "It is like a flower that grows." Having reached this threshold of pain, they wanted nothing more to do with the command responsibility that might lead to more suffering (many volunteered to be truck drivers). The behavior was so widespread that doctors gave it a name, "old sergeant's syndrome." This pattern of emotional numbing, panic attacks, and acute distress is now part of the definition of post-traumatic stress disorder.

If mariners survived emotionally to sail another day, it probably was due in part to necessity, in part to their complex relationship with the sea, and in part to their conservative respect for rituals and other traditions. They mourned their losses, and good shipmasters not only gave them leave to do so but provided rituals for mourning and grieving. That captains could be empathic may come as a surprise to readers of terse first-person accounts like *Before the Wind*, Charles Tyng's memoir of sailing life in the early nineteenth century, which became a surprise top seller when it was finally published in 1999. Such narratives may seem to demonstrate that mariners were men of iron with hearts of granite. If most accounts of accidents at sea seem bloodless, it is because they are official documents, like police reports, or because they were written by highly reticent men to whom public display of emotion was anathema. A seaman of the late nineteenth century probably came closer to the truth of these captains' souls when he described "that strange mixture of great seamanship, ruthless conservatism, blasphemy, and strange inarticulate warmth that was the Atlantic Captain in those days." The power of these documents lies less in what was written than in what was left unexpressed.

That the sea need not drown tender feelings is clearly proved today by the competitors in single-handed around-the-world sailing races. In *Godforsaken Sea*, Derek Lundy describes the bonds between these men and women that maintain a sense of community and meaning in this Other World:

> In the Southern Ocean the fragile lines that connect the sailor to humanity are stretched to the limit. Sometimes they break. The sailors in these races depend for help on their connections with one another far more than on any remote and uncertain source of aid from land. Some skippers have been lifted almost literally out of the sea by fellow racers. Most wouldn't have survived long enough to be picked up by diverted ships or to be reprieved by lifesaving equipment dropped from planes—if they happened to be within reach of them. And in some races a boat and sailor have just disappeared without word or trace.

It is that vulnerability that connects them. One of the most successful of these remarkable racing seamen, Philippe Jeantot, admitted to Lundy his feelings of fragility when sailing alone in the Southern Ocean. "During all that time you are cold, you feel so lonely, you are frightened. You have to admit that, you know."

SUCH VULNERABILITY IS NOT A PRODUCT of the modern era of men's emotional liberation. Samuel Eliot Morison, who had seen many deaths in combat while serving as a historian of naval operations in the Second World War, observed: "For some reason that goes deep into the soul of a sailor, he mourns over shipmates lost through the dangers of the sea even more than for those killed by the violence of the enemy." Two more recent disasters at sea confirm Morison's and Lundy's observations that the sea inspires intense relationships.

One of these catastrophes was the 1987 capsize and sinking of the roll-on, roll-off car ferry *Herald of Free Enterprise* in the English Channel after water poured in through her broken bow doors. Britain's worst peacetime maritime disaster since the sinking of the *Titanic*, it left 193 people dead. The survivors of this accident have been closely studied by psychologists (as of March 2002, the database of the library of the National Center for Post-Traumatic Stress Disorder included thirty-three professional studies of the disaster and its effects). Among the findings is one that adds substance to Morison's speculation about the bonds among seamen: disasters may stimulate the creation of several communities of vicarious victims. After the *Herald of Free Enterprise* sank, psychologists were surprised to discover that some of the people who were most deeply affected were workers on other Channel ferries who were remote from the accident physically, though not emotionally.

Thirteen years after the sinking of the *Herald of Free Enterprise*, in August 2000 many old enemies mourned the sinking of the Russian submarine *Kursk*, with 118 sailors and officers aboard, during a training exercise in the Barents Sea. Even as the Russian government concocted a bizarre campaign to throw blame for the sinking on the U.S. Navy, American sailors responded with warm sympathy engendered by their many years sharing the dangers of the deep sea in their own claustrophobic vessels. Admiral Carlisle A. H. Trost, a former U.S. Navy submariner, spoke of "a bond of camaraderie" between American and Russian submariners that always transcended the Cold War. Christopher Drew, an authority on modern submarine spying, identified the common concern in language that, with small alterations, could describe the fears and empathy that bind all seamen: "Still it is the image of men possibly huddled in the hull, banging for attention as the air turned foul and the sea churned through their sub, that will linger most."

THERE ARE FEMALE VICTIMS TOO, but with the exception of the occasional passenger or captain's wife, until recently most of them were obliged to suffer ashore, like the three widows in the house on Cape Cod that Thoreau was discouraged from visiting. When the women were honored, it

Running before a gale, a small boat is in bare control unless the sails can be doused. No less frightening than a storm itself are the words "lost at sea." Mariners usually did all they could to recover victims. Illustrations like these were commonplace in nineteenth-century publications. (Author's collection)

often was indirectly—for example, in the name "widow's walk" for that rooftop lookout where wives spent days, as Mary Shelley had, hopefully if not desperately staring out to sea through telescopes as their emotions and economic fortunes rose and fell on the fate of their husbands' vessels. A whole school of romantic creative work was devoted to women waiting ashore. Poems, ballads, and paintings portrayed them as victims of a cruel sea that in one stroke could shatter them emotionally and, by implication, economically. Typical is the poem "The Three Fishers" by the Victorian era writer Charles Kingsley. On the coast of Devonshire three fishermen go to sea, leaving wives who stay up all night in the lighthouse looking for their boat, only to find their three corpses on the beach the next morning. The lesson for women is clear:

> For men must work, and women must weep,
> Though storms be sudden, and waters deep,
> And the harbour bar be moaning.

In a painting by Frank Bramley, a sad old woman consoles a girl—a new widow, it seems, because through the window we see the flying spray of a gale. Bramley's title, "A Hopeless Dawn," says all that had to be expressed in words. More recently, in the song "White Squall," written in the 1970s from the point of view of a merchant seaman on the Great Lakes, the Canadian singer-songwriter Stan Rogers described the loss of a deckhand from a freighter and the despair of his girlfriend: "tonight some red-eyed Wiarton girl lies staring at the wall, / And her lover's gone into a White Squall."

Only recently have the women who were left behind received proper recognition. In 2001 Gloucester, Massachusetts, placed on its waterfront a memorial to what its sponsors aptly describe as "the faith, diligence, and fortitude of the wives of fishermen and mariners everywhere." A statue showing a woman and two young children looking out to sea, the Glouces-ter Fishermen's Wives Memorial reportedly is only the second memorial to the female survivors of commercial fishing (the first stands in Norway). The memorial stands near the memorial cenotaph to fishermen who died on the Banks, the Gulf of St. Lawrence, and elsewhere during the nineteenth and twentieth centuries.

UNLIKE WAITING WOMEN and families ashore, the men on board at least had the satisfaction of being able to address their predicament directly through action. The deepest emotion was reserved for the death of a shipmate. Mariners perceived themselves as warriors, and the warrior's code required them to bury and mourn their own. All who died at sea deserved a decent burial to speed their passing to the underwater paradise, Fiddler's Green, and to restore their survivors' faith in a world governed by order and decency.

If the unpredictability and miseries of a seagoing life spawned superstitions, they also provided the glue for deep friendships. The breaking of bonds through a shipmate's death profoundly unsettled mariners after months or years of regularly standing side by side as they struggled with storms, brutal officers, miserable food, bad water, and other assaults on their humanity. A ship, like an army in war, was a community comprising many small communities. What Leo Tolstoy wrote in *War and Peace* about a spirited, tightly bonded artillery battery in combat could be said of a watch aboard a vessel. He called the battery "the family circle—separated from all else." The more difficult the circumstances, the tighter the circle. The fact that the bond was not acknowledged astonished one outsider, the writer Stephen Crane, who after a shipwreck spent thirty hours in a lifeboat with the injured captain, a cook, and one of the engine oilers. In "The Open Boat" Crane wrote:

> It would be difficult to describe the subtle brotherhood of men that was here established on the seas. No one said that was so. No one mentioned it. But it dwelt in the boat, and each man felt it warm him. . . . It was more than a mere recognition of what was best for the common safety. There was surely in it a quality that was personal and heartfelt. And after this devotion to the commander of the boat there was this comradeship that the correspondent, for instance, who had been taught to be cynical of men, knew even at the time was the best experience of his life. But no one said that it was so. No one mentioned it.

Crane noticed what anybody who has been aboard a vessel in a storm knows—that in trying conditions at sea, the distinction between a survivor and a rescuer is artificial. Everybody in the group plays both roles; nobody is a passive victim. This insight about the dual role of seamen suggests how mariners can maintain their morale in terrible circumstances. As was well known long before the disasters of September 11, 2001, on-site rescuers frequently show unusual resilience, very often drawing strength from the experience even in the grimmest situations. A study of one disaster concluded that fully one-third of the rescuers found the experience rewarding, and the proportion who were highly rewarded was larger among ground zero workers than among those who were remote from the disaster site. "Active involvement to a clear purpose seemed to lead to a sense of having contributed in a worthwhile way," concluded the psychologists conducting the study.

If the family circle was threatened by storms or broken by the disappearance of one of its members, it re-formed and tightened through traditions, rituals, and memorials, to the benefit of all survivors. A burial at sea followed a meticulous order prescribed by prayer books and tradition. The ship's business often was brought to a halt for a proper ceremony after the sailmaker sewed the corpse into his hammock or a length of cloth, being sure to take a final stitch through the nose as a guarantee both that the man was dead and that he would remain securely in his last berth. With the promise of "the resurrection of the body, when the sea shall give up her dead," the sailors committed the body to "the deep." If cannons were fired, there was an even number of shots; an odd number was unlucky.

The austerity made the ceremony intensely moving. After Margaret Fuller's friend Seth Hasty died of smallpox on the *Elizabeth* at Gibraltar, his body was wrapped in sailcloth and placed aboard a lifeboat, which the United States consul's barge towed out into deep water surrounded by an honor guard of ships. In one of her last letters, Margaret described "the decent array and sad reverence of the sailors, the many ships with their banners flying, the stern Pillars of Hercules, all veiled in roseate vapor," and at the burial itself, "the little angel-white sails diving into the blue depths with the solemn spoil of the poor good man."

Here is a verse in the song "The Sailor's Grave":

Cheeks they grew pale, each heart grew weak.
Oh the tears that was seen on the brownest cheek.
A quiver displayed on lips of pride
As we lowered him down by the ship's dark side.

Often there was no corpse to lower over the side. When the sailor was lost overboard, the crew was left profoundly unsettled. Except in storm or battle, after a sailor fell overboard, small boats were quickly launched and, in the belief that loud noises would raise a body, guns were fired, horns blown, drums banged, and bells rung. Many seamen believed that a bundle of straws, or a loaf of bread in which some quicksilver or mercury was inserted, would "swim" directly to a body. The failure to recover the body stimulated intense concern. In 1852 the New York newspapers ran the notice of the death of a Captain John D. Hasty (his relation to the first captain of the *Elizabeth* is not known), who "was lost overboard Saturday evening, June 19, in spite of superhuman exertions by the crew to save him. In the sight of a crew who loved him as a father, and friends whose agonized hearts were breaking, the mighty waters closed over one of the noblest spirits and bravest sailors that ever trod a vessel's deck. 'Til the sea give up its dead, rest in peace." The well-known last line is from the hopeful vision in the Book of Revelation of the coming of an apocalyptic spiritual world—the New Jerusalem at the end of time—when the sea not only will disgorge all those lost bodies but will itself disappear forever (Rev. 20:13, 21:1). The vision reflects the truism that most seamen who died at sea were literally *lost*, their bodies never found even after the most strenuous effort.

In *Two Years before the Mast* Richard Henry Dana Jr. described the difficult time following the loss of a shipmate who had fallen from the rigging. A search was quickly made as Dana and other men leaped into the longboat. "We pulled astern, in the direction in which he fell," Dana recalled, "and though we knew that there was no hope of saving him, yet no one wished to speak of returning, and we rowed about for nearly an hour, without an idea of doing anything, but unwilling to acknowledge to ourselves that we must give him up." Although the crew was all too well acquainted with death at sea, the ship's community was broken. Encouraged by the captain, they promptly set about repairing their shattered bonds in a somber ritual:

> This was a black day in our calendar. Death is at all times solemn, but never so much as at sea. A man dies on shore; his body remains with his friends, and "the mourners go about the streets"; but when a man falls overboard at sea and is lost, there is a suddenness in the event, and a difficulty in realizing it, which give to it an air of awful mystery. . . . Then, too, at sea—to use a homely but expressive phrase—you miss a man so much. . . . You miss his form, and the sound of his voice, for habit had made them almost necessary to you, and each of your senses feels the loss.

For several days thereafter the ship was quieter, the crew and officers gentler with one another. "The oath and the loud laugh are gone." Sentiments about the lost shipmate all conclude with a mention of God and heaven because, Dana wrote, "sailors are almost all believers, in their way."

This ritualized seeking of meaning and of community in terrible events helps explain how fishermen could maintain their sanity when their war with the sea cost so many lives. Other support systems helped sustain their communities ashore, where relatives and friends at least had the satisfaction of being thoroughly practiced—all too well practiced—in grieving and recovery.

4

The Escape of the *Calliope*

Samoa, 1889

*"It was one of the grandest sights a seaman or anyone else ever saw;
the lives of 250 souls depended on the hazardous adventure."*

—Rear Admiral Lewis A. Kimberly

WE HAVE SEEN how the power of a storm at sea can ripple
outward vast distances from stricken vessels to touch families
and communities and to inspire new myths about the meaning
of the storm itself. Some storms have affected the world community and the fates of nations. One of the defining events in
English history was the summer of storms that in 1588 beat back
the "invincible" Spanish Armada of 130 ships and thirty thousand men. Two hard blows set upon the huge fleet before it even
entered the English Channel, forcing it to disperse and stop

for repairs. A third gale later hit the Spaniards off Calais and destroyed nine ships. Chased by the smaller, more weatherly English vessels, the surviving invaders fled north, doubled Scotland, and sailed down the west coast of Ireland only to be smashed repeatedly by heavy weather and headwinds. In all, Spain lost twenty thousand men and forty-eight ships—not to the Royal Navy but to storms at sea.

Many Englishmen regarded those gales as signs of divine favor. Three hundred and one years later came another storm that also was considered providential, since it helped prevent a war while producing an inspiring legend of heroism and international friendship that naval historian D. K. Brown has called "one of the great epics of the Victorian navy."

I

IN LATE MARCH 1889, the Department of the Navy in Washington, D.C., received a telegram from a remote island in the western Pacific. Signed by Rear Admiral Lewis A. Kimberly, it read, "Hurricane at Apia on March 15. Every vessel in the harbor is ashore, except the English ship *Calliope*, which got to sea." Kimberly's discouraging list of losses included his own flagship, another American vessel, and two German warships. Hinting at both great heroism and great loss, Kimberly's wire left the faces of many policymakers and naval officials red with sorrow and embarrassment. These men also were relieved. For months the United States had been planning to fight a war for which few officials could work up as much enthusiasm as the country's bloodthirsty newspapers.

Just why seven German, British, and American warships happened to be exposed to the weather in the same tiny, poorly protected harbor in the Pacific can be explained by one word: imperialism. This was the first act in the long drama of showdowns between the great powers over control of land and the shipping lanes that provided access to it. "Every island and coastline in the world seemed up for grabs," historian George W. Baer wrote of that time in his history of the U.S. Navy. "In the fever of imperialism, isolation was no longer possible, invulnerability no longer taken for granted." Except in its own hemisphere, the United States had harbored few international ambitions until the new transcontinental railroad opened a gateway onto the Pacific in 1869. This placed the country at a crossroads between its old, introverted identity and a new, more sweeping one. Some latter-day Thoreaus wanted it to remain a collection of atomized, self-sufficient, low-technology communities, like New England fishing villages. Others looked to a more cohesive, industrialized, international force ranking among the world's great powers.

For the internationalists, Samoa represented the new order not because of the coconuts and copra it produced, but because it was a stepping-stone to empire. As American goods began to flow from the West Coast to Australia, New Zealand, Asia, and the smaller Pacific islands, Washington signed a treaty with Samoa to establish a coaling station for navy ships protecting trade routes. Germany and Britain followed suit. Of the three powers, the Germans were the most aggressive. They established coconut plantations that, to the irritation of the Samoans, they staffed with laborers brought in from other countries. Under these outside pressures, an already unstable local political situation evolved into a civil war between competing claimants for the title of *malietoa*, or king. The three powers were neutral until 1888, when the Germans supported a rebel group and sent three warships—the cruiser *Olga* and two gunboats, the *Adler* and the *Eber*—to Apia, Western Samoa. In a land battle in December 1888, a force of the king's supporters, led by Mataafa, killed twenty Germans.

"Germans swear vengeance," the United States consul telegraphed Washington. "Shelling and burning indiscriminately regardless of American property. Protests unheeded, natives exasperated." German chancellor Otto von Bismarck, laboring under the sharp, critical eye of the volatile young Kaiser Wilhelm II, complained darkly about offenses to the Second Reich. President Grover Cleveland issued three aggressive messages to Congress on Samoa. As the Senate appropriated funds to expand the navy's presence there, the Asiatic Squadron's flagship, the cruiser *Trenton*, commanded by Admiral Kimberly, steamed to Apia to join the smaller *Vandalia* and *Nipsic* in a standoff against three German ships. British interests and power were represented by one warship, the *Calliope*, sent up from Australia.

War feeling spread. German and American sailors fought openly in the streets of Honolulu. Kimberly's opinion was that Germany was "aggressive and energetic, unscrupulous and active in furthering its interests, both in trade and politics." American newspapers shrieked about "the hostile officers of the German gunboats" and boasted that if the United States could only assemble a decent modern steam navy, "we could reduce Bismarck's armada to a pile of iron filings." President Cleveland drafted a belligerent fourth note that, in the end, he declined to send because he was leaving office on March 4 and thought that his successor, Benjamin Harrison, should make foreign policy. Tempers cooled when Bismarck suggested negotiations, yet the war fever persisted into mid-March.

THE THUNDERING over an island eight thousand miles from Washington concerned two issues. One was the heating up of a new commercial competition with the old empire of Britain and the growing one of Germany. The other was the debate over the naval technology required to provide the muscle to defend commercial interests.

The United States lagged far behind. Its navy was only the world's twelfth largest, well behind the navies of Britain, Germany, France, and even some Latin American countries. Its technological sophistication lay even further back. "In America, the naval stagnation of that period was something now almost incredible," Alfred Thayer Mahan (who helped end that stagnation) would write in his aptly named autobiography, *From Sail to Steam*. Most warships in 1884 would have looked at home in the Civil War. Wooden or iron sailing vessels with only modest armaments and auxiliary engines, they were called by traditional names like "sloops of war" and were expected to provide no more than coastal defense. Navy doctrine was so dominated by the technology of "sticks and string" that in the 1884 edition of Commodore Stephen B. Luce's 673-page seamanship manual for Naval Academy midshipmen, only 38 pages were devoted to handling vessels under steam power alone. Such was not the case elsewhere. In Europe engineers and steel producers were developing the technology of a powerful all-steam fleet with range long enough to reach deep into the Pacific and enough horsepower both to carry heavy guns *and* to advance into the teeth of a gale that would stop a "sticks and string" ship dead in her tracks.

Presidents, defying the traditionalists and atomists, pressed to build larger, steam-powered ships. If the country was to make good on this opportunity to become an international economic power (went the new argument), it needed a navy to protect American ships in the Pacific, and that meant establishing naval bases and coaling stations to serve as stepping-stones across the ocean.

~

IN MARCH 1889, therefore, Samoa was at the intersection of three crucial disputes, one between Germany and the United States concerning authority and territory in the island itself, the others concerning the future of the world's economy and navies. A hurricane settled all arguments. On March 12 the navigator of the U.S. Navy ship *Nipsic* noted "a peculiar, coppery red sunset." The sky was clear the next day, but with an unseasonal calm and a falling barometer. On March 14 the glass continued to drop, and the seven captains took in their topmasts and got up steam in case they had to power against a hard blow to keep from dragging anchor. The open, V-shaped harbor of Apia was no place to be trapped by a storm. The naval officers knew it, and so did the many visiting merchant captains in their trading schooners.

The storm's first historian knew it too. He wrote scornfully of "the so-called harbor of Apia" and added, "such a creek in my native coast of Scotland would scarce be dignified with the mark of an anchor in the chart." That historian was Robert Louis Stevenson, the best-selling author of *Kidnapped, Treasure Island, The Strange Case of Dr. Jekyll and Mr. Hyde, The Master of Ballantrae*, and other adventures. He formed his negative opinion of the harbor on entering it for the first time in December 1889, nine months after the storm. There before him, "broken like an egg," the German gunship *Adler* lay on a reef.

Then thirty-nine, with hemorrhaging lungs, Stevenson had fled cold Britain for the Pacific. There he found enchantment, raving about "this precious deep" of the South Seas, where there were "fine, clean emotions; a world all and always beautiful; air better than wind; interest unflagging; there is upon the whole no better life." When it came time to settle down he chose to live at the most westernized of the Polynesian islands, Samoan, because it provided the access to telegraph cables and regular steamer service that he needed to carry the manuscripts of his travel articles and books back to his London publishers. In his farm on the mountain above Apia, Stevenson wrote more adventure novels, played at gardening, and immersed himself in the intricate local politics, which featured characters who rivaled Long John Silver in both charm and craftiness. Stevenson allowed himself to became so wrapped up in the Samoa drama that he foolishly attempted to play peacemaker, at one point risking his life by riding horseback into rebel territory. His mediation attempts failed, but he did go back to doing what he did best and wrote a book about Samoa's time of troubles, *A Footnote to History*, in which he laid out the tribal feuds and the international intrigues that had collided with a hurricane.

The Samoan drama intrigued Stevenson because so many outrageous characters were at odds in such a lush setting. As remote prime ministers and presidents played what they believed was a noble game of global politics, Polynesian chiefs pettily warred over titles, traders bickered over slices of commerce, and navy officers kept their sharp eyes open for a little action. Finally, at stage right, roared in the star of the show—the great storm that humbled everybody, with one heroic exception. The true Samoan story was as exciting as *Treasure Island*.

Besides this human circus, Samoa had the flaw of geography that Stevenson identified when he first saw the wrecked *Adler*. As his readers are aware, this son of lighthouse builders knew how to distinguish safe harbors from dangerous ones. Apia's port fell into the second group, with its wide mouth open to the sea. "The entrance gapes three cables [six hundred yards] wide at the narrowest, and the formidable surf of the Pacific thunders both outside and in. There are days when speech is difficult in the chambers of shore-side houses; days when no boat can land, and when men are broken by stroke of sea against the wharves." The anchorage itself was dubious. It looked roomy enough at high tide, but as the water ebbed, sharp coral reefs emerged on either side to leave barely enough room for a dozen sizable ships. The only soft shore was a beach near the mouth of the Vaisinigo River. The river's normally modest flow brought dirt down from the mountains and deposited it on the harbor's hard coral bottom to make a layer of holding ground for ships' anchors.

Danger, declared Stevenson, "is therefore on all hands." He was writing in terms of geography, but human dangers are never far from the foreground in *A Footnote to History*. The creator of such characters as Long John Silver and Dr. Jekyll, Stevenson understood the menace of pride and greed as well as he did that of an exposed harbor. After settling in Apia, he quickly recovered from his naïve enchantment with the South Seas and saw through the posturing and intrigues of both the natives and the white merchants, diplomats, and naval officers whose ambitions the hurricane interrupted.

⌒

THE FIRST SIGNS of a storm appeared on March 14. The American, German, and English naval officers understood the risks clearly. In such a place, when the barometer falls and the swell rolling in from the ocean begins to rise, it is time for a good seaman to slip anchor cables and leave— unless there are greater pressures to stay. Here those pressures, which were intense, had nothing to do with seamanship. Stevenson remarked, "That any modern warship, furnished with the power of steam, should have been lost in Apia, belongs not so much to nautical as to political history." As seamen, the captains were inclined to vacate Apia harbor, but as representatives of foreign policy they of course had to keep their eyes on their opponents and so were playing a risky game of chicken.

The decision on the morning of the fifteenth to stay in harbor was made easier by local pilots who promised that it was too late in the season for a hurricane and that in any case the harbor was safe. Warships had held their stations in Apia during several recent gales. Their officers prepared to do so again by laying out more anchors, striking their ships' yards and topmasts to reduce windage, and building up steam in anticipation of what they believed would be a few hours' powering ahead to relieve the anchor cables. With four or five anchors dug into the layer of mud on the coral bottom, each of the seven warships rode out what appeared to be a soggy but dying gale. Torrential rain cut visibility until lookouts could hardly see the other ships, and the shore and reefs were out of sight altogether.

Just as the pilots had promised, the barometer leveled off and began to climb early on the afternoon of Friday, March 15, indicating that the storm had moved out to sea. But to everybody's surprise, the glass plummeted a second time. The storm had looped back over Samoa. (It was a wild day in the western Pacific: this huge storm was felt 1,200 miles to the east in the Society Islands, another hurricane formed 1,000 miles to the west of Samoa in the Coral Sea, and a third violent storm raced across the Tasman Sea toward New Zealand.)

The wind rose and shifted into the north so it blew directly into Apia harbor at seventy to one hundred knots. According to Captain Henry Coey Kane of the Royal Navy's *Calliope*, the situation at dawn was "as bad a one as you would care to enter."

~

AS THE GALE BUILT far above the pilots' predictions and became Samoa's worst storm in memory, the issue shifted from politics to physics. Could the ships' engines beat the wind and seas? Even at full steam ahead and with stokers working frantically to feed coal into the boilers, anchors slid across the bottom, rodes snapped, and the ships slipped toward the reef and each other. There was so much spray and flying debris that even in daylight the captains could catch only glimpses of shore to determine if the anchors were dragging—and all of them were. Near dawn, the German gunboat *Eber* drifted under a ledge, capsized, and was pounded to pieces with the loss of all but six of her crew of eighty. The waves then tossed the thousand-ton *Adler*, the other German gunboat, onto her side on the reef. Among the fifteen men lost was an officer who went insane as he lay trapped in his cabin. Observing these accidents, the captain of the dragging American *Nipsic*, which was spouting sparks out of her destroyed funnel, intentionally grounded her on the small beach in the mouth of the torrential river.

With all that wind heaving against the wild outflow of the rain-soaked river, the harbor was the roughest anybody had seen. On the *Trenton*, according to Kimberly,

> sheets of water were thrown up from the bows, and borne by the wind over the lower mast-heads, then falling on deck deluged it faster than the scuppers could free it; at times there must have been a foot or more of water in the spar-deck waterways. The air was filled with foam and spray, both salt and fresh, for in the squalls it was raining in torrents. In the gusts you could hardly look to windward, the eyes could not bear the pain of the constant beating spatter.

The *Trenton* handled it well enough until seas washed away her steering wheel, her rudder became unshipped in a collision with two sunken merchant ships, and her bowsprit ripped away. Water poured down ventilator holes into the hull as the crew of 450 struggled to plug the gap with hammocks and a table (a man was killed in the attempt). The rising water extinguished the boiler fires, and the four anchor rodes snapped. The ship drifted toward the coral reef with almost half her crew pumping and bailing.

Out of this chaos, Admiral Kimberly looked astern and saw a remarkable sight. "The large black hull of a ship looming forth in the dim distance . . . was slowly, very slowly advancing right for us, now high up in the crest of some sea, and then down so low that only her tops could be seen." It was HMS *Calliope*, hazarding an escape.

Based in Australia, the 235-foot British corvette commanded by Captain Henry Coey Kane had been roaming the Pacific on imperial duties such as chasing down smugglers in sampans off the coast of East Asia. The son of an Irish chemist and educator, Kane had joined the Royal Navy as a cadet. In 1882, during a rebellion in Egypt that threatened British control of the Suez Canal, he led naval shore forces on a forced march that ended in a victory. He was wounded, and after two years ashore he was named commander of the *Calliope*.

After arriving at Apia in February, the charming, forceful, black-bearded Kane won the friendship of Samoans by instituting cricket matches and gained the respect of the Germans and Americans by thrusting himself into the ominous political stalemate. He was quick to identify a crisis and then act to end it. Learning one day that the Germans were about to fire on the Samoan rebels, he came aboard their flagship uninvited and warned them to call off the attack. When they refused, he blocked them by planting Union Jacks in the targeted area and placing a British ship in the line of fire. When he later ordered a German to stop harassing a visiting American commercial steamer, the U.S. Navy contingent responded by having its band strike up "Rule Britannia."

II

IMPRESSIVE AS WAS HIS Samoan career before the hurricane, it is Henry Kane's behavior during the storm that makes his and his ship's names bywords for courage, up there with Nelson and the *Victory* in British naval annals.

At first light on the storm's second day, the barometer is well into its second plummet, the sea is becoming impossible, and Henry Kane sees that he must act soon. "It was the most ticklish position I was ever in," he will report with a hardened professional's understatement. The cables to most of his five anchors are parting one by one. Ahead is the helpless American *Vandalia*, bearing down on him on her way to the reef. The German *Olga* is swinging dangerously close to his starboard side. To port the reef is snapping at him. He considers beaching the *Calliope* on the sand, but at 9:30 he decides his only hope is to escape the harbor altogether. That will entail getting up a full head of steam immediately and holding it without damaging his engines for however long it takes to bang ahead five miles dead into a hurricane.

Kane knows his vessel is exceptional. As old-fashioned as she looks, with her full bark rig, the *Calliope* is the most modern and powerful ship in the harbor, if not the whole Pacific. She represents the new thinking in ship design that the traditionalists have been resisting: a swift, heavily armed warship designed and built to survive the worst possible weather. Built almost entirely of steel, she has immense compound engines that develop one-third more power and one-fourth more speed than the larger *Trenton* can call on.

Now, if she is to avoid the fate of the *Adler* and the other ships, Kane must get her out to sea. "I slipped the cables and went hard ahead calling up every pound of steam, and every revolution of the screw," he will report. "In making the passage, the vessel literally stood on end, the water coming in at the bows as she dipped, running aft immediately as she rose. I really wondered how the machinery and rudder stood the strain of the tremendous sea that was running." Although the *Calliope* can make fifteen knots in smooth water, in this appalling weather her advance is almost imperceptible. "The engines worked admirably," Kane will report, "and little by little we gathered weigh and went out, flooding the upper deck with green seas, which came in over the bows, and which would have sunk many a ship." She pitches so far that her seventeen-foot propeller occasionally lifts free. A resilient engineer named Milton spends many hours with his hand on the throttle, easing it back when the propeller rises into the air to prevent the shaft from racing to self-destruction, pushing it forward when the stern slaps down again.

The escape route is crowded, and Kane must wind his way between the reef to port and other ships to starboard and ahead. ("Almost every vessel was at one time or another in collision with some other vessel," Kimberly will remember.) A lookout on the port side will recall, "The sight appalled and fascinated me; one moment I was looking out at the reef, which was like an exposed cliff, at another I saw nothing but a seething caldron." To hold the *Calliope* on something approximating a steady course, Kane assigns ten men to the steering wheel and many more below to lines led to the lower-deck tiller. The two steering gangs communicate with each other through a voice pipe improvised from a length of fire hose. The *Calliope*

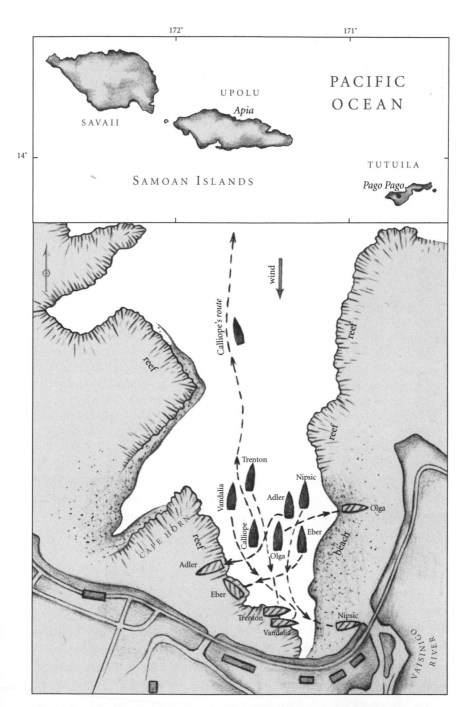

The 1889 hurricane blew straight into "the so-called harbor of Apia," as Robert Louis Stevenson called Western Samoa's main port. The anchorage was surrounded by reefs except for the beach around the river mouth *(lower right)*, where two ships grounded while the *Calliope* escaped.

yaws by the *Trenton* close enough for one of her yardarms to pass over the *Trenton*'s deck.

At this moment comes an astonishing expression of bonding among mariners. "As her stem slowly passed our bow," Kimberly will say, "I was so extremely anxious for her safety and success that I felt by a concentration of mere will I was helping her seaward. It was one of the grandest sights a seaman or anyone else ever saw; the lives of 250 souls depended on the hazardous adventure." Deeply moved by the British crew's courage, Kimberly orders his own sailors and officers to the rail to cheer the *Calliope* on. No less emotional, Kane and his men respond with their own cheers. Kane later wrote:

> Through the whole gale nothing affected the crew of the *Calliope* and myself so much as when passing the American flagship *Trenton*, which was lying helpless, with nothing to guard her from complete destruction, the American admiral and his men gave us three such ringing cheers that they called forth tears from many of our eyes, they pierced deep into my heart, and I will ever remember the mighty outburst of fellow feeling which I felt came from the bottom of the hearts of the noble and gallant admiral and his men. Every man on board the *Calliope* felt as I did; it made us work to win. . . . God bless America and her noble sailors. If the Americans stand as nobly to their guns as they bravely faced that tremendous hurricane, the United States need fear nothing.

Averaging only one knot against the typhoon, the *Calliope* at last clears the harbor entrance at five o'clock that afternoon and steams on with almost no headway for another three hours before the storm eases.

III

As ADMIRAL KIMBERLY watched the stern of the escaping British cruiser slowly disappear in the spray, the *Trenton* drifted south, bounced off the German *Olga*, and grounded on the reef alongside the *Vandalia*. The *Trenton* had only one fatality, but the *Vandalia* was much less fortunate. A wave swept her deck and knocked her captain, C. M. Schoonmaker, unconscious against a gun. The next wave washed him and several other men over the side, and she later ran up on the reef and lost even more sailors while they tried to get a line ashore with the help of Samoans. Forty of her crew died that day. The survivors climbed up into

As shown in this romanticized illustration from the *Trenton*'s point of view, the *Calliope* inched by as the Americans cheered. "I will ever remember the mighty outburst of fellow feeling," said the British captain, Henry Coey Kane. (Auckland War Memorial Museum, C30813)

When the *Calliope* steamed back into Apia after the storm, her crew saw every vessel either wrecked or sunk. From left to right are the U.S. Navy ships *Nipsic, Vandalia,* and the flagship *Trenton*. (Auckland War Memorial Museum, C10702)

the rigging and hung on until the *Trenton* nestled against her and offered shelter.

That there were only 147 fatalities in all was due to good seamanship, good luck, and the rescue efforts of Germans, Americans, Englishmen, and Samoans, many of whom labored through the worst of the storm in human chains to save more than 200 lives. The United States government awarded medals to many Samoans and presented a longboat to a chief, Seumanutafa, who had commanded a rescue boat out to the *Trenton*. As the port began its slow recovery, Kimberly assembled the navy band and paraded it around the shattered town playing "Hail Columbia." Two of the six grounded or sunk ships were refloated with the help of the *Calliope*'s diving suit. During salvage operations, the divers discovered why the anchors dragged so quickly: the brisk flow from the river had scoured all the dirt off the harbor bottom.

The *Calliope* returned to Apia three days later—it took that long for the seas to stop breaking at the harbor mouth. She had lost all her small boats, several anchors, much woodwork, and some rigging, but not a single man. Finding no other vessel intact or floating in Apia, Kane fired off a telegram to England: "The *Calliope*, I thank God, is left afloat and sound in hull." Before his crew went ashore to help clean up the town, he assembled them on deck and thanked them in a speech of such caring and conviction that someone present remarked, "This has been a means of grace." Soon Kane received a note from Kimberly: "You went out splendidly, and we all felt from our hearts for you, and our cheers came with sincerity and admiration for the able manner in which you handled your ship. It was a gallant thing, and you did it so well it could not have been done better. We could not have been gladder if it had been one of our own ships, for in a time like this I can say truly, . . . 'blood is thicker than water.'"

The *Calliope* came to be widely known by a colorful nickname—"the Hurricane Jumper." Kane was cited by the Admiralty for his "nerve and decision," given the high honor of command of HMS *Victory*, promoted to admiral, and knighted.

IV

THE FIRST CONSEQUENCE of the hurricane was that it silenced the war drums. The lost ships probably cost more than the territory they had been sent to win. Even the bellicose newspapers back in the States became reasonable. "The awful devastation wrought in the harbor of Apia makes our recent quarrel with Germany appear petty and unnatural," editorialized the *New York World*, which only weeks earlier had been rabid. There were numerous claims that God had spoken for peace by sending the storm.

Whatever the agent, the three countries agreed to form a tripartite ruling order and to stop taking sides in Samoa's internal politics. Ten years later Germany and the United States partitioned the Samoan archipelago under an arrangement known as the condominium. The eastern part was taken by the United States, which still controls the islands around Pago Pago. The western portion went to Germany, which lost it to New Zealand during World War I. Western Samoa is now an independent nation. When the *Calliope* was finally broken up in 1953, the steering wheel of the survivor of the storm that played such an important role in Samoan history was presented to the government of Western Samoa. The ceremony was held within sight of the rusting hulk of the *Adler*.

LIKE OTHER STORMS, the Samoan hurricane inspired its unique mythology. Two years later a U.S. Navy meteorologist took time out from a dry technical analysis of the storm to exult that the story had "already become part of the history of mankind," especially "the breathless pause of expectation when the gallant *Calliope* slipped her chains." It was not just that the *Calliope* had escaped so dramatically, but that she accomplished her flight before the eyes of so many other hopeful English-speakers in the *Trenton* and the other American ships. Her community, in fact, stretched far beyond the coral and sands of the port of Apia. When she returned for repairs to her home port, Sydney, thousands of Australians came down to the wharf to cheer her. Eight years later a local folk poet named "Banjo" Paterson—the creator of "Waltzing Matilda" and "The Man from Snowy River"—wrote an anthem obviously modeled on the popular songs of imperialism's bard, Rudyard Kipling. "The Ballad of the *Calliope*" opened, "By the far Samoan shore, / Where the league-long rollers pour." When Kane ordered his crew to cut the cables and get up steam,

> the answer came with cheers
> From the stalwart engineers,
> From the grim and grimy firemen at the furnaces below. . . .

The German gunboat *Adler* lay on the reef after the storm—"broken like an egg," according to Robert Louis Stevenson—and was still there more than sixty years later. (Auckland War Memorial Museum, C17094)

The author of *Treasure Island* and *The Strange Case of Dr. Jekyll and Mr. Hyde*, Robert Louis Stevenson (top center, next to his wife, Fanny, at a gathering of islanders and sailors at his farm) came to the South Seas for his health and initially idealized "this precious deep." (Auckland War Memorial Museum, C10629)

And as she slowly passed the *Trenton,*

> Without a thought of fear
> The Yankees raised a cheer—
> A cheer that English-speaking folk should echo round the world.

That cheer was built up into something far more grand. In the *New York Times* obituary for Kimberly in 1902, he was described as having brought the *Trenton*'s band on deck to play "God Save the Queen." The scene's ludicrous impossibility—drummers pounding away as the water floods around their knees, trumpeters grabbing at unfamiliar sheet music in the seventy-knot wind—only inspired more magnificent nonsense. After the storm's greatest hero, Henry Kane, died fifteen years later, the *Times* told how, "as the *Calliope* steamed past the wrecked American warships, he had his band on deck playing 'The Star-Spangled Banner,' which their officers and men heard above the howling of the tempest and cheered."

A HERO KANE SURELY WAS, but he was the first to recognize that the *Calliope* survived not solely because of determination and seamanship but owing to the technological advances represented by Banjo Paterson's "stalwart engineers." The well-known advantages of this new kind of ship helped seal the tomb of the "sticks and string" navy and encourage the rise of a new, deadlier technology of combat.

Robert Louis Stevenson remarked that the storm "founded the modern navy of the United States." That was only a slight exaggeration. More accurately, the escape of the *Calliope* provided a timely, real-life proof of the new imperialist theory of an all-steam fleet. Late in 1889 the secretary of the navy, Benjamin F. Tracy, complaining about "old fashioned engines and defective steam power" exemplified in the wrecks at Apia, called for the construction of twenty heavily armored, all-steam warships. Also in 1889, the all-important intellectual justification for naval expansion was provided by U.S. Navy captain Alfred Thayer Mahan's *The Influence of Sea Power upon History,* one of the most influential books ever published in English. The necessary technological support came in 1890 when the steelmaker Andrew Carnegie overcame his pacifist instincts and agreed to manufacture the nickel-steel plating crucial for the new type of warship. "Around 1890, then, the United States Navy gave itself a new mission and a way to explain it," historian George W. Baer has observed. Only the world's twelfth largest navy in 1889, the U.S. Navy would be ranked third in 1914 and first in 1916.

So it was that, although Captain Henry Coey Kane served under the White Ensign of the Royal Navy, his race to the Pacific helped bring about the arms race that left the Stars and Stripes the dominant flag on the high seas. "In a sense the cheering of the *Calliope* by the *Trenton* as she steamed away into the open sea was symbolic," the British naval historian Oliver Warner has maintained. "Great Britain was then enjoying a high hour in her destiny; that of America was about to come. Both nations would be challenged and endangered by the Germans, and would twice defeat them. The tradition of sea power built up during the course of the eighteenth and nineteenth centuries by the Royal Navy would be taken up by America in the twentieth."

Most of the players in the drama of the Samoan hurricane were far off the public stage by the time America rose to world power. Robert Louis Stevenson was the first to go. His last days had little of the bliss that he had anticipated when he came to the South Seas. In 1893, the year after *A Footnote to History* was published, he admitted that his enchantment with "this precious deep" had faded, telling a friend, "The truth is, I have a little lost my way, and stand bemused at the crossroads." Stevenson missed dark old Scotland after all. Before he could rejoin his old life's path and return home, late in 1894 Stevenson suffered a fatal cerebral hemorrhage in his farmhouse in the mountains overlooking Apia.

5

The Loss of the *Portland*

Massachusetts Bay, 1898

"I am now eighty-seven years old and I live that terrible storm over and over again."

—Mrs. Harmon S. Babcock

THANKSGIVING 1898 was a day of triumph for Americans. In the nine months since the battleship *Maine* exploded in Havana Harbor, the army and new steam navy had won a victory over Spain that was almost as painless as it was quick, with only 385 battle casualties. "The skies have been for a time darkened by the cloud of war," President William McKinley declared in his Thanksgiving proclamation, "but as we were compelled to take up the sword in the cause of humanity, we are permitted to rejoice."

The holiday's weather also offered cause to rejoice. A minor early winter storm left New York and southern New England looking like a picture out of a Currier and Ives calendar. "The day seemed old-fashioned-like," reported a journalist, who complained only that a hard wind "blew the flakes aslant." The U.S. Weather Bureau predicted that the brisk, fair weather would continue into the weekend. But early the next morning, as telegraphed reports from its 150 observing stations poured into the Weather Bureau's Washington headquarters, meteorologists in charge of making the nation's forecasts concluded that the situation had changed dramatically for the worse. A large low-pressure system sweeping in from the Great Plains was over Michigan and, they believed, would quickly advance on the East Coast. At 10:30 A.M., with the crisp precision of an agency that until eight years earlier had been a U.S. Army department, the Weather Bureau ordered that gale warnings be flown from New Jersey to Maine. Over the next eight hours the storm slowed and changed course. Some shipmasters ignored the gale warning and took their vessels out to sea. One was Hollis H. Blanchard, captain of the queen of New England passenger steamers, the 280-foot sidewheeler *Portland*. Right on schedule at 7:00 P.M., he ordered his crew to cast off lines from Boston's India Wharf and headed out into Massachusetts Bay on her eighty-five-mile overnight run to Portland, Maine. Half an hour later, however, snow began to fall gently, and at 9:30 the *Portland* was steaming into a fifty-knot nor'easter. Out in the bay near Cape Cod, seas were churning up the bottom so madly that an underwater telegraph cable snapped and enough sediment was suspended in the waves that crews were shoveling sand off the decks.

It was the worst storm to hit New England since the blizzard of March 1888. "Havoc in New England," read a headline three days later. The wind reached sixty miles an hour in many locations and ninety-seven on Block Island. While an occasional entertaining anecdote surfaced (like the report that hyperenergetic Theodore Roosevelt was trapped in a snowbound train), most of the news was catastrophic. The storm killed more people in thirty six hours—at least four hundred—than died in combat during the entire Spanish-American War. From New York to eastern Maine, train and ferry service ground to a halt, harbors were torn to pieces, river mouths were shifted, ocean liners went adrift, lightships were blown off station, and at least 350 vessels were wrecked or disabled. Cape Cod was cut off by flooding for days, and its reports had to be relayed by telegraph to France and then back to the American mainland. As corpses washed up on the cape, barns became morgues and life was characterized as "one unending funeral." A clergyman at the outer tip of the cape in Provincetown, whose harbor was wrecked, said in all humility, "Cape Cod has seen the world's agony this week, and has learned to have a heart of sympathy for all the world."

The appalling storm lacked a focus and a name until a single tragedy arose among the many. This was the disappearance of the *Portland*. For two days New England juggled rumors about her. It was known that Captain Blanchard had headed out on schedule after discussions (or arguments) with officials in both his shipping line and the local office of the Weather Bureau. After she cleared Boston harbor, the huge white sidewheeler was seen or heard from six times over the next fourteen hours—the last time at about 9:30 A.M. on Sunday a few miles north of Cape Cod. As the rumors flew around Portland, home of almost half the ship's 192 passengers and crew, all the people held their collective breath. The Portland *Daily Eastern Argus* ran a hopeful headline, "No News, Good News." Everybody hoped that Blanchard had found an isolated harbor of refuge to hunker down in, or that he had escaped into the ocean, where the ship was drifting without power.

But eventually news that was not good arrived from Cape Cod. On Sunday evening, a lifesaving station surfman walking the beach near Race Point, at the cape's very tip, came upon a lifebelt labeled "Steamer *Portland*." A tide of wreckage followed—milk cans from a creamery in Maine, mattresses, electric light bulbs, windows, chairs, doors, and paneling in such small pieces that they appeared to have been spat out from an immense grinder. Several hours later another surfman came upon another mess of wreckage, and alongside it the body of a black man wearing a *Portland* life belt. More bodies washed ashore on Monday, every pocket watch stopped at between 9:30 and 10:00.

The full horror unwound in newspaper headlines. "Not One Saved," the *Argus* announced on Wednesday. By Friday the paper was counting corpses: "Twenty-One Recovered." When the trains began running again, families streamed to Cape Cod where, desperate for news, they waited at the doorways of the improvised morgues. A headline portrayed the death watch:

Trying Scenes
Along the Wreck-Strewed Coast
of Cape Cod
IMAGINE THE PICTURE

Only forty bodies of the ship's passengers and crew were identified. Long after the police announced there were no more remains, families refused to return home but continued to crowd the morgues and the offices of the Portland Steamship Company, describing loved ones to patient officials who could only shake their heads. Nobody even knew how many people had been aboard the ship; if an official passenger and crew list ever was made, the only copy went down with the *Portland*. (The best estimate, compiled in 1998 by Peter Dow Bachelder and Mason Philip Smith in *Four Short Blasts*, is that 127 passengers and 65 crew members were aboard that night, for a total of 192 men, women, and children.)

I

OVER THE PAST hundred-plus years, legends about the *Portland* have grown alongside the steady stream of bitter recriminations against Captain Hollis Blanchard. Eager to sample some good news, people latched on to a few tales of happy premonitions. As the ship pulled out, it seems that a cat sprinted down the gangplank and leaped onto India Wharf. That wise cat may have crossed paths with the thirsty passenger who (it was reported) had gone ashore to buy a bottle of liquor to share with a friend but, to his immediate disappointment but eventual joy, returned a few minutes after 7:00 and watched the *Portland*'s stern disappear into the cold darkness as his friend shouted derisively from an upper deck, "I told you so." There is no way to disprove these tales except to quote an observation by Edward Rowe Snow, a New England maritime historian. "If all the stories were true," Snow quipped, "the *Portland* could have never sailed, for the over-loaded craft would have gone down at the pier."

Tales of the *Portland* bubbled up for decades as "the night the *Portland* went down" became one of those few events against which people measure time, often with considerable feeling and imagination. One of the strangest of many strange stories had it that at approximately 9:30 on that blizzard-bound Sunday morning, a shoemaker named Linus Shaw, standing in his henhouse some twenty miles inland from the bay, experienced a vision of a white steamboat being rammed and sunk by a black schooner, followed by the drowning of all the steamer's people. That tale can be either believed or dismissed. More can be read into another story of the *Portland*. In 1950, after Edward Rowe Snow presented one of his radio dramatizations of the *Portland* disaster, Ethel Campbell wrote the station a long letter in which she recalled in considerable detail her travels aboard the ship and ashore on the night of November 26, 1898, as she sold copies of a Salvation Army newspaper, the *War Cry*. She claimed she heard the "I told you so" shouted by the unlucky man on the ship, and also a conversation between Captain Blanchard and another master who warned him (unsuccessfully) not to sail. Ethel Campbell's keenly visual memories of people she encountered on the *Portland* haunted her most. "I can still see some of their faces in my mind." Those faces were wary and even gloomy. "The usual hum and rush of people hurrying to and fro seemed absent that night." The seamen were not enthusiastic about sailing, and the chief cook, one of the ship's many African American crew members, never arrived. Another black man had to be found ashore to take over the ship's galley. One of Ethel Campbell's customers that night was a striking African American woman with a child—"a young colored woman with a very pleasant countenance, a lovely young mother, standing at the door with a handsome boy of about nine, they both had wonderful dark eyes, and the boy had dark curly hair, they stood looking out at the water, across the upper deck, and I could detect a feeling of uneasiness in her voice." Ethel Campbell stepped ashore, heavy (she remembered) with foreboding.

ALTHOUGH THE MOTHER AND CHILD Campbell described so sensitively are not further identified there or elsewhere (including in reconstructions of the passenger list), her memory accurately testifies at least to one undisputed fact—the prominence of African Americans aboard the ship that night. Besides an unknown number of black passengers, between thirty and forty African Americans were in the *Portland*'s crew of sixty-five, most of them from the Portland area. More than one-third of the Portland residents who died in the ship were black. More appalling yet, the loss of the *Portland* decimated Portland's black community of three hundred (out of approximately one thousand black Maine residents) and helped destroy the city's oldest organization of African Americans, the Abyssinian Church. At least seventeen members and two deacons of the Abyssinian Church died in or near the *Portland*.

In 1898 most Americans would not have known that the sea was a workplace for African Americans, but there was a long tradition of black seafarers. At midcentury, one man in six aboard New England whaling ships was black, and almost half of Portland's black men worked in the maritime trades as fishermen or longshoremen. So many black families in Maine had been fishermen that at least five islands along the coast were called "Negro Island." After Irish immigrants took over stevedore jobs on the Portland wharves, African Americans shifted over to the passenger steamships, taking personal service jobs as barbers, stewards, and guards. Some black women also served aboard the ships as stewardesses.

Portland's African Americans who worked around or on the sea formed a stable, solid community. While many white seamen in the late nineteenth century had (and deserved) reputations as riffraff, black mariners tended to be family men who settled permanently in their towns and built local institutions, the most prominent in Portland being the Fourth Congregational Church. Known as the Abyssinian Church because of its black congregation, it was founded in 1827 by African Americans, led by Reuben Ruby, who were tired of being forced to sit in the balconies of churches dominated by whites. Ruby paid $250 to build a sanctuary that reportedly is the country's third oldest African American religious building and still stands on Munjoy Hill in Portland. The church ran the city's "colored school" and became active in the abolitionist movement. Not all Maine African Americans were Congregationalists (or for that matter Protestants). The state had three hundred black Catholics in the late nineteenth century, and Bishop James Augustine Healy was the country's first black Roman Catholic bishop. But the Abyssinian Church came to be identified with black New England. At the time of the *Portland* disaster it was struggling to hold its own against a new black church, Mount Zion Methodist, an evangelical congregation founded by a group of younger people, and headed by an energetic bootblack named Moses Green, who preferred an enthusiastic liturgy over the staid Congregational order. A few of Mount Zion's members were aboard the *Portland*. The older church suffered far worse.

The magnitude of the impact was reflected by the unusually lengthy local newspaper coverage of the Abyssinian Church's memorial service, which was attended by a number of white clergy. According to one paper, the Reverend T. A. Smith preached a "powerful descriptive memorial sermon of the recent distressful disaster that befell a great number of constant worshipers at the church. . . . The close of the sermon was delivered with a will sent forth from the living to those noble heroes who perished while in the discharge of their duty."

By 1912 the church was down to only seven parishioners. After it was dissolved four years later, a local newspaper observed that the "great blow" was the loss of all those prominent members in the wreck. The Munjoy Hill building was sold, the pews going to a Finnish church. The building went through decades of mixed use and was a tenement when seized for back taxes in 1991. Seven years later, at the centennial anniversary of the *Portland* disaster, the city sold the building for a token $250 to a descendant of the church's founder, Reuben Ruby, and a restoration effort was begun. On the weekend after Thanksgiving, a centennial memorial service was held outside the old Abyssinian Church and a wreath was laid at the waterfront in memory of the ship's dead.

II

THAT WAS BY NO MEANS the first memorial to the *Portland* and her people. Several years after the disaster, families of men and women who were lost formed an organization called the *Portland* Associates and held annual memorial gatherings at India Wharf on Thanksgiving weekends. As they aged and passed on, their dedication was carried on by their children, who were led by the individual who more than anybody except Hollis Blanchard was identified with the *Portland*. This was the maritime historian, writer, and lecturer Edward Rowe Snow—America's best-known storm chaser and romanticist of the sea, in whose world sentimentality and the gruesome strolled hand in hand with history.

The descendant of mariners, Snow was born in 1902 in Winthrop, near Boston, and knocked about as a young man, in part crewing in sailing ships. He entered Harvard at twenty-seven and wrote his senior thesis on Boston harbor's islands under the supervision of Samuel Eliot Morison, the crusty, thoroughly unromantic historian and biographer of

Christopher Columbus. (Snow later led a successful drive to create a public park on the islands.) Snow taught high school for several years, then after service in the Second World War went out on his own as a freelance writer and lecturer specializing in New England's history in general, and especially in the more colorful and violent aspects of its maritime history and legends. Although he did do solid scholarly research, Snow knew how to enliven a story with swashbuckling and showmanship. He opened one story, "John Phillips, whose head was brought to Boston in a pickle barrel," and his more than fifty books had titles such as *The Vengeful Sea, Incredible Mysteries and Legends of the Sea, True Tales of Buried Treasure,* and *Piracy, Mutiny, and Murder.* "Some of his favorite words were 'unbelievable,' 'astounding,' and 'the most incredible rescue in the history of New England,'" Judson Hale of *Yankee* magazine said fondly of Snow. He opened his radio show, *Six Bells,* with the clanging of a ship's bell and went on to dramatizations of shipwrecks and piracy. On his lecture circuit, he carried a display that his promotional flyers referred to as "Selected curios from Mr. Snow's famous $17,000 traveling museum." Now at the Peabody Essex Museum in Salem, Massachusetts, these curios include a wooden leg, some daggers, a number of ship's bells that he claimed were from the *Andrea Doria* and other wrecked ships—so many bells, in fact, that he could not always keep them straight—and two skulls that he cheerfully claimed were the last remains of the pirates William Kidd and Blackbeard (whose skull was spray-painted silver).

As part of what he called "my 43-year search for unusual sea adventures," he did not leave all the adventuring to historical figures. He took long canoe voyages, hiked the Atlantic coast at a record pace, and celebrated his sixty-second birthday by diving from near the top of Minot's Light lighthouse. Especially enamored of lighthouses ("There is something about a lighted beacon that suggests hope and trust and appeals to the better instincts of all mankind"), Snow suited up as "the flying Santa" every December for more than forty years and flew around New England and other parts of the country in small airplanes, dropping Christmas presents to lightkeepers and their families.

In a fiftieth anniversary report to his Harvard class, Snow explained his philosophy of life by quoting the famous lines from Tennyson's "Ulysses": "Come my friends / 'Tis not too late to seek a newer world." More accurately, Snow dedicated his life to recreating an *older* world. If his promotions occasionally ventured over the top, few people seemed to mind. His warm heart, coupled with his love of good stories and New England history, found him friends everywhere he traveled.

Snow's favorite story was the mystery of the *Portland*. In his private museum were a number of her artifacts, including splinters from her woodwork that he sent to anybody who was interested, a flag, some cork from one of the ship's life preservers, and a pair of baby shoes that, he claimed, were taken off a young victim who washed up on Cape Cod. Every year he helped the *Portland* Associates organize their annual memorial (including arranging for press coverage), and he was always on hand to read his dramatization of the disaster.

Snow also was deeply attentive to the feelings of survivors. Psychologists who work with disasters speak of "interventions" and "debriefings"— individual or group sessions in which specialists help survivors and rescuers recover from trauma-induced stress. Well before post-traumatic stress disorder was first defined in 1980, Edward Rowe Snow was serving as an intervener and debriefer for many members of the community that formed when the *Portland* sank. On his lecture tours and in his broadcasts, newspaper columns, and books, he invited descendants of victims to write him. Out of these initiatives came more than twenty new names that were added to the list of passengers and crew that had been estimated in 1898, as well as a remarkable correspondence between Snow and elderly people who had lost parents, siblings, or friends to the deep.

A few of these letters in the crabbed handwriting of old age show a little humor. One man, for instance, was absolutely certain that his life was saved because a problem with his luggage prevented him from boarding the *Portland* on the Saturday after Thanksgiving, *1889*. He was furious that Snow and every other historian insisted on dating the accident to 1898. But most of Snow's correspondence from the *Portland* community was poignant. "We were a young couple at the time and it was the most terrible experience one could go through with," Mrs. Harmon S. Babcock, the widow of a victim, wrote him in 1956, adding, "I am now eighty-seven years old and I live that terrible storm over and over again." (Snow assured Mrs. Babcock that he would help her in any way within his power.) A man who did not have a birth certificate asked Snow to certify that his parents had been on board the *Portland* so that he could qualify for Social Security. (Snow wrote the government.) Often Snow could only sympathize. A woman wrote from Florida to report that one of the *Portland*'s dead was a little girl who had been named for her. Another told him about her favorite schoolteacher, Sophie B. Holmes, who was one of the many Thanksgiving vacationers returning home to Portland on November 26. A third said that after her father died in the *Portland* her mother was left so destitute that she was obliged to put her daughter—who was the writer—out for adoption.

And there was the telephone call informing Snow of a sister and brother-in-law's failure to return from a honeymoon, of a father's despair in the kitchen, and of the speaker's sad memory of the first time she had seen a man weep.

III

SNOW AND MANY OTHERS devoted years to trying to solve the double mystery of the *Portland*. The first concerned what happened to her; the second, what compelled Captain Blanchard to head out on such a night. Solutions to these mysteries necessarily demand some speculation, yet they need not be so elaborate as to be strangers to everyday experience and the fundamentals of seamanship. Let us first attempt to re-create the ship's loss.

On many days of any year between the 1830s and the 1930s, passengers boarding a comfortable "night boat" in Boston or a Maine city on a late afternoon can count on arriving at their destination early the next morning. If the weather is kind and passage smooth, they can also count on being rested and well fed. The *Portland*—called "the finest vessel that will travel Eastern waters" when she was launched in 1889 after an expenditure of $250,000—raises the stakes from mere comfort to sheer luxury. Her elegant three-story superstructure has gold and white painted trim, forty-three "cool and airy" cabins, a "Corinthian style of architecture," and an elegant Grand Saloon with carved mahogany stairways and furniture, rich upholstery, velvet carpets that withstand the tests of time and seasick passengers, and the new marvel of electric lights.

Her luxuriousness does not mean there is no schedule to meet. Whether to stick to the timetable in light of the gale warnings is the subject of several afternoon telephone and telegraph messages and conversations between Blanchard and his Portland Steamship Company superiors and their colleagues in Maine. Red gale warning flags have been flying since late morning, yet there are indications that the gale the Weather Bureau says is

The 1898 Portland storm was named for its largest victim, a 280-foot sidewheeler with luxurious accommodations. With her shallow hull and tall, heavy superstructure, she was unseaworthy in a storm. (Maine Maritime Museum)

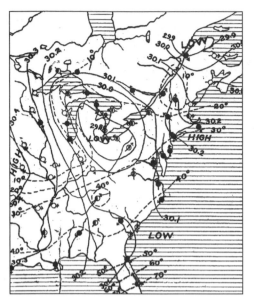

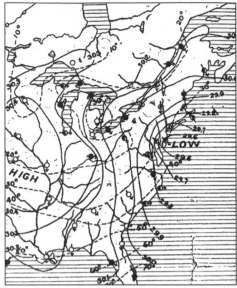

At 8 A.M. Saturday *(above)*, a dry, cold, low-pressure system was sweeping in from the Great Lakes while a small, humid low was coming up the Atlantic coast faster than anybody thought. The *Portland* sailed from Boston at 7 P.M., and an hour later the two storms were merged *(above right)*. By 8 A.M. Sunday *(right)*, the immense double storm was centered over Cape Cod, near where the ship was fighting to survive. (Blue Hill Meteorological Observatory)

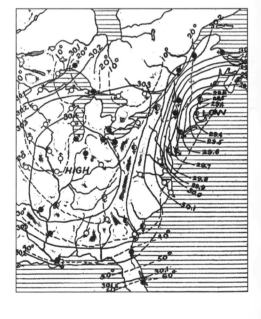

People waited for days in the steamship company's offices, hoping for good news of the ship. This illustration showing a black woman talking with company officials ran in a newspaper over the caption, "He was a cook, Sir." Thirty to forty African Americans were in the *Portland*'s crew of sixty-five. (*Boston Herald*)

New England historian Edward Rowe Snow, his full head of white hair characteristically blowing in the breeze, presides at a *Portland* Associates memorial service in the 1970s. (The Portland Newspapers)

This was how Boston Harbor appeared to Captain Blanchard as he looked out from India Wharf on Saturday afternoon—calm and nonthreatening. The sidewheeler in the slip is the *Portland*'s near-sister ship, the *Bay State*. (Courtesy Robert Mortimer)

moving in from Michigan has slowed. The weather in Boston is fair, the wind light. Still, the captain of the line's other sidewheeler on this run, the *Bay State*, has decided against sailing from Portland. She would have to run west toward the predicted gale, not *away* from it as the *Portland* would.

These messages and conversations are somewhat confused and even contradictory. They are brought to an end when the company manager in Portland runs out to catch a train to Boston to attend the Boston funeral the next day of the line's senior captain, Charles Deering. At that point everybody appears willing to leave the decision up to Blanchard. As usual, he pays a visit to the Weather Bureau, where he studies the charts and is told about the storm approaching from the west. There may also be a few words about a small low-pressure system that appears to be forming on the south Atlantic coast; but exactly how much detail he is given about that system will never be known. The meteorologists on duty will vehemently declare that they precisely predicted every weather feature that appeared that night and the next day, and particularly the extraordinary "double storm" in which the low from the west and the other from the south raced nearly perfectly into an explosive embrace that carried them as one into Massachusetts Bay and the path of the steamship *Portland*. Still, something about that visit leaves Blanchard confident that he can outrun the gale to Portland should his superiors in the shipping line permit him to cast off.

When the *Portland* heads out on schedule at 7:00 P.M., the barometer is stable, the sky overcast, the wind and sea calm. Later, in the luxury of afterthought, other mariners will recall that this weather was *too* calm. "The greasiest evening you ever saw," one captain will claim, meaning that the water is too slick and "oily" to be up to any good. Other old salts will remember an orange-yellow glow in the sky. If Blanchard, who has studied the weather, hears these warnings, the hard-nosed, factual, and aggressive shipmaster dismisses them as unscientific nonsense. The water is slick in any calm, and all that's needed for an orange light are haze, clouds, and low crepuscular sun rays shining through or off them.

Soon it becomes obvious to Blanchard that this storm—or some other storm altogether—has overtaken him with unusual violence. At 9:00, as the *Portland* approaches Gloucester, on Cape Ann, the barometer falls off the edge of the table and the northeast wind rises to near hurricane force, blowing in dense streaks that a survivor of the gale describes as "veins" (one of these veins will slice a twenty-five-foot-wide swath through a forest on Orr's Island, near Portland). At the eastern end of Cape Ann at 9:45, bucking and heaving, the ship is more than an hour behind schedule and running out of the shelter of the Massachusetts shore into the open Gulf of Maine. The *Portland* makes almost no progress whatever through this erupting sea.

LACKING BLANCHARD'S TESTIMONY about the weather off Cape Ann, we can cite a report of similar conditions in the same area by the captain of a much larger modern ship. In March 1974 the 660-foot oil tanker *Amoco Virginia* was making the Boston–Portland run in a heavy nor'easter. When she rounded Cape Ann, the sea was so high that solid green water battered her bridge. The captain decided to heave-to (slow down drastically with the waves slightly to one side) rather than risk destroying his ship by blasting into it or being rolled over by lying beam to. For almost seven hours he held this position until the storm and sea eased. Reviewing the weather, he discovered that two depressions—a cold one sweeping in from Michigan and a warm one coming up the coast—had unpredictably merged to form an unusual double storm whose explosive violence was far greater than the sum of its two parts.

If a tanker built for ocean crossings could not handle these conditions, there is no reason to expect it of the *Portland*, which is both an anachronism and a compromise. A long, wide, shallow platform built to lug large loads up rivers, she can carry seven hundred passengers and four hundred tons of cargo, yet her hull has none of the traditional ship's knife edge. From above and below it looks like an immense pumpkin seed–shaped three-story wedding cake. She is sixty-eight feet wide (counting the large guards overhanging the two paddles), with a draft of only ten feet, eight inches. Built massively of wood instead of the lighter steel or iron that goes into modern ships, the *Portland* is heavy everywhere and in every way; even the ship's bell weighs 522 pounds. Because she is so shallow in draft, much of that great weight of necessity is up high in the "top hamper," with relatively little weight low in the hull to counter it and provide stability. Out of the top of her towering two-deck superstructure churns the thirteen-foot walking beam that transmits engine power to the paddles, driving the great ship at up to thirteen knots. Off to the sides under the massive guards are old-fashioned wheels, unlike the lightweight feathering paddles used on other new steamers.

For all her roominess and luxury, therefore, the *Portland* is not such a fine vessel in terms of seaworthiness, with all that area exposed to seas and all that weight up high. Should a big wave roll her over on her side, she might well keep going. "She is only fit for smooth water," one captain has complained of his sidewheeler. "My greatest care is not to get caught out with her on the first part of this route. If I do, it means getting in out of the wet at the first chance, and favoring her in every way, shape, or manner." No wonder, then, that sidewheeler captains have a reputation for extreme caution. Samuel Eliot Morison, a veteran of night boats, will tell of the wary sidewheeler master who anchored in a dense fog lying under a blue sky. When a passenger, pointing up, demanded to know why they were wasting so much time, the captain snapped, "We're not bound that way."

Hollis Blanchard is not that sort of captain, but after three decades of sidewheeler service, he knows the importance of keeping big waves on a vessel's pointed ends—her bow or stern—and not her sides. To lie broadside leaves the guards and wheels exposed to breaking seas that can lift them right off the ship and open the hull like a can of sardines—if those waves don't first roll the ship right over.

As THE UNEXPECTEDLY FEROCIOUS nor'easter blows up in Hollis Blanchard's face, he knows he cannot get his sidewheeler "in out of the wet" on this black night in a thick blizzard. The first candidate for a port of refuge is Gloucester, but it lies behind numerous rocks, shoals, and islands like Norman's Woe, where Longfellow wrecked his poetic *Hesperus*. On this night, the only way to locate Norman's Woe precisely is to run the *Portland* right up on it, and that is a risk Blanchard does not wish to add to his many other problems—the wild seas, the breath-catching wind, and the heavy layer of snow pressing down on his wide deck and making his already tippy ship even more unstable.

It is 10:00 P.M. and the *Portland* shoulders into the terrific sea toward a low island known as "Thacher's Woe," where in 1635 Anthony Thacher and his wife survived a wreck, though they lost their four children. In a break in the blizzard, Blanchard sees the lights of Gloucester and neighboring Rockport. He knows that more than a few residents there are peering out their windows and marveling that the great *Portland* is out on this night. He thinks through his problem: He cannot get to Portland without having the ship torn out from under him. Turning back toward Boston will take

The sidewheeler *Portland*'s nightly run was between Boston and Portland, Maine, around Cape Ann, where Gloucester is located. The northeast storm probably forced her captain to head downwind toward Cape Cod, where her whistle was heard. She was last seen near Race Point.

him back into the storm, and also into waters full of distressed ships. So all there is to do is to find refuge at Cape Cod, forty miles to the south and downwind. In an inspired act of seamanship, Blanchard locates a smooth spot in the volcanic sea and turns his ship without being caught in the trough. With his stern to the breakers, he slowly runs southward toward Provincetown, not knowing that even that snug port is in ruins. He must not arrive before dawn; he will need daylight to guide him in. Tracking down Provincetown in this blizzard is not merely like finding a needle in a haystack. It is like threading that needle.

In this sea, setting a course is far easier than steering it. The immense breakers overtaking her from astern swing the ship's bow wildly, first this way, then that. Her progress is like the descent of a falling leaf, turning to one side and then the other, sometimes lifting a paddle clear on one side and digging her deck in on the opposite. Waves tear away signs and woodwork. The water jets below through vents and extinguishes the boiler fires as the ship's stokers struggle to pile on dry coal and start them anew. Groaning with strain, the *Portland* heaves furniture about the cabins, along with the passengers and crew in their life preservers.

About twelve miles southeast of Thacher Island, a fishing schooner bursts out of the blizzard directly at the ship. The schooner captain, horrified by the sight of this immense steamer rolling down on him, lights a flare and with a hard lunge at both steering wheels the two vessels skim by each other. Almost an hour later another schooner appears, happily at a safer distance. In the wheelhouse Blanchard stares into the blizzard, half expecting to see Race Point at the tip of Cape Cod loom out of the sea ahead. The long night passes. At about 5:30 A.M., the waves shorten and steepen, telling Blanchard that he is in shoal water near the cape, not as he intended on its protected western side but, instead, on its windward side. To gauge how close he is to shore, he sounds his horn four times and hopes that someone ashore will appreciate his predicament and light a flare. There is no reply (Blanchard does not know that a lifeboatman ashore has heard the signal and is dutifully gathering a crew to launch a boat). Blanchard turns the ship and heads back north away from the cape into deep water, where he hopes to hook around to Provincetown. With every passing wave, her hull groans and paddles and superstructure shake. He fears the one big one that will peel off the deck.

As anxious, exhausted, and bruised as he is, Hollis Blanchard also is thrilled, proud, and hopeful. For twelve hours his ship has survived the worst storm of his long experience at sea. While there are reports that cabins and open areas are wrecked and passengers are injured, the superstructure and hull are still together. He may make Provincetown, and even if he cannot, he can heave-to and wait out this storm, the likes of which he never wishes to see again. Just after 9:00 A.M., the wind suddenly drops almost to a calm and a hole opens in the blizzard. The storm's eye is passing. Ahead he sees two vessels, a schooner, and a steam freighter that he recognizes as the *Pentagoet*, out of New York. Both appear to be in far worse distress than he feels. The good news is that no land is nearby.

The respite is brief. The wind builds again, not from the northeast but from the northwest as the back of the storm swings over. The seas, already breathtaking in their ferocity, grow even larger and whiter as the waves kick in from the new direction, crossing the old. This is the most desperate time. Out of the foam appears the wave of waves, a monster rogue that hurls the ship on her side while ripping at her. First go the paddles, then the deck, and last the wheelhouse, its windows smashed through. Ripped apart and gutted, the *Portland* falls sideways and down, like a hollow lead weight.

IV

FIFTY-ONE YEARS after the *Portland* disappeared, Hollis Blanchard's former church in Portland—the First Congregational Church, from which the Abyssinian Church had been spun off—received a letter, probably from Edward Rowe Snow, asking for the captain's photograph. A member of the church replied but did not enclose a picture. He did not have the heart to approach Blanchard's grandchildren, he explained. "Controversy at this late date would be but an unholy saturnalia." The dreadful accident half a century earlier "must have had an evil effect upon their own emotional lives," he speculated. "In the normal routine, they too suffered, for they had a loss felt just as deeply as the next person."

Hollis Blanchard was one of the most notorious figures in New England history—a Yankee ogre up there with Lizzie Borden and the witch hangers of Salem. He had no admirers after November 1898, once it was believed that he had willfully sailed out into a double storm that had been perfectly predicted by the U.S. Weather Bureau. The newspapers made a football of Blanchard's character. He had taken chances "which no man in his position had a right to take," ran one representative editorial, which also accused him of engaging in either "criminal ignorance" or "criminal negligence." The disaster was "one so far from accidental, one in which the fixing of direct responsibility is so easy." Why did he not do as the other shipmasters did? The captain of the *Bay State* had decided to stay in Portland, and a Captain C. H. Leighton reported that he had declined to sail as a passenger in the *Portland* because he lacked Captain Blanchard's confidence in his ship's ability to beat the bad weather to port. As he remembered the conversation (which apparently was overheard by Ethel Campbell, the Salvation Army newsgirl), he told Blanchard, "By George, Captain, I really don't think this is a fit night to leave port." Blanchard replied, "I don't know about that. We may have a good chance." Leighton felt strongly enough to take the train home to Maine.

Various theories were presented to explain Blanchard's motives. He wanted to attend his daughter's debutante party in Portland. Or he was ambitious to run the *Bay State* and tried to upstage her captain. Or (said his family) his superiors thought he was too careful and ordered him to head out.

None of those makes much sense. But what do we make of Hollis Blanchard?

AN EXPERIENCED PILOT and ship's officer in his mid-fifties, Blanchard had been given command of the *Portland* only two weeks earlier after a long tenure as the ship's pilot, or navigator. He was known to be both cautious and independent—a captain who took the time to visit the Weather Bureau but was not afraid to reject its advice, and surely not the sort of master who had spent his career anchoring when it fogged up. His reputation was for boldness. "The captain unquestionably believed he would be able to run down ahead of the storm, as he had done many times before," was the evaluation of the historian of the Portland Steamship Company, writing many years later.

That conclusion was also in the longest, most balanced evaluation of the man, and the only one that neither demonized nor sanctified him. It was offered by a sidewheeler captain, John W. Craig, who had often sailed with Blanchard and was interviewed by the Portland *Daily Eastern Argus*.

> A cooler man I never knew and I doubt if there was his superior on any boat that plies the Maine coast. He was honest, faithful, fearless. I have never seen in all my seafaring experience a man who could run a boat better in storm or calm. But

—a crucial *but*—

> when he was pilot with me on the *Tremont* he never wanted to admit that the weather was bad. He couldn't seem to see bad weather, and didn't like to talk about it. Sometimes I would ask him if he did not think it was blowing up a storm, or if the prospect was not rather dubious, but he would seldom

admit it. . . . I cannot hardly believe that Captain Blanchard put to sea against orders. But

—another crucial *but* from Captain Craig—

if he had been given to understand that she would be likely to go out at 9 o'clock or had construed the order as meaning that he was to use his best judgment in the matter, then it was not surprising that he started. It had not then begun to snow and he probably thought he could beat out the storm.

Other captains—even ones who had turned back—also defended Blanchard's decision to take his ship out into the calm, or at least his right to make that decision. The deep, these captains were saying, is too demanding and too complex for any decision concerning it to be guided by self-appointed experts ashore.

V

WHILE HE MAY HAVE BEEN as energetic a storm racer as Edward Rowe Snow was a storm chaser, Hollis Blanchard was not operating in a vacuum. Two institutions had the power to affect his plans. One was the U.S. Weather Bureau, the other the Portland Steamship Company.

If it seems unlikely that any licensed shipmaster, no matter how aggressive, would ignore a clearly stated forecast for an unusually violent storm sweeping across his course, such a decision verges on the improbable in the case of Hollis Blanchard. While many captains of his generation distrusted the Weather Bureau's scientific approach and preferred the old rules of thumb they had learned as boys, Hollis Blanchard had learned to read weather maps, and he habitually visited the bureau's Boston office for briefings before heading out.

In the more than half century since Robert Fitzroy and William Redfield demonstrated how to predict storms using barometers and wind direction, and since Matthew Fontaine Maury began collecting wind data at sea, meteorology had become a science. Although one of Maury's goals was to distribute storm warnings by telegraph, the first government agencies to provide them were not in America but in the Netherlands and Britain. The development was slow. After Fitzroy confidently founded the British Mete-

Left: An experienced sidewheeler captain, Hollis Blanchard had a reputation for racing storms. His name became one of the most hated in New England. (Courtesy Robert Mortimer) Above: When the gale hit, Blanchard would have seen a sight like this. After snapping this photograph of a hurricane from a steamship, the photographer noted, "Taken from the top deck. Height of wave, 65 feet. A wall of water." (G. J. Tregar, Courtesy Peabody Essex Museum, Salem, Massachusetts)

orological Service in 1859, he was so hypersensitive to the inevitable criticisms of mistakes and doubts expressed by old shellbacks that he unraveled completely and in 1865 committed suicide.

In the United States, the first national weather service was founded in 1870 not by seamen but by the Army Signal Corps, which was in charge of the telegraph facilities necessary to transmit reports and forecasts over the vast country. By 1881 army meteorologists, trained in the corps's own school of meteorology, were exchanging reports and issuing forecasts over more than five thousand miles of telegraph lines, while also sending out synoptic weather maps by mail. Before long the Signal Corps was transmitting more than thirteen thousand storm warnings annually. As weather forecasting came into demand by farmers and other civilians, the government transferred the service to the Department of Agriculture in 1891 and renamed it the Weather Bureau.

The bureau's military heritage showed in the clockwork precision of its operations and also in the centralization of its forecasting service. The Washington headquarters produced most weather maps, regional forecasts, and storm warnings, although offices in Boston and a handful of other cities were permitted to act independently when local weather was concerned. In 1898 there were 150 reporting stations operated by professionals and more than 2,300 volunteers, and equipped with barometers, thermometers, wind indicators, and other gauges, all calibrated to the same elevation so that reports had a common standard. Twice daily, at 8:00 A.M. and P.M. Washington time, each station wired its readings to headquarters. There, meteorologists incorporated these data into forecasts, which were usually telegraphed to hundreds of regional offices by 10:00 (because facsimile machines would not be developed until the time of the Second World War, weather maps were mailed). The system looked like a bicycle wheel, with the hub at the Washington headquarters and the spokes standing for lines of direct communication, called "circuits," that ran to and from regional offices. All offices on a circuit were able to read reports and forecasts on it, but the circuits were isolated from each other.

With seven hundred staff members and a $1.5 million budget, the U.S. Weather Bureau tirelessly promoted itself in two ways that might seem conflicting. In many brochures, speeches, and articles in popular magazines, bureau chief Willis L. Moore and his colleagues described it both as "a strictly scientific bureau" on the cutting edge of modern research and as a practical-minded, problem-solving agent of material progress. Moore's speeches were filled with dollar signs: so many millions saved when the Weather Bureau warned Florida fruit growers of imminent freezes, Ohio Valley farmers of threatening floods, or Great Lakes mariners of arriving storms. In the world of weather, it seemed, minutes meant everything. For years Moore promised that the bureau could provide probable forecasts on thirty-six hours' notice; in April 1899 he upped the ante to forty-eight hours. The scientific, modern professional meteorologist, he declared, would always outperform the weather sense of the weatherman and the flimflammery of "the pseudo scientist and the astrologer." Moore had a knack for snappy language and clever public relations. When he asked President William McKinley for funds to expand the Weather Bureau during the Spanish-American War, Moore declared that more wars were lost to bad weather than to enemies and cited the fate of the great armada that was sent to England in 1588 by America's current enemy, Spain.

For all his swagger, Moore could be extremely prickly. He did not want it known that the Weather Bureau was imperfect. In 1898 "a strictly scientific bureau" was believed to be incapable of making a mistake. That it did occasionally miss a forecast was widely known. Many New Englanders in 1898 remembered vividly the forecast for March 12, 1888, that anticipated "colder, fresh to brisk westerly winds, fair weather." That was the day of the great blizzard of '88—another double storm caused by the merger of a cold, dry, continental low-pressure system sweeping in from the Midwest with a warm, wet maritime low working its way up the Atlantic coast. Two years after the *Portland* gale, on September 7, 1900, the Washington office forecast "possibly brisk northerly winds" and fair weather for coastal east Texas, which the next day was assaulted by a hurricane that destroyed Galveston. After a Houston newspaper criticized the national Weather Bureau as useless, "for certain sections of the country at least," Moore fired off a five-page letter in which he claimed, against all evidence to the contrary, that Washington had issued a timely storm warning.

As Willis Moore varnished the bureau's reputation (and his own), other people cooperated by polishing the surface to an impossibly bright sheen. In a typical uncritical magazine article published in 1905 under the cheery title "Our Heralds of Storm and Flood," Gilbert H. Grosvenor (founder of the *National Geographic*) ignored the decades-long international development of forecasting to characterize it as "a distinctly American product" and a modern miracle. Yet the bureau was not quite a well-oiled machine. Although Moore claimed there was plenty of time for carefully and accurately processing the forecasts, one of his meteorologists, Alfred J. Henry, admitted in 1900 that the central office devoted only thirty minutes in the morning and forty minutes at night to tracing and forecasting severe storms and other bad weather for the entire country.

People who looked into the forecasting methodology also discovered that it involved far more guesswork and "feel" than Moore let on. To cite just one example, so that storms and areas of low and high pressure could be clearly identified on weather maps, isobars—the lines linking observations of equal air pressure—were averaged out to make fair curves. That was a mere drafting problem. Whole forecasts were subject to estimate, at best. Geographer Mark Monmonier has observed, "Despite the local importance of regional anomalies, turn of the century storm forecasting was very much a process of early recognition, informed guessing, and careful tracking." And that says nothing about the problem of quickly and accurately communicating forecasts to the people who need to know them.

WHAT DID THE WEATHER BUREAU KNOW and when did it know it? That is one of two questions about November 26. The other, which is something else again, directly concerns Hollis Blanchard and his reputation: What did the captain of the *Portland* know and when did he know it? When J. W. Smith, head of the Weather Bureau's Boston office, wrote in the bureau's magazine, the *Monthly Weather Review*, that the *Portland* had been "fully warned by the Weather Bureau," he did not specify what "fully" meant. There is good reason to believe that it did not include the small low racing up the Atlantic coast or the double storm (like the great blizzard of 1888) that it formed with the Michigan low. Very likely, until the violent upheavals of Saturday night, neither the bureau nor Blanchard believed that the problem was anything other than a single gale coming in from the west.

The bureau's own history of its work in the storm in the *Monthly Weather Review* begins at 8:00 A.M. Saturday, when wires from reporting stations noted a large low-pressure system sweeping east from Michigan and a small low off the coast of Georgia. At 10:30 the meteorologists decided to issue gale warnings for the coast from Sandy Hook almost all the way to the Canadian border. By noon the Michigan low was over Pittsburgh and the coastal low was off Cape Hatteras. By 3:00, said the Weather Bureau in its official history, the lows had merged off Norfolk, Virginia, and the new double storm was moving north up the coast. The lows had raced toward this encounter at over seventy miles per hour, twice the usual speed of a winter storm.

An early indication that something very rare was in play came in the early afternoon when the leading edge of the double storm reached New York. At 10:30 Saturday morning, the schooner yacht *Magic* (famous then as the winner of the first United States defense of the America's Cup in 1870) set out from Greenport, on eastern Long Island, on a delivery to New York. At that time, her crew would have known nothing of the first gale warnings, which the Weather Bureau in Washington was just beginning to telegraph to local stations. At about 1:00 P.M., *Magic* was suddenly overwhelmed by a blizzard so thick that the crew could not see the bow from the cockpit and a wind that quickly built to hurricane strength. (*Magic* then was approximately thirty miles from Block Island, which recorded a wind strength of almost one hundred miles an hour.) She drifted under bare poles for hours and eventually dropped two anchors close to the Connecticut shore east of New Haven, where she was nearly run down by a steamship.

THAT THIS FAST-MOVING CELL was not recorded by the Weather Bureau until midafternoon Saturday suggests that almost all the data coming into its offices concerned the storm from the west. Because it came across land, the Michigan low was easy to follow. The coastal low could not be tracked at the time until it came ashore because ships did not yet have wireless radios with which to report weather from sea. There are other indications that the coastal low was lost by the Weather Bureau. The *Monthly Weather Review* referred to the Michigan low as "predicted" but the coastal low as merely "indicated." Also in the *Review*, J. W. Smith, in referring to the morning gale warnings, insisted that they should have been clear enough to cover any new conditions that appeared later in the day. Another indication that the coastal gale (and the double storm) was unknown for many hours was a brief weather forecast in the *Boston Post* on Saturday predicting that the coastal low would go safely out to sea—information that could have originated only at the Weather Bureau.

Before anybody could leap on these and other indications that he was not entirely on top of the situation, Willis Moore seized the public relations initiative on Sunday afternoon. In a statement to the *New York Herald*, he claimed that the bureau had always expected the double storm, and had tracked the coastal low all the way from North Carolina. The Michigan storm played only a minor, supplemental role in these developments, Moore declared, apparently forgetting that his bureau had been tracking it minutely for two days and had issued dire warnings about it. He was certain of one more thing, he told the reporter: "The temperature will moderate during Monday." (It did.)

VI

MOORE'S COVER-UP does not absolve the storm racer on the bridge of the *Portland* of all responsibility. Even if the barometer was steady on Saturday afternoon and Boston harbor was in a flat calm, the Weather Bureau did warn Hollis Blanchard about the Michigan storm. When he returned to India Wharf, the red gale warning flag was still flying. He still decided to head out to sea. Why didn't his superiors stop him?

That a steamship line hired an aggressive captain should not be surprising. Schedules must be kept. But it would be shocking if a well-established line placed a prized ship entirely in the hands of such a commander without putting him on a short leash. When the Portland Steamship Company promoted Blanchard from the *Portland*'s pilot to her captain in mid-November, it undoubtedly felt confident that its management would provide the necessary checks on Blanchard's daring. That this is exactly what did *not* happen suggests that responsibility for the disaster lay in part with the company, as it did with the Weather Bureau, Blanchard himself, and the wiles of nature.

On the evening of November 26, 1898—probably the most important moment in its history—the Portland Steamship Company was a mess. Every person who should have taken part in this crucial decision was new to his job. Worse, the three men who could have prevailed upon Blanchard to be cautious were not on hand to advise him at just the moment when his aggressiveness needed checking. There was no shortage of communication; the problem was that this communication was ineffective. On Saturday several telephone calls and telegrams passed between the company's Portland headquarters and its Boston office on the subject of the weather and the ship's schedule. After the Weather Bureau wired a storm warning to Alexander C. Dennison, the captain of the *Bay State*, the other ship on the Boston–Portland route, Dennison told Blanchard that he intended to stay in Portland rather than head west into the forecast Lakes storm. In reply, Blanchard told him that he would sail. Sometime after the captains conversed, the line's general manager, John F. Liscomb, telephoned from Portland in search of Blanchard, could not locate him, and ended up leaving a somewhat different message with the line's Boston agent, C. F. Williams: the *Bay State* would not sail on time and might not sail at all. He instructed Williams to advise Blanchard to hold off departure until 9:00 P.M. and, if conditions worsened, to cancel. The manager then hung up and rushed to the train station to get to the funeral in Boston. Subsequently, in legal proceedings brought to determine the line's liability for the accident, Liscomb denied that he had directly ordered Blanchard to do anything. His and Dennison's calls from Portland were intended to *inform* Blanchard, he said. (The judge in the proceedings decreed that the accident was an act of God beyond the steamship company's ability to protect against.)

Thus the line declined to exercise its authority to keep the *Portland* tied up at India Wharf. There is no way to know for sure if that was a conscious decision, but the evidence at hand indicates not only that the Portland Steamship Company was in a period of transition in late November, but that on November 26 it was in organizational chaos.

First off, nobody involved with the decision—the line's general manager, its local agent, Blanchard himself, and Captain Dennison of the *Bay State*—had been in his job longer than three weeks. After the general manager died in early November, Liscomb was promoted from Boston agent to the top operational position at the Portland headquarters, while Williams succeeded him in Boston. Liscomb was the man to make the ultimate decision about departure, yet, as we have seen, he declined to do more than make a recommendation whose strength was diluted by mixed signals and communications snafus. Then he abdicated his authority by jumping aboard a train.

The reason for his hasty trip to Boston was itself a distraction to the entire company at precisely the time when it needed to focus on only one issue—whether its ships should sail. The line's senior captain, Charles Deering—the master of the *Bay State*, who had been going to sea for fifty-two of his seventy-three years—had died on Thanksgiving Day, and his funeral was scheduled for Sunday. Attending the funeral besides manager Liscomb were Blanchard's right- and left-hand men on the bridge of the *Portland*. These were the pilot and the first mate (the second was related to Deering), whom he excused from the Saturday trip to Portland. After Deering's sudden death, Dennison was promoted as captain of the *Bay State*. On only his third day in command, Dennison was placed in the ticklish position of sitting at one end of a long-distance telephone line and advising the line's senior captain not to follow his own instincts and take his ship to sea.

On the most threatening day of her nine-year existence, therefore, the sidewheeler *Portland* was in a situation that would be the despair of any well-run organization. Leaders had not adjusted to their new roles, priorities were out of balance, lines of communication were down, and everybody was distracted by the death of an old friend. Meanwhile, the most important matter at hand—the state of the threatening weather—was neither thoroughly known nor receiving the full attention it demanded. In this state of organizational meltdown, risk management was out of control. The single crucial decision to be made on that or any day—whether it was safe for one of the line's vessels to sail—was left to the one man who, despite his many strengths, was temperamentally least qualified to make the correct decision.

In short, one of the worst disasters in New England's history occurred for banal reasons having to do with bad luck, bad timing, and misunderstandings.

AND SO THE *PORTLAND* casts off her lines from India Wharf at 7:00 P.M. on the Saturday after Thanksgiving 1898. The barometer is stable, the sky overcast, the wind and sea calm. Trusting in his understanding of the weather forecast and his own weather eye, feeling challenged by superiors and colleagues, Captain Hollis Blanchard has a competitive glint in his eye. He is setting out to race a storm that, he believes, is slowly overtaking him from the west. If he pushes hard, he will beat it to Portland.

6

Hamrah and the Ameses

The North Atlantic, 1935

*"The action of those who were left was dwarfed by
the grandness of what had just taken place."*

—Charles F. Tillinghast Jr.

LATE ON THE LAST NIGHT of June 1935, a damaged sailboat with
a Persian name sailed slowly into Sydney, Nova Scotia. The boat
tied up off the yacht club, and in the morning three exhausted
young men came ashore, found their way to the telegraph office,
and wired distressing messages to their families in New England. They checked into the Isle Royale Hotel, and after their
first hot baths in almost a month, they were located by a
reporter for the local newspaper, who heard their astonishing
and tragic story.

The headline the next day ran:

Ship's Arrival Reveals Sea Tragedy;
Boston Realtor and 2 Sons Perish
Boys Lose Lives in Efforts to Rescue Father from Death

The shocking story of the ketch *Hamrah* was immediately picked up by
other newspapers, and as it raced across America it was treated not as a
usual disaster tale but as an epic of Homeric proportions. "For generations, there will be told this tale of Robert Russell Ames and his sons,
Richard Glover and Henry Russell," ran a representative commentary in
the *Boston Herald*. "The story will inspire other young men to live fine
lives and dare hard deeds when duty demands. It will be cited in acade-
mies and colleges all over the land as an example of what young Americans can be and what they will do. . . . Happy is the family which
provides such traditions for our citizens." To speak of *Hamrah* and her
people is to speak of family and deep convictions. Some of these beliefs
called the Ames men into the middle of the North Atlantic where a cruel
accident destroyed almost an entire family in less than twenty minutes.

I

WHY WERE A MIDDLE-AGED real estate developer from Boston and five
young Harvard men in a sailboat in the middle of the cold North Atlantic
Ocean, six hundred miles from the nearest land?

Hamrah's crew were part of a large, distinctive, influential middle-class
culture that was grounded in vigorous physical activity, first ashore and
then afloat. The Ames family's connection with the sea began in 1889, when
Robert Ames's father, Professor James Barr Ames of the Harvard Law
School, bought a 250-acre saltwater farm near Castine, on the coast of
Maine. Castine had a long, important history as a French trading post; as
the setting, during the American Revolution, for the worst naval defeat in
American history before Pearl Harbor; and until the late nineteenth century, as a shipbuilding center surrounded by farms and fishing villages. As
shipbuilding died in Maine, so did the old economy of self-sufficiency.
Many families left the sea and went to work in the new canneries and mills,
if they did not leave New England altogether. ("The only place that's growing is the cemetery," Yankees half-joked.)

Land was eagerly sought by city people called "rusticators" or "cottagers," who flocked to the coast in passenger steamers in search of vacation homes. The "insatiable thirst of the cottagers for land," in the words of Charles B. McLane, a historian of coastal Maine, was sated by the ready availability of peninsula and island farms. Some were acquired by real estate promoters with plans for summer resorts with exotic names like Sorrento. One of the most ambitious projects, the New England Tent Club, was assembled on Dirigo Island (the former Butter Island) in Penobscot Bay. Promotional flyers for Dirigo described it as an "Arabic-like town of tents and cottages" devoted to the interests of "the young merchant, club man, college student, graduate professional man, of good social standing and reference." Children were discouraged, and tennis courts, a golf course, and a large casino were installed. The Tent Club collapsed when the automobile diverted people from the single-destination vacation, and the island, back to its original name, today shows no sign that it was ever an exclusive resort for city folk.

Most rusticators decided to go it alone on old farms. Although they often waited decades before modernizing, they did add a few familiar conveniences and institutions such as automobiles, sailing clubs, and summer chapels (thirteen Episcopal chapels were built along the Maine coast around 1910).

The farm that James Barr Ames bought in 1889 was on Perkins Point, just north of Castine. Perkins Point became so closely identified with the family that, even in that tradition-bound part of the world, it came to be known locally by the name of its new owner as "Ames Point." Ames worked the farm in summers with his two sons and a dozen farmhands. He kept the place simple; upstairs plumbing was not installed until the 1920s, and electricity was not introduced for another decade after that. This was not his only property in the area. One June in the 1890s, while on a ferry in Penobscot Bay, he noticed a farm spilling down the south slope of Cape Rosier. He stepped ashore at the next stop and at the general store learned that the two-hundred-acre farm on Condon Point was for sale at a bargain price. He bought it on the spot, and for many decades it was the family's favorite picnic ground. A century after he purchased Condon Point, his granddaughter Phyllis Ames Cox and her husband Archibald Cox, the former Watergate special prosecutor, were living in the farmhouse year-round.

~

ALTHOUGH HE RARELY if ever represented a client, James Barr Ames was one of the giants of the legal profession. A professor at the Harvard Law School beginning in 1872, and its dean from 1895 until his death, he helped lead the transformation of the law from a trade to a profession for which its members qualified in rigorous postgraduate study under a faculty of scholars. An authority on the law of contracts and medieval English legal history, Ames employed the innovative and controversial case method of instruction. Assuming that the law is a science whose precepts can be learned through experiment, Ames and the law school's dean, Christopher Columbus Langdell, turned the lecture hall into a legal laboratory in which students, instead of sitting passively as principles were pounded into their heads, vigorously debated lawsuits and court decisions. Ames, said a Harvard colleague, "baptized men in brain fire."

Ames's life had not been easy. A bright but sickly boy, he had been forced by illness to take a year off from Harvard College. Instead of staying home, he worked as a farmhand. The outdoors activity revived his body and his spirits. Back in Cambridge, he headed his college class, captained the baseball team, did well in law school, and was appointed professor of law before he ever advised a client. Physical activity was in his deepest convictions. "He loved strenuous physical work as he loved to wrestle with a legal problem or to help a student," a colleague said. Ames got around Cambridge at a fast clip, running from his house to the law school in the morning, from his office to the classroom, from the classroom to lunch— on and on until he trotted back home in the afternoon in his now wrinkled suit. When someone politely suggested that he slow down for his health, Ames challenged him to a two-mile race. Convinced like many people in his and the subsequent generation that the best life is a rural life, he became a passionate rusticator. With the proceeds from the many legal casebooks and other teaching materials he published, Ames eventually purchased more than a thousand acres of land in southern and midcoast Maine.

Perkins Point was his favorite place. There he worked along with the hired hands, chopped firewood by the cord, led his two sons, Robert and Richard, on long rambles, and swam and boated on the pond and the cold waters of the Penobscot. Come nightfall, he settled down to study law by candlelight.

~

To PREVENT CONFUSION among the prominent branches of the Ames family in Massachusetts, each has been given a nickname. One is known as "the shovel Ameses" because of its successful shovel-manufacturing business. Professor James Barr Ames's branch is "the intellectual Ameses." His son Richard was secretary at Harvard Law School for many years, his grandson and namesake was a partner of a prestigious Boston firm, and his great-grandson Charles clerked for a justice of the United States Supreme Court.

It may seem surprising that the first of "the intellectual Ameses"—the scholarly author of treatises on statutes in medieval English law—happily devoted his summers to chopping wood and baling hay. Like many of his contemporaries, he believed that a righteous life was a hard life, a perpetual state of challenge that balanced urban and rural pursuits. This code gained a name from Theodore Roosevelt: "the strenuous life," which was the title of a martial speech he gave to a group of Chicago businessmen in 1899. "The highest form of success comes not to the man who desires mere easy peace," Roosevelt said, "but to the man who does not shrink from danger, from hardship, or from bitter toil, and who out of these wins the splendid ultimate triumph. . . . It is only through strife, through hard and dangerous endeavor, that we shall ultimately win the goal of true national greatness."

Despite that flag-waving, tooth-and-claw Darwinism, the code of the strenuous life was widely accepted primarily because of the spiritual benefits it promised. Some were grounded in competition. "Run with perseverance the race that is set before us," says the Bible (Heb. 12:1), and both the athletic and the religious implications of that instruction guided the competition-happy schools, youth groups, and other service institutions that blossomed around the turn of the last century. The early Young Men's Christian Association was half church, half gym (basketball was invented in a YMCA in 1892), and one of the best-known revivalists, Billy Sunday, was a former outfielder for the Chicago White Sox. Yet the code of vigorous, challenging living also offered a sweeter, less competitive spirituality of discovering a truer life in nature. Percy Bysshe Shelley and the other romantics had the same idea, but they went about it differently. Strenuous lifers did not merely *go outdoors* in search of picturesque views. They thrust themselves *into nature* and strove with and against it. Here is John Muir, Roosevelt's favorite environmentalist, rejoicing as he climbs into the high Sierra:

We are now in the mountains and they are in us, kindling enthusiasm, making every nerve quiver, filling every pore and cell of us. . . . Just now I can hardly conceive of any bodily condition dependent on food or breath any more than the ground or the sky. How glorious a conversion, so complete and whole-some as it is, scarce memory enough of old bondage days left as a standpoint to view it from! In this newness of life we seem to have been so always.

A nautical expression of this sense of "glorious conversion" to a truer life came later from Maurice Griffiths, an English boating writer and yacht designer. Here is how he described his feelings on heading out in a small cruising boat:

I found my pulse beating with suppressed excitement as I threw the moor-ing buoy overboard. It seemed as if that simple action had severed my con-nection with the life on shore; that I had thereby cut adrift the ties of convention, the unrealities and illusions of cities and crowds; that I was free now, free to go where I chose, to do and to live and to conquer as I liked, to play the game wherein a man's qualities count for more than his appear-ance.

MUIR'S REFERENCE to "old bondage days" and Griffiths's sensitivity to social judgment both point to the therapeutic nature of the strenuous life. Some of its most eloquent spokesmen were so unhappy that their addictive adventuring has the features of an antidepressant. Muir's boyhood was a miserable one under a brutal father. Bad health pushed Richard Henry Dana Jr. and James Barr Ames—two early proponents of what Roosevelt would call the strenuous life—out of Harvard classrooms into the out-doors. Roosevelt as a boy suffered debilitating asthma and loneliness, from which he escaped into flights of fancy about noble heroes and, on his own part, bouts of extreme physical activity that included boxing, long horse-back rides, and (as we saw in chapter 1) difficult sailing trips in small boats. "From the age of eleven," remarks one of his biographers, H. W. Brands, "his self-esteem had been intimately entwined in his conception of his physical prowess." After his mother and his wife died on the same night in 1884, Roosevelt attempted to work through his despair on a ranch in the Dakota Badlands. (Like many such escapes, his was imperfect; he dressed in custom-tailored cowboy outfits and insisted that his ranch hands call him "Mr. Roosevelt.") The experience provided some solace, but it was not complete. Looking back on this time of recuperation, Roosevelt wrote,

"Black care rarely sits behind a rider whose pace is fast enough, at any rate not when he first feels the horse move under him." (This sentence, which has achieved the status of a proverb, is usually quoted without the important qualification that begins "at any rate.")

If Roosevelt was the most visible embodiment of the code of the strenuous life, its leading thinker was another brilliant, depression-prone mind inside a body that twitched not only for activity but for activity with a moral purpose. This was the influential Harvard psychologist and pragmatist philosopher William James. Like Muir and Roosevelt, James had lived under the burden of "black care" as a young man and had seriously considered suicide. James kept depression more or less at bay with strenuous exertions of willpower, activity, and romance. Life, he said, is "the everlasting battle of the powers of light with those of darkness," in which can be found "heroism, reduced to its bare chance, yet ever and anon snatching victory from the jaws of death." What the world needed was a "moral equivalent of war" to wean boys from debilitating softness, excessive individualism, and too much reliance on brainpower. "We of the highly educated classes (so called) have most of us got far, far away from Nature," he told some schoolteachers. The answer was hard manual labor.

James and Roosevelt raced through their lives as though each moment would be their last, pressing their energies and bodies to the limits of endurance. For that they paid the harsh price of painful middle-aged illnesses and relatively early deaths—James at sixty-eight ("He had worn himself out," his wife said) and Roosevelt, his era's embodiment of vitality, at a mere sixty.

FROM A PURITANICAL regional ethic, the code grew into a national movement that shaped many Americans and institutions in the first half of the twentieth century. People looked for new heroes and found them not (as their parents had) in pulpits or combat but in unpaid, vigorous, and sometimes quirky activity. The new heroes included the lone voyager Joshua Slocum, "Teddy" Roosevelt with his boxing matches in the White House, Charles Lindbergh and Amelia Earhart with their flying adventures, and years later, the Kennedys with their addiction to football and risky living.

Besides strenuous activity, "character" became an idol around the time that young Robert Ames was spending summers at Perkins Point. No qualifiers were called for: either one had character or one did not. The reasons for not having it included the decline of rural values, "nervous exhaustion," over-work, and the inability of modern men to preserve "an ethos of fortitude." The enemy of that ethos was the new America of large cities, smoky factories, elaborately organized corporations, and ethnic diversity (the strenuous life movement was not immune to anti-Semitism and other prejudices).

That was the side of darkness. The side of light could be found among the Boy Scouts, football players, mountain climbers, sailors, farmers, and the heads of boarding schools where middle-class boys and girls lived in spartan simplicity in a regimen of cold showers, muscular Christianity, and daily scrimmages on the playing fields and ice-covered ponds of New England. The bylaws for the strenuous life were written by Ernest Thompson Seton in his nine guiding principles for the Woodcraft move-ment, a predecessor to the Scouts: "1. This is recreation. 2. Camp life. 3. Self-government guided by an adult. 4. The magic of the camp fire. 5. Woodcraft pursuits. 6. Honors by standards. 7. Personal decorations for personal achievements. 8. A heroic ideal. 9. Picturesqueness in all things."

Missing from this mixed list of romantic ideals and pragmatic guide-lines is a tenth injunction that Seton did not have to mention because all strenuous lifers observed it. That rule was *Play the game*, a phrase we saw a few pages back in Maurice Griffiths's lovely leap of joy on casting off. It means to engage directly and unselfishly with the world, in sports and in all life, without trickery, conceit, and overt ambition. The rule was laid down in ringing mandates passed on to several generations of boys and girls. Rudyard Kipling, the most popular writer of the early twentieth cen-tury, is said to have declared that "the playing of the game is more than the game." Later the American sports writer Grantland Rice laid out the rule in a short didactic poem:

> For when the One Great Scorer comes
> To write against your name,
> He marks—not that you won or lost—
> But how you played the game.

"Playing the game" defined a particular view of life and duty. In his appropriately named history of the early scouting movement, *The Charac-ter Factory*, Columbia University literary historian Michael Rosenthal remarks, "At once a political ideal and a moral injunction, it constituted, for those reared in the system, an all-embracing principle of conduct applicable to every circumstance in which an individual might find himself. Good people do it and bad people don't—and these deficient ones would get better quickly if they only would."

THE SEA WAS NEVER FAR from the thoughts of strenuous lifers. When William James insisted that for their own good boys should be conscripted into hard labor, his list of suitable venues included mines, hotel kitchens, and "fishing fleets in December." Rudyard Kipling provided a fictional example of the character-building qualities of seafaring in *Captains Courageous*, his best-selling novel of 1898 that tells how a spoiled brat is shaped into a decent young man by the rough-hewn but good-hearted sailors of the Gloucester fishing schooner *We're Here*. In that spirit, Roosevelt sent his son Archie off for a week of cruising with Joshua Slocum in his yawl *Spray*, where the boy discovered that Slocum knew by heart many of Kipling's poems of soldiers and battle. The president apparently wished that he, not his son, had gone out with the old captain. He received Slocum in the White House and told him he well appreciated how Slocum felt about "the sheer loneliness and vastness of the ocean" because Roosevelt had exactly those feelings about the American wilderness.

If a boy's character was best developed in hardship, within the community of men in action, the perfect community was the one between fathers and sons living vigorously on the water. An example was presented by an unlikely man in an unlikely setting. In 1900 Harvard president Charles W. Eliot—a founder of the modern university and the man who named James Barr Ames dean of the Harvard Law School (and like Ames a Maine rusticator)—spoke on the subject of a proper education to a gathering of teachers and school administrators at the convention of the National Education Association. He chose to say nothing about classrooms and libraries but told the parable of the Gott Island boy, which can be summarized as follows:

One winter morning a Maine lobsterman and his son head out from their island home in their lobster boat to tend traps. As the father pulls the traps the son keeps an eye out for hazards. He spies bad weather and cries out, "Father, there's a northwester coming!" There follows a life-or-death struggle against wind and sea. With rime forming on their lips, the father and son turn to the task at hand and capably sail the little boat home to Gott Island. The lesson was clear, Eliot told his audience of educators, who may have been a little bewildered by hearing the distinguished president of Harvard University expound on the educational opportunities of lobstering. The point of the story was that the education this boy gained on the water was superior to anything he might learn in a classroom, especially an urban classroom. "Now that is a magnificent training for a boy, and the sheltered city offers nothing like it," he concluded. "The adverse forces of nature, if not so formidable that men cannot cope with them, are strenuous teachers; but in modern cities we hardly know that the wind blows, or that the flood is coming, or that bitter cold is imperiling all animal life."

THE STRENUOUS LIFE DOCTRINE has been closely identified with Anglophiles, especially old-line New York and New England families like the Roosevelts and Eliots. Yet the code is by no means socially circumscribed, and—despite the best efforts of the worst bigots to make it an exclusive club—it has had followers from across America and Britain and among male and female members of all social classes and ethnic groups.

The code may be criticized on many counts. It can be a smug enforcer of rigid rules of comportment. President Eliot, for example, was outraged by many tactical developments in sports, including imaginative deceptions such as fake handoffs in football and curve balls in baseball. Hearing some students praise a Harvard pitcher who was famous for his good pickoff move, Eliot cried, "Why! Why! They boasted of his making a feint to throw a ball in one direction and then *throwing it in ANOTHER!*" His put-down of youthful gamesmanship was mild compared with the racial and social exclusiveness that sometimes surrounded the strenuous life. Believers in the code also could be relentless and even bullying in their worship of blind optimism, hyperactive group activities, and the seeming virtues of going to war. Introverts often were marked as pariahs. But at its best the strenuous life builds resilience, self-sufficiency, physical health, and a sense of fair play— each a shield against alienation and other afflictions of modern life. "Playing the game" encourages the most important belief of them all—that life, after all, is at least worth living fully and long until its inevitable end.

II

AFTER JAMES BARR AMES died in 1910, his two sons and their families continued to return every summer to Perkins Point, where they farmed and played to their hearts' content.

The oldest son was Robert Russell Ames, the captain of *Hamrah*. Born in 1883, he became a real estate man. His younger brother, Richard, like his father, was a nonpracticing attorney connected with the Harvard Law School, in his case as its secretary for many years until he took up farming. Between them they had four children, three boys and a girl, all born between 1911 and 1914 and raised as equals. Robert and his wife, the former Margaret Fuller Glover, had Richard and Henry, known as Harry. The elder Richard Ames married Dorothy Abbott, the daughter of another distinguished law school dean, Nathan Abbott, and their children were James Barr (named for his grandfather) and Phyllis Ames.

"We were inseparable. Ours was an extraordinary relationship," said Phyllis Ames Cox, the survivor of the four, in the spring of 2001 as she looked through photo albums. Raised in nearby houses winter and summer, the children spent hours together near Boston and at Perkins Point. There were farm animals to care for, softball and touch football to play, canoes to paddle, rafts to dive from on the pond, trees and barns to climb. "We were always outdoors, and we were never still except to sleep and read. On a rainy day we would go up to the big barn and play in the hayloft, swinging around on ropes, and then we'd go to the big house and sit around the round table and work on our stamp collections." Many snapshots show young Phyllis in the middle of melees, and sometimes above them as she stands, arms raised in triumph, on a barn roof. ("I have to say I was a tomboy," she said with a laugh. "I can't get away from it, can I?")

Their athletic, fun-loving fathers were often on hand. Robert Ames, a head shorter than his wife, Margaret, was the extrovert of the two—constantly in motion, his voice so loud that his secretary wondered why he needed a telephone, since all he had to do was bellow out the window. On his way home from his office in Boston he often stopped at a famous establishment called Jack's Joke Shop to pick up dribble glasses, whoopee cushions, and other entertainments for the youngsters. His brother Richard, a balding legal scholar, was somewhat quieter and more focused. But as far as their youngsters were concerned, they were cocaptains. On weekends they led the children into the forests for hours of tree felling. "They both loved to chop wood," Phyllis Cox remembered. For the two men and the four children, cutting firewood was what sailing had been to Percy Bysshe Shelley: an escapist reverie so enchantingly timeless that they forgot all about the hour. Margaret Ames would have to come out and hunt them down for dinner, but she understood. As she wrote in her husband's obituary, "For reasons best known to themselves it was always necessary to call them for Sunday dinner—taking watches wouldn't do. Those walks back through the woods on crisp, bright mornings are lovely memories."

Their main household was at Wayland, near Boston. In early June, the two families went down to the Boston waterfront with their bags and suitcases and Phyllis's pony and boarded the Bangor boat. The next morning they disembarked at Bucksport, where one of the men from the farm met them in a horse-drawn buggy or an automobile called Napoleon ("an almost completely brakeless model T Ford," according to Margaret Ames). All piled in except Phyllis, who rode her pony down the peninsula to Perkins Point, where they settled in for the summer. It was a life of physical and intellectual vigor. Robert and Richard's mother, James Barr Ames's widow, devoted her mornings to reading Greek, her afternoons to going into the woods with books and a hatchet to cut kindling and pick flowers. "We were always raised to *excel*," Phyllis Ames Cox remembered (on the day she took her first steps, she also tried to climb a ladder). The four children's mornings were taken up with farm chores, including gathering vegetables for meals. At noon the family swam in the pond. After lunch they were free to play. Adventure lay everywhere. In 1924 two barnstorming pilots named Sparks and Fogg working their way up the coast from Florida appeared one day in their tiny biplane and took the cousins up for a novel view of Castine. Generally, however, competition ruled. Richard Ames awarded prizes to the children for their first swim across the pond, and when they were shagging fly balls, he offered twenty-five cents to whomever caught an easy fly, fifty cents for a hard one. Occasionally he offered higher stakes, and one day he shouted, "*A sailboat!*"

When they were little, Dick and his cousin Jim would sit astride porch chairs and pretend they were driving motorboats, but when it came seriously to boats there was only one kind, like Richard Ames's gaff-rigged sloop *Petrel*, moored out in Wadsworth Cove. Dick caught that fly ball, and his uncle produced a fifteen-foot daysailer called *Jackie* with sails sewn by a maid. Richard Ames taught the children how to sail in that simple little sloop, and they spent many summer afternoons out in her more sophisticated successors. When the boat occasionally capsized and swamped, fishermen in the busy harbor towed them back.

Dick spent several summers in an even more vigorous setting at a sum-

ABOVE: "We were always outdoors, and we were never still except to sleep and read," Phyllis Ames Cox said of her childhood. Here she is in the late 1920s with her brother Jim *(left)* and cousin Harry *(center)*, sailing near the Ames farm on Perkins Point at Castine, Maine. (Courtesy Ames family)
BELOW: Margaret Fuller Glover Ames and the Ames children at a picnic in the late 1920s. "Those were golden beautiful years," she would write out of her sorrow. "Weren't we lucky to have had them?" (Courtesy Ames family)

mer camp that has been described as Maine's "ultimate expression of the Rooseveltian age." Situated on a lake near Waterville, Merryweather Camp was owned and managed by Henry Richards—"the Skipper," as the boys called him with veneration. From its founding in 1900 at the recommendation of the Reverend Endicott Peabody, the rector of Groton School, to its breakup in 1938 after Richards's retirement, Merryweather turned out 999 boys, many of whom went on to attend elite boarding schools and Harvard. The outdoor activities included "Scouting" (despite its name, a simulated war) and "Around the World" (a grueling fifty-six-mile canoe trip). The home and family spirit was maintained by the Skipper's compulsively cheerful wife, Laura Howe Richards, a daughter of Julia Ward Howe.

ENERGY, OPTIMISM, BRAINS, and a loving family guided the Ames boys and girl into adulthood. Dick Ames graduated from Milton Academy in 1930 near the top of his class in academics, leadership, and athletics (at his graduation, the class valedictorian recited Kipling's dictum that "the playing of the game is more than the game"). At Harvard, Dick won the top scholarship for scholar-athletes, was elected president of the student council, and at graduation was appointed to the prestigious position of second marshal. As a wrestler he accumulated a record of thirty-five to one, losing the finals of the 1933 intercollegiate 175-pound championship to a man with an obvious knee injury that Ames declined to exploit. During summers he was a counselor at Merryweather Camp, where he developed a close relationship with the Skipper's granddaughter, Laura, that had all appearances of moving toward marriage. Harry, four years younger than his brother, was not the all-around star his brother was, but he did well in academics and was developing into a fine wrestler.

Within the family, Dick Ames served both as his father's right-hand assistant in his ambitious outdoor activities and as a confidant to his mother, from whom he inherited his lanky frame and blinding smile. Margaret Ames enjoyed one of those relationships with her tall older son that mothers (and sons) dream about. From wherever he was—boarding school, Europe on vacations, Merryweather Camp, Harvard—he seems to have written her a letter or postcard weekly or even more often. The usual tone of these notes is lighthearted, but toward the end of some of them Dick, even as a teenager, changes roles from son to counselor. In June 1931, for example, between practices for the rowing race against Yale, he reported an excursion on J. P. Morgan's enormous steam yacht *Corsair*, where he had come across a packet of Morgan's personal stationary and had been unable to resist taking a sheet to write a letter. From that cheerful prank, Dick turned abruptly to family responsibilities, asking his mother, "Have you got tickets on the Bangor Boat for Sat. Night?" Such concern suggests that young Dick Ames not only was as sensitive as he was talented but that he had assumed a key role in the family psychology.

IN ABOUT 1930 Robert Ames decided to commission a family cruising boat. With William Dyer, a Castine neighbor, he developed plans for a fifty-four-foot two-masted sailboat with a traditional husky appearance. To build her, Ames went to Machiasport, at Maine's far eastern corner, to one of Maine's many small, family-operated boatyards. It took two years for the brothers Dan J. and Murray O. Stuart, working alone, to complete the boat. With her hefty hull, long bowsprit, and steering wheel projecting from a box overlooking the small cockpit, she resembled the chunky coasting and fishing schooners that were still common along the Maine coast. Yet her construction was that of a yacht, with planking and deck of teak, an exotic hardwood that grows only in Southeast Asia, fastened with the best-quality bronze screws and bolts. Following his ideals of rural simplicity, and like many owners of new boats built around that time, Ames did not install a motor. An engine may have delivered him to Maine on the overnight boat or a train from Boston, but he was not about to use one while rusticating.

His new vessel was unusual in a few striking ways. In place of the usual black or white, her topsides were painted green, a color sometimes considered unlucky for boats and ships. Her masts, booms, and sails were arranged in the newly popular three-cornered Bermudian or Marconi rig (it was replaced by the old-fashioned gaff rig in 1934). And in naming her, instead of following the old Down East tradition of honoring women (*Elizabeth*, for example), their owners (*C. G. Matthews*), or the weather (*Snow Squall*), he chose a Persian word, *Hamrah*. Perhaps Ames was taken with the then popular Arab legend of the beautiful, clever Scheherazade, who charmed her king with stories for a thousand and one nights—much as a boat might enchant her owner. *Hamrah* means "fellow traveler" or "friend"; today in Iran, a mobile phone is called a "telephone hamrah."

After the Stuart brothers launched *Hamrah* in 1932, at the end of Dick

Ames's sophomore year at Harvard, she got to work as the family boat. Snapshots show Robert Ames usually at the helm with his son Dick standing by, and the cousins sprawling, studying charts. The strenuous life was a masculine life, to the irritation of a female member of another Down East family of sailing rusticators—Eleanor Roosevelt. She complained, "I never get a chance to sail the boat myself. There are always men around. . . . One has always to let the men do the sailing." It was no different at Perkins Point. Boat decisions were Robert Ames's, but women were welcome aboard *Hamrah*.

Many years later, in one of the rare times when she mentioned the boat, Margaret Ames described for her niece and nephew a typical day after a cold front swept away the humidity and left Penobscot Bay sparkling under a fresh, clearing northwest breeze:

> On northwest days Uncle Robert would get up, look out the west window, and say, "Can you be ready for twenty [minutes] by 9:00?" Thanks to that extraordinary Kathleen I could. This was when we had the *Hamrah*. I would telephone for Mrs. Vogell. I'd drive to the village for steaks and onions— Kathleen would prepare rolls and a vegetable in the big gallon jug—and we'd be off down the bay. I never knew whom Uncle Robert had invited until I saw them appear.

Robert Ames's ambitions aimed much higher than spontaneous afternoon sails on Penobscot Bay. Photographs show him practicing taking sextant sights. After two summers of daysailing and cruising around Castine, Ames entered *Hamrah* in the biennial 660-mile race to Bermuda with Dick, his stockier younger brother Harry (also a star Harvard wrestler), and several friends, most of them college age. Their cousin Jim, who was concentrating on a legal career, was not on board (Phyllis, meanwhile, was attending Smith College). The ambitious new direction in her husband's and sons' sailing plans certainly would have made Margaret Ames anxious. In late May 1934, soon before Dick's Harvard graduation, the Ames boys and their father went up to Machiasport, where the Stuart brothers, for an unknown reason, had converted *Hamrah* from the Bermudian rig to the traditional gaff rig, and the new rigging had to be gone over. Dick cooked up another of his funny, teasing, and eventually reassuring letters. He reveled ironically in his graduation ("I'll give you one guess as to whether I am glad to be through Harvard College. I am pining away with grief and am getting pale and wan"), gossiped about a bean supper at Machiasport's Baptist church (where a pretty girl flirtatiously asked him how to play post office), and carried on in that teasing way for eight pages until finally he came to the words he knew his mother was most eager to read: "To get more to the point the boat is in fine shape and ready to slide in on Saturday if the tides be high enough. I have been working the cheek blocks, cleats, and other appurtenances which will make for easy reefing in rough weather. We are just about ready to run the new running rigging and bend on the sails." If anything could have eased his mother's mind it would have been that Dick was preparing the boat for a storm.

TWENTY-NINE BOATS STARTED the race to Bermuda in a near-calm on June 24 off New London, Connecticut (subsequent races have been started at Newport, Rhode Island), and found enough wind to pull them out of Long Island Sound. In a thick fog they sailed on the southeasterly course toward Bermuda, passing fifty miles from the replacement for the Nantucket lightship, which the White Star liner *Olympic* had cut in half five weeks earlier, with the loss of seven lightkeepers. On the second day the sky cleared for a full moon, and they were soon fighting the usual squalls and building sea in the bright blue, weedy water of the Gulf Stream. Came another day of windy weather and the fleet, by now spread out over almost two hundred miles, had a pleasant sail into Bermuda, albeit close-hauled with the wind well ahead. Slow when sailing in a headwind and rough water, *Hamrah* covered the course in just under four days and six hours, beating only two boats.

Losing so badly did not appear to bother the Ameses in the least. The boys, then twenty-two and nineteen, and their friends delighted in Bermuda's island world, where automobiles were banned except for the local doctor. Dick and Henry celebrated by acquiring tattoos. It was in Bermuda that the Ameses were told, very likely for the first time, that their unusual but beloved yacht might have serious shortcomings. The message came from Alfred F. Loomis, an experienced sailor and respected yachting writer with high standards. In his history of ocean racing before 1936, Loomis described it as "the only recreation or dogged pursuit or turbulent pastime—call it what you will—in which man pits himself against his fellow and against the eternal elements as well." For that enterprise, a crew required an able, weatherly vessel, which he believed *Hamrah* was not.

When he forthrightly passed this opinion on to Dick and Harry in the clubhouse of the Royal Bermuda Yacht Club, he probably expected at least an argument; sailors do not accept demurrals about their boats with grace. But the Ames boys charmed Loomis with their modest self-confidence:

> In a few minutes spent in conversation with the sons of the owner I formed a keen admiration for them. They recognized the deficiencies of their packet. She was slow and poor to windward, but she was a lot of fun to sail. They were full of enthusiasm, and I'll never lose the mental image I have of them standing in the clubhouse at Hamilton, the one tall, the other short, both smiling and talking 300 to the minute and telling me with the greatest good nature in the world that they didn't blame me for having advised a young friend of theirs and mine not to take the chance of sailing with them. Though they were too kind to say so, the mere fact of their arrival in Bermuda had branded my fears as false.

Intending to shame the boys into thinking twice about again taking *Hamrah* offshore, Loomis only felt shame himself for questioning these charming young men.

III

AFTER RETURNING FROM BERMUDA, Robert Ames and his sons decided to enter *Hamrah* in the next summer's 3,200-mile race across the Atlantic Ocean to Norway.

In early June 1935, forty-four sailors were at Newport, Rhode Island, preparing six boats for the start of the race. Already anxious enough about the prospect of sailing such a distance across the cold North Atlantic so early in the summer, they were further discouraged by reports that the seventh entry and the single Norwegian boat—a forty-seven-foot converted lifeboat, *Sandefjord*, commanded by a well-known oceangoing yachtsman—had lost a man and almost sunk in a gale while coming across the Atlantic.

Sandefjord's captain, Erling Tambs, was one of the first romantic, hard-scrabble family cruising adventurers. In 1928 he had set out in an ancient pilot boat called *Teddy* on a long cruise with his wife and a dog and almost nothing else; he could not even afford a barometer, a sextant, or reliable charts. Over the next four years his wife gave birth to two children and *Teddy* made it to New Zealand, where Tambs got around safely without any charts at all. The boat was later wrecked on a Tongan reef because she was too slow to sail out of a foul current in light wind; his wife barely escaped with her life. Tambs returned to Norway and wrote a successful book about the voyage that was translated into English. In 1935 he borrowed *Sandefjord* and entered her in the race. First, though, he had to get her to Newport from Norway. On May 17 she was about four hundred miles south of Bermuda in a sea that Tambs described as "tumbling about in a vicious, drunken manner, suddenly joining to pile up huge towers and form tremendous combers where one least expected them." A monster breaker from astern hurled her into a violent somersault, pitching the crew many yards into the sea. Tambs and three others crawled back aboard, but one man was never seen again. The survivors patched her up and inched toward Newport, eventually arriving five days late for the start of the race to Norway.

IF ANYBODY WAS FOOLISH ENOUGH to believe the race would be easy, *Sandefjord*'s discouraging story, relayed by a freighter she encountered, would have shown otherwise. When Alfred F. Loomis spoke of "the soft repose of trans-Atlantic racing," it was with irony.

Leading the community of sailors in Newport was George Emlen Roosevelt, the commodore of the race's sponsor, the Cruising Club of America. A son of a first cousin of Theodore Roosevelt, he was a successful investment banker, brilliant mathematician, and experienced ocean sailor. As a frequent commentator on the sport in *Yachting* magazine, George Roosevelt was a leader in the new pastime of amateur ocean racing. Although his *Mistress* was well crewed and thoroughly prepared, Roosevelt was deeply concerned about the upcoming voyage. Two boats, *Stormy Weather* and *Vamarie*, were also ready for the race, but Roosevelt had serious reservations about the other three. One was a Gloucester fishing schooner named *Vagabond*, manned by a crew of Yale undergraduates. The second was a ragtag German ketch called *Störtebeker* that had been shipped to America and was sailing around Newport Harbor flying the Nazi party flag.

Then there was *Hamrah*, over which there was much the same handwringing that Loomis had done in Bermuda a year earlier. Although she passed the safety inspection, Roosevelt attempted to persuade Robert Ames that his boat and his crew of five young men might not be up to the race. Sailing seven hundred miles to Bermuda in late June and eighty-degree water temperatures was hard enough, but battling 3,200 miles of the North Atlantic called for serious caution. We know only that this tense conversation took place, not what was said, but surely Roosevelt pointed to the pilot chart for June. A graphic display of all known hazards for the month, it showed small icebergs, called growlers, in the area of the course, plus water and air temperatures in the forties, winds often at gale force (stronger than thirty knots), and twelve-foot waves much of the time. A few years earlier, in *Yachting*, where he often wrote sound advisories and commentaries on sailing offshore, Roosevelt had laid down a sensible fundamental law of seamanship: "Sending a bunch of inexperienced enthusiasts to sea strikes me as courting disaster. Sometimes a good crew can save a poor boat, but an *inexperienced crew* is liable to *lose* any boat." So now he would have told the master of the *Hamrah* that if someone as experienced as Erling Tambs had come to grief a thousand miles south of this tough race route, perhaps the Ameses should reconsider this adventure.

Roosevelt made no secret of his own fears, which he frankly described in on-the-record interviews with newspaper reporters. He told them it was his ambition to be the world's oldest ocean-racing sailor. He was hardly alone in his concern. "Their nerves were jumpy" was how one knowledgeable boating journalist, William H. Taylor, summarized the feelings of the sailors in Newport. Only the Nazis in *Störtebeker* seemed eager to risk their necks.

George Roosevelt was unable to sway Robert Ames. Despite a problem gathering a crew and despite Margaret Ames's worries, *Hamrah* stayed in the race. At least one father of a prospective crew member consulted an experienced sailor and then ordered his son to stay home. After some scrambling, the Ameses finally signed up three of the boys' friends from Harvard or boarding school, Sheldon Ware, Roger Weed, and Charles Tillinghast Jr. Ware had no experience, Weed had some, and Tillinghast was the most salty of the six, having sailed all his life, including two races to Bermuda.

Margaret Ames, meanwhile, was expressing her own considerable concern while she provisioned the boat with a month's worth of food. When she insisted that the crew always secure themselves to the boat with safety lines and life belts (the ancestors of today's safety harnesses), her husband promised that he would require the five young men to tie themselves on but declared that he would not observe the discipline. He wanted to feel free to move around the boat. He did assure his wife that *Hamrah* had many safety features, including her sturdily built hull, the low lifelines around the rail, the emergency lines to toss to people in the water, and a rowboat on deck. He also would have tried to console his wife with the sport's well-known safety record; in sixty-nine years of ocean racing, fatalities could be counted on two hands.

The six boats sailed across the starting line on June 7 under an overcast sky and before an anxious spectator fleet. The send-off was muted, with only a few horn blasts and a couple of waves as the competitors disappeared into a dense fog bank. With such inherent tension, the start was reported in papers from as far inland as Cincinnati and Little Rock. As if to explain the anxiety, the writer from the *New York Times* put the start in the larger context of sailors venturing out into the deep and the Other World: "Here was the drama of the waves, the Magellan motif, men against the sea, the perils of the deep, all wrapped up in 44 men and a few boats starting an event that was more than a sport, bigger than a mere test of seamanship, and fraught with hardships which few athletes care to face."

IV

IT WAS A NEW SPORT, this pastime of amateur sailors racing relatively small boats across oceans. The first amateur race across the Atlantic had occurred only seven years earlier, in 1928, and then across mild waters to Spain. The very idea struck old-time mariners as heretical if not crazy, as one of the newspaper reporters in Newport in early June 1935 discovered when he stopped by a seamen's hangout. There, fishermen expressed total bewilderment that anybody would go to sea without being paid for it. They assured the journalist that they were not critical of the amateur sailors as men. "They merely failed to understand why anyone would take a beating like that who didn't have to." The reporter concluded, "Well, it's that kind of thing. Either you see it or you don't, and there's no half-way feeling."

Professional sailors had been racing across oceans for many years, beginning in 1866 in big schooners more than twice the size of *Hamrah*. That year three rich young men, Pierre Lorillard, Franklin Osgood, and James Gordon Bennett Jr., bet $30,000 each on a race between their *Vesta*, *Fleetwing*, and *Henrietta*. The stakes were held by Leonard Jerome (Winston Churchill's grandfather), who sailed across with Bennett, the only one of the three owners to actually race. The race was held in December—a terrible month to venture into the North Atlantic in any vessel, much less a hard-driven racing schooner. Although several amateurs sailed, they were passengers; all the work was done by fifty-six professional sailors whose lot is suggested by the nickname of the captain of *Henrietta*, Samuel "Bully" Samuels, a former clipper ship master who referred to the 107-foot yacht as "the little plaything." Despite premium wages, the nerves of prospective crews and their families were even more tender than they would be in Newport in 1935. A journalist portrayed a chaotic, emotional scene at the wharf before the yachts headed out: "Some difficulty was experienced in securing seamen to cross the Atlantic in such vessels in such weather," he wrote. "The men were willing enough to engage, but their mothers, wives, and sweethearts interfered and persuaded them not to sign articles."

And for good reason. On the ninth day out, December 19, a southwest gale overtook *Henrietta*, and in the wild sea the ship's carpenter went berserk and even Bully Samuels felt obliged to heave-to, turning his bow back almost into the wind and shortening sail until she slowed almost to a stop.

Vesta missed the worst of it, but *Fleetwing* kept pushing through the storm and paid a terrible price, as her captain admitted in the middle of an otherwise dry log entry:

> *Wednesday, Dec. 19.*—This day commences with a light breeze from S.S.W. 2 P.M., in all light sails, gale increasing with heavy sea. 7 P.M., blowing a gale; running under two-reef foresail and forestaysail. 9 P.M., shipped a sea, which washed six of the crew out of the cockpit; hove-to for five hours under two-reef foresail. 2 A.M., kept off; latter part moderate, wind hauling to west; set squaresail. Lat. 47-20, Long. 37-27. Distance run, 199 miles.

That cryptic mention of six sailors drowned is the sort of thing that leads readers to wonder whether ice water or embalming fluid flows through the heart of a shipmaster. A plunging sea swept the deck and rolled *Fleetwing* so violently that two of those men, who were steering, took the wheel spokes with them. She eventually staggered to the finish. In six subsequent transatlantic races between 1869 and 1931, only one other sailor was lost.

"To get the marrow out of yachting," a writer observed in 1890, "requires leisure, patience, and money." Twenty years later, that formula also included "energy," "daring," and "irreverence." When average people began to go to sea as amateur sailors early in the twentieth century, they sailed in the same spirit of heroic strenuous living that propelled the Ameses and other wood-chopping rusticators to Maine.

The sponsor of this pastime is often thought to be Joshua Slocum, the fifty-one-year-old experienced sea captain who, unable to find work in the dying trade of merchant sail, between 1895 and 1898 circled the globe in a solitary fashion in a thirty-six-foot fishing boat. His book, *Sailing Alone around the World*, inspired hundreds of long-distance sailors. While Slocum's example was influential, he was not the man to marshal the forces of amateur sailors in small boats. It was not that he discouraged people from going to sea ("To young men contemplating a voyage," he wrote at the end of *Sailing Alone*, "I say go"). Rather, he had no interest whatever in the developing technology and competitiveness that imbued the new sport of amateur yachting and brought a new golden age of sail to succeed the old one replaced by steam power. Slocum's interest in the sea had less to do with energy and teamwork than with traditional spirituality—a word he was not embarrassed to use in his book and lectures. "Everything in connection with the sea should be eminently respectable and be told in spirituality," he wrote to a friend in 1903. "No man ever lived to see more of the solemnity of the depths than I have seen, and I resent, quickly, a hint that a real sea story might be other than religious."

Interior improvement under the divine dome of nature was not the primary interest of Thomas Fleming Day and the other founders of the pastime of modern amateur yachting. They also sought spiritual meaning, but in less overtly religious and more energetic ways. In his magazine *The Rudder*, which he edited from 1890 into the First World War, and his many books, Day updated the old idea of the sea as a playground for escaping the shore world's woes by adding three new ingredients, one idealistic, the second commercial, and the third instructional. The first was the notion that a risk-filled strenuous life purified human existence—an idea Day passionately believed in and on which he repeatedly staked his life in his own adventurous voyages. The second was that such a life lay within the grasp of average people thanks to the advancing technology of boat building. As it turned out, this technology was proprietary to the firms that happened to advertise in *The Rudder*. Day's self-interest and deepest personal concerns engaged in the same enterprise to create one of the first consumer magazines that provided services to readers in both its editorial and its advertising columns. Enveloping all this was Day's fervent conviction that the sea was no dangerous primal force but, rather, a maternal, safe habitation fit for humans in small boats.

To suggest that he was a heretic is to put the case mildly. Where Slocum had mildly proposed, "The sea has been much maligned," Day went so far as to speak of the deep as a benign, nurturing presence. His enthusiasm for a loving sea surpassed even Shelley's. Day went so far as to call the sea "our great green mother." His enthusiasm seems startlingly naive. "Did you ever hear a seaman, an old and tried voyager, descant on the dangers of the sea?" he asked. The answer to this question, of course, should be a firm *yes*, but with characteristic willfulness Day decided that an old sea dog would think otherwise:

> Often he will preach of the dangers of the vessel but he knows well enough that the sea never destroys purposely and malignantly. He knows that it never has or never will murder a vessel; that every vessel that goes down commits suicide. Because men go to sea in badly designed, poorly constructed, or rotten craft, is the sea to blame if they disappear? Make your vessels seaworthy, ably man them, carefully fit them out, and they will perform your voyages in safety. That there are dangers of the sea, such dangers as no man can guard against and no human foresight or precaution prevent, I readily admit. But the same dangers menace the dweller upon land.

It is too easy to make fun of this. Thankfully, Day did not trust solely in dreams but backed up his sunny idealism with detailed instructional and technical articles in which he and his writers taught his readers about boats and seamanship. He clearly did not want people heading out there unprepared—just unafraid. Knots, navigation, yacht design and construction, food, storm sailing—all and more were covered in his pages with the understood message, *you can do it* because the sea is at least as safe a place to live as the land, and far more rewarding. His focus lay less on tradition and awe than on the heretical enterprise of turning the deep and ships into a technical problem that amateurs could manage without professional assistance in small sailing boats of their own.

THE TRADITIONAL ROMANCE and awe of the deep that Day rejected bubbled up in a luxurious manner in a building erected in (of all places) the middle of Manhattan Island by (of all people) J. Pierpont Morgan. This was the clubhouse of the New York Yacht Club, which opened in 1901, five minutes' walk from Times Square. Writing to Morgan, in his role as the club's commodore, the architect Whitney Warren proposed that the club present itself not as "an ordinary social institution" but as one whose mission was "the furtherance of naval architecture from the amateur point of view." Warren's inclusion of the adjective *amateur* is telling. Amateurs romanticize their interests; professionals usually do not. The building's nautical and maritime theme is clear from the street, where three huge galleon-style windows push out over the sidewalk with an outpouring of sinuous braids of seaweed and octopus tentacles, and the face of the sea god, Poseidon, presides over the front door. Through the windows passersby can see the club's immense model room, with its hundreds of models of yachts and ships surrounded by seaweed, sea monsters, snails, shells, dolphins, lightning bolts, clouds, and stars. A visitor to the model room said, "Except for the absence of motion, one might fancy oneself at sea."

TOM DAY AND THE GENERATIONS of amateur sailors who came of age between 1900 and 1940 introduced a second golden age of sail on the heels of the death of commercial and naval sail. This age was one of small boats, most of them no longer than sixty feet. "In a large vessel a man is on the sea," Day wrote, "but in a small one he is *with* the sea." In 1904 he sponsored the first long-distance race for amateur sailors—330 miles from New York City to Marblehead, Massachusetts, over the tricky shoals near Nantucket and Cape Cod. The winner of the trophy donated by Sir Thomas Lipton was a thirty-five-foot sloop, *Little Rhody*, from Providence, Rhode Island, sailed by Charles F. Tillinghast, the father of a crew member in *Hamrah*. Day also sailed in this pioneer race in his twenty-six-foot yawl *Sea Bird*, which was not much more than a big dory. He finished way back, unapologetic as ever. "She is heavily built, ugly, and very slow," he admitted. "Her only redeeming virtues are ease of handling and fine sea qualities." He proved it in 1911 by sailing her to Naples, Italy. In 1912, as a stunt promoting *The Rudder*'s advertisers, he and a small crew took a thirty-five-foot power-boat with a small gasoline engine from Detroit to St. Petersburg, Russia. All the while Day sponsored ocean races for sailboats across the treacherous Gulf Stream to Bermuda. As he moved toward retirement in 1917, he declared victory: "My work is, I believe, bearing fruit and rapidly driving out of men's minds the foolish and unfounded fear of the sea, and no less silly belief that small boats, because they are small, are unseaworthy."

Amateur ocean sailing benefited indirectly from the First World War, when a number of young men were introduced to the sea through duty in the arrow-thin 110-foot submarine chasers. The leaders of the next generation of boating magazine editors came out of the subchasers. One of these men was Alfred F. Loomis, who would be so impressed by the Ames boys. Another was Herbert L. Stone, the publisher of *Yachting* magazine, which for half a century dominated boating commercially and otherwise in a way matched by few, if any, publications in any other activity. In 1923 Stone revived the race to Bermuda, which in turn inspired other long offshore races off Florida, California, and England.

The spirit of the times was proclaimed by a brash former subchaser commander, William W. Nutting, who taught himself how to sail while taking long voyages and wrote magazine articles pumped full of strenuous life braggadocio. "Is 'Safety First' going to become our national motto?" he asked rhetorically. "In this day when life is so very easy and safe-and-sane and highly specialized and steam-heated, we need, more than ever we needed before, sports that are big and raw and—yes—dangerous." Nutting founded a national organization for sailors, the Cruising Club of America, which aimed to straighten America's spine with daring outdoor activity in small boats, and which adopted the motto, Nowhere is Too Far. Keeping to these convictions, Bill Nutting and three shipmates headed off to Labrador in 1924 and disappeared near an ice pack.

That tragedy only seemed to inspire more adventurers to carry on. By 1935 a dedicated sailor could participate annually in two or even three races totaling some 3,500 miles. A large, international community of ocean-racing sailors quickly formed. In the appendix of his history of ocean racing, Alfred F. Loomis listed the names of almost two thousand men (and the few women) known to have sailed in one or more of the thirty-eight ocean races between 1866 and 1934—a million miles of sailing by 350 yachts, with a total of only ten fatalities (six of them in the first race). Almost all of these sailors were amateurs, and many of them raced often; more than 120 men sailed in at least three ocean races between 1923 and 1935.

By the thousands, sailors cruised or raced across miles of ocean with no hope of financial benefit. One of the intangible satisfactions was the strong family feeling aboard many boats. George Emlen Roosevelt often sailed with his brothers, sons, and cousins (including Theodore Roosevelt III). The first truly modern ocean racer, *Dorade*, won the 1931 race to England with a seven-man crew that included her owner, Roderick Stephens Sr., his twenty-three- and twenty-one-year-old sons, Olin (the boat's designer and skipper) and Rod Jr. (who had supervised her construction), and two of their boyhood friends. *Dorade*'s design, unlike *Hamrah*'s, stressed weatherliness, or the ability to sail fast close to the wind in rough seas.

THE FAVORITE IN THE RACE to Norway was a fifty-four-foot yawl, *Stormy Weather*, an evolution of *Dorade*. Commanded by Rod Stephens Jr., she was sailed by her crew of seven young amateurs with a band-of-brothers exuberance and discipline that would have pleased Theodore Roosevelt or Henry Richards. When they were not sailing, sleeping, eating, or keeping a watch for ice, they often assembled the ship's orchestra—two accordions, a guitar, a clarinet, and three harmonicas—and played exuberantly, with varying degrees of skill. The sailing aboard *Stormy Weather* was far more adept than the musicianship. When one of her crew, Kenneth Davidson, went home after the race, he inscribed a sailor's supreme compliment in the log: "It has been a great privilege to sail in *Stormy Weather* and to share, very humbly, the spirit of seamanship which has always prevailed." She finished at Bergen on June 27 after little more than nineteen days, or just five hours slower than the much larger seventy-two-foot ketch *Vamarie*. When the handicaps were figured she was presented the trophy put up by King Haakon of Norway. After George Roosevelt's *Mistress* came in a day later, Roosevelt admitted that he had been so "scared pink" that he had averaged only three hours of sleep a day as he kept a constant watch on his navigation and a lookout for ice. The Germans took thirty-five days, ten more than the Yale students on the *Vagabond* who, when they crossed the finish line, sent up distress flares; they needed a doctor to attend to a crew member who had recently broken his arm.

That was not the only accident or close call. Early on, two of the boats were almost run down by a passing ocean liner coming at them out of the fog. *Vamarie*, owned by a colorful Russian named Vadim S. Makaroff (who was known as "the caviar king" for his success as a specialty foods importer), lost her professional skipper, Alexander Troonin, overboard one day while he was on the bow setting the spinnaker. After the boat sailed right over him, the thoroughly keelhauled Troonin somehow managed to grab the logline—the spinning line dragging astern that measured speed—but it snapped, leaving him in a big ocean of 40-degree water watching the stern of his vessel rapidly shrink as she sailed on toward Norway. The helmsman was Sherman Hoyt, a legendary old seaman whose adroit steering had helped win the America's Cup in 1934. He spun *Vamarie* 180 degrees, leaving her stopped dead with her bow in the wind and her sails useless. Like *Hamrah*, *Stormy Weather*, and George Roosevelt's *Mistress*, she did not have an engine, which meant she had to make her way back to Troonin under sail. As the crew cleared away the mess, Hoyt got her moving again, and only eight minutes after Troonin went over the side, he was back on board.

V

HAMRAH, ALAS, was not so fortunate. Her accident can be reconstructed from survivors' accounts:

After the starting gun, the green ketch beats slowly into the fog with no hope of keeping up with *Vamarie*, *Stormy Weather*, or *Mistress*. (Margaret Ames will not even board a liner for Norway until June 24, more than two weeks after the start.) The captain is fifty-two-year-old Robert Ames. Dick Ames, twenty-three and recently accepted by Harvard Business School, is navigator and self-appointed safety officer, daily reminding his shipmates to move around carefully and hook on their life belts (although he cannot make a dent in his father). Harry Ames—as like his short, stocky father as his brother is like their tall, lean mother—is twenty now, with that sunny, kindly, energetic Ames disposition. Harry recently completed his first year at Harvard and captained the freshman wrestling team. With them are three young men who have much in common with the Ames boys; all have been with them at Harvard, and all but one have also been at Milton Academy. Roger Weed was in Dick's class, and Sheldon Ware is Harry's Harvard roommate. The single outsider is only marginally so: Charles F. Tillinghast Jr., son of the winner of Tom Day's pioneer race in 1904, was raised in Providence and attended another boarding school before Harvard. The most experienced offshore sailor of the six, Tillinghast at twenty-one has already sailed in two Bermuda races.

The breeze freshens and, unluckily for *Hamrah*, goes into the east—on the nose, exactly where the bluff-bowed ketch does not want it as she slowly pounds into the sloppy seas. After three days of this Dick announces that they are off Cape Sable, Nova Scotia. The breeze pulls aft, allowing

LEFT: Amateur sailing in the early twentieth century followed the heretical assumption that the sea posed technical problems that amateurs could solve. But it also attended to tradition, for example, in the temple of nautical symbolism that is the clubhouse of the New York Yacht Club in Manhattan. This is the fireplace in the model room. (Guy Gurney/New York Yacht Club) BELOW: Traditional in appearance, *Hamrah* sails before the start of the 1935 race from Newport, Rhode Island, to Bergen, Norway. She is still towing the dinghy (not shown) that will soon be placed on deck near the steering wheel. (© Mystic Seaport, Rosenfeld Collection, Mystic, Connecticut)

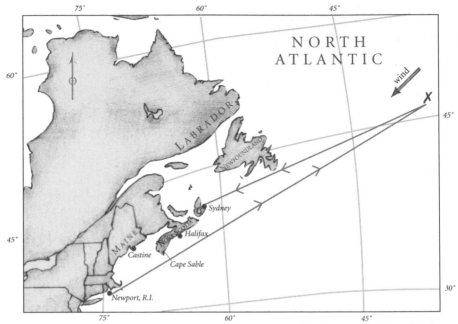

Based in Castine, on the Maine coast, the ketch *Hamrah* was raced by the Ameses and their friends to Norway. The accident occurred at approximately forty-six degrees north, forty degrees west, half-way between Boston and England.

them to finally reach directly toward Europe under full sail. Low-pressure systems come and go, with small gales and shifting winds.

After a week of this, at the change of watch at eight o'clock on the morning of June 19, *Hamrah* reaches on the port tack at nine knots. There is a hard nor'easter—a gale of wind blowing against the prevailing westerly swell—and through this rough sea the ketch plugs along, deeply reefed and with mizzen furled. Alone on deck and at the helm, Charlie Tillinghast looks around and estimates that the seas are as high as *Hamrah*'s fifty-foot mast. Tillinghast's watchmate, Robert Ames, has finished his breakfast below and is pulling on layers of wool sweaters and socks, topped by his heavy oilskins and sea boots. He swings up the ladder through the companionway and, under Tillinghast's watchful eye, crawls across the swaying, wet deck to the port side, where he throws himself down on the bottom of the upturned dinghy near the cockpit.

The two men sit in this wild setting with its big white-capped sea, all gray and white in the confusion between the old westerly swell and the new

gale's easterly swing. The younger man is more energetic as, eyes glued on
the compass, he wrestles the long-spoked wooden steering wheel to muscle
twenty tons of boat on course. She surges, rolls, yaws, and dives across and
through the tumultuous sea. The sounds of the rigging's whine and the
bow's roar are often broken by a wave's whack against the vessel's side or
onto her deck—the *thump!* of Leviathan's tail, the ancients might have
said—and then the loud, heavy sluice of water across the deck.

After an hour the two men are almost accustomed to *Hamrah*'s jumpy
motion when, with startling, surprising velocity, the bow drops and the
stern rises. Out of the corner of his eye Robert Ames spies a white wall
advancing from astern. He cries out—too late. Six feet of water sweep forward from stern to bow, filling the whole surroundings with white water.
Barely hanging onto the wheel's spokes, stinging salt filling his eyes, Charlie Tillinghast looks around to find the boat whole, her rigging standing,
her cockpit full but draining—and Robert Ames no longer on the dinghy
but in the ocean astern. The wave has thrown him the full width of the
boat and over the leeward lifelines and into the ocean, where he is now
barely afloat as *Hamrah* sails away.

Tillinghast yells as he turns the wheel hard to starboard to bring the
boat off the wind and jibe back toward the struggling man. As the bow
swings down, Dick Ames, in his underwear, leaps up the companionway,
spots his father, and with hardly a pause grabs the emergency line tied to
the boat and dives overboard. He is only a few feet from his father when
the boat jerks the rope from his grasp. He swims on and embraces his
father as *Hamrah* jibes and comes toward them. Robert Ames is so passive
that Roger Weed, following Dick up the hatch, is convinced he does not
know how to swim.

Tillinghast brings the bow to within fifteen feet of the two men. The
others toss a life preserver and a small life raft just as a breaking wave sepa-
rates the rescuers from the victims. Although the raft is blown away, the
swimmers have the life preserver, which offers enough buoyancy to
support them as Dick holds his father's head up. Harry is frantic to dive in
after them. The others persuade him to stay: without an engine, they need
him to help sail the boat.

Tillinghast jibes again, and as the reefed mainsail bangs across in the
second jibe, the boom and gaff break, leaving the sail billowing uselessly.
Now many yards downwind of the Ameses with only a small jib set, Til-

linghast, Ware, and Weed pause to clear away the damage with a hatchet and hacksaw and then set the mizzen. Harry, meanwhile, is untying the dinghy and sliding it into the water. Charlie Tillinghast again begs him to stay with *Hamrah*. They need sailors to handle the boat to get to his father and brother. Harry pushes the boat over the side and leaps in and applies his wrestler's arms to the oars.

Days later, when Charlie Tillinghast describes these dreadful moments in an article in a Providence newspaper, his Yankee self-discipline holds his bitter frustration in check:

> While we were putting the mizzen on her, Henry, the younger son, launched the small rowboat and reached his brother, whom he got aboard. His father was by this time possibly drowned; at any rate I did not see him. The rowboat was to windward, so we jibed again and sailed as close to the wind as possible, hoping that the small boat would be able to back downwind to a point where we would get it. Unfortunately, it was swamped at this point. It was then clear that we were going to leeward more quickly than was the swamped small boat.

Heaving the mess of the broken boom and torn mainsail overboard, they finally can try to beat toward the Ameses, who by now are barely visible five or six big waves upwind. The last they see of the Ameses, Dick and Harry sit side by side on the bottom of the upturned dinghy, waving. A wave breaks. They vanish.

VI

HAMRAH AND THE THREE SURVIVORS circled until nightfall, finding nothing more. The gale increased, and they had to heave-to for two days in the same area where their friends and shipmates had drowned. Perhaps they welcomed those two days as an opportunity for quiet reflection. Charlie Tillinghast, who had gone through the Naval Reserve Officer Training Corps program at Harvard, took command. They decided to sail west to America. Although St. John's, Newfoundland, was closer, they chose the nine-hundred-mile route to Sydney, Nova Scotia, to avoid ice and because they had better charts for that area. They sailed into shipping lanes in hopes of finding a vessel to take a message, perhaps even the liner that was carrying Margaret Ames to Europe, but the report had to wait until after a long beat to windward in moderate wind. The ubiquitous fog thickened near land, and there was little sleep over the last few days as *Hamrah* felt her way, entering Sydney on the night of June 30.

We know almost nothing of that ten-day passage, but judging from the thoughtful statements that Tillinghast and Weed provided newspapers after they arrived, the young men seemed in firm command of their emotions. On their arrival in Nova Scotia, the only outward signs of strain were their exhausted faces. Weed and Tillinghast later said they were satisfied that they had done the best they could. It may have helped them that, as sailors, they were used to dealing with risk, chance, and an environment that is beyond human control and often hostile. But even more important may have been the phenomenon (discussed in the notes to chapter 3) that even when rescue efforts are futile, rescuers who are closest to the scene may feel rewarded for their efforts.

WITHIN TWO DAYS OF THEIR ARRIVAL in Nova Scotia, their story was in headlines across America. Not everybody knew it right away. Early on the morning of July 2, at Merryweather Camp in Maine, young Holton Wood, a friend of the Ames boys, was sorting the mail when an automobile roared up. The old Skipper, Henry Richards, leaped out and demanded that he hand over all the newspapers. The boy dutifully hefted the stacks of Boston and local papers into the car, whereupon Richards raced off. Not until that afternoon did Holtie Wood learn that the Skipper was protecting his campers, counselors, and granddaughter from reading the dreadful news about their friend Dick Ames before he and Laura Richards had a chance to tell them gently.

After the first shock wore off, people looked at the accident more carefully, and not always uncritically. There were a few boating magazines that, no doubt jittery about the concerns of some advertisers, improbably denied that there was anything to worry about when going to sea in small boats. Yet more sensible commentators were not afraid to confront the ambivalence inherent in the tragedy. Herbert L. Stone, the publisher of *Yachting* (who had inspected *Hamrah* before the race and found no reason to disqualify her), observed that while there could be no dispute about the nobility of the Ames boys' heroism and family devotion—"their act rises above eulogy," he rightly asserted—they should have remained on board to help sail the ketch to their father's rescue. An editorial in the *New York*

$\mathfrak{Boston}\ \mathfrak{Post}$

THE GREAT
Breakfast Table Paper
OF NEW ENGLAND

TUESDAY JULY 2 1935 **   *Established 1831.*   TWENTY-EIGHT PAGES—TWO CENTS

BOYS DIED IN VAIN
TRY TO RESCUE DAD

Two Sons of Robert Russell Ames, Noted Yachtsman of Distinguished Family, Perish in Raging Sea Attempting to Rescue Father, Hurled From Ship by Giant Waves----Shipmates Helpless on Stricken Vessel

The Ames story was headline news, and it was not surprising that Dick and Harry's efforts were prominently featured.

LEFT: The crew before the start of the race to Norway *(left to right)*: Robert Ames, Harry and Dick Ames (with their powerful wrestlers' builds and tattoos), Roger Weed, Sheldon Ware, and Charles Tillinghast. The unprotected steering station and sagging lifelines reveal that safety equipment was not as carefully policed then as it is now. (© Mystic Seaport, Rosenfeld Collection, Mystic, Connecticut)

BELOW: Three decades after the accident, *Hamrah* enjoyed a second life as a family cruiser under the name *Samba* in the Gulf of Mexico. She was still sailing in 1980. (Courtesy Ethel C. Radzewicz)

Herald Tribune (probably written by William H. Taylor) identified the core issue, that accidents will occur whenever people strive with or against nature: "It is this very circumstance—this pitting of small human skills and fabrics against the treacherous enormity of the sea—which brings entries into ocean races. Blue-water racing is not extra hazardous. But neither is it completely safe. That is why there are blue-water races; and, as in mountain climbing, the rare tragedy is the price that must be paid for a kind of adventuring that is itself humanly worthwhile." Living a careful life is one thing, but a life of absolute comfort and safety is no life at all, and sometimes—many people wanted to make clear—a reminder of that truth can be brutal. The *Hamrah* accident caused at least one father to ban his two sons from ever sailing offshore in the same boat.

Ocean racing survived and eventually thrived. The Germans sponsored a transatlantic race in 1936 but—whether out of fear, respect for the Ameses, or political feeling—there was only token American participation. The Second World War ended long-distance sailing for almost a decade, but since the late 1940s there have been thousands of scheduled races in almost all the oceans and seas, with turnouts of as many as three hundred boats and more than two thousand sailors. Large numbers of amateur sailors went to sea to cruise for much the same reasons that had driven the Ameses when they ventured out into the deep in *Hamrah*—to build character, to bring together the generations, and to reaffirm values that they believed were truer than many found ashore.

The accident inspired improvements. Boat inspections became more rigorous, better boats were designed, tighter safety rules were imposed, and when young sailors (like me) received our first lessons in seamanship, it was with a certain amount of finger-wagging that we were told and retold the story of *Hamrah* and the Ames boys. "If someone goes overboard, never go in after him," an older watchmate would say. "Get the boat to him. Remember the *Hamrah*."

VII

FROM SOON AFTER THEIR ARRIVAL in Sydney until they reached the haven of their families in New England, Sheldon Ware, Roger Weed, and Charles Tillinghast were public figures eagerly sought by reporters. One even hunted Weed down while he was changing trains in Bangor, Maine, at 1:30 in the morning. In late August the Ames family hired a crew to sail *Hamrah* to Machiasport, and she eventually made it after two weeks of mishaps that began when one crew member developed appendicitis and had to be put ashore, then ran through a week of gales and an onboard fire. Under storm sails, she finally tied up in Machiasport on September 7. She was sold over the winter and went on to a long, rewarding life under later owners.

The three surviving crew members—Ware, Weed, and Tillinghast— picked up their lives, which followed somewhat parallel lines in peace and war, although only one survived into old age.

The youngest, Sheldon Ware, was no sailor but had been a friend of Harry Ames at Milton Academy and his Harvard freshman roommate. After graduating in 1938, he took a job with a manufacturing company in Pittsburgh, where he spent his spare time playing sports, flying small planes, and advising groups of boys. After the war broke out he joined the Army Air Corps and piloted a B-25 bomber in the Pacific. One of thirty-two members of his Harvard class of just over a thousand to die in combat, he was shot down over the Netherlands East Indies on the day after Christmas, 1944, leaving his wife and infant son.

Roger Haydock Weed, four years older than Ware, was Dick Ames's classmate at Milton Academy and Harvard, in the class of 1934. After his exuberant but financially pressed father committed suicide in 1931, he spent his summers away from Boston, often around boats. He worked one summer in an oceanographic research vessel and another as a sailing instructor on Long Island, New York. My father, who was one of his charges, remembered Weed, as many did, as warm, funny, and encouraging. While at Harvard Law School, he acquired a share in an old schooner that he sailed off the New England coast. He worked in New York until he enlisted in the navy soon after Pearl Harbor. After officer training, he was sent to the South Pacific where—in either an astonishing coincidence or a rare case of matching a duty assignment to an individual's experience— Weed joined an interservice air-sea rescue operation for recovering downed pilots. It was, he later wrote, "very gratifying in wartime to measure accomplishment in term of lives saved rather than people killed, and also a little unusual." At one time or another he was assigned to a submarine, two battleships, three command ships, three aircraft carriers, and the command centers of the Central and Southwest Pacific Theaters. At three amphibious landings, he ran air-sea rescue operations that saved dozens and perhaps hundreds of lives.

After the war, Weed worked in a Connecticut law firm until his life began to be unraveled by alcohol and depression. He moved in 1958 with his family to Denver, Colorado, where he took a public relations position in a bank and was an active outdoorsman. The next year, on the occasion of his Harvard class's twenty-fifth anniversary, he wrote a long, apparently self-confident autobiography in which he said that the *Hamrah* accident—which he referred to as "the story of Dick Ames"—was one of the most important events of his life along with his distinguished and exciting war work. He blamed the accident wholly on the boat: "It seems to me, in retrospect, inevitable that a set-up like the *Hamrah* would get into some kind of trouble. It is only unfortunate that the trouble she got into was so severe." He ended his report on a note of optimism, but two years later he was badly burned in an automobile accident. In December 1962, after leaving a despondent letter, Roger Weed walked into the woods near a high mountain pass, fell, and perished in a blizzard.

When the snow melted the next spring, more than 120 people gathered to conduct a successful search for the body of the man who himself had been a searcher for the lost in both the Pacific and the Atlantic Oceans. "A gifted but modest classmate" was how Roger Weed's Harvard class secretary described him after his death, which was ruled an accident despite his despairing state of mind. His daughter, Hilary, now a nurse living in rural Maine, was fifteen when he died and does not recall her father's mentioning the *Hamrah* accident or, for that matter, any of his worries. "We share a lot more about feelings today," she said late in 2000, speaking for many daughters and sons of the Second World War generation. "Today we are more free to talk about life and death."

CHARLES FOSTER TILLINGHAST JR. was twenty-two years old when he commanded *Hamrah* on the return from the accident. Born in Providence, Rhode Island, he was brought up in and around boats there and in neighboring Bristol, at the head of Narragansett Bay. As a boy he sailed with his father, who had won Tom Day's first long-distance race in 1904, and his best friend, George "Sim" Matteson. On one cruise in a small boat, the two boys were blown by a gale to a spot so remote that a couple of days passed before they could get to a telephone. When Sim called home collect, his eight-year-old sister, Rose, answered but stayed on the phone only long enough to hear the operator identify the caller and where he was calling from. That was all she needed to know, so Rose hung up, as any true Yankee would.

After returning from Nova Scotia, Tillinghast wrote a graceful, understated account of the accident for a Providence newspaper (it was reprinted in *Yachting* magazine and elsewhere). When the Cruising Club of America presented him its Blue Water Medal, the sport of yachting's most respected award for seamanship, Tillinghast deflected all personal praise in the equally modest acceptance letter that he sent to George Roosevelt. This award, he said, properly belonged with Dick and Harry Ames. "The action of those who were left was dwarfed by the grandness of what had just taken place."

With that Tillinghast shut the door on celebrity. After working for several years in the family-owned textile company in Providence, Tillinghast went on active duty in the navy in 1940 and married Rose Matteson a year later. His heroics were not over. As a gunnery officer on the cruiser *Vincennes*, on August 9, 1942, Charles Tillinghast took part in the devastating First Battle of Savo Island, when (as we saw in chapter 2) eight Japanese ships caught the Allies literally asleep near Guadalcanal and sank the *Vincennes* and three other Allied warships. In a letter to his brother-in-law, Tillinghast described the scene as the ship was abandoned:

> Such a mess, Simbo! Her decks looked like a sieve and you could see fires raging below, and the hanger was a furnace. I went forward to look for wounded, after we got the fantail cleaned up, but most of them had been picked up, stuffed into life jackets, and thrown over the side. Bodies lay everywhere, many of them burned to crisps with several arms and legs lying around with no owner. I swam for an hour, then picked up a raft and about 7 A.M. got picked up by a destroyer. From the water you couldn't tell whether she was Jap or American (luckily she was U.S.).

Tillinghast did not mention that he had given his life jacket to a seaman who could not swim.

After several months on the staff of Admiral William Halsey, and several months more helping commission a new cruiser, Tillinghast was named commanding officer of a new destroyer escort, the *Weeden*. He took her into the Pacific in 1944, and the next March, near the Caroline Islands, while the *Weeden* was escorting a convoy to the Philippines, a near typhoon pounded her for four days. He had been through *Hamrah*'s gale and, worse still, the great hurricane of 1938 that smashed through Rhode Island, and here he was at sea in a 306-foot destroyer escort. "I like the sea itself so I like this duty," he wrote his parents, "for in many ways you are in much closer contact with it than on a big ship." The storm blew her 150 miles off course and at one point knocked her over almost seventy degrees, perilously close to the end of her positive stability. Tillinghast described the typhoon to his parents:

> The sea became all white and the wind picked up the tops of the waves and blew the salt water as high as the mast in what amounted to the heaviest rain you ever saw. Visibility was cut down to about 200 yards if you looked down wind, and you couldn't look the other way without goggles. With them it was like looking through the port of a diving suit—water all around. The wind went around the compass complete three times during the course of the storm and as it never stayed from one direction for more than a few hours, it made a very choppy irregular sea which broke all over us, but no mountainous seas. We were lucky for we had no casualties or trouble of any kind.

Once again Charlie Tillinghast was both concise and modest. His executive officer gave him full credit for properly ballasting the *Weeden* so she would not capsize.

At war's end he wanted to stay in the navy, but his wife had no taste for the peripatetic life and they ended up far inland. Rose Tillinghast loved horses and he liked farming (when the *Vincennes* went down off Savo Island, he took his seed catalogs), so they moved to the Piedmont of North Carolina, where he helped one of her cousins manage a farmers' cooperative near Asheville. In time he became an independent grower of gladiolus, whose voluptuousness contrasted so greatly with his own austerity. Every year he rented fifty or seventy-five acres of fertile bottom land where he nurtured the bulbs and eventually sent out the cut flowers. Although Charlie Tillinghast missed the sea, rural life pleased him. "He wasn't a fancy-minded kind of guy at all, not the country club type," his daughter Harriet remembered without a trace of disappointment. If he was a little remote— a sort of Gary Cooper in his upright taciturnity—he more than compensated with his displays of decisive character. "He was a real hero, my father, and he never would admit it," she said. She went on to mention the time he ended a frightening standoff between two migrant workers, one with a knife and the other with a gun, simply by stepping up and ordering them to drop their weapons. She remembered: "*They knew.*"

Busy as he was all summer with his bulbs, the horses, and camping trips with his wife and two daughters, he had almost no time to sail. His only regular connection with the sea was the U.S. Navy ROTC program that he helped run in a local college. On trips back to Providence, he sometimes borrowed a cruising boat and sailed around Narragansett Bay and Block Island, dismayed at the increasingly crowded waters he had sailed on so freely before the war. In the early 1970s Tillinghast returned to the sea. He bought a used Columbia 29 class fiberglass sloop that he was convinced would take him long distances to uncluttered waters. *Little Auk* had been designed by Olin Stephens, whose *Stormy Weather* had been so different from *Hamrah*. For eleven years, for as much as six months a year, in good weather and bad, Tillinghast energetically cruised in her with his family and friends, but sometimes single-handed. Most years he was in the cold waters off New England and the Canadian Maritimes, but he twice sailed up and down the rugged Labrador coast and also crossed the Atlantic— long, ambitious voyages in such a small boat. His seamanship was as tradi- tional as his disregard for discomfort, and he navigated by sextant and depth soundings. His wife remembered a rough night passage across tide- swept Cabot Strait from Newfoundland that ended with a perfect landfall at the small island chain of Saint-Pierre and Miquelon, France's last toe- hold in North America.

Until then Charlie Tillinghast, like so many other men of his genera- tion, had said very little about his wartime experiences, and nothing at all of *Hamrah*. Nobody asked, as Rose recalled: "We knew how he felt about it and that he didn't want to talk about it. It was such a desperate affair." But now that he was under sail again, he started to talk. "Those were very good years," Harriet Goodrich said. "Daddy was a Yankee. He had no patience whatsoever with people who could not move on from their problems. His personality changed, and I got closer to him. When we were sailing up to Labrador, with the boat heeled way over and water up to the cabin ports, and the wind vane set so she steered herself, he sat in the cockpit and told me about the sinking of the *Vincennes* and the navy seaman he saved who couldn't swim."

In 1982, when he was sixty-eight, *Little Auk* was returning to Scotland from the North Cape of Finland—a feat even for a skipper half his age in a boat twice his vessel's size—when she was dismasted off northern Norway. Unable to find a replacement mast, he shipped the boat back to Rhode Island. That was his last long cruise. In 1986 Charlie Tillinghast suffered a stroke, and in time he went into a nursing home, where until his death in 1995 he sat quietly in his darkened room, reviewing his memories and recounting them to his family, including more details about the *Hamrah* tragedy and recovery. His daughter remembered: "When Daddy spoke about *Hamrah*, he indicated that he knew he had done everything he probably could have, but there was a wistful tone in his voice. He said he begged the last Ames son not to go over. He knew it would be a disaster, he *knew* Harry would be lost. When he spoke about the accident, there was a sadness in his voice about Mrs. Ames."

VIII

As USUAL, the deep left widows. On June 19, 1935, Margaret Ames was in New England, preparing to board a ship for Norway, and in no position to know that she was losing her entire family. She did not learn of the accident until two weeks later when, as she waited in Norway for *Hamrah* to sail into Bergen, a telegram arrived from Boston. One of the boys' friends, William Wolbach, accepted it and gently broke the news. Her anguish was made more acute by knowing that the liner that carried her across the Atlantic very likely crossed tracks with *Hamrah* as the ketch slowly made her way to Nova Scotia. Her hair turned white almost overnight, and back home, a neighbor caught glimpses of her pacing the floor of her room, wringing her hands.

Other than a handful of relatives and close friends, few people heard her speak of the accident in the forty-eight years that passed until her death in 1983. Margaret Ames never remarried, and yet she moved on, working through her grief to make a new life for herself. Warmhearted and responsible as a young woman, she could have shut herself off in her misery. Instead, she opened herself to other people and, by her example, led others to recovery. "She was our inspiration, a beacon to point the way," Phyllis Cox said. "It's a wonder to me that Aunt Margaret managed to pick herself up. What saved her was doing things for other people. She did not want to dwell on the past. She wanted to move on in order to avoid a terrible pain."

A close family friend, Donald Straus (whose father met her at the boat when she returned from Norway), described the transformation this way: "She became a stronger, lovelier, more outgoing lady. She threw out love to people, and they threw love back to her."

In the beginning, her close counselor in emotional survival was Laura Howe Richards, whose "understanding and teaching helped me to face life again," Margaret wrote. Then eighty-five, Laura Richards, wife of the Skipper of Merryweather Camp, was a prolific author of children's books (her novel *Captain January* was made into a movie starring Shirley Temple) and carried the banner of one of New England's most famous families. Her father, Samuel Gridley Howe, had directed the Perkins School for the Blind, the first large American institution dedicated to training the disabled for active lives. (Laura was named for her father's most famous student, Laura Bridgman, who was as well known in the nineteenth century as Helen Keller would be in the twentieth.) Laura's mother, Julia Ward Howe, was even more famous as a public speaker, proponent of women's rights, poet (she wrote the mystical lyrics to "The Battle Hymn of the Republic"), and prolific author. She also was a person of fierce moods, and to cope with them her daughter developed into a flinty optimist. Like another optimist, Theodore Roosevelt, she befriended the melancholy Edward Arlington Robinson, the author of bleak poems such as the often-anthologized "Richard Cory" and "The House on the Hill," which opens:

> They are all gone away,
> The house is shut and still
> There is nothing more to say.

Like Edward Rowe Snow, that other merry New Englander, Laura Richards seemed incapable of imagining that there is "nothing more to say." She understood Margaret Ames's need in the wretched months after the accident to learn how to cope without having to sacrifice her honorable grief.

She succeeded. A year after her family sailed out from Newport, Laura Richards told Margaret that there was a "radiance in your face, beside the tears that will still spring." She had regained the "spring of life," Richards continued; she had grown spiritually with "the strength that has been given you, not only to comfort and cheer, but to enrich and enliven life for others." She ended: "I think of this year as one of victory; I think of Robert and Dick and Harry, surrounding you with their love and inspiration. I have no fear for you, Margaret, anymore." She reengaged with the world and became an energetic dispenser of good thoughts and deeds to people in trouble. "So you must be up and doing again!" Richards wrote to her in 1937. "They all come to you, my dear; or if they have not the heart to do so, you go to them; steadying, comforting, uplifting. No need to remind you how directly and clearly all this comes from your own sorrow; from those deep wells you draw those draughts of cheer and comfort."

Resilience can take many paths and forms, any one of which Margaret Ames might have chosen. She could have acted out her grief in bizarre behavior, or worn widow's weeds to attract sympathy, or like Dickens's Miss Havisham, made mourning a weapon that she turned simultaneously inward on herself in self-contempt and outward in revenge. But what Margaret Ames did in her remaining half-century of life was to make grief her fellow traveler, her *hamrah*, as she worked toward a better life. People who have suffered depression sometimes speak of "the A.A. thing"—of helping oneself by helping others through support groups. Margaret Ames took on the world as her group.

About the accident she expressed two feelings that may seem contradictory. One was a grieving mother's love for her dead sons, the other her admiration for the way they died. "I think Aunt Margaret was so proud of her boys that they knew what to do and what they *wanted* to do," Phyllis Cox remarked. "They did not let her down." While many of us might find this tension wrenching, she was comforted. The knowledge that her immediate family had been destroyed in a few minutes in a remote corner of the sea, with no opportunity for her to bid them farewell—all that must have been too terrible to contemplate without the solace of believing that Dick and Harry had been motivated by the purest motives. With high Victorian floridness, Laura Richards laid out this ideal in an ode dedicated to Margaret that ends,

> They sprang to answer, swift and free,
> And dying, left for you and me
> Immortal as the stars shall be
> Their shining story.

Margaret Ames honored the boys' memory in memorial plaques, prizes, and athletic trophies that she established at Milton Academy, Harvard, and

Castine's sailing and golf clubs. In the Castine cemetery she placed a stone inscribed with the names of her three Ames men and a passage from David's lamentation for Saul and Jonathan: "They were lovely and pleasant in their lives, and in their death they were not divided" (2 Sam. 1:23). This moving passage, which she quoted in other memorials to her boys (and which is partially inscribed on the Margaret Fuller memorial), suggests that the ideals of friendship and nobility can ease the disintegrating forces not only of a storm but of loss.

In the obituary for her husband that she composed for his Harvard class, she wrote: "In times which are disturbed and upset, it is a strong rock of comfort to know that Robert Russell Ames stood for what is fine in our rather bewildering world." The "bewilderment" she mentioned in the obituary would not go away. So fortunate in many ways, her family was unusually unlucky in others and lost several members to accidents or cancer. In 1941 Richard Ames, who as her brother-in-law was her last link to her husband, died in an out-of-control brushfire on Perkins Point. The farm was left in equal shares to her and to Richard's son and daughter, the two survivors of the band of four who had so delightfully made the Point their playground. Understandably, painful memories as well as practical considerations led them to sell the property half a century after old Dean Ames had acquired it in the first wave of the rusticators.

Richard's son, the younger James Barr Ames, spent his vacations at the summer place of the family of his wife, a descendant of the two Adams presidents. After his first wife died, he married a cousin of mine, and at a family gathering I asked him about *Hamrah*. A vigorous man who exuded responsibility, he appeared short-circuited by my question, which I regretfully realized was painful. He looked at the ground, shook his head, and murmured, "Dreadful, dreadful." As an "intellectual Ames," he was born and bred to the law and chose the practice of trusts and estates, whose daily concern lies with clients' intimate personal problems. At his memorial service in October 2000, his son Richard, in his eulogy, provided insight not only into his father's heart but into his family's beliefs:

> He did indeed take on the troubles of others, not just in his professional world, but in all parts of his life, public and private. He didn't know how to turn his back on trouble. He would just wade in—ever optimistic that a solution would be found, that a lonely person could be made to feel less lonely, that one last conversation could be tried before the next appointment. He

didn't always succeed, he was often late to the next appointment, but you always knew that he was doing his best, and he did succeed more often than not in finding a solution, in making life for someone better than it had been.

PHYLLIS AMES, the former tomboy of Perkins Point ("I ran everywhere," she remembered. "Everybody said I was just like my grandfather") remained in close touch with Maine. After graduating from Smith College, she was considering a career as a teacher when she met Archibald Cox, a young lawyer and Harvard Law School professor. After they married, they lived on her father's old farm near Boston. While raising three children, she managed the horses, chickens, and a vegetable garden, rode in horse shows, played on a pickup basketball team called "the Tired Mothers," and was at her husband's side throughout his long, remarkable career. He served as solicitor general and Watergate special prosecutor (until Richard Nixon had him fired), and headed the public-interest organization Common Cause. "There is honest, and then above that there is Archie Cox," Bostonians would say. The Coxes spent summers at Condon Point, which her grandfather had sighted from a steamer's deck before the turn of the century. Eventually they retired to the farmhouse, with its view across Penobscot Bay.

When her son was a young boy, Phyllis Cox wanted him to learn to sail but worried that this might upset her aunt. Although Margaret Ames still loved to look out to the sea and gloried in its changing colors and textures, she never again set foot in a small boat. Phyllis went to her with the problem, prepared for any answer. Her aunt told her, "I would love him to take to the water."

MARGARET AMES was not born to deep self-analysis. In her circle, if mention of Freud or Jung triggered any reaction at all, it was laughter. But as she attempted to make sense of the terrible accident, she moved into the world of the examined life. "Finding closure" was a concept that Margaret Ames would not have recognized. She would not have understood such a thing, and even if she had, she would not have welcomed it. At some point in her old age, in notes that she jotted down under the heading "Longevity," she laid out the foundations of her new existence in which pain and joy moved hand in hand. "My own sons gave their lives in their early '20s," she began. That was the definition of her life, her declaration of dependence. From that baseline she went on to explain how, after that loss, she had succeeded in carefully building a new, meaningful, and happy life for herself. It took hard work, she said, and also something more—a combination of the spiritual and the pragmatic:

> All this planning is of little avail however unless one is tranquil in one's decisions. Tranquility comes strangely enough from two sources—inner dependence on God, faith in life with all its sorrows, faith in life to come— all these are on one side—on the other is a vital interest in worthwhile things—a hospital, civic work of any kind as long as one's strength is adequate. After that some special hobby.

She ended with lines from a poem by William Reed Huntington, a nineteenth-century Episcopal priest: "Be strong to live. Desponding heart be strong, / Strong to submit, to trust, to wait." Intended perhaps as an outline for a talk to a group, these straightforward guidelines are the testimony of a troubled soul who after much suffering found solace in learning how to get through the day without losing touch with her grief. Most of her hobbies were unremarkable—needlework, weaving, travel, tennis, studying art, reading, letter writing. The exception was a literary project that developed into a book to help people who, like her, were grieving. What used to be called "an occasional book" (because it was published for a particular occasion or need), *For Those New to Sorrow* began as a suggestion from Laura Richards. "When I first lost my family, she told me to write down the things that helped me most," Margaret Ames wrote about the desperate year of 1935. "Once, when I asked her how I could ever repay her for what she had taught me, she answered, 'Pass it along, my dear, pass it along. Have your little book published,' adding with her dear bright smile: 'I don't expect you to do it in your 50s, nor yet your 60s; but your 70s—now *there* is a decade.'"

Margaret Ames was seventy-three when *For Those New to Sorrow* was published in 1962. The book gathered writings of comfort and solace that, at Laura Richards's suggestion, she began collecting after she heard of the accident in 1935. She had kept them in a small black three-ring binder that eventually bulged with poems, prayers, biblical passages, and other material that she found or that had been sent to her in sympathy (including several poems in honor of her three men). Although she was a Unitarian, she received considerable encouragement and assistance from the Reverend Edward O. Miller, the social activist rector of New York's Saint George's

Church and the summer rector of Castine's Episcopal church, across the street from her house. Running throughout the 146 selections and materials concerning the three Ames men is the constant theme of new life for the dead, and also for the survivors. She included the stanza from Shelley's "Adonais" eulogy for John Keats that opens, "Peace, Peace! he is not dead, he doth not sleep— / He hath awakened from the dream of life."

She and her family and friends distributed thousands of copies of *For Those New to Sorrow* to hospitals, nursing homes, and like facilities and to people who had endured a tragedy. The initial print run was exhausted, and the second printing in 1974 ran out, too.

FOR YEARS SHE MOVED back and forth between Castine and Boston, all the time keeping in touch with a community structured around her sons that included the men who had desperately tried to save them. Harry's schoolboy friend Donald Straus described her warmly as "the essence of motherhood and kind of a foster mother who taught me how to handle the death of a family member. She rose above it with her sorrow. She has remained in my life."

Margaret Ames also kept up with the subsequent owners of the boat off which her husband and sons died. The family sold *Hamrah* to a man in Salem, Massachusetts, who put an engine in her and eventually resold her. She went through several hands and names until she reached Carl G. Bowman, captain of the United States Coast Guard Academy training ship *Eagle*. In 1959 he took the boat (renamed *Lydia*) to New Orleans, but finding that he was unable to sail as much as he wished, he sold her to Paul and Ethel Radzewicz of Jackson, Mississippi. They renamed her *Samba* and shaved two feet off her keel so she could sail in the shoal waters of the Gulf of Mexico, out of New Orleans and Biloxi, Mississippi. Proud of her strong construction and traditional gaff rig, the Radzewiczes lavished attention on their vessel and spent many happy weeks in her with their children. "*Samba* was breathtaking under full sail," recalled their daughter, Maureen. They even purchased colorful lightweight nylon sails for downwind sailing and gamely entered *Samba* in races, in which she invariably trailed much more modern boats. The Radzewiczes were once awarded a trophy engraved with words that would have pleased the Ameses: "To those who finish last, not least, who race gallantly but slow." When the Radzewiczes wrote Margaret Ames to ask about the boat's history, she sent information

Charles Tillinghast commanded *Hamrah* after the accident. Like the two other survivors, he served in the Pacific in the Second World War. After retiring from the flower business in North Carolina, he cruised adventurously in the North Atlantic in his small *Little Auk*. Here he is in her cabin. (Courtesy Rose Tillinghast)

The dedication page for Margaret Ames's book *For Those New to Sorrow*.

This anthology was compiled in memory of

ROBERT RUSSELL AMES
February 12, 1883–June 19, 1935

and his two sons

RICHARD GLOVER AMES
April 1, 1912–June 19, 1935

and

HENRY RUSSELL AMES
December 16, 1914–June 19, 1935

who gave their lives in an effort to save their father when he was swept overboard during a storm off the coast of Newfoundland in the Transatlantic Race to Norway, June 19th, 1935

They were lovely and pleasant in their lives, and in their death they were not divided.

II SAMUEL 1:23

and said she was glad the old *Hamrah* was bringing pleasure to children once again.

When Camille, the worst hurricane in Gulf history, hit Biloxi on August 17, 1969, *Samba* broke away from her mooring and was carried by the tidal surge up onto the shore and against a restaurant. Holed so badly on her port side that she was a total loss, she was moved to a nearby beach and lay there for two years until the family, who had purchased a fiberglass boat, sold her to Joel Lee, a twenty-six-year-old airman. Although Lee knew nothing about boats, he became enchanted by *Samba* as he drove by during his daily commute to and from work at the local Air Force base. As romantic and ambitious as Thomas Fleming Day, Lee labored single-handed for two years, replacing twenty-five broken frames. By 1974 she was sailing again under a new sloop rig and a new name, *Joel's Ark.* "People laughed at me for trying to fix the old boat up, just like they laughed at Noah," Lee told a local newspaper. He kept her for seven years before selling her and moving to California. Nothing more is known of the old *Hamrah.* The boat may not have been perfect, but the dreams and satisfactions she provided people for half a century, despite storms and tragedy, remained as real as her thick teak planking.

MARGARET AMES was still thriving in 1981. Living year-round in Castine, she sat out on her porch in fair weather so she could talk with passersby, invited children in to play with toys she kept in a large bureau, and had her son's friends and the midshipmen from the local maritime academy over for Sunday dinner. "She was an Aunt Margaret for everybody," said Virginia Graves, her housecleaner for many years. She was two months shy of her ninety-fifth birthday when she died in 1983. Among her many bequests was a grandfather clock for one of Dick's roommates. She was buried in the Castine cemetery in the family plot whose centerpiece was the memorial stone that she had erected for her sons and husband almost half a century earlier.

Her works and spirit survived her. After the space shuttle *Challenger* exploded on nationwide television in 1986, interest in *For Those New to Sorrow* revived, and Phyllis Ames Cox and James Barr Ames brought about a third printing with the assistance of Holton Wood, from whom the Skipper, on that July morning in 1935, had seized the newspapers with their bleak headlines. The brother and sister wrote in the introduction: "We have undertaken this reprinting in memory of our remarkable Aunt, in the hope that those new—and old—to sorrow will continue to gain strength and courage from these pages." In 2000 Wood had 550 copies of her book and, in the pass-it-along spirit, was prepared to mail one to anybody seeking succor. "I do it," he said, "because it's the kind of thing Mrs. Ames would like us to do."

ONE MARCH DAY IN 1963, perhaps inspired by a warm south breeze carrying the first hints of spring, Aunt Margaret had a happy memory of the old days when boats were at the center of their lives and her impulsive husband would scoop up the family and carry them out onto Penobscot Bay in *Hamrah*. "Dear Jim and Phyllis," she wrote to her nephew and niece, "we will always remember the picnics at Condon Point . . . , the picnics 'Down the Bay.' Those were golden beautiful years. Weren't we lucky to have had them?"

7

The Wreck of the *Pollux*

Newfoundland, 1942

> *"At the beginning you're damn sure 'It' is going to happen to someone else, not to you. But something happens that changes your thinking from 'I expect to get back' to 'I probably won't get home.'"*
>
> —Henry Strauss

Two months after Pearl Harbor, "Admiral Winter" was in full command of Cabot Strait as a submarine-wary convoy of U.S. Navy ships pounded through a southeast gale toward Newfoundland. Burying their bows and rolling their rails in forty-foot seas, the tight formation of three ships worked its way northeast toward the Argentia navy base, all the while zigging

189

and zagging in hopes of confusing any enemy submarine lurking in what sailors fearfully called "Torpedo Alley."

The focus of the convoy's attention (in fact, its entire reason for being) was the supply ship *Pollux*. Fast and armed, with a trained fighting crew, she had been running alone in these waters for months until a special, top-secret cargo demanded an escort with much more firepower. She carried 233 men in crew and troops, tons of mundane essentials—paint, toilet paper, lumber, cash for payroll—plus (and here was the reason for the convoy) bombs and something rumored to be a cutting-edge advance in the new science of radar. So on February 17, 1942, two destroyers, the forty-year-old *Truxton* and the new *Wilkes*, flanked the *Pollux* on her wild run to Argentia.

The *Wilkes* was in charge, but the anxious officers on the bridge of the *Pollux* doubted her navigation. Concerned that the gale was pushing the convoy inexorably toward Newfoundland's coast, they proposed breaking the formation and heading out to sea. The *Wilkes* responded sharply: the convoy *will* maintain formation; the *Pollux will* sail her assigned course.

The stage was set for one of the worst accidents in American naval history, an event so extraordinary (and inexplicable except to a few men on the bridge of the *Pollux*) that the navy would at first refer to it in mythological terms as a "tragic drama of the sea," as though beyond human control and understanding.

I

THE TENSELY WORDED MESSAGES to and from the *Wilkes* that night were sent and received via light signal by one of the *Pollux*'s quartermaster signalmen, twenty-six-year-old Isaac Henry Strauss, whose life was dramatically and permanently altered by the consequences of those orders.

Wiry and scrappy, Strauss was not one to give in easily to difficult circumstances. He had, for example, hardened himself to the rigors of North Atlantic duty by turning himself into a human icicle. While on watch on the bow of the *Pollux* on frigid nights, he patiently stood stock-still and allowed a thick shell of ice to form around his body as a barrier against a wind so strong that it sometimes blew his diminutive frame across the deck as though he were wearing skates. The grandson of Jewish immigrants and the son of a lace importer, Strauss had been born and raised in New York City. Preferring to be called Henry, he was the sort of Henry whom most people, on first meeting, instantly called Hank. At New York University, despite his small stature, he had been a diving champion and, by his own admission, "a tough kid" prone to picking fights and taking long motorcycle trips. He also was a sailor. During summers he sailed and paddled little boats, some of which he built himself, off Far Rockaway, near Brooklyn. In the late thirties he paid a boat builder $500 to construct a small cruising boat named *Nanki-Poo* in honor of the playful wandering minstrel prince in Gilbert and Sullivan's *Mikado*. He and his wife, Jo, took their honeymoon cruise aboard her.

An aspiring writer, Hank Strauss scrambled for assignments while serving in the naval reserves, anticipating service as an officer when the inevitable war came. In due course he was called to active duty. The navy, however, had determined that an ensign's monthly pay of $120 could not support a family, so it illogically required him to sign up as an enlisted man, earning only a third of that amount (fortunately, Jo Strauss supported herself as a nurse). A college-educated enlisted man was an anomaly in that era's navy. Hank Strauss still had to be pugnacious to deal with the harassment thrown his way. As he would recall, "College got me into a lot of fights."

ONE STANDARD that this feisty young man respected was his ship's intense combat readiness. "We had to keep our mouths shut about a North Atlantic run," Strauss said during a series of interviews almost sixty years later. Spies were expected in each saloon, submarines on every square mile of ocean. Even in vicious gales like this one in February 1942—a storm that was leveling Quonset huts in naval installations up and down the coast—U-boats were known to materialize out of the night and fire torpedoes.

At least the men of the *Pollux* had confidence that they could defend themselves. They were not like the career merchant mariners on board the slow, lightly armed civilian freighters making the Murmansk run, for whom the transition from peacetime mariner to wartime target was abrupt and terrifying. Morale in those ships was so bad in 1942 that American, Canadian, British, and Norwegian psychologists assembled in New

York for the Conference on Traumatic War Neuroses in Merchant Seamen. The consensus was that for the first time in the experience of these
mariners, their homes, friendships, way of life, and entire resources were
under assault by an enemy against which they were all but defenseless. A
psychologist said, "The big problem of prevention is to harden seamen to
a particular situation"—in other words, they must be prepared for the
fact that this was not business as usual in which they had to contend just
with the sea. New training programs were developed to address what,
almost forty years later, would come to be called "post-traumatic stress
disorder."

If life was more secure aboard the *Pollux* it was because, as Hank Strauss
acknowledged, she was a well-armed vessel in the Naval Auxiliary whose
crew was trained to fight:

> Sure, we were scared of wolf packs, particularly in the North Atlantic, but we
> were young and we believed that "It" would always happen to *the other guy*.
> It all had to do with being able to fight back. Unlike the Merchant Marine,
> we felt independent and to a much greater degree under our own control.
> We were trained in our weaponry, and everyone had his assignment. Mili-
> tary training, in addition to skills and automatic responses, has a great effect
> on your mind and motivations. Who wants to train in football and never
> leave the bench? There's a big difference between feeling you are in a fight as
> opposed to feeling you are a helpless target.

EVEN A SELF-CONFIDENT SHIP at sea worked under a blanket of security
so tight that seamen and officers had to make one of the greatest sacrifices
that any sailor or soldier could make—not to smoke at night lest a sharp-
eyed German peering through a periscope catch sight of a flaming match
or a glowing cigarette. Troops might as well have been ordered not to write
home, so greatly did they depend on cigarettes for solace and encouragement.

The intimate relationship between the military and cigarettes seems
astonishing today, but then it was well known and even encouraged.
"There is magic in cigarettes," it was said. That claim was made not in a
Camel or Chesterfield advertisement but in an official government book-
let. *How to Abandon Ship* was distributed to all sailors in ships running the
world's "Torpedo Alleys" to help them prepare for the possibility—even
the probability—that they would have to abandon sinking ships in life-

boats. In the chapter on morale, the first topic was cigarettes. Food, water, clothing, and sleep came later, as did the advice on how to resist the temptation to commit suicide ("Take it out on the wind and sea"). Smoking was crucial to survival. Any sailor abandoning ship must be sure to take all the cartons from his slop chest and give them to the lifeboat commander to ration out, especially after sunset. "Cigarettes are most important at night to the men on watch," the authors declared, presumably under the assumption that an enemy submarine would care little about a lifeboat. "It is then that they supply the very essence of morale—courage and confidence." Smoking was long known to relieve stress and provide boosts of energy. Today, tobacco is recognized as an antidepressant. Specialists in post-traumatic stress disorder who work with Vietnam veterans report that heavy smoking increases in direct proportion to the amount of combat or psychological stress they experienced when in the field.

Smoking also provided individual or group comfort on demand. Anybody who has endured military life knows how important a moment of privacy can be in that authoritarian setting. During the Second World War, the era of celebrity testimonials for cigarettes, it certainly did not harm one's self-image that cigarettes—which tobacco companies provided free to the armed forces—could temporarily transform an anxious teenage draftee into a grown-up, successful man and even a hero like Joe DiMaggio. Self-image meant a lot in groups. Far from the security of family and friends, young men regularly facing the possibility of immediate extinction found that a cigarette provided admission into a close-knit support group. There were no secret handshakes among smokers, only stained fingers and teeth and the bulge of a pack of cigarettes through a pocket. Few events were more comforting and symbolic of human connection than a buddy's offer of a cigarette or a match or the glimpse of a tiny bit of burning ash across a field or a ship's deck. That a lit cigarette was also a visible symbol of safety certainly added to the appeal. When the smoking lamp was lit on board a ship at sea, it meant that the enemy was not close at hand. At least for a moment, everybody could breathe more easily (at least metaphorically and emotionally, though not physically). But when the smoking lamp flicked off and men had to make it through another bleak night without a light, what was at hand was not comfort or community, but death itself.

II

THE *POLLUX* CONVOY BLASTS through the storm on Cabot Strait. Its situation appears difficult, even nearly impossible. On each bridge, officers and enlisted men struggle to keep track of the convoy's formation and position. They peer through the snow squalls and sea smoke to try to spot the other ships and, when blinded by the blizzard, they take a chance on sonar readings on the other ships' propellers, setting off the "pings" that draw an enemy submarine as honey draws a bear. Under a regimen of radio silence, the limited communication between the bridges is by signalmen operating lights—large blinkers by day, narrowly focused rifle-type ones by night.

Navigating is even more difficult. On this sunless, starless voyage there has been no celestial fix since the convoy left Portland, Maine. The navigators are struggling to gauge their positions using primitive electronic devices: none too reliable radio direction finders that acquire approximate compass bearings on radio towers, and ping-transmitting depth sounders that come up with highly approximate water depths to compare with charts. The navigators apply themselves to the half art, half science of dead reckoning navigation, or figuring progress toward a destination by estimating how far the vessel has progressed in a given direction over a known period of time. In such wild conditions, with the wind and current pushing so hard on one side, the actual speed and heading may be far different from the readings on instruments. This gale blows from the southeast against the ships' starboard sides, setting them some unknown distance to the north, where the land lies.

On the bridge of the *Pollux*, where signalman Henry Strauss is awaiting orders, the captain, Commander Hugh W. Turney, and navigator, Lieutenant Junior Grade William C. Grindley, are bickering about the ship's position and their obligations to the convoy. Their instructions are to follow orders issued by the *Wilkes*, to observe the predetermined course changes that are part of the elaborate choreography of submarine avoidance, and to stay in formation within sight of the other ships at a range of about one mile. The ships are expected to accomplish all that despite the blizzard, the hurricane-strength wind, the breaking seas, and Grindley's serious concerns about whether the *Wilkes* is on top of the navigation. A former Merchant Marine officer with seventeen years' experience at sea,

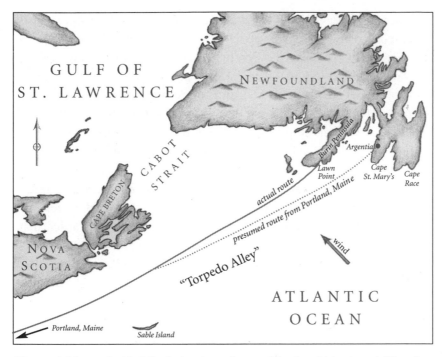

The route of the supply ship *Pollux* in the winter of 1942 took her from Maine through "Torpedo Alley" to Newfoundland. She grounded on the east side of Lawn Point.

Grindley believes that the frequent course alterations at the ships' high speeds are compromising navigation. He recommends that the convoy slow from fifteen to eight knots, but he is turned down. Grindley will later estimate that the storm set the convoy to the north at a rate of almost two knots, causing a course error of eleven degrees to port (toward land). Telling Turney that he cannot guarantee a position within fifteen miles and that he fears they will run up on Newfoundland's Burin Peninsula, he urges his captain to break formation, turn ninety degrees to starboard, and head out to sea. That radical step is turned down too.

In late afternoon Signalman Strauss is told to flash a message to the *Wilkes* relaying Grindley's doubts about the convoy's position and progress toward Argentia. The task force commander on the *Wilkes*, Commodore Walter W. Webb, who has already reprimanded Turney for not following orders, firmly disagrees: "We will arrive Argentia 0400." In other words: "*Steam on.*" This confidence seems to Strauss to be misplaced, given the conditions. An experienced sailor, he will say, "One of the things a sailor should be sensitive to is that there's a lot of guesswork."

Turney does alter course ten degrees to starboard to offset most of the set to port. The signal reporting that course alteration is misunderstood by the *Wilkes*, so the ships diverge. Much time and energy are expended through the rest of that bitter night on finding the *Pollux* and re-forming the convoy.

At twenty-three minutes after midnight, the *Wilkes*'s depth sounder identifies a fifty-fathom depth that her navigator has expected to cross one hour later. This indication that she is approaching land earlier than expected is properly logged but is not analyzed for another three hours. Everybody is distracted by the storm, the search for the *Pollux*, the submarine avoidance maneuvers, the unreliable communications, and a confusion about the chain of command. That sounding is like a can of rat poison in the cellar that looks like dog food. Everybody knows it should be checked and rechecked and rechecked again, yet somehow the poison ends up in the dog's dish. Not until 3:30 A.M. does an officer of the *Wilkes* review the log, discover that sounding, and draw the correct conclusion—that the ship is much closer to land than anybody thought.

Also on the *Wilkes* at about that time, the operator of the convoy's only radar device observes a "pip" on the scope off the ship's bow, indicating a rock or perhaps another ship. Radar is new and not universally trusted. The captain, on hearing this news, instructs the operator to climb the mast and clear off the ice that (the captain is convinced) is misleading the receiver. At 4:00 A.M. the radar scope displays a Christmas tree of pips a mile directly ahead of the ship. The *Wilkes* is put into full reverse—too late to stop her from running her bow onto rocks on the west side of Lawn Point on the Burin Peninsula. One minute later and three miles to the east, the other destroyer, the *Truxton*, piles straight into Chambers Cove and pins herself between two rocks.

The *Pollux* strikes last. Running at fifteen knots between and slightly behind the two destroyers, she rams the edge of a rocky shelf on the east side of Lawn Point. The next sea picks her up and tosses her onto the shelf. Below in his bunk, Hank Strauss is heaved onto the cabin sole, bunk and all. Amid earsplitting groans from the wracked ship and the roar of the seas breaking on her, he assumes that the ship has collided with one of the destroyers. Staggering to the deck, he discovers that the *Pollux* has grounded and is already breaking up and that the nearest land, barely visible through the wild spray, is a near-vertical cliff reaching hundreds of feet into the bleak predawn.

Strauss and his shipmates then commence to behave in a way that blends silliness, selflessness, and the very highest degree of heroism.

III

Viewed from a distance, a disaster has facets enough to satisfy almost every search for meaning. Extroverted advocates of the nobility of heroic action, introverted believers in spiritual disciplines, cynics, pessimists, optimists—all can find a corner of a catastrophe that illustrates their views, yet none may quite grasp the whole complicated story in the way the victims themselves experience it.

A view of disaster from the extroverted point of view was William James's take on the 1906 San Francisco earthquake. The philosopher of the strenuous life was visiting Stanford University when, just before dawn on April 18, 1906, an earthquake shook northern California and triggered fires in San Francisco. James's immediate response to being heaved out of his bed was exuberance. "I felt no trace whatever of fear," he recalled a few weeks later in a magazine article; "it was pure delight and welcome." That upbeat mood remained with him as he viewed the wreckage of the quake and the succeeding fire in San Francisco. He happily noted how the disaster had broken down barriers between people. There was a strong sense of community, a few individuals were discovering their skills as leaders, and the entire event was providing exactly the right spirit of "moral equivalent of war" that he believed brought out the best in people. James wrote to his brother Henry, "San Francisco seemed in a good hearty frame of mind."

He knew that there was suffering somewhere, but he did not seek it out. He found only three people who were emotionally overcome. "Physical fatigue and *seriousness* were the only inner states that one could read on countenances." The typical attitude was selflessness: "There was a temper of helpfulness beyond the counting." Anticipating the discoveries of other psychologists that rescuers at the sites of even gruesome accidents found the work rewarding, James hypothesized that the public perception of a disaster was directly related to physical distance from it. Misery seemed to increase with distance from ground zero:

> In our drawing rooms and offices, we wonder how people ever *do* go through battles, sieges, and shipwrecks. We quiver and sicken in imagination, and think those heroes superhuman. Physical pain, whether suffered alone or in company, is always more or less unnerving and intolerable. But mental pathos and anguish, I fancy, are usually effects of distance. At the place of action, where all are concerned together, healthy animal insensibility and heartiness take their place. At San Francisco the need will continue to be awful, and there will doubtless be a crop of nervous wrecks before the weeks and months are over, but meanwhile the commonest men, simply because they *are* men, will go on, singly and collectively, showing the admirable fortitude of temper.

Keenly observant as he was, James missed two features of postdisaster behavior. Those who are distraught are not merely "nervous wrecks" but may be completely helpless. And much behavior at ground zero defies logic. In what psychologists call the "period of recoil" soon after a disaster, a few people are calm and rational, a few others are irrational and even hysterical, and most are simply stunned. John Leach refers to "an overwhelming of the senses" during this time after the disaster, when "so much information strikes the victim that he is unable to process and comprehend it and consequently becomes bewildered and numb." Many victims go into a "dream-like reality"—a sort of instantly created living myth at whose core lies a deep denial that there is any risk.

RATIONALITY AND IRRATIONALITY, heroism and foolishness, tenderness and frustration—each strode the deck of the *Pollux* as she teetered on the ledge off the Burin Peninsula. The one nearly universal constant was what James called "a temper of helpfulness." A delicate concern for shipmates was all but ubiquitous. For example, among frantic fears that the ship might soon capsize, Commander Turney took the time to open the ship's canteen for the sailors to take all the food they wanted. He also laid out his ration of cigarettes. Smokes and all they symbolized were a common obsession. In the next cove over, where the destroyer *Truxton* was in as precarious a situation as the supply ship, a seaman who rushed below to retrieve his wallet also stopped to gather all his cigarettes and store them in prophylactics so they would stay dry. The ship soon rolled over.

Aboard the *Pollux*, Hank Strauss noted behavior from across the wide spectrum of possibilities. "I guess people have a strange reaction when they're facing catastrophe," he observed almost sixty years later. One reaction was out-and-out denial:

> I went on deck with the other quartermaster signalmen and when we looked up and saw the cliff we started laughing. There we were: forty-foot seas breaking over the ship; the deck smashed into kindling; heavy bunker oil pouring out of the ship everywhere and covering everything; officers telling us that the ship was likely to roll right off the shelf and sink at any moment. All that was happening, and all we could do was laugh. It seemed so funny to us that *those stupid officers* had actually run the ship into a cliff! We took the oil in both hands and smeared the pilot house with it, that same pilot house that we'd polished every night. It was a crazy act of defiance.

When a shipmate drowned while trying to swim ashore, Strauss found himself briefly hypothesizing that the fellow had at least died happy because he had visited a brothel back in Maine. "When he went down in the water, I thought, 'There's a lucky guy. At least he's been *laid*.' " (Recounting this weak attempt at humor in 2001, Strauss scolded himself for being so disrespectful to the memory of friends. "I'd known many of these guys for years. I even knew their wives and sisters.")

This jocular denial, which protected Strauss's and his surviving shipmates' sanity, continued much of the day, even after the ship began to fall apart. A wave picked up the ship's bow and foredeck, broke them off from the rest of the ship, and moved them twenty feet to the side. As rolls of toilet paper and cans of paint spilled out of the storage compartments, Strauss tried to take the edge off his fear with more levity. Recalling how President Franklin D. Roosevelt described United States wartime naval strategy with the phrase "two-ocean war," Strauss thought, "Here's the *two-ship* war." If he sought escape in mad humor, others found it in an equally mad observance of regulations. When the deck cracked, seamen who rushed to the ship's store for wooden planks to bridge the gaps were firmly instructed by the storekeeper that they had to sign for everything they took, as though they were assembling a gangway while on normal duty in Portland harbor. Stranger still was the sad end of the fellow who was assigned to look after the log books. So that they could be sunk in case the ship was captured, all logs were in lead jackets. This man threw them over his shoulder (lead jackets and all), leaped over the ship's side, and was not seen alive again.

As DAWN CAME to the hellish seascape and their predicament sank in, denial slowly gave way to constructive action. On the *Wilkes*, the crew jumped up and down on the afterdeck to depress the stern and lift the bow off the rocks. Leaking badly, she backed off and hovered just offshore as her crew attempted to launch rafts and let them drift downwind to the *Pollux*. But when seamen tried to crawl aboard, they were held back by the tarlike bunker oil covering the sea.

Fully exposed to the waves rolling onshore, the *Pollux* took a dreadful beating, first from the breakers coming in, then from the heavy backwash going out. There was a constant deluge of motion and sound as the great waves fell on the ship and twisted and ground her onto the shelf. "I spent twelve hours on that ship while the storm was flinging her against the rocks," Strauss recalled. "The noise was just *tremendous*. It was like being in the middle of a thunder and lightning storm cracking all around you. But when the order finally came to abandon ship, guys were yelling, and they seemed even louder than the ship."

After the bow broke off at about noon, Commander Turney encouraged his men to abandon ship. He soon regretted it. More than a hundred sailors went down the cargo nets into the churning water and tried to swim to the cliff. Some men smeared their bodies with oil as insulation, the way swimmers did before attempting the English Channel, but it made little difference, since everybody became covered with the gooey stuff, which Strauss described as "halfway to tar and inches thick." While fighting the oil, the waves, and the freezing water, many men beame so exhausted that they could not hold their arms down to prevent their partially secured life jackets from rising up and off their torsos. They had only enough energy before drowning to shout warnings to their shipmates to stay on board. Bodies floated everywhere. Some men who made it to shore said they were so cold and numb that they just wanted to die in peace (one even walked right back into the water). When Turney saw what was happening, he ordered everybody to stay on board; men near him reported that he was in tears.

The *Pollux* breaks up in the seas. "The noise was just *tremendous,*" Henry Strauss remembered. "It was like being in the middle of a thunder and lightning storm cracking all around you." (Donald W. Cady)

Men look up from the ship at the precipitous cliff surrounding the cove. There were only a few ledges to stand on. The inset shows the same cliff from a distance. (Donald W. Cady)

Grace is a theme of many stories of that day and night. A seaman named George Coleman said that after a drowning friend warned him to stay on board, he was so badly shaken that he started reciting the prayers he had not said since childhood. "Help me, Mother of God," he prayed repeatedly until he finally calmed down. He came upon an obviously frightened teenage seaman who was sitting alone and looking out to sea to the *Wilkes*. According to Coleman, they sat together for a while until the ship's stern fell off the *Pollux* and the deck became broken by deep cracks that left them isolated. Coleman decided to try to swim to shore, but as he was stepping over the lifelines the boy asked him for his cigarettes and matches. Coleman climbed back, and as they sat together smoking what he was certain were their last cigarettes, four men appeared and rescued them. Coleman said he never did learn the boy's name. In such a story, it makes little difference whether every detail is factual or whether it is another of those sanity-preserving legends founded on a few truths and an underlying structure of meaning.

Many men, meanwhile, were struggling to get a line ashore in a whaleboat and a life raft. They capsized and a few men crawled ashore into small caves in the base of the cliff. At about 4:00 P.M., a light messenger line was sent over on a grapnel hook that grabbed the cliff. Strauss volunteered to climb across this line carrying a heavier rope. First he went below and retrieved a photograph of his wife so that if he died she would be told that he was thinking of her. He tied the rope around his waist and started out on the light line, hand over hand. He was almost all the way to the shore when a wave knocked him off. Although he was a champion diver, he could not swim a stroke. "I couldn't move a thing," he remembered. "All I could think was, 'This is stupid. The bastards are letting me down.'" On the ship, the rope was too slippery for anybody to grab and pull him out. A powerfully built bosun's mate, Glen Wiltrout, ingeniously solved the problem by wrapping some of the rope around his torso and slowly spinning in place to pull Strauss to the ship.

Eventually men were sent across one by one in a bosun's chair to the cliff base, where they perched precariously on narrow, wet ledges. There they discovered their continuing vulnerability. As Strauss would put it, they were "rescued but no longer rescued." They would somehow have to make their way up a three-hundred-foot sheer slope. Under a black sky and with the rising tide lapping at their feet, they encouraged each other, singing "There's a long, long trail" and other First World War songs that their fathers had taught them. Strauss protected himself from the cold with his trick of standing stock-still and allowing a coating of ice to build up. From time to time the doctor passed around a bottle of raw rubbing alcohol. "You could feel that like a knife blade following the course of your stomach. It etched the intestines, but it warmed me up," Strauss recalled. As the tide climbed up the cliff, picking men off their narrow roosts, Strauss chanted his own prayer: "I have to make it, I have to make it."

<h1 style="text-align:center">IV</h1>

"Is anybody down there?" A voice floated down the cliff:

"You bet your life, Charlie!" a bosun's mate named Lloyd shouted back.

Earlier that day, two local boys out hunting had walked to the other side of the cove and seen the wrecked *Pollux*. They rushed the news back to the general store in the village of Lawn, where a group of men with black smudges on their foreheads were sitting around a hot stove. It was Ash Wednesday, they had all been to church, and they were not inclined to believe the boys. Lawn and the neighboring village of St. Lawrence had recently suffered setbacks. A tidal wave in 1929 had wiped out many docks, the cod fisheries had given out, and the local fluorspar mine was paying low wages while its workers were getting sick from miner's disease.

A man named Manning volunteered to check the boys' story. He saw the *Pollux* hard aground and breaking up, surrounded by corpses, and rushed back to the village. He rounded up men, horses, and gear and led them on the ten-mile hike through the mountains to the top of the cliff, beneath which the survivors were desperately hanging on.

(In the next cove eighteen-year-old Edward Bergeron, a survivor from the capsized *Truxton*, swam ashore and climbed the adjoining cliff, cutting hand- and footholds into the ice. He made his way to the fluorspar mine and found help. These rescuers attempted to lower a dory on ropes to the few men who survived as the ship broke up. On the first try, the wind blew it right back to the top, so a young fisherman climbed aboard as ballast, and the improvised elevator eventually saved several lives.)

At the scene of the *Pollux* wreck, the local men—miners, fishermen, and farmers—split into groups, some to go down the cliff and form human chains to help bring men out of the water, others to haul the Americans up on a rope. A few of the Americans died of hypothermia or other causes on the way up. The survivors who reached the top were helped over the lip and taken to a bonfire by people so large and strong that they seemed to be giants. Not until a reunion of rescuers and rescued in 1988 did the Americans realize that their rescuers were not much different from themselves. Hank Strauss was so blinded by the oil in his eyes and so addled with exhaustion that when he reached the top of the cliff he mistook a tree that was burning on the fire for an aircraft carrier and then decided that the thing to do was to walk back to New York and find his wife. The *Pollux*'s navigator, Lieutenant Grindley, grabbed him after he had taken a few steps and gently led him back to the group around the fire, where one of the local boys took off his gloves and gave them to Strauss.

Strauss and the others were loaded on a horse-drawn sled and taken to homes, where women scrubbed off the layers of black bunker oil. A family named Rose took charge of Strauss, cleaned him up, and put him in bed with hot bricks as bed warmers. There was some confusion about Lanier Philips, a steward from rural Georgia, whose skin would not whiten no matter how hard the women scrubbed. They had never seen an African American. "These people gave me a different outlook," Philips said at the reunion forty-six years later. "An entire community treated me as a human being and not as a black man. They made me see there were people in the world who were not racists and bigots. Not only did they clean me, but they fed me and they clothed me and they put me in their bed."

In all, 140 wreck survivors were recovered alive and taken to the warmth of the villagers' homes. Of the 203 men who died on or near the *Pollux* and *Truxton*, the bodies of 138 were found and buried in Newfoundland. One man's family was so grateful to the clergyman who conducted his funeral that they contributed funds for a cut-glass communion chalice for his church. After the war the United States government donated a hospital to the region in thanks for the extraordinary rescue effort. Like the Prince Edward Islanders in the Yankee Gale almost a century earlier, the Newfoundlanders did not make much of all this. When asked why they had gone to so much effort, the villagers mumbled, "It was the right thing to do" and rushed to change the subject.

Although the groundings were front-page news in America, the U.S. Navy was extremely reticent about the disaster, even declining to tell victims' families much about its circumstances. Disciplinary proceedings against officers led to reductions in rank or prohibitions against future commands. Curiously, the harshest penalty was imposed on the officer who had been the first to warn about the developing situation. William C. Grindley, the navigator of the *Pollux*, was threatened with a dishonorable discharge. When he complained to his senator, the punishment was changed to a permanent rank of Lieutenant Junior Grade. Grindley resigned from the navy and returned to merchant ship duty.

HANK STRAUSS, who had observed the navigator's prescience up close, judged the navy's treatment of Grindley to be scapegoating. Immediately after the disaster, however, he was most concerned about himself. Believing he was permanently blinded by the oil, Strauss set his exhausted mind on suicide until doctors promised him he would regain his sight, as he soon did. The scope of the accident came home to him in two routine events. On the troop transport carrying the survivors to Boston, nobody had to be told to wear a life jacket. Later, in the first mail call since the accident, many names were greeted by deep, distressing silence.

As he recovered, Strauss found himself speculating about what to make of his close call. "At the beginning you're damn sure 'It' is going to happen to someone else, not to you. But something happens that changes your thinking from 'I expect to get back' to 'I probably won't get home.' It really doesn't occur to you at first that you'll lose the 'I expect to get back,' but when things are really big, there's no room for extraneous thinking." Already, after his ship ran hard aground and his future seemed uncertain at best, Strauss had promised himself that, should he survive, it would be a sign that he was called to do work that touched people's lives in a unique way.

When his eyes cleared and he got back on his feet, he was made an officer and assigned to command a submarine chaser in the Pacific. He was strafed by Japanese aircraft in the Solomon Islands, and his subchaser sank under him in the Tasman Sea. As trying as those moments were, they did not compare to the misery he had felt on the ledge under the cliff on Lawn Point. Strauss had already begun to build something out of that pain.

I was going nuts in the hospital, so I guess as therapy I took notes on my experiences. After the navy gave me a direct commission and sent me to sub-chaser school, I put the notes together in an article that I thought I'd send to *Life* magazine. By then I was receiving letters from parents of sailors in the *Pollux* asking me how their sons had died, and I changed my mind about the article because I didn't want to risk offending them. "You must have known so and so," people would write. Eventually I wrote an article that ended up in *Reader's Digest*. People *still* write. Every year without fail there are e-mails, letters, phone calls. After the boy who alerted the village died, I got calls from his family. They tracked me down because they knew I would like to know.

He received one letter from a family in backwoods Kentucky who said their boy had been such a good swimmer that they couldn't understand how he could possibly have died. Because his body was not recovered, they had buried an empty coffin next to his brother. Years later, in a letter that reflected the other half of this agonizing story of missing sons, a New-foundlander told Strauss that as a boy he had seen a corpse wash up on the shore sixty miles from Lawn Point. Now he wanted to know more of the story.

THE ACCIDENT LED DIRECTLY to Hank Strauss's career. "The navy shaped my life tremendously and prepared me to do what I said I was going to do, which was something that would touch people's lives." While undergoing training, he noticed that many sailors were not well motivated to learn their jobs. He blamed it on insensitive instructors. Later, while command-ing the submarine chaser in the Pacific, he experimented with training methods and discovered that what worked best was not merely to pass on information but to provide an emotional message. Trainees should know how and why *this* subject would help *them*. In the military context, that meant persuading them that if they mastered the subject, they might save their own lives.

Although he had envisioned a career as a writer, Strauss went into film-making because, as he put it, "Film is the only emotional medium." Although he made many movies on travel for Pan American Airways and one on art appreciation that was nominated for an Academy Award, his special interest was training films that he produced for clients such as AT&T, the U.S. Army, General Electric, IBM, and the Episcopal Church. He called these productions "attitude films." One of the first of them dealt

Several months after the disaster, Henry Strauss was sworn in as an ensign by his former commanding officer, Commander Hugh W. Turney. Strauss later commanded a submarine chaser in the Pacific. (U.S. Navy)

Henry Strauss *(left)* at a *Pollux* reunion in 1988. By then he had retired from filmmaking after specializing in training films teaching tolerance and ethical behavior. (Courtesy Henry Strauss)

While recovering in the hospital after the accident, Strauss drew this sketch of the disastrous initial attempt to abandon ship. (Henry Strauss)

with white-collar workers' prejudice toward blue-collar workers. Strauss summarized the theme in a rhetorical question: "Do you think you're a better man than he is just because you're a foreman?" The answer came directly out of his own experience in the storm:

> The navy, and especially guys like Glen Wiltrout—who made a winch out of himself and saved my life—taught me that intelligence was not necessarily related to position or rank. It was a very humbling experience for me then, when I was an enlisted man *and* a college graduate. I learned in the navy, and also noticed later on when we spent winters in Grenada, that when living is hard, human life tends to be valued more and there is more interdependency. Where I live in Connecticut, it seems that you have to have a friend in order to have a relationship. It's rigid. In the navy and in Grenada and other places, the relationship is in the situation.

A related message infuses another of his films, *Inner Man Steps Out*, which has been described this way: "A supervisor who knows the 'book rules' for human relations finds himself in trouble when trying to apply them to people on the job." In *A Matter of Balance*, which he made for IBM, the issue is the challenge of trying to behave ethically in settings where unethical behavior can be rationalized. *Are You Listening?* concerns attentive listening, a skill that former "tough guy" Hank Strauss had developed after the *Pollux* disaster by (among other arts) learning how to express his views in thoughtful rhetorical questions.

For Strauss, these values were not merely noble, abstract ideals applicable only to corporate clients or to other people in exceptional times of crisis. In the patient but decisive manner that he believed he had first discovered in Newfoundland, the man who had figured out how to stay warm by becoming a human icicle lived his values concretely in his own life. For example, he quietly challenged the genteel anti-Semitism that used to be commonplace in America by settling in Darien, Connecticut, and joining exclusive yacht clubs. A sailor since his youth, he became an avid, extremely competent yachtsman with a forty-two-foot boat that he sailed every year between his winter home in Grenada and his main home in Connecticut.

One summer in the mid-1980s, Hank and Jo Strauss flew to the French island chain in the Cabot Strait, and joined a friend who was cruising in the area in his own boat. As they neared Newfoundland, Strauss decided to look for the Rose family of St. Lawrence who had cared for him after the accident. In the years since the war, the town had paved its roads, closed the mine, and built a fish factory on the waterfront.

Starting at the factory, Strauss found himself in a large, busy business office telling a young woman that he hoped to locate someone named Rose whose first name he could not recall. When she replied that several Roses lived in town, he provided an outline of his story—how he had been wrecked in the *Pollux* many years ago, and how this kind family had taken him in and scrubbed the bunker oil off him. By the time he got to the hot bricks that had warmed his bed, the office was silent. "Everybody must have heard the story of the wrecks and the rescues, and now they realized that it was all true. It was as though Moses had walked in the door, and people discovered that this man they had heard so much about really existed." The disaster, in fact, had become the reason for one of the town's most important events. Every year on February 18, St. Lawrence holds a memorial service during which the story is retold in order to teach the values of community service and self-sacrifice to the town's children. The woman who told Strauss about the ceremony explained it simply: "Greed has not yet come to Newfoundland." The memory is kept alive in other ways: St. Lawrence has a street named for the *Pollux*, and the schools include a teaching module on the disaster.

Strauss's visit led him to help organize a reunion of the surviving rescuers and rescued in 1988. Afterward, he spoke about the experience at his yacht club in Connecticut. Although he had been living in the area for many years, until then most of his friends were unaware of the disaster, much less his involvement with it. The first question came from his daughter Jan, who wanted to know why he had said so little about these events. She was annoyed that she had known nothing of the story until she was eighteen.

Hank Strauss was not surprised either by her concern or by his own previous reticence. "Most of the guys I sailed with in the *Pollux* never told their families about it, either. Some of them didn't say a word for twenty years. Isn't it strange how all those people buried it all those years?

"But of course they didn't bury it. I never thought it was blocked out of my mind at all."

8

Derelicts

The *Mary Celeste*, Azores, 1872, and *First Draft*, Gulf Stream, 1996

"*When I wrote a yarn round the incident, it was done irresponsibly and I never imagined it would be seriously analyzed. Of course it won't stand it.*"

—Sir Arthur Conan Doyle

"*It is what it always was: do or die. Have too many good things going for me.*"

—Miles Necas

UNTIL NOW we have been following a chronological path. We will now move from chronology to three timeless themes concerning storms at sea. First, there are the violent storms that do not destroy vessels but empty them, leaving mystifying drifting derelicts known to history as "ghost ships." Then, in chapter 9, we will consider redeeming storms whose violence transformed the lives of two men for the better—one an Old Testament prophet, the other the author of one of the most popular of all hymns, "Amazing Grace." Finally, we come to a modern understanding of the storm at sea as something to seek out for ultimate adventure in remote corners of the world where Beryl Smeeton, one of these modern-day mariners, said she found "a feeling of exhilaration, a feeling of battle."

A DERELICT ALWAYS POSES an unpleasant dilemma. It is a mystery, and though a mystery may break up the tedium of a long watch on a ship at sea, its memory may haunt for years.

One midsummer dawn sometime in the late 1970s, I was in the crew of a thirty-foot sloop sailing along the Connecticut coast of Long Island Sound toward the finish of an overnight race. In the remnants of the cool night breeze that was slowly dissolving in the hot morning air, the new sun glistened off the dewy, lush lawns of the Gold Coast mansions on the shoreline, just upwind of us to the north. Besides a handful of our friendly competitors, the only other vessel within view was a small cabin cruiser half a mile or so directly ahead, quietly chugging along not much faster than our low speed.

"Do you see that powerboat?" someone asked the helmsman.

"Yes. Does he have lines out astern?" Why else would a powerboat be under way slowly at 6:00 in the morning other than to hook a fish? And if so, we mustn't pass too close for fear of tangling his tackle.

Up went the binoculars. "No lines. You can pass close by."

"No lines? Why would he be out here? What's he doing?"

The boat crossed our bow, headed toward shore on a long, smooth arc.

"That's odd," whispered the fellow with the binoculars.

"What's odd?"

"There's nobody in the cockpit. He's on autopilot."

"That's not odd. It's damn strange."

A pause. "She doesn't look right."

We all nodded. This boat simply did not fit: seemingly empty, yet inscribing a perfect clockwise circle around us; working her way to the east before coming back at us from astern. The sea tolerates no perfect courses, or, for that matter, any perfect *anything* of human devising.

The morning took on a November chill as our imaginations processed what at first seemed to be a normal, rational encounter into something else entirely. There was among us an unstated, desperate passion to see a man in the cockpit holding a fishing rod, or a woman at the steering wheel, or a child chewing an apple, or to hear the yipping of one of those annoying small dogs that some boating people think make cute shipmates.

"What should we do?" The steerer's voice was tense.

"You know what *I* think?" We certainly did want to know. "What *I* think is that he lashed the helm and went below to use the head."

"Or to take a nap!"

"Or get laid!"

"He's on the radio calling his buddies to find out where the fish are!"

With miles to go before the finish, and other promises to keep, we sailed straight on and left the powerboat circling in our wake. I returned to my house and my sons, went about my life, and avoided speaking of my disturbing sighting for many years. Strangely, I cannot remember the year when that boat appeared. I know precisely where I was when I heard that the Kennedys and Martin Luther King Jr. were shot, when Bucky Dent hit his home run to beat the Red Sox in 1978, and when Ronald Reagan was first elected president. Although these and many other distant improbabilities have stuck in my memory, I cannot pinpoint the time when this one so deeply unsettled a perfect morning.

DERELICT VESSELS are more common than we might think. From 1846 to 1850, 680 British sailing ships were abandoned by their crews and left to sink, burn, or drift for thousands of miles. In his sobering book *Disaster at Sea*, Edgar A. Haine reports that a few derelicts were seen so often that they were given nicknames, like the "White Ghost" (aka the *W. L. White*), which, after being abandoned in the Caribbean in summer 1888, rode north and east up the Gulf Stream at a rate of twenty to forty miles a day and finally sank off Scotland, 5,780 miles from where her crew had given up on her. Thirty-six ships reported encountering her during that long, skipperless passage. The nineteenth-century longevity record for derelicts was held by the *Fannie E. Wolston*; after her crew abandoned her in October 1891, she drifted for 859 days and seven thousand miles. In 1904, according to Haine, "it was estimated there were 100 to 150 phantom ships moving across the shipping lanes, day and night, in storms and in calm." The problem has lessened but not disappeared. During a fifty-two-month period in the 1990s, 116 derelict vessels were reported in the North Atlantic.

Although derelicts pose an obvious risk of collision, they threaten more than the physical well-being of mariners. Our deepest insecurities are touched by people and objects that were once whole and orderly but have become split. An otherwise healthy vessel floating handsomely but empty of crew is like a friend whose mind had gone elsewhere—another Miniver Cheevey who, in Edward Arlington Robinson's poem, dreamed of the days of knights and armor and "kept on thinking . . . and kept on drinking." Another human derelict narrates Samuel Taylor Coleridge's epic poem about a floating derelict, *The Rime of the Ancient Mariner*. Both he and the ship are

> Alone on a wide wide sea:
> So lonely 'twas, that God himself
> Scarce seemèd there to be.

The sight of a near derelict deeply disturbed the young Joseph Conrad. As he recalled in *The Mirror of the Sea*, on an unusually beautiful day— "one of the days when the might of the sea appears indeed lovable, like the nature of a strong man in moments of quiet intimacy"—his ship came upon a dismasted, waterlogged brig that had been kept barely afloat for days by her exhausted crew. In that ship Conrad for the first time recognized the sea's "unfathomable cruelty."

I

AT LEAST CONRAD had the satisfaction of rescuing sailors before the ship sank. No such luck attended the crew that came across the abandoned but still sailing *Mary Celeste* in 1872.

The *Mary Celeste* has inspired more speculation than any other seafaring mystery. The few known facts and the many legends about her have touched the lives of a great many people, among them Sir Arthur Conan Doyle, the creator of Sherlock Holmes. Early in his career, Doyle helped create the myth of the "ghost ship" by building a wild fictional tale around the skeleton of the

Mary Celeste story. His work stimulated any number of irresponsible speculations and out-and-out frauds until, late in his life, Doyle bitterly regretted
that he had ever written a word about the *Mary Celeste*. As we will see, the
only theory about the causes of her abandonment that meets the demands of
all the evidence (and that satisfies the Holmesian standard, "I never guess")
concerns a storm of a particularly violent and terrifying kind.

ON DECEMBER 4, 1872, in fine weather following a gale, the brigantine
Dei Gratia, out of Nova Scotia, came upon the ninety-nine-foot half-brig
Mary Celeste at 38°20′ N, 17°15′ W, between the Azores and Portugal. Ini-
tially the encounter pleased the *Dei Gratia*'s master, Captain David Reed
Morehouse. He was a friend of the other ship's captain, Benjamin Briggs.
They had dined together a month earlier in New York, the day before the
Mary Celeste had headed out on her passage to Genoa, Italy. Briggs's wife,
Sarah, and their two-year-old daughter, Sophia Matilda, were aboard.
Briggs, who had suffered more than his share of troubles with unruly sea-
men, told Morehouse he was well pleased with the crew of seven.

Morehouse's initial pleasure quickly dissolved as a close look at the
Mary Celeste persuaded him that she was not right. She was sailing a slow,
meandering course to the west—opposite the one to Italy—under a
severely reduced rig, with her sails luffing. When hails went unanswered,
Morehouse, worried about an ill or disabled ship's company, sent the mate,
Oliver Deveau, and two other men over to inspect. They found no captain,
no passenger, no crew, and no ship's boat. There was some damage, though
hardly enough to be catastrophic. The rigging was in disarray, the binnacle
was toppled and its steering compass smashed in, the rail forward had been
shaved down, and (most strangely) though the galley and cabins were partially flooded, there was only three to four feet of water in the bilge—
nowhere near enough to almost sink a ship of that size. On deck lay the
ship's sounding rod, a metal rod that was inserted into the pipe for the
bilge pump to measure the bilgewater. Two deck hatches were open, and
their covers lay on deck.

In the hold was a cargo of 1,701 red-oak casks of alcohol, bound for Italy
where it would be used to fortify wine. Besides the boat, the only missing
items were the sextant, the navigation tables, and the ship's chronometer.
The lockers and drawers contained the crew's and passengers' clothing and
foul-weather clothing. The last log entry, for November 25, gave a position

six miles off the eastern point of the island of Santa Maria in the Azores. Since then the ship apparently had sailed more than three hundred nautical miles without a hand at the wheel.

A careful search discovered the merest hint of violence: beneath a bunk lay a sword whose blade had a reddish tint. Intending to claim salvage, Morehouse ordered Deveau and a crew of two to sail the derelict to Gibraltar.

IN GIBRALTAR, an investigation of dubious quality was held by J. Solly Flood, the British Admiralty proctor. The first of many cranks and other outrageous characters who have long fouled the reputation of the *Mary Celeste* while enlivening her story, Flood was obsessed by the nature of the cargo. Benjamin Briggs was an abstemious family man, a churchgoer who read a chapter of the Bible daily, and a captain who kept a "dry" ship. Flood, assuming that seamen would do anything for a drink, decided that this crew had no other interest than to get at the kegs of alcohol, which (he reckoned) required that they slaughter the captain, his wife, and their baby daughter, along with the mate. Flood determined that the red stain on the sword was blood and that after using it on the Briggs family and the mate, the mutineers had made off in the ship's boat. Flood explained the hacked-up rail with a theory that the mutineers had slightly damaged the ship in order to persuade the captain of a passing vessel that they were in deep distress and deserved saving.

Even before Flood made his ruling, his intentions were so clear that the ship's owner, who had hired the crew, fled Gibraltar before Flood could issue a warrant for his arrest as an accessory to murder. By the time Flood issued his judgment, the *Mary Celeste* was back in service. In 1884 she was wrecked off Haiti, reportedly by her crew under directions from an owner eager for the insurance money. By then it was well known that Flood had concealed the report of a consulting chemist that the stain on the sword blade was rust, not blood.

IN THE SAME YEAR that the ship sank, the mystery was revived sensationally by an unsigned story in an English magazine about a derelict brigantine named the *Marie Celeste*. In the tale, titled "J. Habakuk Jephson's Statement," Jephson, the narrator, is a doctor from Brooklyn who is aboard the ship when she is taken over by an African American passenger named

Septimus Goring and the black crew members. They slaughter all the white people aboard except Jephson, who is saved because he carries a magic stone cut from an African statue. After the bloody mutiny, the ship sails to Africa. The author of "J. Habakuk Jephson's Statement" clearly intended the story to be fiction by giving the ship a different name—*Marie*, not Mary— and changing several other crucial points. All the same, a Boston newspaper suggested that this account offered a new insight into the old mystery of the ghost ship, and Solly Flood furiously drafted a lengthy report defending his own theory of serial murder by alcoholics.

Among readers who correctly believed it to be made up, there was speculation that the tale was written by Robert Louis Stevenson, who was known for plucking the core of his stories from the newspapers. But "Habakuk" had been turned out by a twenty-four-year-old English medical doctor and aspiring fiction writer, Arthur Conan Doyle. Between attending to patients, he worked on short stories, a few of which reflected his experiences at sea. Encouraged by the twenty-nine guineas he earned for the story, the doctor kept writing and developed a series of highly original mystery and horror tales featuring a brilliant detective called Sherlock Holmes. The stories were strikingly contemporary, with modern touches that, alas, included the nasty racism that permeated the tale of the *Marie Celeste*. Doyle became successful enough as a writer to drop his medical practice altogether.

If more ink came to be spilled concerning the *Mary Celeste* than almost any other vessel, it was in part because Doyle first made his name prominent by taking an interest in the ship. Other than Solly Flood's fantasy, "Habakuk" was the earliest of many imaginative efforts in the field of what came to be called "Celesteana." A bibliography published in 1942, twelve years after Doyle's death, listed sixty-nine articles and books about the *Mary Celeste* that had been published in the United States, Britain, and Germany. The library of Celesteana was so large—and so full of crackpot ideas—that when a new, serious theory for the abandonment of the *Mary Celeste* was published in 1950, the author, Gershom Bradford, gave it the tongue-in-cheek title, "*Mary Celeste*. No, Not Again!" Much more was to come, including a novel in Italian and a bunch of publications in the 1970s around the centennial of the abandonment. Edward Rowe Snow, the New England sea romanticist and storm chaser, weighed in with a chapter in a book with a far less ironic title, *Adventures, Blizzards, and Coastal Calamities*.

As one indication of the broad interest in Celesteana, one of its leading

scholars, Frederick J. Shepard, lived hundreds of miles inland from salt
water in Buffalo, New York, where he headed the city's public library. (The
online catalog for Buffalo's libraries today lists more than three times as
many books concerning the famous old ghost ship—fourteen, including
one by Shepard himself—as are in the Boston Public Library's catalog.)
Another respected Celesteanist, Charles Edey Fay, was a New Englander
who took up the subject while serving as an executive at the ship's insurer,
Atlantic Mutual Insurance Company (which kept the "Vessel Disasters"
scrapbooks about shipwrecks mentioned in chapter 2). When Fay wrote
the most reliable book about the incident and its succeeding controversy,
he lost all chances of peace and privacy. "Although my book was written 14
years ago," he wrote in 1956, "hardly a month passes without an inquiry of
some kind about the case."

WHEN FAY SUBTITLED HIS BOOK *The Odyssey of an Abandoned Ship*, he
must have been referring not so much to the vessel herself as to her reputation, which has wandered both sides of the equator between fiction and fact.

The *Mary Celeste* was once a public obsession, and like all public obsessions this one inspired far more than its share of fictions. Among them
were: everything was in perfect order; the ship's boat was still on board; a
half-eaten breakfast was on the cabin table (as were cups of hot tea); a cat
was dozing in a locker; all the sails were set; and the ship's company totaled
an unlucky thirteen. The most imaginative stories concerned the culprits.
Here are a few theories as to who was responsible:

> The crews of the *Mary Celeste* (that mutinous, alcoholic mob), the *Dei Gra-
> tia*, or an unnamed third vessel (perhaps a disabled freighter).

～

> A mad captain. In a fit of fundamentalist religious mania, Briggs butchered
> the crew. Alternatively, Briggs was driven insane when a piano broke loose
> and crushed his wife; he subsequently heaved himself overboard, leaving the
> crew to dispose of the piano and themselves.

～

> A mad seaman. A one-armed crew member was treated so badly by the first
> mate that he went insane and heaved the crew and passengers overboard,
> one by one. This is the plot outline of a 1936 horror movie variously titled

The Mystery of the Mary Celeste, The Secret of the Mary Celeste, or *The Phantom Ship* and starring Bela Lugosi in one of his post-*Dracula* roles.

∾

Barbary pirates far from home. They impressed the crew, most of whom died of fever.

∾

Nobody. It was all a scam by the two captains, Briggs and Morehouse, to gain salvage money.

∾

A huge octopus, or maybe a devilfish. In this scheme, proposed in 1904 and perhaps inspired by Jules Verne's *20,000 Leagues under the Sea,* a monster patiently snags sailors off the deck, one after another.

∾

Who knows? According to a man from Cincinnati in 1909, the whole thing was explained in a cipher message that, unfortunately, nobody was able to read.

∾

Mystical agents, possibly extraterrestrial beings. They became interested when the ship sailed over the lost city of Atlantis. Such ideas continue to be associated with the *Mary Celeste* by New Agers.

Given this erratic history of interpretation, no wonder the Buffalo librarian Frederick J. Shepard titled his book *The Mary Celeste: A Sea Mystery, the Facts of Which Have Been Clouded by Romances.* No better example exists of the human need to account for all the details of a disaster of the deep through mythologizing. As another thoughtful Celesteanist, MacDonald Hastings, remarked, "The mystery of *Mary Celeste* is largely a mystery of wish." This is not to deny that the mystery has attracted charlatans. J. G. Lockhart, the creator of the theory of the wild piano, also published another theory altogether. The speculation about a conspiracy between the two captains arose from a journalist who called himself alternately Charles Keating and Lee Kaye, and whose book *The Great Mary Celeste Hoax* itself was a hoax that claimed as its main source a nonexistent "survivor."

Besides good sense, the chief victim of these schemes was Arthur Conan Doyle, who assumed responsibility for the mess. "When I wrote a yarn round the incident," he complained late in his life, "it was done irresponsibly and I never imagined it would be seriously analyzed. Of course it won't stand it."

Doyle cleverly got his revenge with a little-noticed parry in one of his last stories, "The Adventure of the Sussex Vampire." There is a quick mention of a ship inhabited by an animal that Holmes refers to as "the giant rat of Sumatra, a story for which the world is not yet prepared." The name of this rat-infested vessel is the *Matilda Briggs*. In this obvious reference to Sophia Matilda Briggs, the daughter of Captain Benjamin Briggs, Doyle announced to the world that he felt sucked dry by the mystery of the *Mary Celeste*.

OTHER THAN THE NOTION that the sea is off limits to normal human activity, those wild ideas share a complete absence of any of the usual concerns of mariners. There is nothing in them about storms, other natural phenomena, dangerous cargo, a leaky hull, torn sails, or errors in judgment. Other speculations about the abandonment of the *Mary Celeste* are more attentive to nature and seamen. According to a recent theory, a seaquake, or underwater earthquake, shook the vessel enough to start a fire, cause leaks in the kegs of alcohol, and stimulate among the crew a terror of God's imminent judgment. Captain Briggs then gave the order to abandon ship, taking the navigation equipment with him. Unfortunately for this ingenious proposal, the salvage crew of the *Dei Gratia* noted no sign of fire.

The potentially explosive cargo also is the centerpiece of the most influential solution to the *Mary Celeste* problem, which is that the alcohol was heated by the presumably hot Azorean climate until it became a gas and either blew up or threatened to do so. Briggs collected the navigation equipment, had the ship's boat launched (after planing the railing to speed the launching), and abandoned ship, keeping the boat connected to the ship by a long rope to see what would happen. In his haste to get off the ship, however, he left some sails set, and when a breeze came up and the ship gathered speed, either the painter broke or the crew cast it off, fearing that the boat would capsize. The *Mary Celeste* sailed on while the boat foundered. This ingenious theory faces an insurmountable hurdle: the water and air temperatures near the Azores in late November (when the ship was abandoned), are hardly tropical but average sixty to sixty-five degrees, less than half the boiling temperature of alcohol and, more significant yet, about the same as the water and air temperature near New York in late October, when the ship was loaded. If there was no danger from exploding kegs when they were put aboard—and presumably there was none—the chances of that danger in the same climate a month later should have been no greater.

A SHIP OFF THE AZORES in late November is at far greater risk of being hit by a storm than by a heat wave. A sailing guide to the archipelago advises staying away after September 15, "based on the experience of many wrecked and sunken ships down through the ages." This leads to the most persuasive *Mary Celeste* theory of the lot: that she was caught in a storm and took on water in such a way that Briggs became convinced the ship was sinking, even though she was not.

Supporting the theory that the ship was hit by an extraordinary storm are four pieces of evidence provided by Oliver Deveau, the *Dei Gratia's* mate, during Solly Flood's hearing. First, the rigging and fittings were in disarray or damaged. Second, Deveau testified that there was "a good deal of water between decks": the galley was half-flooded, several cabins were soaked, and there was water damage everywhere. Third, there was a little less than four feet of water in the bilge—some but not a lot. The fourth bit of evidence was Deveau's report that the rod for sounding the ship's bilge was on deck and the pipe it fit into was open. Obviously Briggs had been concerned about flooding. When Flood asked the mate to explain the abandonment, Deveau pointed to the sounding rod. "My idea is that the crew got alarmed, and, by the sounding rod being found alongside the pumps, that they had sounded the pumps and found a quantity of water in the pumps at the moment, and thinking she would go down abandoned her." The sentence may be convoluted but its meaning is simple: Briggs was convinced that his ship was sinking.

THE *MARY CELESTE* MYSTERY comes down to one question: How could an experienced captain like Briggs be frightened into leaving a vessel that was not sinking? The most persuasive answer is that he was caught in a certain type of storm with unique characteristics—a waterspout. Writing in the scholarly maritime history journal *The American Neptune* in 1950, Gershom Bradford proposed that the *Mary Celeste* was hit by a waterspout coming out of one of the storms that was reported on November 25 in the area of Santa Maria, near where the ship was sailing. Bradford was an experienced seaman, an authority on nautical terminology and maritime history, and a career employee in the navy's Hydrographic Office. The waterspout theory is impressive for three reasons. First, waterspouts were known to occur in that stormy season in the Azores. Second, they are terrifying. And third, a waterspout has unique features that explain the evidence discovered by the salvagers: the modest damage to the ship; the large amount of water in the cabins; the small amount of water in the bilge; and the presence of the sounding rod.

Like tornadoes except that they occur over water, waterspouts are tight swirls that drop suddenly out of clouds to create a freestanding vortex of intensely low atmospheric pressure reaching down to the water and stirring up a terrific mess. One witness to a waterspout remarked on "the black monster cloud above" and how at the spout's base, "the sea was lashed into a mass of white foam and spray that mounted upward as high as the masts of a large schooner." The unpredictability and strong winds of a waterspout are as spectacular as its appearance. In December 2001, during the annual ocean race from Sydney, Australia, to Hobart, Tasmania, waterspouts dangled out of the clouds and caught several racing boats on only a few minutes' notice. As the winds accelerated from twenty-eight to sixty-five knots in a matter of seconds, even extremely experienced sailors were intimidated. "We had a helpless feeling, where this freak of nature was chasing us down," said one world-class skipper, John Kostecki. "Nobody on board has ever experienced anything like this, and we all hope we never do again." The skipper of a seventy-nine-foot boat confessed, "I really feared for my life. It was the most unbelievable thing I have ever seen. I saw it coming and tried to outrun it. It looked like it was going behind us, but then it turned and got us. I was looking up a tunnel of water and could feel my jacket riding up my back."

Although waterspouts caused little serious damage to the boats in that race, they have destroyed much larger vessels. In September 1917 the *Alice Knowles*, a 115-foot whaling ship out of New Bedford, was capsized at night by a waterspout near the Cape Verde Islands in the eastern Atlantic Ocean. The only survivor, Quentin DeGrasse, told a vivid story:

> At two o'clock a terrific roar came out of the blackness. No man could hear another's shouts. The waterspout enveloped the ship, dragging her onto her beam's-ends. She remained there a brief moment, and the captain attempted to smash in the cabin skylight to release his son in the steerage and any others of the crew. Before he had struck half a dozen blows, the vessel was turned keel-up—the crew was trapped below or thrown from the deck into the boiling ocean.

The *Mary Celeste* as she appeared when she was discovered. Her sails were luffing and her rigging was in disarray, but she was still sailing. Many wild theories were bandied about concerning her abandonment, but the theory that makes the most sense accounts for a sailor's worst fear, which is that a ship is sinking in a storm. (Courtesy Peabody Essex Museum, Salem, Massachusetts)

Waterspouts are much feared by mariners, and for good reason. As this 1873 drawing suggests, they have sunk ships. A survivor of a waterspout said the wind was so strong and loud that he feared he would lose his mind. (Courtesy Historic National Weather Service Collection, NOAA)

Some crew members were already in a lifeboat and lowering it into the water when the ship rolled over, tossing them and the boat onto the keel. DeGrasse and another man managed to save themselves by hanging onto the remains of the shattered boat and, after fighting off sharks for four days, were finally rescued. The other man soon died, leaving only DeGrasse to tell a terrifying tale in which his worst memory was neither the blackness of the waterspout nor its destructiveness, but its terrible shriek. Recalling his first hours in the water, he said, "The waterspout and gale had passed, but a thundering noise still deafened me."

SUCH NOISE IS ONE of the features of a waterspout, along with its violence, the flying water, and the plummeting air pressure inside the vortex. The roar of waterspouts and tornadoes has often been compared to the sound of many locomotives racing by. Intense noise can destroy resolve, resilience, and judgment while dropping a wall between people who are only a few feet apart. The writer and sailor Lincoln Colcord wrote of a storm that "the noise of the wind was deafening, the tremendous liquid power of it benumbing." He added, "I could no more have heard the man at my elbow than I could have heard a man on another planet."

More recently a single-handed racer, Dominique Wavre, reported a "very high stress level" as he sailed his sixty-footer through a storm. "The noise was unreal. Both infernal and incredible at the same time." The sound was so ferocious that it kept him awake for twenty-four hours. In the big catamaran *Team Adventure*, racing at speeds of twenty knots and more across the southern Pacific toward Cape Horn, Larry Rosenfeld laid out how unpleasant sailing can be: "The drivers [steerers] require lots of concentration because they are steering at these speeds into the blackness of the night and dark water. Goggles or visors are a must because the spray hits your face like a fire hose. The noise is amazing—a high pitched wail that sounds like a falling bomb in WWII movies—as our finely-tuned machine slices mostly over and sometimes through the waves." Noise, then, is a weapon against sanity and community.

Besides noisy violence, a waterspout has two other extreme features that pushed Benjamin Briggs over the edge to abandon the *Mary Celeste*. One is a tremendous volume of flying water caused by torrential rains, hail, and the sea being sucked up to the cloud. The other is the extremely low air pressure inside the storm. The sailor in the 2001 Sydney–Hobart race experienced it when his jacket rode up his back. Another example is that of a family cruising boat that was caught in a waterspout on Chesapeake Bay. The wind was so loud that the husband, on deck, was convinced he was going insane, and the boat was tossed so violently that his wife, below in the cabin, felt as though she was being shaken in a corn popper. Then what the couple called a "vacuum" descended on the boat. They blanked out for a few moments until the sound of shattering wood snapped them back into alertness. A slide in a hatch had exploded outward. The cause was the great differential between the low air pressure outside the hull and the normal pressure inside the boat. The boat, in effect, had exhaled through its weakest point, which was the hatch cover. The pressure in the center of a tornado has been known to drop several inches and cause a violent updraft that will tear the roof off a house unless the air has somewhere else to go (people in tornado-prone areas open doors and windows as the twister approaches).

HERE, THEN, IS WHAT probably happened on board the *Mary Celeste*:

A line of thunderheads approaches the vessel, with dark waterspout tails dragging in the water surface. A spout roars at her, knocking the ship far over on her side and destroying the binnacle and compass, and covers her in a drenching rain and earsplitting thunder.

Briggs, struggling to think analytically through this chaos, knows enough about these storms to be aware of the risk of the vessel's being blown apart. To attempt to equalize the air pressure and prevent the ship from blowing herself up, he orders the crew to open all the hatches, doors, and ports, shouting as he must into each sailor's ear. As the cabins are flooded in the downpour, a sailor crawls across the nearly vertical deck and pushes the sounding rod into the pump. When the ship rocks upright, he extracts the rod and finds water ten or more feet deep. Terrified, he shouts to Briggs that the ship is sinking.

Briggs, harried by the screams of his wife and daughter and the reports of flooding, is unable to appreciate that the vacuum around him is pulling the water up the pipe, the way a thumb over the end of a straw pulls water out of a glass. He presses the crew to launch the boat.

Santa Maria is only six miles away, a short enough row, once this short storm passes. Briggs anxiously prepares to abandon ship. While the ship's carpenter prepares the rail for a quick launch, he scoops up his wife and daughter and his navigation instruments.

The crew of *Illbruck* rush desperately to clear the deck of sails and other gear as a waterspout roars down at them during the Sydney–Hobart race in December 2001. Sailors reported that the spout appeared and swept by in only two minutes. (Illbruck Challenge/Ray Davies)

Few sights at sea stir up as much misery as that of a derelict or floating wreck. Joseph Conrad recognized the sea's "unfathomable cruelty" when he saw his first drifting ship with a half-dead crew. (Author's collection)

The boat is in the water, the men jump in, and Briggs hands his wife and daughter and the navigation instruments to the mate and slides down after them. The boat is pushed away and rowed off in the breaking seas. Briggs pulls out a compass and sets a course, then looks back at the *Mary Celeste* and is surprised by how high she floats. She is not sinking or anywhere near it as, with her sails in disarray, she slowly sails into the shadow of the next thunderhead, which brings along the next waterspout. Beyond it Benjamin Briggs can see more towering clouds and, under them, more black vortexes. As little Sophia Matilda snuggles under his coat, the horrified Benjamin Briggs prays that they will miss him and not leave him to the merciless deep.

II

ANOTHER DERELICT APPEARED 124 years after the *Mary Celeste* was discovered, and some 20 years after I was mystified by the circling boat on Long Island Sound.

"We have an emergency!" The shout came down the companionway minutes before the 0800 watch change. A much smaller sloop had popped out of the murk of a rain squall almost dead ahead. It was July 3, 1996, and we in *Toscana*, sailing back to Rhode Island from Bermuda, were in the middle of the Gulf Stream. A spot two hundred miles south of Cape Cod and almost three hundred miles east of Maryland hardly seemed the place for this lightly rigged pocket cruiser, which was much better suited to a quiet bay or lake. How inappropriate she looked, with her bizarre mixture of seamanlike self-sufficiency and abandoned disarray. Her mainsail was loosely furled on the boom, the lowered jib waved about, more or less lashed to the foredeck. The hatches lay wide open, a fishing pole jutted over her side with a line out, and a Bimini top sagged, like a half-opened umbrella, over the cockpit. Lines to two sea anchors hung over her bow, and a regular metal anchor and rode lay near the mast. Like the crew of the *Dei Gratia* when they came upon the *Mary Celeste*, we had many questions. Did the crew, whoever they might be, have their wits about them? Who would try to dig an anchor into a bottom eight thousand feet underwater? And why did nobody greet us?

The vessel lacked personality. Black plastic Maryland state registration numbers adhered to her bow, yet no name or hailing port marked her

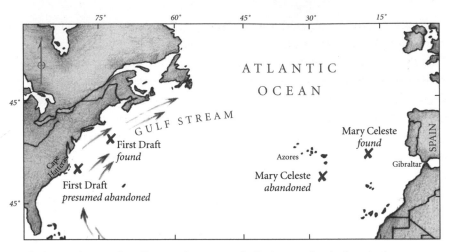

The *Mary Celeste* was found between the Azores and Gibraltar. One hundred twenty-four years later, *First Draft* lost her captain and only crew, Miles Necas, off Cape Hatteras and was then carried more than two hundred miles by the Gulf Stream.

transom, and our repeated shouts over our rail and radio stirred no response. The silence from the sloop was as deep as the ocean.

THE LITTLE BOAT showed no sign of life as we circled her, shouting and blowing horns. We debated what to do with no consensus. A few felt obliged to stop and make an inspection; perhaps the crew was sick and helpless. Others argued that this was none of our business and potentially risky ("insurance scam" was one of the examples bandied about). The first group won out, and we set a course to intercept the little lost sloop, which in due course appeared out of the rain squall.

The crew of *Toscana*, a fifty-one-foot sloop, was remarkably well prepared for the task. John St. Coeur was a fireman and emergency medical technician, and Tom Conley was a policeman. Conley hastily assembled a pack of helpful gear for John, including rubber gloves should medical work be needed. With the engine on, Eric Swenson, the owner, nudged *Toscana*'s bow, well padded with fenders, alongside the skittish sloop, and John stepped aboard. Half an hour later he was back with his backpack full, reporting that the boat lacked both a crew and all sense of order. The bilge overflowed, the tiller was broken, there was a crack in the cabin floor, the outboard engine's fuel tank was empty, as were two tequila bottles, and clothing and tools were strewn about.

He had found a marine radio, a handheld global positioning system electronic navigation device, a baseball cap with the logo of a marina near Norfolk, Virginia, a jacket with the logo of a communications industry union, cans of food, various bills of sale and licenses, an electronic date book, some personal letters, statements from a securities brokerage account, an English-language Gideon Bible, a collection of poetry in Czech, and a chart marked with a sketchy position near Cape Hatteras dated June 24. No safety equipment was aboard, and neither was there a wallet or a log book.

John and Tom spread the documents on the cabin table and sat down to a meticulously professional inspection, holding each item by a corner as though it constituted evidence in a murder case—which, of course, there was a chance it did. They soon reported an identity for the derelict: she was *First Draft*, a twenty-seven-foot fiberglass sloop built in 1971 in California. Her owner of record was a fifty-three-year-old Czech named Miles Necas. We knew nothing else about him except that he had visited Norfolk, Virginia, he probably worked in communications, his boat was two hundred miles and nine days from that charted note at Cape Hatteras, and he was nowhere to be seen.

There was nothing else to do except bring the U.S. Coast Guard up to date and resume our course to Newport, satisfied that we had made an effort to relieve the distress, if not of Miles Necas, at least of his family and friends. Thirty hours later, on Independence Day afternoon at Newport, we handed our finds to a flabbergasted young coast guard rating who could not understand why we were not keeping the electronics. They were ours to retain under salvage rights, she explained. St. Coeur, the fireman, patiently replied that we were giving her what she would need to conduct a proper investigation. The radio was set to the channel of the last transmission, and the GPS had memory programmed with waypoints (geographical positions of buoys and harbors) that would tell where Necas was headed. Shaking her head, the young woman accepted the instruments and walked off.

After a coast guard airplane found the little boat, a relay of cutters towed *First Draft* to Woods Hole, on the heel of Cape Cod. In December 1996, the coast guard issued a 165-page accident report that represented more than fifty-seven hours of work by the agency's Marine Safety Office in Providence and the Questioned Document Unit at the Federal Bureau of Investigation Laboratory in Washington. *First Draft* went into storage in an old air base—a vessel so worn out by time and the sea that the Internal Rev-

The violence of a storm is well known, but not the fearsome noise. "The noise was unreal. Both infernal and incredible at the same time," one ocean sailor reported of a storm he was in. It comes from the scream of the wind in the rigging and also the roar of the sea washing the decks. This is amidships in a fifty-five-foot yacht in a Gulf Stream gale. (John Rousmaniere)

enue Service declined to seize her for the back taxes owed by her owner, about whom much was told in the report and accompanying documents.

BOHUMIL MILA NECAS was born in Czechoslovakia in 1942 and taught in colleges there until the Russian invasion in 1967, when he fled to the West. Ending up in the United States, he worked as a translator and computer programmer. In the nineties he worked for a graphics company in Washington, D.C., but things began to turn against him. After losing his house by foreclosure, in November 1994 he bought *First Draft* from Dan and Kris Beach for $1,850—the low price reflected the boat's age and worn gear, including a broken inboard engine—and moved aboard her at a marina in Annapolis, Maryland. He packed the boat full of electronic equipment, including a computer, and installed a television, refrigerator, and stereo system (none of which was seen by John St. Coeur). Burdened by financial problems and, some of his many sailing friends believed, unhappy at the end of a relationship, he began planning a long cruise south in search of a new life.

The boat had been named by the Beaches, who had bought her in their first stab at sailing. Dan, a fireman, and Kris, who worked in a university computer center, were typical dreamers who liked the way sailboats looked and valued their leisure time together, so they bought a boat. They proceeded to teach themselves how to sail catch-as-catch-can, and after a couple of years in *First Draft*, they moved on to a bigger boat and sold her to Miles Necas.

Most liveaboards are friendly souls, but the charismatic and charming Necas ("a daring Czechoslovakian adventurer," according to Kris Beach) was unusually amiable. He helped the Beaches with their new boat and served as the marina's social secretary, organizing parties for the couples and families that lived aboard or came around on weekends. Training for his projected single-handed voyage, he often went out alone in *First Draft*, even in rough weather, from which he returned with scary stories about his hair-raising adventures. In July 1995 Necas said good-bye and headed south. He got only as far as the mouth of the Potomac River, where he settled in for the winter at a marina in tidewater Virginia. As a member of a fun-loving trio of liveaboard men who called themselves the Three Amigos, he maintained a festive atmosphere. Along the way his seamanship improved somewhat. When the Beaches last saw him, in late 1995, Necas

As the author was crossing the Gulf Stream, this small cruising sloop appeared out of a rain squall after drifting from Cape Hatteras after a storm. "*First Draft* is a darling boat," her owner, Miles Necas, wrote in his log. "Smart and sturdy. But she is not a blue-water craft!" (Shelley St. Coeur)

"How inappropriate she appeared, with her bizarre mixture of seamanlike self-sufficiency and abandoned disarray." *First Draft*, July 1996. (Shelley St. Coeur)

described a stormy nighttime sail on the Potomac when he fell overboard but pulled himself back on deck using the safety harness he was wearing. At least he had not romanticized the risks.

WHEN HE SET OUT AGAIN in June 1996, Miles Necas was bound around Cape Hatteras for the Intracoastal Waterway and then south to Florida, perhaps as far as the Keys. He kept a log, which coast guard inspectors found in the boat's bilge, too waterlogged to read until it was restored by the FBI. His entries, which he wrote at the end of each day, provide a view of an optimistic, devout, resilient, perhaps even stubborn individual who was in a little over his head but was working hard to develop the right stuff. Miles Necas may not have been an especially talented sailor, but he was a cautious and often imaginative seaman who understood very well the dangers he was risking by sailing out in such a small boat. He usually wore a life jacket, he often wore a safety harness to keep from falling overboard, and he installed a sturdy lifeline and devised both a self-steering arrangement and a system of safety lines and a ladder that, he hoped, would help him climb on deck should he fall overboard. This was no Percy Bysshe Shelley carelessly staking his life on a gamble that nature and the sea are merely picturesque preserving energies.

His troubles with dragging anchors, storms, and fear as he worked down Chesapeake Bay toward the Atlantic did not undermine the good fortune he felt. Necas thrived emotionally, though not necessarily physically, as he indicated in a log entry: "Got good beating. Fell asleep at the table. Morning revealed I was less than 300 yards from the light after making perfect slalom run through fish traps. Never saw them. God Loves Me!" In a sudden thunderstorm off Cape Charles, at the shore's southern tip, the boat careered so wildly out of control that all he could do was hang on. He cheerfully described his reaction this way: "Fucked the mast for 15 minutes and peed in my pants." The concerned crew of a nearby large powerboat sent a distress alert to the coast guard. That night: "Fell asleep at the table, too tired to eat. Woke up when hit the floor. 1:00 A.M. checked anchor and drag. OK?" As usual, he ended the entry, "God Still Loves Me."

The next day, June 12, he made a risky landing under sail against a seawall— "Just a kiss. Perfect! Nobody saw me! Damn, what a seamanship!" —and went ashore to see *Mission Impossible*, which had been shot in his native Prague. After an hour the theater manager alerted him to an approaching storm, and Necas spent half the night fending his little ship off the tar-soaked seawall. Two days later he anchored off a wildlife refuge and attended to his seamanship while keeping in tune with the nature around him: "At 7:00 P.M. dragged and drifted about one-half nautical mile. Panic. Set second hook at 29 feet, all 200 feet of rode. Sets good. First has only 100 feet—not enough aspect [scope] especially in sand. What a gorgeous evening. Watched pelicans in perfect unison wingbeat for wingbeat a few inches from the water! How do they do it?? God Loves Me."

NECAS PLANNED TO SAIL OUT of the bay, then 120 miles south around Cape Hatteras to the North Carolina coast, where on Independence Day he would meet a friend and head down the Intracoastal Waterway to Florida while developing an idea for a new business venture.

The first part, around Hatteras, was the most demanding stage. Even in good weather, a short passage down the Atlantic coast can be far trickier than most dreamers think, with a single-handed sailor's problem of both resting and standing watch during long night passages, and with the chances of strong currents spinning off the edge of the Gulf Stream and erratic winds from ahead. If the Cape Hatteras region is even more littered with shipwrecks than the funnel into New York, it is owing not to space aliens, as "Bermuda Triangle" buffs would have it, but to the climatic clash there between cool, dry air blowing off the continent and the steamy, volatile air carried along by the superheated waters of the Gulf Stream, which sweeps northeast only a few miles offshore.

The wind to fear is one from the northeast. Though favorable to a vessel sailing south, it blows square into the teeth of the Gulf Stream, with its three- to four-knot current. The conflict kicks up a horrendously confused sea that can break boats and crews. The circumnavigator Eric Hiscock described sailing in such a sea in his heavy thirty-footer *Wanderer*: "At times the motion was almost indescribably violent, though Susan got fairly near to it when she said it was like sailing among a lot of concrete blocks." The tossing and rolling were such that the Hiscocks were unable to do much more than cook and clean up as the boat sailed herself. They were steady only when in their bunks: "It was as if we lived a kind of hospital existence—bedridden, but fortunately free from bedsores." The Hiscocks' *Wanderer*, so uncomfortable in these conditions, weighed almost three times more than Miles Necas's twenty-seven-foot, 5,600-pound *First Draft*, which as she rounded Cape Hatteras found herself reeling in a hard nor'easter.

～

FIRST DRAFT'S EXPERIENCES over the following grim days are laid out in Miles Necas's log. His progress is extremely slow. It is no help that his boat is unsuited for the open sea and rough water. "Our boats don't leak! All boats given time leak!! Untangled rigging umpteenth time." As the wind kicks up on June 23 he deploys a sea anchor (improvised from a canvas bucket) off the bow to hold it in the waves. "Sea anchor useless." A day later: "Drift is huge, up to 30 degrees off course." The tiller breaks, and his diet is down to Dramamine.

On June 25, as he approaches Diamond Shoal, a dozen miles off Hatteras, what comes in but a northeast gale with waves whose heights he estimates at six to nine feet, towering over his low deck and cabin. He anchors in fifty feet of water and settles down to ride out the storm, which rages for two days:

> First Draft is getting a spray bath with every wave. Riding the anchor beautifully. Can't go topside or in cockpit so I stay in, take a pill, and sleep, sleep, sleep, sleep. . . . Unable to go topside or in cockpit. It is a miracle I am not seriously hurt. Several times got caught on wrong foot amidships and literally flew from port to starboard side landing with a thud.

He radios the coast guard to report his position and the damage to his steering. He does not request assistance; his courage rises with his exhaustion.

> I lost 20-plus pounds this cruise, feel clumsy, fat, and old for this shit. But I am too stupid to quit. It is what it always was: do or die. Have too many good things going for me. New venture I know will be success and with success comes money and with money *a new boat*. First Draft is a darling boat. Smart and sturdy. But she is not a blue water craft!

He finishes off that entry with a detailed plan for steering the tillerless boat using the sails. Ending, "God Still Loves Me," he turns the page in his log book and writes, "6/27/96 Thur."

THOSE PROBABLY ARE his last words. At the end of its investigation, the coast guard will conclude in a general way, "It is likely that he was in a weakened state from five straight days at sea with little sleep or food, suffering from seasickness, and therefore was unable to survive the ordeal."

On Thursday the nor'easter gradually fades to fifteen knots and the wind shifts into the northwest, leaving an extremely confused sea over Diamond Shoal. Unsteady yet aware that the worst has passed, and elated that he and his pocket cruiser have ridden out a gale at one of the most dangerous spots on earth ("Damn, what a seamanship!"), Miles Necas decides to get under way. The brazen self-confidence that has carried him this far now works against him. What psychologists call "the period of impact" is past; now he is in the apparent—but only apparent—lull of the "period of recoil," when less obvious but more insidious threats wait to fall upon the careless survivor.

He staggers forward on the lurching deck, weighs anchor, starts the wheezing outboard motor, and sets sail, steering with the engine as the tillerless rudder swings around uselessly. His stomach grumbling after several days of enforced fasting, he sets out a fishing line and rigs the Bimini top to protect him from the hot sun. But before he can make the day's log entry that would undoubtedly have ended with an even more fervent declaration of divine love, a leftover rogue sea snaps the boat into a roll, and his beloved *First Draft* hurls her captain into the sea.

From water level, the deck of even a twenty-seven-foot boat might as well be the peak of Everest, except that Everest is stationary and *First Draft* is moving away, leaving her captain in her wake, saying his prayers. The amoral little sloop works her way toward the coast until the gas tank empties. Another boat comes alongside. Her curious crew board the derelict, drink the tequila, and steal the wallet, computer, and stereo system—almost all Miles Necas's worldly goods. Again the little sloop is left alone. For days the Gulf Stream carries her into the ocean, until one morning she drifts out of a black squall into the path of *Toscana*.

Capable enough to survive a storm under appalling conditions, Miles Necas was unlucky enough to die accidentally in its aftermath—another lost seaman who, if the biblical promises are true, will be found again when there comes a new and better world.

9

"Amazing Graces"

The Prophet, the Apostle, and the Hymn Writer

*"There I continued till noon, almost every passing wave
breaking over my head; but we made ourselves fast
with ropes that we might not be washed away."*

—John Newton

WITH THE EUPHORIC Miles Necas in *First Draft*, we have come
full circle over almost 175 years since Percy Bysshe Shelley also
attempted to escape personal shoreside tribulations in a small
boat but had his dream come to grief in a storm. We now turn
to the most extreme response to a storm—to regard it not as
an accident or a punishment but as a purifying experience,
a test sent by God or fate or conscience to awaken us to the
possibility of a better life. We begin with the flawed biblical

prophet Jonah's survival and conversion in a storm at sea, move on to
the gale in which the Apostle Paul demonstrated superhuman abilities,
and end with the blow in the North Atlantic that converted John Newton and led him to write the hymn "Amazing Grace." In the final chapter
we will see how this ancient idea of purification is kept alive, though
usually in a more secular form, by modern-day sailors seeking extreme
challenge as they venture into the wild Southern Ocean "because it is
there."

I

THE OLDEST AND STILL the most powerful story of a storm at sea and its
consequences is a brief account in an ancient language of a gale that
struck a ship sailing across the Mediterranean Sea. Here is how a standard
translation begins the narrative:

> But the Lord hurled a great wind upon the sea, and there was a mighty tem-
> pest on the sea, so that the ship threatened to break up. Then the mariners
> were afraid, and each cried to his god; and they threw the wares that were in
> the ship into the sea, to lighten it for them.

This is superb storm writing. The anonymous author who wrote the
Book of Jonah pulls readers into the story with strong verbs (the storm
does not simply appear but is "hurled") and sympathetic characters who
make their feelings known through their actions, not an accretion of adjec-
tives and adverbs. We can hear the groans of the straining vessel and the
despairing shouts of the sailors as they desperately lighten ship and pray to
their own gods.

The author sets these pious, resourceful men against the wretch who lies
sleeping in the ship's hold, unconscious both to their heroic efforts to save
his life and to God's attempt to attract his attention. He is Jonah, the story's
central character and antihero, a man so dead to feeling and unaware of his
situation that even a storm cannot awaken him. By this stage in the story
we already know two other things about Jonah. First, despite his prickly
nature, this is a holy man—a prophet gifted with an inherent ability to persuade bad people to mend their ways. Second, while he has the tongue of
angels, he has feet of clay. When God instructed him to convert his people's
worst enemies in Nineveh, the capital city of the Assyrian empire, Jonah

declined because he believes the Assyrians deserve punishment, not grace. Certain that God's authority is bounded by the borders of his own country, Israel, Jonah took ship in the opposite direction for Tarshish, a place in remote Spain that was considered the end of the world.

Among the story's many shocks—including an imperfect holy man, admirable heathens, a beneficent storm, a friendly man-eating fish, and enemies of good heart—is the fact that the Book of Jonah is an exception to the rule that stories named for their leading figures usually hold them up as idealized role models. Although the story was probably written by a Jew about a Jewish holy man, to be read and used by Jews in religious rites, the noblest behavior in the storm is not by the eponymous main character but by the idolatrous heathen sailors from other lands who, unlike Jonah, understand who God is and what sort of behavior God expects. As they conscientiously struggle against the gale and pray for their salvation, Jonah lies asleep in the ship's hold, avoiding social contact and devoid of humanity. The Old Testament scholar Phyllis Trible has observed that the prophet and the idolatrous sailors are exact contraries. He is alienated and passive; they are involved and engaged. "As the activity of the sailors increases, the activity of Jonah decreases. Lying down to sleep in the innards of the ship, he is close to becoming an inanimate object, a replacement for the wares that the sailors have hurled overboard." According to Trible, the Hebrew words describing Jonah's state are not generally applied to ordinary healthy sleep but indicate a near-death state. In a word, he is numb.

OF ALL THE SURPRISES in this brief but wonderful story, the greatest is that the healing agent is not a gentle, spiritual breeze but a violent storm at sea, which everywhere else has been regarded as a primal force for evil. Working through direct intervention and shock therapy, the storm restores Jonah's religious faith, and through it his faith in himself. In earlier chapters we saw the violence that a storm can do to human beings, numbing them with hypothermia, seasickness, and noise. Those are the physical sensations that Joseph Conrad referred to when he wrote, "The disintegrating power of a great wind is that it isolates one from one's kind." But Jonah is not alone because of the storm, and neither does he suffer *from* it. Rather, this storm is a healer. It is a theophany, a manifestation of God, through which God attempts to cure Jonah and end his suffering by calling him to obedience, which also means fulfilling Jonah's own best nature.

In the Talmud, the compilation of Jewish oral laws and commentaries, Jonah's sufferings are described as coming upon him "because of the anguish of his soul." To put it in more modern language, Jonah is numbed by traumatic despair. After the terrorists' destruction of the World Trade Center in New York, Dr. Bessel A. van der Kolk, a psychiatrist, observed emotional blankness among the rescuers at ground zero and the health workers who attended to them. The telltale sign of trauma was their emotional numbness: "The worst thing that happens in trauma is that people shut down and become like zombies. Then people really lose their capacity to engage in and attend to their current environment. Their whole system gets shut down." Jonah's system has been "shut down" not by the storm but by his acknowledgment of his rebellion.

The storm has human agents who pump life back into the flattened, self-defeating prophet. His sleep through the storm is so deep that it is unnatural; he sleeps not peacefully but stupidly, like a drunkard who has passed out. But the ship's captain must see some potential in this wretched creature, for he comes below and awakens him, reproaching him for his unfaithfulness. "Arise, call upon your god! Perhaps the god will give a thought to us, that we do not perish." His conscience and humanity stirred up, Jonah joins the crew on deck. When they cast lots to determine who is to blame for the storm, the lot falls on Jonah, as it must. Fessing up to his duty, he tells enough about himself and his god to cause the sailors to convert on the spot. His story has turned their abject fear of the storm into awe—far more awe, in fact, than he can drum up in himself. He tells them to throw him into the sea as propitiation. Decent people that they are, the sailors pray to Jonah's God and labor harder to save the ship. Their own efforts are not enough for, as the author tells us, "the sea grew more and more tempestuous against them"—meaning that God wants Jonah off the ship. Finally acceding to his wishes, they throw (or "hurl," according to some translations) him into the sea. The storm subsides, and the ship is saved.

But Jonah is not lost. A lifeboat in the form of a "great fish" appears to rescue him. In the fish's belly, Jonah at last recognizes his dangerous plight and offers thanksgiving for his rescue from "the heart of the seas." After three days and nights, the fish vomits (again, some translators prefer "hurls") him out onto the shore. Reborn and with his selfish concerns apparently in check, Jonah travels to Nineveh and fulfills his calling brilliantly by converting the king and all the wicked Ninevites.

~

THE JONAH STORY, of course, is about a lot more than storms, although it shows how important storms are to the world as symbols of human transformation. Its 1,400-word text is short enough to fit easily on a page in a modern newspaper. (Publishing the story there every now and then would not be a bad idea; it would at least remind readers of their limitations.) The anonymous author needed no more space to strike to the heart of a crucial question of the human condition—where a person is to fit in the immense divine and human order. Part satire, part legend, part parable, and part theological tract, it is the story of the travails of a self-absorbed person who never quite seems to get life sorted out, yet recovers because of divine mercy. Nobody knows who wrote this story, or even when. By considering the Hebrew, the historical references, and other factors, biblical scholars can confidently date many texts to within a couple of decades, yet when it comes to the Book of Jonah there is broad bafflement. The best anybody can determine is that it was written between about 800 and 200 B.C., probably after the Babylonian exile of the fifth century exposed Jews to foreigners (the book's notable tolerance of non-Jews is also a theme of another postexile biblical short story, the Book of Ruth). Besides nudging readers out of their xenophobia, the story of Jonah's storm and its consequences also illustrates the fallibility of human judgment and the fallacy that there are simple solutions to life's problems—as well as the fallacy that good deeds are accomplished only by the best people. What holds the story together is Jonah's awkward humanity.

It was a stroke of genius by the anonymous writer to situate the narrative in two territories that every reader would have been convinced were hostile. One was Nineveh, which was to that time what Saddam Hussein's Iraq is to ours. The other was a storm at sea, where the prophet-in-spite-of-himself found order. According to one authority on the Book of Jonah, Karin Almbladh, the Israelites considered the sea "a nonworld," "a land of darkness." As the Talmud says to highlight the sea's terrors, "Most ass drivers are wicked, while most camel drivers are worthy men; and most sailors are pious." Jonah tells why in his hymn of thanksgiving after he is saved:

> The waters closed in over me,
>   the deep was round about me;
> weeds were wrapped around my head
>   at the roots of the mountains.

He was cast into Sheol, the Other World of chaos and death, from which
the fish saves him. The best-known episode in the story, Jonah's three days
(a period of time that in the Bible means "a journey") inside the great fish
are usually presented in popular art as extremely tame—more a soothing
sauna than the wake-up cold shower that it is in the story.

"JONAH IS EVERYWHERE," says biblical scholar James Limburg. The story
may be better known today than at any other time in history. There are at
least eighty-two children's books with "Jonah" in the title, plus a vast
number of works of art inspired by the story that range across the spectrum of taste and quality from Michelangelo's Sistine Chapel to the Dis-
ney cartoon movie *Pinocchio*. Many people learn about the foolish
prophet and his extraordinary adventures in their youth. "When I was a
child, the wondrous story of Jonah fascinated, frightened, and filled me
full," recalls Phyllis Trible, the Old Testament scholar quoted earlier.
"When I became a college student, I did not put away childish interests
but began to transpose them into critical reflection." After writing her
doctoral dissertation on the book in the 1970s, she watched as Jonah studies became "an industry."

    This is not the first time the story has had a wide following. Archaeolo-
gists working on digs from the early centuries of Christianity have found
twenty times more images of Jonah than of Noah and even of Jesus' bap-
tism. Just why this was so is suggested by another parallel between that era
and ours: both faced great insecurity. Then, Christians were persecuted;
today uncertainty is rampant. In such times, the example of an "every-
man" who rises above his own human limitations brings comfort.

    Jonah is one of us. Like him, we know that to follow any unpopular but
necessary vocation imposes risks—the greatest being that we might succeed. That fear of success has been called "the Jonah complex" by the
father-son team of André and Pierre-Emmanuel Lacocque, one a biblical
scholar and the other a clinical psychologist. "What the book of Jonah is
teaching us," they write, "is that we are called to give unique responses to
life's unique demands." If we do not respond appropriately, our disobedi-
ence invites despair and a storm sent by God or conscience.

    We remember Jonah's fragile humanity in odd ways. Someone who
brings bad luck to a community is called "a Jonah" (even though the thrust
of Jonah's story is that no matter how fallible this reluctant prophet, he

somehow succeeds in bringing about good ends). His humanity is no-where more visible than at the end of the story. The same man who in the belly of the whale offered thanksgiving for his own salvation somehow cannot bring himself to do other than to demand that God slaughter all those thousands of Ninevites whom he has just converted. In Jonah's nar-row, authoritarian definition of justice, there is no room for tender mercy—except the mercy that he selfishly extends to himself. Like the ship's captain, God (or Jonah's conscience) sees through Jonah and makes a demand of him: "Do you do well to be angry?" The tone of the question may strike some readers as sarcastic and others as gentle, like the "still, small voice" that came to the prophet Elijah earlier in the Bible (1 Kings 19:13). Either way, the point is the same: Do not Nineveh's helpless deserve the same divine love and protection that have been granted to Jonah? To remind him of the les-son he should have learned in the storm, God creates a large gourd plant to protect Jonah from the hot desert sun and the sirocco wind. Then, just as easily, God destroys this natural umbrella. The story closes with a comic scene in which, under God's benevolent gaze, the moody prophet sits bak-ing, still struggling with his conscience and his fallible humanity. It is hard to believe this is Jonah's last wake-up storm.

The Jonah storm story has long played a crucial part in Jewish and Christian devotions. In ancient Israel, during droughts, after earthquakes, before attacks by enemies, or in other times of calamity, Jews gathered for fasts and chanted the Book of Jonah as a request for divine grace. Today, on the Jewish fast day of Yom Kippur, the Day of Atonement, Jews chant the story of Jonah to remind themselves (as S. Y. Agnon wrote in his great book on the High Holy Days, *Days of Awe*) that "no man can fly away from God," that "God pardons and forgives those who turn in *Teshuvah* [repentance]," and that "the compassions of God extend over all that He has made, even idolaters." At the end of the reading, congregations add verses from the book of the prophet Micah that tell how God "wilt cast all our sins into the depths of the sea" (Mic. 7:19).

Christians have long read the Book of Jonah in their annual cycle of Scripture readings, including in the liturgy of Holy Saturday at Eastertide. There also are readings in the gospels of Matthew and Luke in which Jesus directly compares himself with Jonah. These sayings make use of an argu-mentative method of interpretation called typology, which, by presenting an event in the New Testament as an improvement on or fulfillment of one in the Old Testament, is intended to demonstrate to potential converts that the new faith is superior to Judaism. In both gospels Jesus declares that if Jonah was a sign of divine judgment to Nineveh, Jesus himself will be a sign not only to one city but to the entire present generation. "Something greater than Jonah is here," Jesus says, indicating that he will produce more repenters than the prophet. Matthew alone has Jesus compare his forth-coming resurrection from "the heart of the earth"—the grave—as some-thing greater than Jonah's dramatic yet less miraculous survival from the heart of the sea—the fish's belly (Luke 11: 16, 29–32; Matt. 12:38–42).

The purifying storm, therefore, is the agent by which the reluctant believer is led through despair to a more profound and authentic life.

II

JONAH'S STORM may well be an unacknowledged character in the story of the Apostle Paul's storm and shipwreck at Malta. The New Testament's sea disaster, it is the mirror image of Jonah's storm and seems also to say, "Something greater than Jonah is here."

This story is told by Luke in chapters 27 and 28 of the Book of Acts, the history of the early church. While most scholars agree that this storm occurred during the winter of 60–61 A.D., there is little consensus on whether it happened as Luke describes, with its miracles and Paul's sur-prising mastery of navigation and weather forecasting. According to one persuasive view, the story started out as a typical storm account of the sort found in *The Odyssey*, into which an editor inserted six appearances by Paul. In any case, it is told as vigorously as Jonah's, though with much more detail about seamanship and weather, and with less sympathy than calcula-tion.

The ship is a grain carrier bound for Italy, and Paul is on board as a pris-oner after his arrest in Jerusalem for disturbing the peace. As a Roman citi-zen, he may choose to be tried in Rome, and that is his preference. While the ship is moored at Crete, he warns the Roman centurion who is in charge that bad weather is approaching and recommends wintering there. The centurion prefers to rely on the judgment of the captain, which is quickly proved to be poor.

Once at sea, the ship is overtaken by "a tempestuous wind, called the northeaster"—a hard blow feared by sailors everywhere in the Northern

Hemisphere. The wind is so strong that the ship cannot make her way to windward toward a harbor of refuge. In the temporary shelter of a small island, the sailors reef the sails ("lower the gear"). According to Luke (or whoever wrote in his name), the sailors also "undergird the ship," meaning to reinforce a weak hull by binding it tightly in ropes, from the deck around the bottom of the keel and up the other side. Only then do they set out.

At least the wind is in the northeast, which allows them to scud before the rising storm that Paul has accurately forecast, despite the demurrals of the non-Christian captain. It is not made clear where Paul gained such competence as a weatherman and (as we see later in the story) as a seaman. The New Testament tells us that he often traveled by sea and that his chosen trade was tent-making, which might have involved making sails. Whether those life experiences taught him something about seamanship, the real point here is not what the real Paul knew but the way in which this Paul asserts himself in the crisis with a bold confidence and sincere dutifulness that are strikingly un-Jonahlike.

As the gale worsens on the third day, the sailors demonstrate admirable seamanship. They secure the lifeboat on deck, lighten ship by jettisoning cargo, and take down some spars ("the tackle of the ship") both to decrease windage and to lower the center of gravity and thereby increase stability. They also attempt to ease the ship's motion in the rough seas by dragging a sea anchor or drogue overboard. Yet their prospects are bleak. Rain and spray drench the passengers and prisoners huddled on deck, and despite the drogue the ship rolls and pitches violently and all the crew, passengers, and prisoners are too seasick to eat. Adding immediacy to his story by assuming the voice of an eyewitness, Luke records this chilling memory: "And when neither sun nor stars appeared for many a day, and no small tempest lay on us, all hope of our being saved was at last abandoned."

Paul again steps forward decisively to urge the crew to "take heart." An angel has come to him, he says, and the angel has promised that they all will survive because there is a divine plan for Paul to reach Rome. Whether or not the Romans believe him, after two weeks of misery and terror they sense that they are nearing shore (probably because they feel the waves steepen as they sail over shoal water). They anchor, and some mutinous sailors escape in the lifeboat. The next morning Paul, again promising that all will survive, encourages the remaining ship's company to eat the bread that he distributes after saying a few words reminiscent of the Christian formula at Holy Communion. The fortified sailors cut the anchors' cables and sail the ship onto a shoal, where the stern breaks up, leaving everybody to float ashore on wooden planks. Although the soldiers want to kill the prisoners to prevent them from escaping, the centurion demurs. He likes Paul and wishes to save his life.

"And so it was that all escaped to land" exactly as Paul predicted, and with his wise, heroic assistance. The land is Malta; despite the great storm, they have sailed five hundred miles without the loss of a single life. Paul proceeds to miraculously save two lives. He himself remains unharmed after he is bitten by a poisonous snake, and by the laying on of hands he saves the father of his host on the island. With that, every sick person on Malta comes to Paul and is healed. Paul is acclaimed as a god, a being far greater than poor obtuse Jonah.

A PARALLEL READING of Paul's and Jonah's storm stories suggests that the two storms are contrasting tests of faith and men, and that, without referring directly to Jonah, Luke seems to have him always in mind. Where Jonah flunked his test, Paul has gloriously passed his. The apostle's behavior is superior to Jonah's in every way. Before the storm, Jonah flees God's call but Paul embraces it. (Earlier in the Book of Acts, on the road to Damascus, the vision of Jesus tells Paul, "You will be told what you are to do" [Acts 9:6].) During the storms, Jonah hides in the cabin, a passive passenger with a bad attitude, but Paul strides the deck, a visionary leader and a skilled pilot and weatherman. In times of doubt, Jonah depends on his heathen captain; Luke shows Paul to be a stronger, wiser man than his heathen ship's master. And so on. The notion that a storm at sea is a test of fortitude is hardly novel. Implying another typology, Luke also wants us to believe that a storm is a test of sanctity that only a Christian can pass. Because Paul is the unJonah—an abler seaman and a more pious prophet—we are meant to believe that Christianity is the fulfillment of Judaism.

Somehow this hierarchy does not work. As noble as Paul appears in Luke's storm story, as admirable and even godlike as his actions seem, the reader's empathy gravitates not to the perfect apostle but to the imperfect prophet. Though there be storms, the wavering prophet muddles through them to the light. Paul may be a saint, but Jonah is our brother.

III

OF THE MANY "JONAHS" who have brought bad luck to ships but have gone on to better things, the best known and least understood may be John Newton, who was inspired by a storm at sea to write a hymn that in all times rough or gentle expresses the quintessence of hope and gratitude. The sustained success of "Amazing Grace" is due to all three of its features—the words that Newton wrote, the tune that was later adopted by those words, and Newton's own remarkable story of personal transformation in a storm at sea. "Amazing Grace" is the offspring of a North Atlantic gale.

WHEN HE WROTE THE HYMN, Newton was inspired by his own experience in a leaking ship in a brutal storm, where for the first time in his riotous life he had a sense of divine protection. Such an undeserved kindness is called a grace or, in the language of devout Christians like Newton, "God's unmerited free spontaneous love for sinful man, revealed and made effective in Jesus Christ." About twenty-five years after that trial, he wrote a hymn expressing his feelings about his conversion. Titled "Faith's Review and Expectation," it opened with these two stanzas:

> Amazing grace! How sweet the sound
> That saved a wretch like me!
> I once was lost, but now am found;
> Was blind, but now I see.
>
> 'Twas grace that taught my heart to fear,
> And grace my fears relieved;
> How precious did that grace appear
> The hour I first believed.

As D. Bruce Hindmarsh, one of Newton's biographers, has observed, this hymn concerns a soul torn between "rebellion and surrender"—a tension represented by several dichotomies: between stark amazement and sweet grace, wretchedness and salvation, blindness and sight, and being lost and being found. Here is another example of the rule for writing laid down by Stephen Sondheim: "Reduction releases power." Newton said as much in his preface to *Olney Hymns*, the collection that included "Amazing Grace":

> They should be *Hymns*, not *Odes*, if designed for public worship, and for the use of plain people. Perspicuity, simplicity, and ease should be chiefly attended to; and the imagery and coloring of poetry, if admitted at all, should be indulged very sparingly. . . . The workings of the heart of man, and of the Spirit of God, are in general the same in all who are the subjects of grace.

Newton was articulating a core concern of the emotion-laden Protestantism to which he was drawn, including the evangelical wing of the Church of England and the Methodist Church. Those successful churches addressed not narrow theological doctrines but people's "workings of the heart." Their liturgy included congregational singing of hymns that were neither triumphant anthems nor poems based on Scripture but heartfelt expressions of the worshipers' deepest concerns. The images in these hymns (which in time came to be known as "gospel hymns") came from everyday life, including the frightening disasters reported in the shipping news in newspapers. "The poetry of all gospel hymnody abounds with sentimental and subjective imagery," writes a historian of church music, Timothy A. Smith, whose list of popular subjects includes "angels, sailors, lighthouses, sinking ships, gardens, warfare, and dying children." It was John Newton's genius in "Amazing Grace" to express the profound feelings of personal religious crisis without exploiting any particular image, including the one that actually helped bring about his own spiritual transformation—a ship caught in a dreadful storm at sea.

THE HYMN'S SOUND, which may be better known than the precise meaning of its words, makes the crisis clear. When "Faith's Review and Expectation" was published in the first edition of *Olney Hymns* in 1779, it had no music. Newton left that to congregations. But like his other hymns—including "How Sweet the Name of Jesus Sounds" and "Glorious Things of Thee Are Spoken, Zion City of Our God"—it has a distinctive sound that combines soothing sibilants and open vowels. In the first line alone, four soft *s* and *z* consonants buzz like bees around the wide-open flowers of the six drawn-out vowels. These words were married to the now-familiar tune in the United States. *Olney Hymns*, which was published in a handy pocket-size edition, was carried to America and used in churches, camp meetings, and revivals from New England to the Mississippi River. Several tunes were tried before "Amazing Grace" joined a tune called "New Britain" in 1835 in a hymnal titled *Southern Harmony*. The tune may have

originated among slaves; more likely, as its title suggests, it originated in
New England. (Tune names can have many types of inspiration. The tune
for "Eternal Father, Strong to Save," which begs God for protection from
"peril on the sea," is called "Melita"—an ancient word for Malta and a reference to the refuge that Paul found after his shipwreck.)

"New Britain" started out as a simple "shape-note" tune—so called
because the notes were printed with distinctively shaped heads to indicate
pitch. That allowed untrained voices to quickly master the music. In gospel
music or "sacred harp" music (the voice was known as "the harp you were
born with"), shape-note tunes have been described as "mournful," "eerie,"
and "a cross between Gregorian chanting and bluegrass." They are the roots
of country music and much rock and roll. "Amazing Grace" has been widely
sung in Methodist, Baptist, and Presbyterian churches for over a century.
Although Newton was an Anglican clergyman, it was not included in the
hymnals of the Church of England and the American Episcopal Church
until the 1980s, soon after the secular world discovered it in top-selling
recordings made by Judy Collins, Elvis Presley, and, in Britain, a Scottish
bagpipe band. By the late 1980s "Amazing Grace" had taken on a new life and
become something like an ecumenical anthem. (A soprano saxophonist
played it with moving effect at my wedding in 1989.)

When church musicians were asked to explain the hymn's popularity,
they proposed that the words and music suit each other, are easily remembered, and according to Sally Campbell, a church organist, are easy to sing
because the range is just an octave. "It's just nice simple music, built firmly
on the major triad of a scale, with some graceful passing notes and a few
nontriadic notes for variety." She added, "I've noticed this: the bugle call
reveille is also built (exclusively) on the triad, so it may tie in, subliminally,
to a wake-up call familiar to all of us, scouts and soldiers or not."

That wake-up call becomes obvious in the fourth word of the second
line, which Newton chose because it spoke precisely to his situation before
the storm at sea brought about his conversion. After that soothing first
line—"Amazing grace! How sweet the sound"—the singer is almost
stopped cold by a word that has all the grace of a train wreck: "that saved a
wretch like me!" Some singers are so offended by the word's harsh meaning
and grating sound that they substitute more pleasing nouns, including
"soul" and "jewel" (which misses Newton's point completely). When Elvis
Presley, who was reared on gospel music and shape-note tunes, sang "Amaz-

ing Grace," he substituted "wreck," which at least approximates Newton's original. (Presley's home, Graceland, was named not for the hymn but for its original owner's Aunt Grace.) Newton preferred "wretch" because that was how he thought of his spiritual state. According to Raymond E. Glover, an authority on church music who calls "Amazing Grace" "a truly remarkable hymn," Newton used the word autobiographically in at least ten other hymns. He surely believed that grace had led this particular wretched individual to undeserved redemption.

To understand why Newton felt this way, we turn to the third of the appeals of his great hymn. After the words and the sound comes his biography, in which the turning point is a storm at sea.

According to one of his biographers, John Newton "had a life so extraordinary that he can seriously be proposed as the original of Coleridge's Ancient Mariner." (Newton's experiences may, in fact, have inspired *The Rime of the Ancient Mariner*.) Like Jonah's fictional life, Newton's historical one had more than its share of reversals and ironies, not the least of which is that the author of one of the very few hymns to have universal appeal, across all races and most ethnic groups, was a slave trader even after the conversion that his most famous hymn celebrates.

The son of a merchant ship captain and a devout woman who died when he was seven, Newton was born in 1725 and at age eleven went to sea on the first of several voyages under his father's command. He was impressed into the Royal Navy as a midshipman, but after going absent without leave to visit the young woman he later married, he was flogged, reduced in rank to common seaman, and transferred to a ship trading along the African coast. In another change in his erratic youthful career, he quit the ship with hopes of making his fortune as a slave trader on an island off Sierra Leone, but ended up waiting on his employer's mistress, who treated him brutally.

A year of this persuaded him that he must resolve to change his life for the better, but once he was given the opportunity by a captain who rescued him at Newton's father's request, he reverted to his old ways. "I was no further changed than a tiger who has been tamed by hunger," he later wrote. "Remove the occasion and he will be as wild as ever." As the *Greyhound* worked the coast, trading for beeswax and exotic woods, Newton drank heavily, lured crew members into foolish escapades, and enraged the ship's

"Amazing grace! How sweet the sound / That saved a wretch like me!" That wretch, John Newton, began to reform his life during a long watch at the helm of a ship that threatened to sink in the North Atlantic Ocean. (Courtesy National Portrait Gallery, London)

captain with his disrespect and blasphemies, even ridiculing the man behind his back. Except for studying some mathematics, he had nothing to do except take nothing seriously, least of all himself. "My whole life, when awake, was a course of most horrid impiety and profaneness." Why the captain (who had, after all, saved him from his servitude and had invited him to share his cabin) did not throw him off the ship must be counted as the first of the several graces granted John Newton before (Jonahlike) his conscience finally caught up with him.

In January 1748 the *Greyhound* headed home to England on the usual circular route of following the trade winds—sailing first west to the coast of Brazil to pick up the southerlies, then north to the Grand Banks of New England for some cod fishing to replenish the larder. On March 1 she weighed anchor and sailed east toward England in the prevailing wester-lies. With nothing to do on this long voyage except further irritate the cap-tain with blasphemies and write love poems to his lady friend, Newton dipped into a book by a religious writer, Thomas à Kempis, who invited reprobates to buttress their consciences and test their virtues by exposing themselves to adversity. Newton read on until guilt overwhelmed him and he tossed the book down. "My conscience witnessed against me once more," he reflected about this moment.

That night, March 10, 1748, there came the storm that changed his life. We know about it from letters that he wrote to a friend and that were published anonymously under the title *An Authentic Narrative of Some Remarkable and Interesting Particulars.*

NEWTON IS SLEEPING in his bunk when a wave sweeps the deck, pours below, and floods the cabin. Awakening to the roar of the water and cries that the ship is sinking, he is clambering up the companionway ladder when the captain, shouting down the hatch, orders him to go find a knife. As Newton searches for the knife, another man climbs up the ladder and is immediately swept overboard. This is the first of the graces that John New-ton will experience that night. Grace number two is that the *Greyhound*'s buoyant cargo of beeswax and wood keeps the ship afloat despite her huge leaks. Newton joins the crew of twelve in plugging the gaping seams with clothing and in pumping the bilge. When a despairing shipmate cries out, "No, it is too late now, we cannot save her, or ourselves," Newton's self-confidence flickers. To his own surprise, he prays for divine assistance: "If this will not do, the Lord have mercy on us." Taken aback by his own words—"the first desire I had breathed for mercy for the space of many years"—he instantly doubts himself: "What mercy can there be for me?" Back he goes to the pumps and his awakened conscience and faith:

> There I continued till noon, almost every passing wave breaking over my head; but we made ourselves fast with ropes that we might not be washed away. Indeed, I expected that every time the vessel descended in the sea, she would rise no more; and though I dreaded death now, and my heart foreboded the worst, if the scriptures, which I had long since opposed, were indeed true; yet still I was but half convinced and remained for a space of time in a sullen frame, a mixture of despair and impatience. I thought, if the Christian religion was true, I could not be forgiven; and was, therefore, expecting and almost at times wishing, to know the worst of it.

Too exhausted to pump any more, he staggers below, throws himself onto his bunk, and lies there weakly, prepared to die, until someone reaches out to him. The captain appears and orders Newton to the helm, just as Jonah's captain snapped the sullen prophet back to attention by reminding him of his responsibility to his shipmates. As he steers for eleven hours, his shipmates pumping and the wind slowly moderating, Newton feels new life rising within him. "There arose a gleam of hope," he will write in *An Authentic Narrative*. "I thought I saw the hand of God displayed in our favor; I began to pray."

The storm passes, leaving the *Greyhound* half derelict, rolling in the leftover seas. After several days of slow, discouraging going, the crew is heartened early one morning by the sight of a mountainous island rising out of the east. Certain that it is Ireland, they polish off the last of the bread and brandy when the rising sun breaks "Ireland" into wisps of clouds. Down to rations of just a small bit of dried fish a day, the sailors turn on Newton, the outsider. "To my great grief I have a Jonah!" exclaims the captain. There is even talk of hurling him overboard before the ship's company takes command of their emotions. As Newton will remark, "We began to conceive hopes greater than all our fears." One day, as "despair was taking place in every countenance," the wind turns favorable and pushes the ship east while heeling her enough to keep the damaged part of the hull free of the sea. As she drifts into Donegal, Ireland, on April 8, the last bit of food is on the stove and the water tank has just been emptied.

During these trials, Newton slowly comes to believe that he is being called to a higher purpose. "Thus to all appearance I was a new man. . . . I consider this as the beginning of my return to God, or rather of his return to me."

AN AUTHENTIC NARRATIVE is an example of the once well-known literary genre in which a sea voyage serves as an analogy for the spiritual life. Newton understood exactly. "My connections with sea affairs have often led me to think that the varieties observable in Christian experience may be properly illustrated from the circumstances of a voyage." He was not alone in noting that thoughts can be deep at sea. As Joseph Conrad wrote in his introduction to *The Mirror of the Sea*, at sea one can live "that innermost life, containing the best and the worst that can happen to us in the temperamental depths of our being, where a man indeed must live alone but need not give up all hope of holding converse with his kind." Like Conrad, Newton developed these insights into universal stories, in his case in hymns. The rule that many human struggles are like those of a voyager can be seen in some great literature, including the biblical story of Jonah, *The Odyssey*, *The Rime of the Ancient Mariner*, *Moby-Dick*, Conrad's novels and stories, Kipling's *Captains Courageous*, and Hemingway's *The Old Man and the Sea*. The genre surfaces also in recent books about storms and shipwrecks that constantly remind us that life is nowhere near as secure and easy as we prefer to believe. Robert Foulke, an authority on sea narratives (and himself a sailor), has written of these parallel stories:

> We embark on voyages not only to get somewhere but to accomplish something and, in Western culture, often to discover more about the ways human beings can expect to fare in the world. The epic voyages of Odysseus, Jason, and Aeneas were freighted with metaphor as well as adventure, and that characteristic has clung to voyage narratives ever since. In this sense voyages are a natural vehicle for the human imagination exploring the unknown, whether it be discovering strange new lands, finding out the truth about ourselves, or searching for those more perfect worlds we call utopias.

The notion that the sea is a school for life is represented also in the nautical imagery that we rely on to describe the highs and lows of living. Take the much anthologized advice to live adventurously that has been attributed to Samuel L. Clemens: "Throw off the bowlines, sail away from the safe harbor, catch the trade winds in your sails." Consider our stormy courtships, after which we sail onto the shoals of marriage where, should we avoid being flooded by emotions, we may succeed in weathering our troubles or, alas, may endure the shipwreck of a divorce, after which we struggle to tack safely away from despair's lee shore.

In John Newton's time, the image of the voyage of life was called on in the context of religion. Some of the best-known stories then were sea-deliverance narratives—moralistic, inspirational tales (like Luke's narrative of Paul's wreck) imposed on real-life storms and shipwrecks with the purpose of finding spiritual meaning in dire, brutal, otherwise hopeless tragedies. The idea was summarized in the title of a book written by an English Puritan in 1682: *Navigation Spiritualized*. American sea-deliverance narratives had titles such as *A Monumental Memorial of Marine Mercy* and *God's Wonders in the Great Deep*. Despite such titles, the authors did not leave everything to God. "Piety was no substitute for seamanship," observes Donald P. Wharton in his introduction to a collection of American colonial sea-deliverance narratives. Many such narratives contain detailed descriptions of navigation and ship handling. Still, these stories were not how-to manuals but inspirational books. The repeated theme is that we all are sailors in a stormy sea, and as we search for our harbor of refuge we peer around hopefully for evidence of kindness and protection. As John Newton wrote in one of his hymns,

> The gath'ring clouds, with aspect dark,
> A rising storm presage
> O! to be hid within the Ark,
> And shelter'd from its rage!

NEWTON'S CONVERSION in the storm was hardly perfect. In his day, unlike ours, people doubted quick change and the perfectability of human nature. If repentance was to be sure, it must be difficult and gradual. Although he no longer mocked religion after the storm, he still felt empty. "I soon began to feel that my heart was still hard and ungrateful to the God of my life." He once observed that faith and assurance are like an island that, though it disappears in the fog, is always reliably there across the water. "Thus it is with respect to many great truths, which you and I have seen with the eye of our minds. There may be returns of dark, misty hours when we can hardly perceive them, but these should not put us on questioning whether we ever saw them at all."

He expressed this idea of a good life as a struggle and a work in progress in another of the original six stanzas in "Amazing Grace":

Through many dangers, toils, and snares,
I have already come;
'Tis grace hath brought me safe thus far,
And grace will lead me home.

Returning from Ireland in 1748, Newton decided to get married. To establish a household, he needed quick cash, and to acquire it he went into the slave trade. After commanding slave ships for several years, he came ashore in 1755, his conscience still clear (although he later became a fervent abolitionist).

Around that time Newton began to speak in churches and at revivals about his storm and the conversion he had experienced in it. In 1764, at age thirty-nine, he was ordained a priest in the Church of England and put in charge of a church at Olney, a village of impoverished lacemakers about fifty miles north of London. Although unprepossessing in the extreme (another cleric referred to him as "one Mr. Newton, a little odd-looking man of the methodistical order, and without any clerical habit"), Newton won a reputation as a brilliant preacher. Meanwhile he started writing hymns. His next-door neighbor was the poet William Cowper, who suffered from a conscience so much more harshly self-reproachful than Newton's that he was on the verge of mental illness. To occupy his friend, Newton proposed that they write hymns for use in weekly services. Newton brought this wreck of a man into his home and tended to him, at one time experimenting with an early type of electric shock treatment. Under Newton's care, Cowper improved a little. His hymns exploiting storm imagery parallel "Amazing Grace" in tempestuous inspiration and hopeful devotion. Despite his better gifts as a poet (Cowper translated Homer), he remained more bleakly woeful than his friend. In the last poem he ever wrote, "The Castaway," there are these dreadful lines:

No voice divine the storm allay'd,
No light propitious shone;
When, snatched from all effectual aid,
We perish'd, each alone . . .

Unlike Cowper, Newton glimpsed all the light. "There was nothing about him dull or gloomy or puritanical, according to the common meaning of the term," said Newton's friend William Jay. "As he had much good nature, so he had much pleasantry, and frequently emitted sparks of lively wit, or rather humor." That vitality found its way into his hymns, which say much less about hell than about mercy and salvation. Over a period of nearly fifteen years, while laboring as a country parson in a town almost broken by poverty and disease, Newton wrote hymns at a rate of about one a week. When his collaboration with Cowper was published under the title *Olney Hymns* in 1779, it contained 348 hymns, 282 of them by Newton.

Many of Newton's hymns were commentaries on the weekly Bible lessons read in his church. The occasion for "Amazing Grace" was the Old Testament story of God's promise to David that he will head a ruling dynasty, to which the former shepherd boy humbly responds, "Who am I, O Lord God, and what is my house that thou hast brought me thus far?" (2 Sam. 7:18, 1 Chron. 17:16). Besides the Bible, Newton was inspired by contemporary events from which he drew highly imaginative, even playful, insights. When a moody lion came to Olney, probably as part of a traveling circus, he looked at the animal and saw himself and his limitations. His description of the lion episode in a letter to a friend in 1778 provides an insight into his long struggle against alienation that began in the storm:

> Last week we had a lion in town. I went to see him. He was wonderfully tame, as familiar with his keeper, and as docile and obedient as a spaniel; yet the man told me he had his surly fits, when they dare not touch him. No looking glass could express my face more justly than this lion did my heart. I could trace every feature. As wild and fierce by nature, yea, much more so, but grace has in some way tamed me. I know and love my Keeper, and sometimes watch His looks that I may learn His will. But, oh! I have my surly fits, too— seasons when I relapse into the savage again, as though I had forgotten all.

He added, "I got a hymn out of this lion."

After *Olney Hymns* was published, unrelated conflicts in his parish forced Newton to move to London, where he served at St. Mary Woolnoth Church. Newton was still preaching in his eighties, and still struggling with his conscience. To the end of his many days, he continued to refer to himself as "the old African blasphemer"—the man he was before his storm at sea.

10

The Ulysses Generation

in the Southern Ocean

"Beryl wanted to get out to sea, well out, and to have her storm."
—Miles Smeeton

THE PURIFYING TRIAL of a great storm has continued to be accepted, though generally not in the old form of testing one's relationship with God. With the rise of amateur adventuring in the twentieth century, the rewards of seafaring have come to be measured no more by conventional religious faith than by the dollar value of cargoes. Now the standard is the personal satisfaction of voluntarily taking on and (with skill and luck) completing voyages into waters whose danger makes them attractive. Jonathan Raban has reflected on this changing meaning of the sea, and he proposed an explanation in an interview in 1993: "The reason I think the sea has become the object of increasingly obsessive attention among lots and lots of people in the past twenty-five to fifty years, and even more in the last ten, has been that it *does* represent the last unfettered, untamed, undomesticated, and unpretty area of nature that we can know at first-hand." The sea is once again the Other World, separate from the compromised world of the land. But unlike the gentle preserving Other World where Percy Bysshe Shelley went to float passively, this one is a volatile setting where strivers go to test themselves and their vessels for ever higher stakes upon the deep.

I

BEFORE LOOKING at the adventurers of the "Ulysses generation," we should spend a moment with a recent vision of the sea in an apocalyptic setting. Long after the dangers it represented seemed to be eradicated, the sea has been regarded as an agent of Armageddon.

At the end of the New Testament there is a sublime vision of the perfect world that arrives when Satan is conquered and the New Jerusalem descends. "The former things have passed away," wrote the visionary in chapters 20 and 21 of the book known as the Apocalypse or the Book of Revelation. There is neither death nor mourning in the New Jerusalem, neither pain nor tears, neither night nor ugliness. All people who have been lost are found, for the sea and Hades give up their dead. In this new world, in fact, there is no sea. The deep is among the former things that disappear entirely, along with everything it signifies—storms, chaos, destruction, despair. Nowhere is the instinctive fear of the sea more clearly displayed than in the verse, "Then I saw a new heaven and a new earth; for the first heaven and the first earth had passed away, and the sea was no more" (Rev. 21:1).

When that stark vision of the end time is revisited by contemporary prophets, the setting usually is land, not the sea. But the deep sometimes plays a part. In a recent apocalyptic sea story that makes Newton's and Jonah's vigorous experiences seem pedestrian, the crew of the yacht *Heart Light* believed they were encountering the New Jerusalem when they were caught off New Zealand in June 1994 in the deadly Queen's Birthday storm (which occurred at the time of Queen Elizabeth II's official birthday). The storm certainly was apocalyptic in force. It lasted four days, with winds clocked as high as ninety knots and seas estimated to be as high as one hundred feet. On the face of it, *Heart Light*'s chances of survival were poor. A not-especially-well-prepared forty-one-foot cruising catamaran sailed by a not-especially-knowledgeable crew, she still survived through most of the storm, because her crew believed they were undergoing an apocalyptic experience of the kind envisioned in Revelation, and must survive it to ascent to the higher realm.

The boat was owned by Americans Darryl and Diviana Wheeler. Diviana was the driving force. A clairvoyant guided by an inner voice she called the Sage, she believed she had special spiritual and psychic powers that first came to her when she was taken aboard a spacecraft at age four. Although the Wheelers knew little about sailing and rarely steered their boat, leaving the helm to the electronic automatic pilot except when docking, they had succeeded in reaching New Zealand. There they took out passengers on what Diviana called "Creative Contact" cruises where she taught spiritual enlightenment. The boat was essential to this work because, as she wrote in her book about the storm, *Heart Light* enabled the Wheelers to carry clients and guests to remote places where there were no interfering electrical surges or what she called "people pollution." While the boat was well equipped for communication with spiritual powers— there was, for example, an inventory of crystal wands, one of which weighed sixty-five pounds—the Wheelers made no preparations for storm sailing other than to carry a drogue to slow the boat in big seas and an emergency position-indicating radio beacon, or EPIRB, so they could transmit an SOS over a long distance. Decisions about sailing schedules and boat checkups were often made after consulting the crystals, the *I Ching*, or messages from the Sage. The Wheelers, Diviana reported, confidently relied on "our guardian angels of destiny."

AS THE STORM OVERTOOK THEM, Diviana decided that it was a part of the Armageddon in which the higher forces of good were battling the forces of evil for world dominance. *Heart Light*, she was sure, was being pulled into the storm's center, an immense, glowing waterspout whose "vortex doorway" would open for a fluorescent green spaceship that would descend, gather up her family and boat, and take them to a higher realm. Bizarre as these convictions may seem, they provided sufficient motivation for the Wheelers to fight for their survival as they sailed toward the vortex doorway. Darryl steered for almost a day in conditions that could easily have capsized the boat had the crew given up and allowed her to lie ahull, drifting broadside to these seas. As Darryl struggled at the helm, with his son massaging his aching shoulders, Diviana was below communing with her spirits. (The son's wife, meanwhile, was perpetually seasick.) Though repeatedly hit by waves and suffering damage, *Heart Light* ran on.

When the captain of a nearby fishing vessel came on the radio and offered rescue, Diviana heard new instructions from the Sage advising that they could now abandon the boat because the doorway had been reached. Below her on the sea bottom was a submerged temple where the crystals belonged. From there they would send a spiritual beacon to the spaceships that would introduce the New Paradigm. A few hours later, the Wheelers were taken off by the fishing boat, which, to eliminate a hazard to navigation, rammed and sank *Heart Light*.

To say the least, this tale is extremely unusual. To say the best, it is proof of the doctrine that the most important ingredient in survival is to have a deeply held purpose and belief system, no matter how bizarre they may seem to outsiders, and to be guided by them with no distractions. As John Leach observes in *Survival Psychology*, "Long-term survival is a lonely state. It is a very personal struggle, and no one can take this burden from the victim." The best survival tool often is the human spirit.

II

IN THEIR UNUSUAL WAY, the Wheelers were storm chasers. While many other modern-day amateur voyagers are also storm chasers, they usually have constructed less elaborate reasons for their risky passages into the windy, wide-open Southern Ocean. That was the area Joseph Conrad was referring to when he remarked, "For a true expression of disheveled wildness, there is nothing like a gale in the bright moonlight of a high latitude."

Among the best known of these adventurers was William Albert Robinson, an American engineer who became entranced by the sea in the 1920s and sailed around the world alone in a thirty-two-foot ketch that he had bought for $1,000. Along the way, he became infatuated by Polynesia: "I fell victim to which might be called 'island disease,' or in this case, more specifically, 'Tahiti disease.' " He bought land in Tahiti, but he returned to

America and during the Second World War built submarine chasers and minesweepers in a shipyard in Ipswich, Massachusetts. After the war he sailed down to Tahiti in his seventy-foot brigantine *Varua* and settled ashore. His domestic period lasted five years until, as he wrote in his elegant memoir, *To the Great Southern Sea*, "I began to wake up and go and study the charts." Pushed by a vague force that he eventually identified as the urge to experience nature at its worst, he planned a voyage almost all the way to Cape Horn, and then up the Humboldt Current to the Galápagos before returning to Papeete.

He knew there would be strong winds, possibly gales, but what Robinson and his small crew of Polynesians, including his pregnant mistress, found some 1,500 miles west of the Horn was what he called "the ultimate storm." When his story ran under that title in *Sports Illustrated* in 1955, the world at large discovered the mysteries and excitements of chasing storms.

This brings up a crucial point about the amateur age of sail that succeeded the commercial age. Until the 1980s most adventurers who went out there did so because it was *there* and they could write about it. From Joshua Slocum on through Robinson, Bill Tilman, and Miles Smeeton, they were amateur sailors but professional authors. The reason we know so much about Robinson's storm in 1952 is that he wrote a book about it, as Smeeton did about the two gales that almost killed him five years later. There is no need, therefore, to speculate about *Varua*'s actions and her captain's feelings, as we must do to come to a satisfactory understanding of the wrecks of *Ariel* and the *Elizabeth*—even though, ironically, their victims included two of the best-known writers of their time, Percy Bysshe Shelley and Margaret Fuller. Other than sea-deliverance and other spiritual narratives by the likes of John Newton, the writing of the first great age of sail was typified by the remote tone of log entries. But the second age of sail comes to us in the intimate voices of sailors who wrote for a general audience—and were engaged in exploring two parallel realities, one internal and the other exterior.

FOR AMATEUR SAILORS, the Southern Ocean that William Albert Robinson set out on is what the Mediterranean Sea was to Jonah—the pathway to the place of ultimate escape. The difference was that Jonah sailed to try to escape *from* something, while the Ulysses generation of post–Second

World War sailors was drawn *toward* something. What that was they could not always say precisely, other than describing an itch to go places under conditions of sufficient "hard and dangerous endeavor" to please Theodore Roosevelt and the other true believers in the strenuous life.

If the Southern Ocean could possibly have been created for any human end, it was to make a home for such people. A wide band of open water in the far southern regions of the Atlantic, Indian, and Pacific Oceans, it lies between forty-five degrees south and Antarctica and rings the globe unimpeded except by the lower regions of South America near Cape Horn. Because there is little land in the way, it has a reputation for predictability and regularity, but in fact it is broken up by weather fronts as much as it is by icebergs and growlers. Descriptions of the region often sound like entries in "Believe It or Not." To quote one old captain, William H. S. Jones, "It is strange, but true, in the high southern latitudes, where seas can be 50 feet high and 2,000 feet long, they roll forward in endless procession with occasionally one sea of abnormal size towering above the others, its approach visible for a considerable distance."

Strange, and also remote and impersonal. Other than a few mountaintops, the Southern Ocean is the world's last sparsely populated territory of storms, bleakness, and solitary misery. To gain a closer, more intimate view of this vast, risky place, there is no better source today than the Internet, where around-the-world racing sailors record their observations in e-mail messages sent back home to their commercial sponsors and the media. In 2001 and 2002, three around-the-world races carried more than a dozen boats and two hundred sailors into the Southern Ocean for weeks at a time.

"Brother is it wet," reported Grant Dalton, a Southern Ocean veteran, from east of Cape Town in mid-November 2001, during the Volvo Around-the-World Race for sixty-foot racing sloops. "It would be impossible for the boat to be any wetter. We bail it (literally) every two hours maximum and the water just pours over the deck. This is not your average heavy spray, more walls of white water which eventually penetrate through everything and through all of this the boat continues to thunder along, now under small spinnaker in a confused sea." That same day another skipper, John Kostecki, reported "the biggest iceberg I have ever seen, eight stories high—maybe even eight mast heights high. It looked like Table Mountain in the Southern Ocean."

The cold and winds make sail handling aboard these boats as demand-ing as it was on the old-time square-riggers. "We had need of every finger God had given us," Richard Henry Dana Jr. wrote in 1840 about a trip aloft near Cape Horn during his two years before the mast. In 2001 Knut Frostad, of *Djuice*, reported from the Southern Ocean:

> Changing headsails in more than 40 knots is probably the most difficult and dangerous change we have. Six guys hooked on with safety lines on the bow, trying to pull down and in the old jib. The boat is still logging up to 20 knots and suddenly a wave washes the bow, pushing the six big guys back at high speed. Then they crawl forward and start all over again pulling the jib in. Soaking wet but still smiling we crawl back together in the cockpit.

From a competing boat, *Illbruck*, Mark Christensen complained, "There is so much water, on deck, downstairs, in my clothes, in my sleeping bag. I tell myself that it is okay; at the speed we are going I won't have to put up with it for as long. But it is still difficult climbing out of wet clothes and into a wet bunk."

That is and was the Southern Ocean at its worst.

THE IMPRESSION THAT SUCH CONDITIONS are permanent—immense breaking seas and steady gale-force west winds running unvaryingly around the globe—is mistaken. Deep depressions roll down the Southern Ocean every few days "like a series of bowling balls gyrating around the world," according to meteorologist and sailor Bill Biewenga. These fronts bring heavy, shifting winds that churn up extremely confused seas, full of rogue waves. The sequence was laid out in February 2001 in a series of daily e-mail reports by a gifted writer and sailor, Cam Lewis, who was racing a 110-foot catamaran around the world.

"The Southern Cross is right on top of us with a million stars," he reported on February 23, 2001. "It's clear, but clouds and moisture are rolling in. My nose is tickled by the incoming humidity." His weather sense was correct, as he noted a day later:

> The smooth sailing of the last couple of days is now a distant memory. The sunshine and full sails are history. We jibed onto port over 30 hours ago and the wind has slowly been building. It has gone through a wide arc all the way to the north and northeast and now back again into the northwest. Sails have slowly been reduced to just three reefs in the main and no headsail and

the forecast is bleak. We will have more of this—30, 40, maybe even 50 knots of wind for a few days, maybe longer. Cape Horn lies 2,100 miles ahead and it looks like it will live up to its reputation as a hard place to pass by unscathed. . . . I very much look forward to getting out of this misnamed Pacific Ocean, past the Falklands and well on our way north up the Atlantic.

Even the wildlife knew something was up: "The birds have felt this low coming and have gone to Bora Bora ahead of us. Yesterday I only saw one albatross and the further we go into the middle of the Pacific and the further from dry land we get, the less birds we will see until we close in on the Chilean coast. It's still a long, bumpy road and we will have to continue with respect and caution. Time to go and get wet, it's my watch."

Two days later: "Wind 35 knots to as high as 67 knots, waves about the same height in feet as wind is in strength if you measure the faces top to bottom." The seas, Lewis said, were "liquid Himalayas." Although he was racing, Lewis was forced to slow down: "My self-preservation instinct kicking in. Thank God for that! You can surf most of them most of the time, but sometimes down here they are such big waves it is just too scary." He added: "If you want to pass the Horn, you have to play the game."

Many veterans of the Southern Ocean say less about the atrocious weather than about the mood of this frontier region, which usually seemed empty of other vessels even in the great age of commercial sail before the opening of what the seafarer-writer Allan Villiers called "the last sail-banisher" and "that Horn-banisher," the Panama Canal.

A few mariners do not mind the loneliness. Once Joshua Slocum cleared the South American coast and was out in the Pacific, "Then was the time to uncover my head, for I sailed alone with God. The vast ocean was again around me, and the horizon was unbroken by land." But he was an exception. To most people the Southern Ocean feels like solitary confinement. Not even the cranky single-handed sailor Francis Chichester was comfortable in the high latitudes, which he characterized as "a great void" that "made for intense loneliness, and a feeling of hopelessness." It is chaotic and so intensely lonely that on a wretched night watch off the Horn, Conrad found himself surprised by the comfort rendered by the mere voice of a shipmate he otherwise disliked. "It is, after all, the human voice that stamps the mark of human consciousness upon the character of a gale."

~

As WILLIAM ALBERT ROBINSON sailed down from Tahiti into the Southern Ocean, tracking the passage on the chart in what he called "the little necklace" of his noon positions, he also ruminated on the emptiness of the great southern sea. Comparing this passage with his previous ones, he would write:

> There had been the solitude before, on the other voyages, but never the out-of-this-world solitude of the Southern Ocean. For six weeks we had been where ships no longer pass, starkly aware of the complete interdependence of our little group of five souls—six according to Ah You's count—and *Varua*. As long as we did everything right we were all right; or should have been, for chance and fate are also to be reckoned with. It was reasonable to think of leaving one's bones in some warm tropical sea, to be stirred now and then perhaps by a tropical cyclone or brushed by the passing shadow of some gay young circumnavigator—but down in this dismal gray remoteness, chilled by the drifting Antarctic ice, was no place to die.

His unease became real fear when he was enveloped in "the ultimate storm." "Anything I had previously seen was child's play compared with what was in store for us during the next 48 hours." The seas heaving on top of the normal high rollers were so immense that they blanketed his sails. Like all good storm writers, Robinson had the ability to stand both inside and outside himself simultaneously, to be both vulnerable and strong while noting fine details and taking in the immense seascape. Here is *Varua* running under lashed helm in "real gale winds" some 1,500 miles west of Cape Horn:

> Nothing was said, but all of us gathered that evening in the saloon. The ship underwent increasingly violent gyrations, and had that cello-like tremble throughout that goes with real gale winds. Through the cabin windows— buried deep one moment, carving great arcs across the sky the next—we caught a glimpse now and then of the growing moon, momentarily visible between flying clouds. I could not help thinking, as I felt the seas crash outside, of the fragile fabric that made up this small ship—man and his little toy—pitted against what was outside. What was more vulnerable, what more dependent upon each individual part? I turned on the radio to drown out the noise of the storm and surprisingly it functioned perfectly. We listened to South American music. We made jokes about South American weather, and laughed too loudly at our jokes.

Modern-day yachts in the Southern Ocean follow in the wake of the old commercial vessels, like this square-rigger, thought to be the bark *Garthsnaid* rounding the Horn in 1924, in a photograph attributed to H. Ibbetson. As Richard Henry Dana Jr. said about a trip aloft in a Southern Ocean gale during his two years before the mast, "We had need of every finger God had given us." (Courtesy Peabody Essex Museum, Salem, Massachusetts)

Such jovial denial is familiar to storm veterans. After the 1979 Fastnet gale blew through, our crew energetically kept themselves entertained, knowing full well that men had died out there.

Robinson thought the storm had peaked, and said as much in his log, but he was wrong. He laid out thick lines as drogues astern to slow *Varua* and ordered his crew to pump dense fish oil out through the toilet to create a calming slick. Robinson steered for more than twelve hours in a wind so strong that it blew even the heavy oil ahead of the vessel on the curl of the breaking seas. He chose to run with his vessel's stern to the seas. The alternative would have been fatal, as Richard Henry Dana Jr. made clear in *Two Years before the Mast* when he noted that only the most gifted helmsmen could steer upwind in such conditions. "It requires a good deal of skill and watchfulness to steer a vessel close-hauled, in a gale of wind, against a heavy sea," Dana reported. "A little carelessness in letting her ship a heavy sea might sweep the decks, or take a mast out of her." The rule was "ease her when she pitches": when waves appear, luff her up a little to spill wind and slow the boat—again, easier said than done, especially in the black of night when the first sign of a big wave is a roar.

Robinson steered in the dark in a sea filled with "white phosphorescent avalanches that I felt towering over my head astern but did not see until they burst down on us and swept by on either side." As the wind rose to hurricane strength, most of the shrieking ended, leaving a "hollow booming that reverberated through the night" as the waves roared past. Robinson remained confident but anxious. "All deep-water sailors feel opposing emotions about the sea," he would write. "Love and hate—even fear—all play their part. Never, before this voyage, had I felt the threat of the sea so acutely; never had my love of the sea been so seriously threatened by the opposing emotions."

Naturally enough, Robinson found himself meditating on what he was doing out in this tempest. In time he decided that the prospect of a storm like this was exactly why he had left Tahiti and headed this far south. He felt that he had been called to the Southern Ocean, not by this storm in particular but by the *idea* of storms, much the way he was called to Tahiti. "Tahiti was not so much a place as an idea," he wrote of the Polynesian island that haunted him when he first visited in 1929—"a dream of the individual who came seeking something that may or may not have existed

William Albert Robinson, shown here during his earlier circumnavigation, sailed into the Southern Ocean in 1951 in search of an "ultimate storm." He found that storm—rather, it found him—and it quickly surrounded him with "white phosphorescent avalanches that I felt towering over my head astern." (Courtesy Peabody Essex Museum, Salem, Massachusetts)

in fact but was firmly entrenched in legend." Similarly, he was seeking the legend of the Cape Horn storm.

It took his mistress, Ah You, to reduce the storm from abstract belief to concrete experience: "It is as if I had been to war. I never thought I would be so brave."

Varua survived with no serious damage and sailed up the west coast of South America. After the baby was born in Panama, the vessel returned to Tahiti, where Robinson and Ah You raised an ever-larger family of daughters and he engaged himself in combating elephantiasis (which affected many Tahitians) and researching Polynesian history. *Varua* took more long voyages—to Samoa, Thailand, and Hawaii—but Robinson did not return to the Southern Ocean or again place himself in the path of the legend of the storm.

III

ROBINSON WAS A MEMBER of a generation of amateur adventurers who were born between about 1900 and 1920 and who set out after the Second World War to cross seas and climb mountains, finding in strenuous, dangerous adventure a modern-day version of William James's "moral equivalent of war." The prototype of these men and women was Homer's hero Ulysses (Odysseus in Greek), who found plenty of adventures as he slowly returned home from the Trojan War. The Ulysses example has been held up by many people, most influentially in print by the poet Alfred, Lord Tennyson. About 1840, he reworked the story of the Greek wanderer in a poem he titled "Ulysses."

Like *The Odyssey*, the poem has a battler's aggressive forward tilt, though in this case he fights not one-eyed giants but old age and boredom. Though in retirement in Ithaca, he is still restless: "I cannot rest from travel; I will drink / Life to the lees." Famous "for always roaming with a hungry heart," he is "a part of all that I have met." Thinking he has one quest left to him, he calls to his old shipmates,

> . . . Come, my friends.
> 'Tis not too late to seek a newer world.
> Push off, and sitting well in order smite
> The sounding furrows; for my purpose holds

To sail beyond the sunset, and the baths
Of all the western stars, until I die.

His and his crew's bodies are no longer strong, but their solidarity will carry them forward, as he promises in the final lines:

One equal temper of heroic hearts,
Made weak by time and fate, but strong in will
To strive, to seek, to find, and not to yield.

Tennyson's "Ulysses" usually is inaccurately read as a call to unusual, solitary, and quixotic physical activity, and for that reason it has acquired an extremely broad range of admirers. Edward Rowe Snow, the athletic storm-chasing chronicler of New England epics and sea disasters whom we met in chapter 5, remarked that "Ulysses" best explained his philosophy of life. In late 2001 Ulysses' call, "Come, my friends. 'Tis not too late to seek a newer world," could be found as an epigram on the Internet sites of the Jet Propulsion Laboratory's Mission to Saturn and of Mystress Angelique Serpent, a dominatrix and self-described "spiritual teacher."

They missed the point. The poem is less about the sweat of vigorous solitary exertion than about the ideal of community. Ulysses is "a part of all that I have met." Tennyson wrote the poem to honor the death of one of his closest friends; the poem, he explained, "gave my feeling about the need of going forward, and braving the struggle of life." There is evidence that he was correct to stress human connection. Psychologists have found that what keeps men alive is not a wistful hope for future heroic activity but a healthy sense of both community and compromise. Reforging old relationships is especially valuable. "Our lives become the sum of all whom we have loved," says a psychoanalyst who has conducted lifelong studies of men. "It is important not to waste anyone."

THE EXAMPLE OF ULYSSES also was called upon by the English writer J. R. L. Anderson to help explain the burst of adventuring after the Second World War. In *The Ulysses Factor*, published in 1970, Anderson considered the lives of 124 twentieth-century adventurers from Slocum on. Writing in a period when grand theorizing was in vogue, Anderson hypothesized that these men shared several aptitudes and values, including physical and emotional courage, coping skills, competence, self-discipline, self-sufficiency, endurance, restlessness, and ruthless commitment to getting the job done *now*. When Ernest Shackleton told his wife, "Sometimes I think I am no good at anything but being away in the wilds just with men," he was expressing many of those values, and especially the last one. (When she learned he had died in the Antarctic, she sent instructions to bury him there.)

Anderson described these efforts as self-centered, but not merely so. "There is some factor in man, some form of special adaptation, which prompts a few individuals to exploits which, however purposeless they may seem, are of value to the survival of the race." It is an elitist argument and one that can be racist, yet it strikes to the core of why a William Albert Robinson would sail into the Southern Ocean hoping for a storm.

Adventuring for its own sake became popular in two activities—amateur sailing and mountain climbing—around 1900. What Anderson said of one sport rings true for the other: "Mountaineering was invented as an end in itself, the achievement of a summit a goal as compelling as the quest in other ages for a route to India." The pairing of mountains and the sea seemed natural, given the crowding on the world's flatlands. The spirit of the Ulysses generation came to be expressed in a statement by the English mountain climber George Mallory. Asked why he wanted to climb Mount Everest, he replied, "because it is there." Whether he offered this out of conviction or exasperation at being asked about his motives one time too many, his reply has reverberated in popular culture ever since he said it in 1923, a year before he died on Everest. Mallory elaborated on his motivation:

> The first question which you will ask and which I must try to answer is this, "What is the use of climbing Mount Everest?" and my answer must at once be, "It is no use." . . . So, if you cannot understand that there is something in man which responds to the challenge of this mountain and goes out to meet it, that the struggle is the struggle of life itself upward and forever upward, then you won't see why we go. What we get from this adventure is just sheer joy. And joy is, after all, the end of life. We do not live to eat and make money. We eat and make money to be able to enjoy life. That is what life means and what life is for.

It is the line "because it is there" that is most identified with adventure to implausible places. After the circumnavigator Miles Smeeton and his wife Beryl rounded Cape Horn on their third attempt—after twice being capsized and almost killed—he titled his book *Because the Horn Is There*. Thirty years later, in his superb book about modern single-handed racing, *Godforsaken Sea*, Derek Lundy asked the French sailor Catherine Chabaud why she chose in 1996 to race across the Southern Ocean—"the outback of the world," Lundy nicely called it—and around Cape Horn. She answered: "It's my Everest. When you like sailing, you want to go to its Everest—to sail in the South, to sail to Cape Horn."

SOME OF THE BEST-KNOWN FIGURES in the Ulysses generation tended to be soldiers and sailors and also mountaineers. Harold William Tilman, between and after fighting ably in two world wars, rode a bicycle across Africa in fifty-six days, spent a decade climbing in the Himalaya (leading a nearly successful assault on Everest), and, after buying his first boat at age fifty-six, devoted two decades to sailing to remote mountain ranges for climbing expeditions. His approach was even more casual than that of the owners of *Heart Light*. He headed out in creaky, damp old pilot cutters with ancient equipment and pickup crews of college students who usually knew even less about sailing than he did. Yet his fifteen breezily written books testify to remarkable self-confidence. For example, take his explanation of why he sailed to southern Chile: "A region such as this has an irresistible attraction for a mountaineer who, late in life, catches sea fever and aspires to making an ocean voyage in his own boat."

Only Bill Tilman could make a cold cruise to Patagonia in a fifty-year-old pilot cutter in order to climb ten thousand feet into a glacier and make it sound like walking down to the corner for the morning paper. His loose detachment from the obvious rigors became associated with other British adventurers as well as with Americans who, like Tilman, were addicted to going where nobody else went, which usually meant venturing into unfamiliar regions, many of them around ice. Tilman kept at it well into his old age. In 1977 his boat disappeared while sailing to the Falkland Islands.

IV

IF BILL TILMAN HAD A MANTRA, it was "we preferred the unknown to the known." If his friends Beryl and Miles Smeeton had one, it was "put on your boots and go." Among the leading figures of the postwar Ulysses generation, this wife-and-husband couple of mountaineer-sailors remained in motion for four decades. We will end our exploration of the ways storms strike and people respond with the near disasters they experienced in the Southern Ocean.

Any discussion of the Smeetons must begin with Beryl, if only because that was the way Miles wanted it. Whatever it takes to deal with stress in horrible conditions, Beryl Boxer Smeeton had it. "A gutsy independent woman who refused to conform to anything" (in the words of a friend), she came from a rugged breed. When she was born in Dorset, England, in 1905, it was considered a mark of accomplishment that of her father's four male blood relations, only one had died in his own bed. The sea and illness at foreign stations had snatched away the other three. A decade later the ratio became one out of five when her father was shot to shreds on the Western Front. By her twentieth birthday, she was demonstrating a tendency toward following "a relentless stream of self-imposed challenges" (to quote her and her husband's biographer, Miles Clark). In due course she traveled alone by horseback and foot through four continents, including spending six months hiking and riding through lower South America. When the Smeetons settled down for a while on a primitive island farm in western Canada, she said she loved the experience because it had "a feeling of exhilaration, a feeling of battle," like mountains and boats in the Southern Ocean.

"Living with Beryl has been one long struggle for survival," half-joked Miles Smeeton, who exercised a lighter touch. He once predicted that should a flying saucer ever appear before them, he, "distrustful and suspicious," would hide behind a bush while Beryl would instantly climb aboard, and off she would go. She was determined to the point of forcefulness, harder edged, hot tempered—in sum, the more traditionally "masculine" member of the pair. He was the softer one: humorous, impulsive, and flirtatious. Not that he was unimposing or lacked fire. An acquaintance said of him, "He's like Odysseus." More accurately, he was like Odysseus' creator, Homer, who understood the full range of the adventurer's situation and character.

In fact, Miles was a poet with a taste that ran more to whimsy than to epics. When cruising he often wrote funny rhymes that he mailed to his daughter and granddaughters. Some concerned humorous if slightly threatening alligators who appear in odd places—airplanes, balloons, and even a sailing yacht, where they sit around, talk about what's new in the world, and shell peas for alligator stew. A small collection of these poems,

Alligator Tales (and Crocodiles Too!), was on the best-seller list for children's books in 2001.

Beryl supplied the fuel and Miles the oxygen for their torch. When Beryl saw a wild sea, her tendency was to instantly dive into it. When he saw one, he explored it. Together they shared a spirit that, for example, caused them to use a hunting horn as a foghorn and to search for experiences that, in the spirit of playing the game, provided the full-hearted sense of risk and independence that they both coveted like life itself. When presented with the possibility of sailing around Cape Horn at age sixty, Miles was exhilarated: "I could swing once more on that rope of youthful enjoyment and adventure that had supported us through thirty years of excitement and vicissitudes, whose strands were wearing a bit thin but which would surely support us a little longer." To that they added a complete sense of independence. Because they had promised that they would never call for assistance should they be in trouble, lest their calls risk the lives of other mariners, they did not carry radio transmitters.

THE SIX FOOT SEVEN Yorkshire-born soldier met up with Beryl—"with her slim figure and long mountaineer's stride"—in the 1930s in India, where he was in the army. She left her husband for him, and they embarked on a permanent adventure largely stimulated by her whim. "Her love of adventure smolders within her like an eternal flame," he would write lovingly. Together they climbed to 23,000 feet with the Sherpa Tenzing (Sir Edmund Hillary's guide on Everest), and one or both of them eventually left a footprint on every continent. After the war, during which he served with great distinction and was wounded, they emigrated from England to Canada (in large part owing to their distaste for socialism) and acquired the island farm in British Columbia. In 1951 the Smeetons bought a cruising sailboat in England with the sole purpose of using it to circumvent currency restrictions that barred their taking money to Canada. Their scheme was to buy the boat with their English assets and sell her in Canada on arrival.

First they had to select a good vessel—a task for which they were pretty much disqualified by their total ignorance of boats. Their first choice was a Norwegian pilot boat, like the ones Erling Tambs had sailed in the thirties. This boat appealed to them because she had run spies in and out of Norway and still carried a bullet in her mast. The owner decided not to sell after all, and they ended up with a forty-six-foot Chinese-built teak ketch named *Tzu Hang* (the name combines the name of the Chinese goddess who protects seafarers with a word meaning a family or community). Their first passage was a sequence of disasters that Miles Smeeton, with his healthy sense of humor and humility, considered a proper lesson. "It was as if the sea was determined to keep me in my place," he mused—"the right place for a beginner, a newcomer to the domain." Delivering *Tzu Hang* to Canada, they found that they liked this domain. It struck them as a far saner life than the one they found ashore in most places, which Miles described in his books as messy Dickensian circuses. Within the next fifteen years the Smeetons logged more than 130,000 miles in *Tzu Hang*, including a circumnavigation of the globe.

THEIR GREATEST ADVENTURE occurred in 1957 when they sailed *Tzu Hang* from Australia across the Southern Ocean with the intention of satisfying Beryl's goal of rounding Cape Horn. With them was John Guzzwell, a survivor of a Nazi detention camp who was taking a leave from his single-handed circumnavigation in a twenty-footer. There also was a cat named Pwe and, if not all the comforts of a Victorian home, at least many of them. At Beryl's insistence, no matter how rough the sea was they always had afternoon tea with a bit of fudge or another sweet she had made. ("Their boat was a private island of old-fashioned High Toryism," Jonathan Raban aptly observed in his introduction to a new edition of Miles's classic, *Once Is Enough*.)

While those who have not sailed long distances may picture the world of an offshore yacht as chaotic and uncomfortable, in fact it is highly structured and orderly, especially in a well-prepared vessel under a competent crew with a minimum of egotism, like *Tzu Hang* and her three sailors. The appeals of such a life transcend the limits of the word "adventure." Watches and meals fall at set hours, there are established routines for every action, and all enjoy plenty of time and opportunity for sleep, reading, and reflection. Miles described another voyage this way: "We were isolated from the past and from the future and enjoying to the full the present moment, as if there was something added, an extra spice of life."

TZU HANG'S PASSAGE east through the Southern Ocean in early 1957 is blissful, with the three sailors and the cat getting along perfectly. Progress is slow in easterly headwinds until six weeks out, when a westerly gale socks in. Miles will remember the view and the fear it arouses:

The sea was a wonderful sight. It was as different from an ordinary rough sea as a winter's landscape is from a summer one, and the thing that impressed me most was that its general aspect was white. . . . I had seen it before, but this moving surface, driving low across a sea all lined and furrowed with white, this was something new to me, and something frightening, and I felt exhilarated with the atmosphere of strife. I have felt this feeling before on a mountain, or in battle, and I should have been warned. It is apt to mean trouble.

Looking at the same breakers, their top fifteen feet all white, John Guzzwell hopes that none of them will swipe *Tzu Hang*.

At 9:00 in the morning on a stormy Southern Ocean Saint Valentine's Day in 1957, nine hundred miles west of the Horn in a wild westerly gale and immense heaving seas, Beryl relieves Miles at the helm. As he climbs down the companionway ladder, he is distressed that he must close the hatch behind him to keep water from coming into the cabin. It is a matter of community: "I didn't want to leave her and to shut the hatch on her, and cut her off from us below."

A little while later, Beryl looks astern over her shoulder, and seeing no horizon, believes she has somehow lost her sight. Then she realizes what is happening. "The whole horizon was blotted out by a huge gray wall. It stretched in a dead straight wall from horizon to horizon." Water pours down the wall's vertical face as it advances on the ketch. The great wave lifts *Tzu Hang*'s stern and hurls it over her bow in a violent somersault. Beryl flies to the end of her lifeline, which snaps when she comes up hard, and she tumbles overboard. She is many yards away when the ketch—missing her rig, her superstructure, and everything else that was above deck—eventually bobs upright.

John Guzzwell is below changing film in his movie camera. "I had a sudden feeling that something terrible was happening," he will recall. "Then everything was blackness and solid water hit me. I was conscious of a roaring sound and that we were already very deep." He fights against the water pouring down and climbs up through one of the holes where the cabin once was. His immediate thought is of other people. "What a bloody shame!" he thinks. "No one will ever know what happened to us." Looking aft he finds Beryl in the white water under a blue sky. She is in a bright yellow slicker that is red with the blood pouring down her face. Distancing himself from the horror of the moment, Guzzwell reflects that right now it would be good to have color film in his camera.

"Living with Beryl has been one long struggle for survival," Miles Smeeton *(left)* half-joked about his remarkable wife. Here they are in the cabin of their ketch *Tzu Hang* with their daughter Clio and their shipmate John Guzzwell before heading out from Australia to Cape Horn in 1956. (Reprinted with permission of Clio Smeeton)

Beryl Smeeton at the helm, enjoying the storm a few minutes before *Tzu Hang* pitchpoled west of Cape Horn. (John Guzzwell)

The old soldier is below, reading, when the boat somersaults and heaves him out of his bunk. Up to his waist in water, struggling to control his terror for his ship and his wife, Miles Smeeton also has one of those out-of-body experiences that, in a crisis, provide a bit of psychic padding around our sanity:

> When I am angry, or stupid and spoiled, or struggling and in danger, or in distress, there is a part of me which seems to disengage from my body, and to survey the scene with a cynical distaste. Now that I was afraid, this other half seemed to see myself struggling through all the floating debris, and to hear a distraught voice crying, "Oh God, where's Bea, where's Bea?"

He scrambles on deck and spots Beryl many yards away, high above him on the face of another wave. She seems to be smiling.

Despite her crushed vertebra, fractured ribs, and head injury, Beryl swims to the wildly rolling, half-sunk boat and reaches up as Miles reaches down. Unable to lift her, he calls for assistance. Guzzwell at this moment is thinking that their situation is so appallingly hopeless that it would be better if he and Miles just jumped in along with Beryl. Yet he goes to Miles and they hoist her on deck.

As Beryl struggles for breath, the two men speak quietly:

"Well, this is it, Miles," Guzzwell says.

"Yes, it looks like it, John."

Miles can only assume that his vessel is sinking. Yet when the next great sea rolls in, *Tzu Hang* lifts to it. "We've got a chance," he shouts.

Beryl says, "I know where the buckets are."

THEY BAILED FOR HOURS, covered the gaping hatches with sails, nibbled on what food they could discover, retrieved the soaking wet, terrified cat, and talked through the capsize. Beryl, self-conscious because she had been steering, worried that if they ever got to land and people learned a woman had been at the helm, she would be blamed for allowing the boat to broach. Miles would hear nothing of this: "If they know you, they'll say that's how they know we didn't broach, and, anyway, we didn't: we just went wham. Let's leave it."

And then they slept. Beryl, though badly injured and unable to move about much, awoke first and got the stove going to make tea. As they bailed until satisfied that the hull was sound, she asked what it looked like outside the cocoon of the boat, with sails now covering the holes left by its broken hatches. To tease her, Miles described the scene as like that in Frank Bramley's sentimental painting *A Hopeless Dawn*, showing women weeping over the loss of their men at sea.

There was, in fact, no sentimentality at all in Beryl Smeeton. "The whole of Beryl's life had been a comprehensive preparation for this moment," Miles Clark wrote in his dual biography, "and there can be little doubt that she was the most determined to live." Miles Smeeton knew it too. His *Once Is Enough*, though ostensibly a narrative of this remarkable adventure, reads more like a long love letter to this even more remarkable woman. In it he recalled how a Chilean friend described her as *"qué buena compañera"*—a term of old chivalry that any old soldier would like because it suggests so much more than a domestic relationship. "There was a flavor of buccaneers and swords about the Spanish words," Miles recalled pleasurably.

THE RECOVERY WAS METHODICAL. Guzzwell, a master carpenter, fashioned a rudder and masts to substitute for the ones that had broken. Eventually they were able to set enough sail to bring *Tzu Hang* up to three knots as she sailed toward Chile. They would look back on these slow days at sea when they improvised their survival as a time of profound intimacy and trust. "There was a wonderful feeling of comradeship between the three of us," remembered Guzzwell. "We all realized that without the other two we would never have survived, and though we all wanted to get into Coronel, I think we all realized that we would never be this close again."

Eighty-seven days out of Melbourne, they pierced the coastal fog and found their way into a port near Concepción, which Beryl had visited during her Andean hiking days.

Over the next eight months they set *Tzu Hang* to rights in a Chilean naval base where, to the amazement of this couple who prided themselves on their independence, assistance was proffered everywhere. Guzzwell was there for much of that time before he departed to attend to his family and continue his circumnavigation.

Once *Tzu Hang* was seaworthy, a hard decision presented itself. Should they sail home to England the easy way or along the challenging route? There were excellent reasons for riding up to Panama on the Humbolt Current, transiting the canal, and sailing to England in relative peace. Miles

According to Beryl Smeeton, the wave that tossed *Tzu Hang* was like this one. Such monsters are not limited to the Southern Ocean; this photograph was taken from another vessel in the North Atlantic. "It was as different from an ordinary rough sea as a winter's landscape is from a summer one," Miles said of that seascape, "and the thing that impressed me most was that its general aspect was white." (Courtesy Steve Dashew)

Miles Smeeton re-created *Tzu Hang*'s pitchpole in these sketches. Although the crew trailed a drogue to slow her as she came down the face of the wave, the heavy yacht still somersaulted like a bathtub toy. (Reprinted with permission of Clio Smeeton)

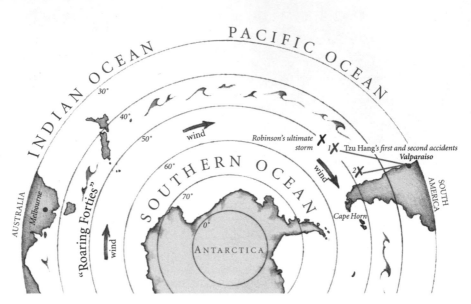

The only deep that circles the globe, the storm-filled Southern Ocean was described by Sir Francis Chichester, the single-handed sailor, as "a great void" that "made for intense loneliness, and a feeling of hopelessness." It has become the arena for some of the most adventurous sailing.

thought that was too tame. He wanted enough risk to ease his anxiety about heavy weather before fear got the better of him. His preference was to cruise south in Chile's protected channels as far as possible, then sprint to the Straits of Magellan. That seemed risky enough, what with the sailing directions for Patagonia promising "almost perpetual rain, thick weather, strong gales; heavy williwaws which must be felt to be believed. . . . Hailstorms and snow flurries even in summer," plus waterspouts. Although he sensed that Beryl shared his concern, the subject came up only belatedly because, he believed, they both were a little embarrassed to admit, at their age, that they wanted to do something because it frightened them.

The ship's warrior had a riskier plan. "Beryl wanted to get out to sea, well out, and to have her storm"—this even though she was recovering from dysentery. And so in early December 1957, *Tzu Hang* headed back into the Southern Ocean and worked her way south against the prevailing headwinds and current. Her two-person crew was at less than peak confidence. Beryl, recovering from her illness, spent long days below, reading with Pwe in her lap. Miles started out feeling nervous and unprepared. At the first sign of heavy weather they doused sails and lay ahull for a while "to reassure ourselves of *Tzu Hang*'s behavior," Miles wrote, knowing full well that his readers would understand that his concern extended beyond the ketch's behavior to his own.

Eleven days out, the barometer dropped 1.7 inches (fifty-eight millibars) in twenty-four hours. The glass was still falling on Christmas Day 1957 as, running before a force 7 gale, they opened their presents from their daughter in England and their friends in Chile. Outside the cabin there were portents of something very serious. Miles described them in mythological terms: "Somewhere to the northwest a dark monster was brooding, sending his messengers on before with the news of his coming, so that his shadow already seemed to brood over the sea, and the ragged clouds came flying, and the sea's long swell came rolling, to tell us that the danger which had threatened for several days was approaching now."

The storm blew for ten hours as *Tzu Hang* lay ahull. When the wave hit, Miles was below thinking of making tea and anticipating that it was about time for the storm to fade. "Almost as I thought this, *Tzu Hang* heeled steeply over, heeled over desperately into a raging blackness, and everything within me seemed to rebel against this fate. All my mind was saying, 'Oh no, not again! Not again!'" Rolled upside down, *Tzu Hang* came up half full of water but in somewhat better shape than the first time. Miles found himself declaring, "By God, we've done it once and we'll do it again!" and became so embarrassed at mouthing words so trite that it took him a moment to discover that Beryl was already hard at work hauling out a sail to tie over the hole left by a broken hatch. As they moved about the boat, making good on the painful lessons they had learned ten months before after the first disaster, Miles sensed that John Guzzwell was still working beside him. Under another jury rig, they worked their way back to Chile.

This time they sent *Tzu Hang* by ship to England, where she was resurrected once again. Ten years later, after a long circumnavigation, *Tzu Hang* and the Smeetons headed toward Cape Horn for the third time, this time from the east. Miles speculated that they were propelled by "something in our blood." This time they made it.

THE OLD TENSION between the preserver and the destroyer went on because it always had and always will.

Before the first accident, as *Tzu Hang* was happily sailing across the Southern Ocean toward Cape Horn—as the ketch, in Miles's Homeric phrasing, "seemed to be singing a wild saga of high adventure"—Beryl initiated a debate about the nature of this immense cold, rough sea on which they were staking their lives.

"Not the cruel sea," she said. "The sea is impersonal. I don't see how you can call it cruel. It's the people who are apt to be cruel. I don't think that you would call mountains or the sea cruel. It's only that we are so small and ineffective against them, and when things go wrong we start blaming them and calling them cruel." Yet nobody, she went on, should ever claim to have conquered a mountain or the sea, no matter how great the struggle to reach the top or a distant shore.

Miles broke in. "You wouldn't like the sea if there wasn't an almost continual struggle."

By "you" he meant Beryl and himself, and he might have named most of the men and women in these pages. Very likely, he would have included a great many of us, too.

Appendix

Storm Strategy and Tactics

Although this book is not a seamanship manual, some understanding of storm seamanship will help readers appreciate the lot of captains and crews. The fundamental challenge can be stated simply: keep the vessel from lying broadside to large breaking waves that might capsize her or at least sweep her deck and cause damage or injury.

The sea itself usually shoots the fatal bullet, not the wind. "The waves, not the wind," sailors say of the worst risks. Because a cubic foot of seawater weighs sixty-four pounds, the power of even a moderate-sized ten-foot breaking wave flying at twenty knots is enormous. Waves are sledgehammers, and they also are sandbags. What they don't destroy, they fill and sink. As boats are pressed lower, they become less stable. Eventually they may capsize. Any sea of moderate size can have breaking waves, because any sea contains rogues—unusually steep or high waves running at an angle to all the others. Oceanographer William G. Van Dorn estimates that one deepwater wave out of five is an irregular rogue, probably caused by a distant gale or shifting winds.

To avoid being smashed by these seas, the boat must be sailed expertly or at least slowed and made controllable, unlike Percy Bysshe Shelley's wildly leaping *Ariel* (chapter 1). There are four commonly accepted techniques, or storm tactics, for getting through a storm: heave-to, lie to a sea anchor, lie ahull, or run with it. None is perfect or easy to implement.

To *heave-to* is to proceed slowly under sail or engine on a heading between close-hauled and a reach—or about sixty degrees off the wind. The vessel is described as being "hove-to." This can be done under power or by shortening sail and adjusting the remaining sails so the boat lies comfortably without requiring a helmsman. Making a little speed both forward and sideways, the vessel absorbs some of the blows of waves. Heaving-to usually works well except in breaking seas, when lying to a sea anchor or running before the storm may be a better tactic. In the 1851 Yankee Gale, the mackerel boats hove-to successfully off Prince Edward Island until their sails blew out and the nor'easter flung them onto the island's shoals (chapter 3). Forty-seven years later, the sidewheeler *Portland* probably was attempting to heave-to off Cape Cod when she was smashed by a rogue wave (chapter 5).

To *lie to a sea anchor* means to stop the boat entirely by putting her bow into the wind and waves and, under bare poles (with no sail set), streaming a parachute on a line over the bow so that the boat lies with the least area exposed to the seas. This method appears to work best with relatively narrow hulls, like those on trimarans and catamarans, that can pierce passing waves with little fuss. Larger boats may sail around the anchor, exposing first one flank, then another, to dangerous waves.

To *lie ahull* is to allow the boat to drift with no sails set. In a confused sea, this can put the boat at risk. The Smeetons in *Tzu Hang* were lying ahull when they were rolled the second time off Cape Horn (chapter 10). This tactic has few fans today.

To *run before it* (or scud) is to sail with the wind directly astern, steering around the worst waves. Unlike the other three passive storm tactics, it requires active steering. There should be enough speed to provide steerage way (a boat cannot be steered unless water passes over the rudder) and to keep the boat just ahead of the waves so she is not pooped (smashed from astern), but not so much speed that the vessel leaps over waves or the steerer loses control, allowing her to broach (roll over on her side) or pitchpole (somersault). Speed may be limited by dragging a drogue—a parachute, a warp (long length of heavy rope or chain), or other drag device—astern. This tactic was used successfully by Hollis Blanchard of the *Portland* until he ran out of sea room off Cape Cod (chapter 5); by the *Greyhound*, with John Newton steering for eleven hours as he struggled with his conscience (chapter 9); and in the Southern Ocean by William Albert Robinson in *Varua* and the Smeetons until *Tzu Hang* was unlucky enough to meet a massive breaking sea (chapter 10).

Although all four tactics have long histories of success, there is no one best tactic for all conditions and vessels. Unfortunately, discussions of storm tactics often stray into bitter, foolish debates about the "perfect" tactic. In their quest for absolute answers, many people become purists, insisting on one tactic and damning the others. But anyone who has been out in a bad gale knows there is nothing pure or absolute about a storm at sea except its danger.

FOR FURTHER READING

The literature on storm seamanship is large and expanding. The following books concern handling smaller boats: Peter Bruce, *Adlard Coles' Heavy Weather Sailing*, 30th ann. ed. (Camden, Maine: International Marine, 1999); Steve and Linda Dashew, *Surviving the Storm: Coastal and Offshore Tactics* (Tucson: Beowulf, 1999); John Rousmaniere, *The Annapolis Book of Seamanship*, 3rd ed. (New York: Simon & Schuster, 1999); and Victor Shane, *Drag Device Data Base: Using Parachutes, Sea Anchors, and Drogues to Cope with Heavy Weather*, 4th ed. (Summerland, Calif.: Para-Anchors International, 1998). Many narratives of individual storms include sections on strategy and tactics, for example, William Albert Robinson, *To the Great Southern Sea* (Tuckahoe, N.Y.: John de Graff, 1966); John Rousmaniere, *Fastnet, Force 10*, rev. ed. (New York: W. W. Norton, 2000); and Miles Smeeton, *Once Is Enough* (1959; reprint, Camden, Maine: International Marine, 2001).

The meteorological aspect of storm sailing is covered in several excellent books, including Michael William Carr, *Weather Predicting Simplified: How to Read Weather Charts and Satellite Images* (Camden, Maine: International Marine, 1999); Steve Dashew and Linda Dashew, *Mariner's Weather Handbook: A Guide to Forecasting and Tactics* (Tucson: Beowulf, 1998); William J. Kotsch, *Weather for the Mariner*, 2nd ed. (Annapolis: Naval Institute, 1977); William G. Van Dorn, *Oceanography and Seamanship*, 2nd ed. (Centreville, Md.: Cornell Maritime, 1993); and Alan Watts, *The Weather Handbook* (Dobbs Ferry, N.Y.: Sheridan House, 1994).

GLOSSARY

Most nautical terms in this book—*bow, compass, mast, starboard*, and so on—are well known or defined in dictionaries, but a few may be unfamiliar to general readers and are defined briefly here.

abaft. Behind.
abeam. Alongside.
aboard. On or in a vessel.
aft, after. Toward the stern.
aloft. In the rigging.
astern. Behind a vessel.
ballast. Weight deep in the hull or the keel to provide stability.
bare poles. Masts carrying no sail.
barque (bark). Three-masted vessel whose forward two masts are square-rigged and whose after mast is fore-and-aft rigged.
barquentine. Three-masted sailing vessel whose forward mast is square-rigged and whose two after masts are fore-and-aft rigged.
beam to, broadside to. With the vessel's side exposed to waves or other objects.
beat, beat to windward. To sail close-hauled.
Bermudian (Marconi) rig. Fore-and-aft rig with triangular sails.
Bimini top. An awning over a cockpit.
binnacle. The support for the steering compass in the cockpit or on deck.
brig. Square-rigged two-masted vessel with a small fore-and-aft sail on the after mast.
broach, broach to. For a vessel to go out of control and lie beam to waves.
breaking wave, breaker, jetting wave, plunging wave. Wave whose top is falling or flying off.
channel. Water deep enough for a vessel to sail in.
chart. Map of a sea or lake used in navigating.
close-hauled. Sailing as close to the wind as possible.
cockpit. Recessed area in the deck containing the steering wheel or tiller.
confused sea. Irregular sea.
course. A vessel's heading.
current. Moving water caused by tide or wind.

depression. Area of low atmospheric pressure, a storm.

dinghy. Very small boat. Also "dory," "ship's boat."

douse. To lower a sail.

draft. A vessel's depth.

drogue. Object towed astern to slow the boat. See the Storm Strategy and Tactics appendix.

ease. To release pressure on the helm or a sheet.

force. One of thirteen categories in the Beaufort Scale of Wind Forces, which indicates average sea and wind conditions. Force 0 is a calm (wind speed zero knots, wave height zero feet). Force 6 is a strong breeze (wind speed twenty-two to twenty-seven knots, wave height ten feet). Force 12 is a hurricane (wind speed sixty-four to seventy-one knots, wave height forty-five feet).

fore-and-aft rig. Sails set along the line from bow to stern, as against the square rig.

forward. Toward the vessel's bow.

gaff rig. Four-sided sails set in fore-and-aft rig. The upper side is on a spar called a gaff.

gale. Wind of thirty-four to forty-seven knots.

galley. Kitchen in a vessel.

growler. Small iceberg.

halyard. Line or wire that pulls up and holds up a sail.

headsail. A jib.

heave-to. To almost stop the boat. See the Storm Strategy and Tactics appendix.

helm. A vessel's steering equipment.

high. Area of high atmospheric pressure, usually fair weather.

keel. The largest fin under the hull. It usually contains ballast.

ketch. A sailboat with two masts the aftermost of which (the mizzen mast) is shorter and forward of the rudder.

knot. 1.15 statute miles per hour.

lee shore. Land onto which a wind blows, pressing vessels onto shoals.

lie ahull. To allow the boat to drift with no sail set. See the Storm Strategy and Tactics appendix.

line. Rope that has a particular use in a vessel.

low. See *depression.*

luff. Flapping in a sail; the forward edge of a sail.

main-. Prefix indicating "largest" or "primary" (mainmast, mainsail).

mizzen. Small fore-and-aft sail set well aft.

navigate. To sail. In particular, to determine a vessel's position.

nor'easter. A gale or storm with the wind from the northeast.

offshore. Away from land.

onshore. Toward land.

pitch. When the bow plunges into waves. To pitchpole is to dig the bow into a wave and somersault over it.

prevailing. Usual or typical; the "prevailing westerly" wind in the Southern Ocean or Northern Atlantic establishes a "prevailing swell" from the west.

reach. To sail across the wind.

reduce sail. Shorten sail.

reef. To decrease a sail's size. Also a shoal composed of rocks or coral.

rig. Arrangement of masts and sails.

rigging. Wires, ropes, and other objects that support the mast and sails, including stays, sheets, and halyards.

rip, tide rip, tidal race, race. Rough water where tidal current runs fast.

rode. Line or chain connecting an anchor to the vessel.

run, run before it. To sail before the wind, with the wind on the stern. Also "scud."

schooner. Sailboat with two masts the aftermost of which (the mainmast) is taller than the other (the foremast).

scud. To run before the wind. See the Storm Strategy and Tactics appendix.

scupper. A drain in the deck or cockpit.

sea. Deep water, the deep.

sea anchor. Small parachute hung over the bow to keep the bow into the waves. See the Storm Strategy and Tactics appendix.

sea room. Enough deep water to sail in.

seamanship. Art and science of handling a vessel competently.

seas, seaway. Waves.

set sail. To hoist a sail.

sextant. Navigating instrument that measures angles to the sun and stars.

sheet. Line or wire that pulls a sail in.

ship. Very large vessel. A full-rigged ship has square sails on all masts.

shoal. Area of shallow water where a vessel may run aground and where waves are unusually steep.

shorten sail. To reef or lower sails.

spar. Mast, boom, gaff, or yard.

square sail. Rectangular sail carried across the vessel.

stability. Resistance to heeling or rolling.

stay. Wire supporting a mast.

storm. Wind of forty-eight to ninety-three knots.

surf. To slide down the face of a wave.

swamp. To be filled with water.

swell, groundswell. A prevailing pattern of regular waves.

tide. Rise and fall of water caused by the gravitational force of the moon and sun.

top hamper. Superstructure and masts above the deck.

topsail. Sail set high in the rigging.

trade wind. Predictable seasonal prevailing wind.

vessel. Any ship or boat.

weigh anchor. To retrieve the anchor and get going.

yard. Horizontal spar supporting a square sail.

yawl. Sailboat with two masts the aftermost of which (the mizzen mast) is shorter and abaft the rudder.

Notes

Chapter 1. *Ariel* and Percy Bysshe Shelley

Note to page 7: "The sea both attracts and repels, calling us to high adventure and threatening to destroy us through its indifferent power," writes Robert Foulke, an authority on sea literature, in *The Sea Voyage Narrative*. Like the west wind in Shelley's poem, water has long been thought of as both preserving and destroying. On the preserving side there is the ancient tradition of "living waters"—freshwater spilling down inland streams, bubbling up from springs, or flowing in other settings. "From water comes life," wrote Carl G. Jung, referring to the amniotic fluid of birth as well as to the Christian baptismal font. "Living waters" did not include salt water and the sea until about two hundred years ago, when Europeans and Americans began to vacation at the seashore and eventually to seek refreshment not only on the beach but in small boats on the sea itself. As we will see in chapter 6, the movement of amateurs to seafaring during the twentieth century was greatly influenced by notions about proper living that were embodied in Theodore Roosevelt's idea of "the strenuous life." This movement peaked after the Second World War when sailors (including the men and women we will encounter in chapter 10) sought ultimate adventures in boats.

As even the most technically skilled sailor will admit, the sea has its romantic side as the Other World. Obsession about it is both common and complex. Some Africans believed that the surface of the water was an interface between life and death, and that on spiritual sea voyages souls crossed the border and were purified and transmigrated to reincarnation. According to an old Cornish tale, on still nights a voice cries, "The hour is come but not the man," and a figure runs down from the hills into the sea. One of the most honest confessions of an obsessive love-hate relationship with the sea is by E. B. White, widely known for his children's books. He wrote of the water and boats as others write of sex: "With me, I cannot not sail." He could not tear himself away from what he called "the cruel beauty of the salt world." White's complex relationship with the sea as the Other World was an addiction that took full account of *all* its features, tragic and life-affirming alike.

The point is often made that we need to acknowledge the existence of wild other worlds if we are to be fully human. As the wise novelist E. M. Forster wrote of the ominous Marabar Caves in *A Passage to India*, to attempt to tame such places would rob "infinity and eternity of their vastness, the only quality that accommodates them to mankind." In *The End of Nature*, Bill McKibben properly worried

294

about the consequences of believing that we can incorporate nature into our daily lives. "Having lost its separateness, it loses its special power," he noted. "Instead of being a category like God—something beyond our control—it is now a category like the defense budget or the minimum wage, a problem we must work out." Rudolph Otto, in *The Idea of the Holy*, introduced the word "numinous" to describe the soulful feeling of the encounter in which both awe and dread are offered in response to the appearance of the divine power in a setting wholly outside ourselves.

Such an acknowledgment of an awesome presence is common at sea. According to Thucydides, before the Athenian navy got under way in 2500 B.C. it paused to worship: "At the herald's signal the customary prayers before sailing were pronounced, rising in unison from the galleys as a single prayer. From end to end of the fleet, captains and soldiers poured libations of wind from cups of silver and gold." Something very like that ceremony is repeated today at the launching of boats and the opening of yacht clubs. That feeling has remained alive for millennia.

In the high latitudes of the Southern Hemisphere in 1938, a grain ship was running in a force 10 gale—fifty knots and more—with the rigging screaming, the decks awash, and four men at the helm. One crewman, Eric Newby, found himself feeling minute and lonely. Then a comfort came over him: "At this moment, for the first time I felt certain of the existence of an infinitely powerful and at the same time merciful God. Nearly everyone in the ship felt something like this, no one spoke of it. We were all of us awed by what we saw and heard beyond the common experience of men." Sailors have acknowledged these powers in rituals for thousands of years.

Yet not all people fear the water and look to land for safety. Studying Indians of coastal British Columbia more than a century ago, the anthropologist Franz Boas discovered that in their vocabulary "seaward" and "inland" had connotations entirely opposite from those familiar to most other people. Some of these tribes spent weeks at sea in their canoes and were so at home there that they believed the place of chaos was the mainland. The ocean was where they lived and found security. Writing of these Indians in *Passage to Juneau*, Jonathan Raban observed that they "were moving on the sea exactly as whites moved on dry land; but the whites steadfastly failed to wise up to this basic transposition of land and sea, place and space." In a nice coinage, Raban described these people as blessed with "water-hauntedness"—a quality not known by Percy Bysshe Shelley. The discovery of the sea by average Europeans began during Shelley's lifetime, in the first decades of the nineteenth century. Alain Corbin, a French cultural historian, has described the feelings people discovered at the seaside: "Right down into the observer's body the emotion arising from the sublime scene causes the experience of the continuum of natural phenomena to coincide with life rhythms." The idea that nature is at the beck and call of "life rhythms" rather than the other way around was revolutionary, considering the ages-long beliefs about the sea as the dangerous Other World.

Note to page 10: The list of maritime superstitions seems endless in both its length and its quirkiness. According to one bizarre belief mentioned by Charles Tyng in his autobiography of a life under sail in the early nineteenth century, recently published under the title *Before the Wind*, whenever a black bear is seen walking on a yard aloft, the crew must spring to the halyards, for the animal's acrobatic trick prefigures a gale. Another notion that was taken seriously by enough people to guarantee that it would be written down was that a drifting coffin containing an open Bible means a wreck is nearby.

Here are more. A skipper should change crew every year, for a new set of hands will bring luck. Sailors must not whistle for wind unless they want more than they can handle, or board a fishing vessel from the port side, or have their hair cut at sea (except during the "crossing the Line" ceremony at the equator, when heads of novice sailors are shaved), or point a finger at another ship (how they *should* indicate a nearby vessel is not specified). Norse traditions instruct us not to start building a ship on Thursday (the domain of Thor, the god of storms) or to weigh anchor on Friday (when Frigg, a goddess of unusual malice, is in charge). An owner must not go to pick up a new boat unless she is perfectly prepared to go to sea; should she be unfinished and the impatient owner forced to go home empty-handed, the odds are extremely high that when they finally do go out she will sink and take a crew down with her.

In keeping with such wondrous beliefs, Jack Tar and other seamen from Egypt to Latin America to Asia have bolstered their courage by inserting pieces of gold and silver under the heels of masts, painting magic eyes *(oculi)* on their vessels, and tossing coins on "lucky" rocks when heading out. They build costly figureheads on ships' bows, they hang votive paintings in cabins, they give their vessels benevolent names (*maru*, seen on many Japanese ships, means "circle" and implies perfection), and they bow to patron spirits such as Saint Nicholas and lucky sprites like the character in an eighteenth-century sailors' song who is "a sweet little cherub that sits aloft, to keep watch over the life of poor Jack."

Note to page 17: Shelley and Williams were by definition in a dangerous setting. Sailors along a coast may not be as skilled and experienced as those who are at sea. More significant, strong winds kick up tremendous waves more quickly in shallow water than in deep water. Add to these risks a summer afternoon, when the heating of nearby land confuses the atmosphere and may set off a downburst of air from the sky. A downburst is "a cloud mass that cools and collapses suddenly" with a great roar, as meteorologist Michael Carr describes it in *Weather Predicting Simplified*. Even a relatively small downburst—a microburst—can cause a jet airplane to plummet to earth.

Add an approaching cold front, and the weather quickly shifts from benign to destructive. The gusts in the rapidly rising air pressure on the back side of the squall line can blow at twice the speed of the prevailing wind and come from new directions. Because the wind's force increases with the square of the wind speed, with an increase of twenty knots raising the effect four-hundred-fold, the impact of the accelerating air on a boat can be as violent as a collision between automobiles.

Note to page 20: William Godwin's pointed command to Mary Shelley was on target. Often the right word from a friend is all it takes to snap a victim out of numb passivity. In the wake of a disaster, writes psychologist Charles C. Benight, "When all seems lost, it may be important to understand that we still retain the most essential ingredient to survival—our ability to control how we think." Relatively fast psychological recovery from disaster depends on a combination of optimism, practicality, and adherence to personal integrity and beliefs. The challenge is to distinguish one's emotional wounds from the practical tasks at hand. "The person who can grasp the problem before him and break it down into simple, ordered, and manageable chunks is paving the way for his survival and rescue," John Leach writes in *Survival Psychology*. He adds, "Simple directed action is the key to regaining psychological functioning." Psychologists have rephrased the ability to "pull up your socks" as "coping self-efficacy." Benight found that survivors of a Florida hurricane who exhibited low measures of CSE soon after the storm—for example, who were incapable of reporting losses to insurance companies—were more likely to suffer chronic distress later on.

Note to page 21: Shelley's dramatic, oversimplified reputation reflected elements of his life and especially of his violent early death, which his admirers perceived as romantic and fitting. "When somebody thinks they have a piece of information in a disaster, they want to tell everyone they know to bring everyone into a consensual reality," Camille Bacon-Smith, a folklorist, said of the flood of e-mails after the terrorist attacks on September 11, 2001. "They want to bring everyone into the group, and with the Internet the group is huge."

The James Dean effect, with its stunning implications about the ways we need to dramatize life, was noted in psychological experiments when subjects were asked to evaluate various life histories that were invented for the occasion. They agreed across age and gender lines that a life that ends on a high note after twenty-five years is superior to a fifty-year life that ends after reversals. A corollary, called the Alexander Solzhenitsyn effect, is that a terrible life is judged to be far better if it ends with a few only moderately bad years than if it ends abruptly before things improve.

Of course, this drama is an abstraction, like the romantic sublime; whether the participants in this study would be content to welcome the chronology into their own lives is another question altogether.

Chapter 2. The *Elizabeth* and Margaret Fuller

Note to page 44: The English travel writer Eric Newby saw the weather sense at work while sailing aboard the 320-foot four-masted bark *Moshulu* as she carried grain across the Southern Ocean. To Newby's initial disbelief, his normally reserved Scandinavian shipmates predicted the imminent arrival of a gale despite the prevailing fair weather.

"Going to vind a little too mooch," said one sailor, colorfully. When another seaman, named Tria, more tersely advised, "Koms to blow," Newby mistakenly believed that was a good thing.

" 'No, no. Not good. Koms to blow bad,' he replied anxiously.

"I asked him how he knew.

" 'I don' know how I know. There's someting fonny, someting noh good in the vind.' "

The skeptical Newby sneaked onto the chart house (which was off limits to deckhands) and, taking a look at the log book, discovered that the barometer had been falling steadily for the past two and a half days. When he returned he began to notice what his shipmates had been seeing: "These seas did not seem to be raised by wind; instead they seemed the product of some widespread underwater convulsion. All around, the sea was surging and hurling itself into the air in plumes of spray, occasionally leaping over the rail by the mizzen braces and filling the main deck with a swirl of white water. The air was bitter; I could see Tria's breath smoking." Within hours they were in a heavy gale.

Note to page 53: The image of a helpless female victim of shipwreck sometimes takes a religious turn. In December 1875 five Roman Catholic nuns who had been exiled from Prussia were among the 157 victims of the wreck of a ship named the *Deutschland* on a sandbar at the mouth of England's river Thames. It was reported that as the ship slowly sank, one of the nuns, clinging to the rigging, shouted, "O Christ, come quickly!" She may well have been crying out in confusion, but the poet Gerard Manley Hopkins sought more meaning in the nun's plea. The son of a marine insurance adjuster, Hopkins had often heard talk of shipwrecks and their consequences at the dinner table. Now, as a candidate for holy orders in the Roman Catholic Church, Hopkins was struggling with his relationship with God. Out of this nexus of accident, family history, and personal need came one of the greatest of all religious poems, "The Wreck of the *Deutschland*," with its portrayal of commitment to God in a seascape where "storms bugle his fame."

Note to page 58: Recently, long-distance single-handed sailors have been experimenting with new types of sleep regimens in order to avoid exhaustion and the mistakes that spin off from it. Advised by Claudio Stampi, a sleep specialist, Ellen MacArthur followed a regimen of "cluster naps" during the 2000–1 Vendée Globe single-handed, nonstop sailboat race around the world, taking a total of 891 naps averaging thirty-six minutes. Most of these naps were in clusters broken by two- to eight-minute periods of wakefulness that allowed her to monitor the boat's performance, yet she still slept an average of almost six hours a day and never went without sleep for longer than nineteen hours during the ninety-day race, which she finished in second place.

Deprivation of all kinds throws people off their moral, physical, and intellectual bearings, making them forget their training. Sleep loss is one of these deprivations; another is long absence from families. "The principal stressor is the social-emotional separation from one's closest persons," reports psychologist Jan Horbulewicz, who has studied offshore fishermen on long voyages. His and others' research has showed that sailors' efficiency plummets as a voyage runs on, with the nadir of morale and effectiveness coming around the cruise's 75th and 155th days. It happens that Henry Bangs and the *Elizabeth* were almost exactly 75 days out from Leghorn when they neared New York on July 18, 1850.

Chapter 3. The Yankee Gale

Note to page 85: For all his sensitivity in recording the rituals of life aboard a ship at sea, Richard Henry Dana Jr., like many sailors who had been at sea far longer than two years, seemed confused by shore life when he reached land. Once ashore, he grew cold and austere. Dana was in his early twenties when he wrote *Two Years before the Mast*—which alongside *Moby-Dick* (which it helped inspire) is one of the greatest of all American sea books. He also wrote a manual for sailors, *The Seamen's Friend*. But by age twenty-nine he was obsessed with social standing and money. Nothing satisfied him, even his legal practice in which he advised seamen on their rights and defended runaway slaves. Political honors he expected never came his way. Believing that his life after his voyage was a failure, Dana rediscovered a modicum of happiness only toward its end, while living in Italy. His remains are buried in the same Roman cemetery as those of Percy Bysshe Shelley, a very different sort of man.

"The grief a community experiences after a traumatic event may become either a developmental crisis or opportunity for that community," note Mary Beth Williams and other trauma specialists in a discussion of community and mourning. "It may stagnate a community's future development or propel a community into new areas of growth."

The delicate rituals described by Dana and others that surrounded a death at sea did not occur on all ships. Fear and prejudice, as always, took their toll on decency. In *Snow Squall: The Last American Clipper Ship*, Nicholas Dean cites the case of a captain who refused even to come out of his cabin to say a few words over the body of the African American cook. Yet most people seem to recognize that rituals help bring meaning that is desperately needed in times of disaster. For example, the bubonic plague set off mass frenzy. Long before the development of germ theory in the nineteenth century, plagues caused widespread fear, in part because of mortality but also because they were inexplicable. The Old Testament relates that when the plague swept through the Philistines in about 1050 B.C., "there was a deathly panic throughout the whole city . . . and the cry of the city went up to heaven" (1 Sam. 5:11–12). When the plague returned in the middle of the fourteenth century, many people were as terrified by its apparent randomness as by its lethal cruelty. According to one highly educated man who watched helplessly as the plague killed one-third of the population of Western Europe, "the most terrible of all the terrors" was the illness's total inexplicability.

After disasters, some or many survivors, rescuers, and others may suffer from post-traumatic stress disorder. PTSD symptoms (whose onset is often delayed) include emotional numbing, dissociation, nightmares, substance abuse, panic attacks, severe anxiety, and severe depression.The National Center for Post-Traumatic Stress Disorder estimates that about 8 percent of Americans experience PTSD at some point in their lives, with women (10.4 percent) twice as vulnerable as men (5 percent). As many as one-third of the survivors of hurricanes, storms, earthquakes, and other natural disasters may suffer from it. Yet most disaster survivors move on healthily. Stephen A. Joseph and other psychologists who studied the aftermath of the sinking of a car ferry, the *Herald of Free Enterprise*, in the English Channel in 1987, with the loss of hundreds of lives, found that three years after the accident "most survivors reported strong positive changes in their outlook on life."

Rescuers' attitudes are often even more positive. Psychologists who studied a devastating train wreck and fire that occurred in Australia in 1977 found two patterns. First, as gruesome as the work was, 35 percent of rescuers came away from it feeling more positive about their own lives; only 10 percent felt more negative. Second, the closer rescuers were to the heart of the accident—for example, serving in direct contact with victims rather than at a remove in a reserve unit or supply center—the more likely they were to feel rewarded. "Active involvement to a clear purpose seemed to lead to a sense of having contributed in a worthwhile way," write the authors of the study titled "Who Helps the Helpers?"

As Dana indicated, rituals are crucial. After a more recent disaster at sea, a psychologist who was on site noted, "Rescue workers as well as others involved often seek to find meaning in the disasters they face." Lasse Nurmi, a Finnish police psychologist who worked with doctors assigned to the task of identifying bodies of many of the 852 victims of the sinking of the car ferry *Estonia* in the Baltic Sea in 1994, found that as he observed this long, difficult, and often grisly task, although his faith in a benevolent God declined, his belief in the importance of rituals increased. Whenever a body was taken to the mainland, Nurmi led rescue workers and nurses in a religious service. Such rituals later were the norm at ground zero at the site of the World Trade Center disaster.

There are all kinds of rituals, of course. Mythmaking is one. An unfortunate ritual that often occurs after disaster is the scapegoating of individuals (alive or, often, dead) who are assigned all blame. After the 1979 Fastnet Race gale near Ireland and Cornwall, in which fifteen racing sailors died and five yachts sank, even before the storm ended there arose an international wave of criticism concerning almost every aspect of the disaster except the storm itself, which brought the third lowest barometer reading for an English August in almost eighty years. Survivors and observers appeared to want to distance themselves as far as possible from the calamity, as if to declare that it could never happen to them.

In *The Perfect Storm*, by Sebastian Junger, a pleasure sailor serves as a foil for other characters' heroism (and in some cases tragic heroism). This yachtsman is portrayed not simply as incompetent but as unethical because, according to Junger, he caused others to risk their lives to save him. Junger made his point of view clear in a revealing interview in the United States Naval Institute *Proceedings*, the navy's professional magazine. When asked about the heroism of rescuers, he changed the subject to this yachtsman: "The reality is that some pleasure boaters do stupid things and take risks they shouldn't take. They don't need to be out there in the first place; it's recreation. We live in a very indulgent society. They get in trouble, and suddenly navy destroyers are being sent out to save them. What a cushy society we have that can afford to do that. Journalistically, I'm much more interested in people who get in trouble doing their jobs. Someone has to build sky-scrapers or drill for oil or catch fish or farm, things that get people hurt and killed. Somebody has to do it to keep the society running. Nobody has to climb moun-tains or sail across the Atlantic to keep society going. The people who are doing something functional interest me much more."

So much for the brotherhood of seafarers. In fact, Ray Leonard, the yachtsman Junger portrayed so darkly in the book, was no careless Pollyanna but far better prepared than some of the professional fishermen in the story. An experienced ocean sailor who had been going out in his boat for seventeen years, he later reported that he was in nowhere near the distress portrayed in the book and film based on it, and that he abandoned his boat only when the coast guard ordered him to.

Chapter 5. The Loss of the *Portland*

Note to page 113: Little note of the *Portland* disaster's devastating effect on Port-land's African American community was made at the time, even in the few surviv-ing newspapers from African American communities. When the *Wichita Tribune*, a weekly serving the fifty-two thousand black people of Kansas, ran three otherwise highly detailed stories on the disaster in its December 3 issue, there was not a word about the race of the victims. The main headline was not "40 Negroes Dead" or the equivalent but, rather

OVER 170 SHIPS WRECKED

179 LIVES LOST IN THE NORTHEASTER

OFF NEW ENGLAND COAST

Since most newspaper reports in white papers in Boston and New York men-tioned black victims, this apparent neglect by a black paper cannot be considered the product of racism. More likely this detail was buried by the catastrophe's immensity. Over a century later, when racial sensitivities were far more alert, in the first days after September 11, 2001, nobody cared how many of the 350 New York firemen who lost their lives at the World Trade Center were white or black or

Latino. Individuals counted, not groups. A few weeks after the suicide attacks, a specialist on post-traumatic stress disorder, Rachel Yehuda, told an interviewer, "People have a real sense of wanting to help their fellow man in whatever small or big way. There are a lot of humble, silent heroes in this that we don't hear about and we don't read about and we don't see. They are just invisible. Real heroes. To me, those are the silent people who are just sitting with people, getting them a glass of water." Another psychiatrist and PTSD authority, Marilyn Bowman, observed after the attacks that particulars tend to be addressed after the first shock wave has passed: "Within our culture, most people of good will and well-intentioned feelings and thoughts acted with upset and outrage and disbelief and then gradually became differentiated into different types of responses."

Note to page 121: As we have seen in earlier chapters, orange crepuscular lights often are considered a reliable predictor of storms; yet as meteorologist Alan Watts writes in *The Weather Handbook*, "They have no prognostic value except to show that the cloud is broken and that the situation is at present stable." What one observer called "veins" of wind in the *Portland* storm have also been referred to by Watts as "corridors of extremely strong winds." Irregularity is common in all winds, in fact. As meteorologist Joseph M. Sienkiewicz has said, "Wind is not a blanket. It is, rather, like a colander."

Note to page 125: Because she had no survivors, the exact conditions of the *Portland*'s loss must be estimated. She probably capsized and sank about ten miles north of Race Point, Cape Cod, on Sunday morning at about 9:30, the time frozen on the watches of victims. Had she survived those conditions another twelve hours, until 9:30 P.M., she would have been seen again. The first search for the ship was sponsored by a Boston newspaper two weeks after she disappeared, and it failed to find her. Subsequently there have been at least two claims of discoveries of the sunken "*Portland*." One is twenty miles north of Race Point in more than 300 feet of water on Stellwagen Bank. This wreck was found in 1989 by a shipwreck research organization, the Historical Maritime Group, using sonar and remote sampling. The other, more reliable candidate lies ten miles nearer the cape on her beam's ends in 144 feet of water. After snagging fishing nets for many years and yielding some doorknobs and other items identified with the *Portland*, she was visited in 1945 by a diver sent down by Edward Rowe Snow. The ship was "practically disemboweled" said Snow.

The proposal that the *Portland* capsized runs against two old theories that she either ran aground on Peaked Hill Bar, the shoal extending almost a mile north of Cape Cod, or sank after a collision with the *Pentagoet*, the freighter that was near her on Sunday morning, or (if we are to believe the shoemaker's vision) a black schooner. If the first were true, her remains certainly would have been seen after the storm; if the second or third, her wreckage would have been mingled with another vessel's. Neither is the case. (Not a trace of the *Pentagoet* has ever been found.)

The *Portland* was inherently unstable, just as the sidewheeler captain said when he observed of his vessel, "She is only fit for smooth water." If the waves don't smash her, they and the wind would press over on her side. Once beyond her limit of positive stability—the last angle of heel at which she still has a tendency to pop back upright—she will capsize. Wide, shallow vessels with a high center of gravity reach that point very early. Stability declines dramatically if there is free water (water, snow, or ice sloshing or sliding from side to side) on deck.

Although sidewheelers went out of style, other beamy, shallow vessels were built in the 1980s as roll-on, roll-off car ferries to run across the Baltic and the English Channel. Two, the *Herald of Free Enterprise* and the *Estonia*, both almost five hundred feet long with wide-open decks designed to carry huge loads of passengers and automobiles, capsized with a great loss of life (193 passengers and crew in the case of the *Herald*, 852 in the *Estonia*). As we saw in chapter 3, the loss of the *Herald of Free Enterprise* was Britain's worst peacetime maritime disaster since the sinking of the *Titanic*. That of the *Estonia* was the worst peacetime sea disaster in Scandinavian history and the worst disaster in Swedish history since a battle against Russia in 1809.

The *Estonia*'s capsize on September 27, 1994, may have been similar to the loss of the *Portland* ninety-six years earlier. With at least 989 passengers and crew (the list was unreliable), many returning across the Baltic to Sweden after a vacation, she set out of Tallinn, in the former Soviet republic of Estonia. Running before a sixty mile per hour wind with waves described as the size of apartment houses, she was slowed from sixteen knots to eight knots, and eventually to only five knots. At 1:00 A.M. the bow hit the backs of large waves and a hinge on a bow door broke. Water poured in, spread as free water on the car deck, and destabilized the ship. The captain brought her broadside to the wind and sea, perhaps intending to put her bow into them and heave-to, but she quickly became unresponsive to the helm. Her engines cut out, and she developed a steep list of up to thirty degrees. By 1:24 the list was sixty degrees—far enough for an engineer escaping the engine room to run up the walls. A passenger on the first deck saw water rapidly rising in his cabin. A Mayday was sent despite interference by a poorly maintained Russian radio station. The nearest rescue center, in Finland, sent helicopters. The alarm for evacuation was sounded, and the passengers and crew on the by now nearly vertical deck threw life rafts into the fifty-degree water, jumped in, and attempted to board them as the rafts capsized and were swamped. The ship sank at 1:48 A.M., less than fifty minutes after the first sign of trouble. Several other cruise ships came to attempt to rescue the people in the water, but the steep seas made that difficult if not impossible as their passengers and crews watched, horrified.

Note to page 134: One of the few newspapers to suspend judgment on Blanchard was the *New York Herald*, which not coincidentally was also one of the few papers to take a serious interest in weather, even running detailed forecasts on its editorial page. Whereas the *New York Times* on December 1 believed everything the Weather

Bureau said and accused Blanchard of criminal behavior, the *Herald* on November 29 and 30 described the storm's origin as uncertain. It declared that not enough had been known about the atmosphere to predict such a gale accurately.

Note to page 136: This was hardly the first or the last storm in history that was not fully predicted, or in which an experienced captain did not fully grasp the potential explosiveness in the environment. Sometimes the fault lies with surprises presented by the weather itself. (Forty years later, the forecast for the day when the 1938 hurricane destroyed much of New England read, "Rain, probably heavy today and tomorrow, cooler.") The involvement in 1898 of warm, moist maritime air near the Gulf Stream added to the double storm's explosiveness. Meteorologist Michael Carr writes in *Weather Predicting Simplified*, "Rapidly developing lows tend to occur in a matter of hours over warm underlying surfaces, such as the Gulf Stream in the Atlantic Ocean and the Kuroshio Current in the Pacific Ocean. Also called meteorological bombs, these systems develop from initial mild disturbances to full-strength storms in 12 to 24 hours." They are characterized by tightly packed, symmetrical isobars (lines of equal atmospheric pressure), by sets of clouds arranged in the shape of a comma, and, often, by rapid falls in barometric pressure at a rate of one millibar or more per hour. Until the relatively recent introduction of weather satellites, which can look down and photograph the distinctive comma-shaped cloud pattern, these storms were extremely difficult to predict over the short term.

Even with today's extraordinary technology, storm forecasts are rarely accurate to the degree that we often expect in other activities. According to a study of hurricane records by Hugo du Plessis, forecasts by the U.S. Hurricane Center are wrong by an *average* of between 47 and 165 miles (for forecasts between twelve and forty-eight hours in advance of the storm, respectively). Obviously, then, it is a mistake to perceive a storm as a defined entity with a clear, predictable track rather than as a wild force rattling around within a large "circle of uncertainty."

The sea is as likely to find a way around defenses as any cunning enemy. Sometimes a weather prediction is correct but the timing is unlucky—for example, during the 1979 Fastnet Race off England and the 1998 Sydney–Hobart Race off Australia. Another example is Hurricane Mitch, which swept through the western Caribbean in October 1998. Although Mitch was carefully tracked using satellite imagery and airplane spotters (devices that not even the futurist H. G. Wells would have imagined in 1898) and its movements were constantly communicated to captains, the storm still surprised everybody by unexpectedly altering course ninety degrees and turning smack into the path of a 282-foot cruise ship, which sank with the loss of all hands. Mystical explanations were offered for the loss of the *Fantome*. It was "like the storm went after the ship. Like the devil itself," claimed the cruise line's founder, Michael D. Burke. Besides diabolical, the hurricane was characterized as a predatory animal—"a huge beast," for example. A man aware that Burke's ships had problems with safety inspections speculated, "Father Time finally caught up with him."

Strange spirits and diabolical fate may make good copy in tabloid newspapers and the science fiction community, but they distract from firm analysis. What really happened was that this cruise ship was allowed to be cornered by an immense storm in the narrow Gulf of Honduras, and success depended entirely on the hurricane's holding a steady course so she could try to slip around it. In the end, Mitch followed its own elusive laws and not the ones that humans attempted to impose on it by cutting safety margins to the bone.

As the experience of the *Portland* suggests, an incomplete forecast may be even more dangerous than no forecast at all. On December 18, 1944, a typhoon three hundred miles east of the Philippines thrust itself across a sizable portion of the American fleet. Three destroyers sank with almost all their people, another twenty-eight United States ships were badly damaged, and a total of 790 officers and men were lost. A partial weather warning had distracted many commanders from personally evaluating the actual sea conditions as they attempted to maintain the ordered course and speed. Pacific Fleet commander Admiral Chester W. Nimitz laid out what amounts to a primer on respecting the weather as it is rather than as meteorologists think it is or mariners hope it will be. "There is no little red light which is going to flash on and inform commanding officers or higher commanders that, from then on, there is extreme danger from the weather," he said. The time for taking crucial safety measures cannot be determined except by the commander's considered personal judgment.

Chapter 6. *Hamrah* and the Ameses

Note to page 150: If I write with so much energy (and ambivalence) about the code of the strenuous life, it is because I was raised in it. One of my great-uncles, Dr. James B. Ayer, a professor at the Harvard Medical School, was described by my father as "a hearty man with a zest for life, which included tennis, squash racquets, and incessant chopping of wood." My father, who was born in 1918, was brought up in the same spirit. The day school he attended in New York City in the 1920s had a classical curriculum but also taught boxing—a skill that served him well when he was assaulted by the street kids who tried to pick on the boy in knickers.

The summer camp I attended in the 1950s, Boothbay Camp for Boys, on an island in the Kennebec River above Bath, Maine, was like Merryweather Camp. It was in its forty-third year of challenging boys with Indian lore, mountain hikes, skinny-dipping, hypercompetitive sports, and woodcraft. We addressed the camp's director, a high school athletic director, as "Coach," but behind his back we referred to him as "One Match," alluding to his goal of making sure nobody went home in August without mastering the art of lighting a fire on the first try, regardless of rain or wind.

Note to page 156: Erling Tambs's second close brush with death temporarily washed much of the romance out of his system. "On rare occasions it may happen that the ocean rises to such violence that even the best of man-made ships will find themselves in serious danger," he wrote at the end of his report on *Sandefjord*'s nearly disastrous voyage. He went to sea again in *Sandefjord* with the purpose of hunting whales in the South Atlantic, or so he told her owner. Tambs ended up in Cape Town, where he tried to sell the boat. Returning to Norway, he wrote another book about his voyages and, during the German occupation, collaborated with the Nazis. After the war he spent his days in prison fantasizing about sailing to Argentina. The last word on Tambs has been offered by a Norwegian who knows his checkered record well: "He was too much a dreamer, I think."

Note to page 165: The around the campfire spirit of ocean racing in the 1930s has been left far behind by today's professional racing sailors, who go out with only one goal in mind—to win the race. To save weight, crews on the first leg of the 2001–2 Volvo Ocean Race around the world were permitted to bring only foul-weather clothing, a pair each of shoes and socks, a couple of T-shirts and pairs of shorts, and a hat. "We get to bring a toothbrush, but they supply the toothpaste," reported one sailor, Keith Kilpatrick, in an e-mail from his boat. Music was banned. Even Walkman-type personal CD players were out. "One of the toughest things for me will be 30 days without music. It'll be silence, and sleep when I can."

Note to page 168: In the postmortems to the *Hamrah* accident, nobody could accuse the survivors of poor seamanship. Although the boat lacked much ability to sail to windward even when undamaged and had no engine, they still got her to within a few yards of Robert Ames. The chief criticism then was that her traditional design and rig left her vulnerable in upwind sailing. "Boats that cannot go to windward at all in a high sea should certainly not be allowed to start in an ocean race," declared Alfred F. Loomis after he heard about the accident. There was more muted criticism about the reaction of the Ames boys, who by going overboard diminished the available crew by almost one-fourth while tripling the potential mortality. Had someone other than Robert Ames gone over the side, he probably would have ordered his sons to stay on deck and help sail the boat.

In any case, it is very likely that nothing could have been done to save Robert Ames, who probably drowned right away. Roger Weed observed that he was so passive that he seemed not to know how to swim, and Dick Ames had to hold his head clear of the water. Ames may well have died immediately after he went overboard owing to the "gasp reflex"—the automatic opening of the mouth in frigid water that can cause drowning or a heart attack.

Note to page 169: Recovery from disaster depends on many factors, including character, training, and treatment. The *Hamrah* survivors probably would have measured high in coping self-efficacy, discussed in the note to page 20, on page 297. They surely had enough practical problems on their hands while sailing a crippled vessel to port to give them renewed faith in their ability to cope. Today, rescue agencies offer and often require counseling services for personnel exposed to corpses and injuries. Some rescue teams on site routinely conduct regular self-checkups called "howgozits" and replace members whose effectiveness appears to be undermined by stress. Very likely the three young survivors of the *Hamrah* conducted their own informal "howgozit" debriefings. Whether they later suffered from the experience is not known except that Weed and Tillinghast spoke of it many years later with obvious deep concern, suggesting that they had been worrying it over. Conceivably it was a factor in Weed's apparent suicide.

Chapter 7. The Wreck of the *Pollux*

Note to page 193: That people respond to pressure and crisis in different ways for different reasons was made clear to psychiatrists who worked with soldiers during the First World War. Some of the variables are listed by Ben Shephard in *A War of Nerves*, his history of psychiatric treatment of soldiers. In the early days of treatment of what was called "shell shock," doctors came to see that a man's capacity to endure in war was determined by many things—heredity, upbringing, "character," the society he came from, how he felt about the war, his relationship with his fellow soldiers, how long he had been fighting, whether his wife had been unfaithful—quite apart from the military circumstances in which he found himself. They realized, too, that in the military context collective factors often mattered more than individual ones. The better the discipline in any division, the less shell shock there was in that division.

Although smoking has long been associated with the stress of combat, it may also say something about men. Research by Jean C. Beckham and her colleagues has shown that Vietnam veterans who experienced heavy combat and veterans diagnosed with PTSD are more likely to smoke (and smoke more) than those with a history of light combat. Veterans also report that they tend to smoke more when they have memories of military service. While only 39 percent of the veterans of low-combat service were smokers, 56 percent of those with high-combat experience and 66 percent of veterans diagnosed with post-traumatic stress disorder smoked, many of them heavily.

In *D-Day*, Stephen E. Ambrose has more than a dozen anecdotes about the importance of cigarettes in the lives of fighting men as they invaded Normandy. One concerns a soldier who was offered cartons of cigarettes as he boarded his landing craft in England but turned them down because he did not smoke. The quartermaster warned him to take them, "because by the time you get where you're going, you will." Forty years later the soldier told Ambrose, "He was right. On that ship I learned to smoke and did so for a lot of years thereafter."

Independent of military service, there appears to be a correlation between gender and smoking in stressful situations, when smoking may serve as an antidepressant while improving concentration. A long-held assumption that only women reach for a cigarette for emotional reasons was challenged by a 1999 study. According to Larry Jamner of the University of California at Irvine, a social scientist who worked on it, the study showed that "contrary to previous assumptions about smokers' attitudes, men smoke to control their emotions just as women do. Smoking, in fact, seems to calm feelings of anger in men but not in women. In some cases, we may have to look for ways to ease anger and sadness among men as we encourage them to stop smoking."

Note to page 200: Studies of behavior in disasters indicate that very few victims immediately act with cool-headed effectiveness. For most people, concerns lie elsewhere. After an immense gas explosion in Nova Scotia in 1917, survivors did not organize themselves into rescue teams to search for victims until after they ran home and checked on their families. Disasters are sometimes broken down into periods or phases. According to the a theory developed in 1951 by psychiatrist J. S. Tyhurst, there are three. The first is the "period of impact." Survivors of that phase go on to the "period of recoil," when they discover that although the initial threat to life and limb has passed, there are other threats. Those who get through that second phase enter the "period of post-trauma," when there may be nightmares, depression, fear, and other emotional distress that, today, are symptoms of post-traumatic stress disorder.

In the "period of recoil," Tyhurst (who studied fires in apartments and ships) found three types of behavior: "effective," "ineffective," and "normal." Out of ten victims, one or two are effective, another one or two behave ineffectively (for instance, they engage in hysterical weeping or screaming), and the remaining seven or eight behave normally, which means they are somewhat muddled and in need of leadership. These proportions of heroes, cowards, and normals seem to apply to most crisis situations.

Some disaster scenarios have a fourth phase that comes first among people who know that a disaster is imminent. This is called the "pre-impact," "warning," or "threat" phase. In all stages people engage in denial. "Very few people will acknowledge a direct threat of an impending disaster," John Leach writes in *Survival Psychology*, summarizing the literature. "A number will report that they became disassociated from the situation in which they found themselves and will go on to describe a sense of dream-like reality. During the period of pre-impact, denial is represented as 'this will not happen to me.' During the period of impact, denial is represented as 'this cannot be happening to me.' " The question, then, is how quickly victims can be made to believe that this is, in fact, not a dream but a reality to attempt to cope with.

Chapter 8. Derelicts

Note to page 220: Despite his frustrations, Arthur Conan Doyle continued to believe in the restorative powers of the sea. At the end of "The Adventure of the Sussex Vampire," Holmes recommends that the best treatment for the youthful culprit is to strengthen his character in the tried and true way. "I think," Holmes commands, "a year at sea would be my prescription." The connection between Doyle's *Matilda Briggs* and the real Sophia Matilda Briggs of the *Mary Celeste* is not noted in the Holmes reference books and the biographies of Doyle that I consulted. Chris Redmond, editor of the Internet site Sherlockian.Net, reports that Edgar W. Smith remarked on it in the *Baker Street Journal* in 1952.

Note to page 227: Nothing attracts a sailor's concern like rising bilge water. In some conditions, a wary crew can be misled. During the 1979 Fastnet gale, several crews became convinced that the water was rising because their boats had been holed and therefore abandoned them for small, unstable life rafts. In fact, the water came from downflooding—water was pouring down through hatches and vents from the decks when the boats were rolled far over, and then sloshing around the interior and dripping off furnishings, giving the appearance that it was rising from the bilge.

Note to page 237: My re-creation of Miles Necas's last hours is the most reasonable possible explanation. There is a possibility that he was robbed and murdered by the crew of a passing boat, yet there are easier ways to steal a computer than to kill a sailor on a rolling little boat off Cape Hatteras.

Chapter 9. "Amazing Graces"

Note to page 257: Related to the sea-deliverance narrative is perhaps the most widely understood maritime symbol outside the storm itself and the one thing that holds a vessel sure against shipwreck—the anchor. Long regarded in ancient times as the ultimate sign of security, the anchor especially appealed to the early Christians because of its resemblance to the cross, their symbol of God's grace through the life and death of Jesus Christ. An early manual of Christian teaching analogizes hope in the lovely formula "a sure and steadfast anchor of the soul" (Heb. 6:19; this verse has long been associated with seaport churches, among them the Abyssinian Church of Portland, Maine, mentioned in chapter 5). A Christian symbol called the "mariner's cross" combines the anchor, a crucifix, and a vessel's steering wheel.

If the anchor symbolizes hope, the shipwreck represents hopelessness. In a study of portrayals of disaster in art and literature, George P. Landow observes of the meaning of the shipwreck: "In part, its very randomness makes it so terrifying and disorienting. . . . Whereas the Christian life journey emphasizes meaningful continuity, connection, and duration, the shipwreck communicates an experience of discontinuity, for the shipwrecked voyager . . . is suddenly cut off from his past and thrust into a terrifying new existence. Finally, whereas the Christian voyager belongs to the community of fellow believers, a community of which God is the center, the shipwrecked voyager finds himself in a condition of essential isolation and helplessness."

Note to page 259: Why despite their many similarities John Newton was able to resist debilitating despair and William Cowper did not may have been due to their differences in personality, background, and sense of community. Newton had survived an actual storm in the company of other seamen. Compared to such vividly recalled threats, the crises that a guilty conscience can stir up may seem small. But if that conscience has no such real-life experience of rescue and is isolated from the world in loneliness, any threat, no matter how small, may seem fatal. The differences may be seen in the two men's relationship. Newton reached out to Cowper like a sailor extending a kind word, a cigarette, or a helping hand to a shipmate on a long, dreary midwatch that they know they must endure in order to reach the dawn.

Chapter 10. The Ulysses Generation in the Southern Ocean

Note to page 275: Studies of men born about 1920 found that happy aging is determined more by coping and compromise than by Ulyssean daring. "It is social aptitude, not intellectual brilliance or parental social class, that leads to successful aging," said Dr. George E. Vaillant, a psychoanalyst and the head of the ongoing Grant Study of Harvard graduates, in an interview with *Harvard* magazine in 2001. The only sure bar to old-age happiness is alcohol abuse. Otherwise what counts heavily is the nature of relationships with other people: "What's critical is allowing yourself to love others, and being able to *take people in*—as in, 'I've got you under my skin.' When someone gives you a compliment, do you cross the street, or do you feel genuinely good about yourself? In a personal encounter, do you come away feeling resentment or gratitude? A simple lesson from the Grant Study is to worry less about cholesterol and more about gratitude and forgiveness."

It also helps to have a strong connection with one's past. In his book *Aging Well*, Vaillant wrote that in old age "our lives become the sum of all whom we have loved. It is important not to waste anyone. One task of living out the last half of life is excavating and recovering all of those whom we loved in the first half. Thus, the recovery of lost loves becomes an important way in which the past affects the present." Self-care also plays an important part in successful aging. "Our defenses are always more mature when we are not hungry, angry, lonely, tired, or drunk. Feeling safe, secure, and 'held' allows us to use more mature defenses." It helps, too, to master some coping skills and to minimize narcissism. "Don't try to think less of yourself, but try to think of yourself less."

Sources

My sources are listed below, chapter by chapter, and there is a brief bibliography on meteorology and storm seamanship in the appendix. First, however, I wish to acknowledge the libraries and archives I consulted. I relied most on five collections: the library system of Columbia University; the Research Libraries of the New York Public Library; the Ferguson Library of Stamford, Connecticut; the immense and growing collection on the World Wide Web; and (hardly least) the library of the New York Yacht Club (William Watson, Librarian), with its superb collection of publications concerning all aspects of the sea.

I also made use of the Burke Library at Union Theological Seminary, New York; the Nimitz Library at the United States Naval Academy, Annapolis, Maryland; the Special Collections Division of the Boston University Library; the Harvard University Archives; the Maine Historical Society, Portland, Maine; the library of the National Center for Post-Traumatic Stress Disorder, White River Junction, Vermont; the library of the South Street Seaport Museum, New York; the G. W. Blunt White Library at the Mystic Seaport Museum, Mystic, Connecticut, including the archives of the Cruising Club of America; the archives of the New York Yacht Club; the Kendall Institute at the New Bedford Whaling Museum, New Bedford, Massachusetts; the archives of Milton Academy, Milton, Massachusetts; the chart and book collection of Landfall Navigation Inc., Greenwich, Connecticut; and the public libraries of Portland (Maine), Boston (Massachusetts), Providence (Rhode Island), and the Borough of Kensington and Chelsea (London, England).

The following libraries, archives, or collections provided valuable assistance by e-mail, postal mail, or telephone: the Maine Maritime Museum, Bath, Maine; the New Jersey State Archives, Trenton, New Jersey; the Cape Ann Historical Association, Gloucester, Massachusetts; the Free Library of Philadelphia, Pennsylvania; and the historical societies of Boothbay, Castine, and Machiasport, Maine.

Chapter 1. *Ariel* and Percy Bysshe Shelley

On Shelley and his group, Claire Tomalin, *Shelley and His World* (New York: Scribner's, 1980), and A. B. C. Whipple, *The Fatal Gift of Beauty: The Final Years of Byron and Shelley* (New York: Harper & Row, 1964), have considerable material on Shelley's sailing and death and are the sources of many quotations. I thank my friend Cal Whipple for his insights about Shelley. Other helpful aids are Kenneth Neill

Cameron, *Shelley: The Golden Years* (Cambridge: Harvard University Press, 1974), and Desmond King-Hele, *Shelley: His Thought and Work*, 2nd ed. (Teaneck, N.J.: Fairleigh Dickinson University Press, 1971). Shelley's reputation is the subject of Karsten Klejs Engleberg, *The Making of the Shelley Myth: An Annotated Bibliography of Criticism of Percy Bysshe Shelley, 1822–1860* (London: Mansell, 1988). Lionel Trilling's reading of "Ode to the West Wind" is in his *Prefaces to the Experience of Literature* (New York: Harcourt Brace Jovanovich, 1979).

I also consulted Betty T. Burnett, ed., *The Letters of Mary Wollstonecraft Shelley*, 2 vols. (Baltimore: Johns Hopkins University Press, 1980); Paula R. Feldman and Diana Scott-Kilvert, eds., *The Journals of Mary Shelley, 1814–1844*, 2 vols. (Oxford, Clarendon Press, 1987); and Emily W. Sunstein, *Mary Shelley: Romance and Reality* (Boston: Little, Brown, 1989). On other key figures in this extraordinary story, see Benita Eisler, *Byron: Child of Passion, Fool of Fame* (New York: Knopf, 1999), and Ernest J. Lovell Jr., *Captain Medwin: Friend of Byron and Shelley* (Austin: University of Texas Press, 1962).

The subject of the meaning of the sea and the myths and superstitious surrounding it is vast. Among recent books, see Alain Corbin, *The Lure of the Sea: The Discovery of the Seaside in the Western World, 1750–1840* (Berkeley: University of California Press, 1994), and Jonathan Raban, *Passage to Juneau: A Sea and Its Meanings* (New York: Pantheon, 1999). Alexander Frederick Falconer, *Shakespeare and the Sea* (London: Constable, 1964), is a guide to Shakespeare's treatment of the sea, storms, and mariners. On Charles II and the founding of English yachting, see John Rousmaniere, *The Golden Pastime* (New York: W. W. Norton, 1987).

On mariners' religious nature (and obsessions), my sources include Eric Newby, *The Last Grain Race* (1956; reprint, Oakland, Calif.: Lonely Planet, 1999); Walter Magnes Teller, *The Search for Captain Slocum* (New York: Scribner's, 1956); and E. B. White's "The Sea and the Wind That Blows," which may be found in many anthologies, including Peter Neill, ed., *American Sea Writing: A Literary Anthology* (New York: Library of America, 2000). "The hour is come but not the man" is in Crispin Gill, *The Isles of Scilly* (Newton Abbot: David & Charles, 1975).

For guidance on Hebrew roots, I am indebted to Leah Ruth Robinson Rousmaniere, and also to Hans-Joachim Kraus, *Psalms 60–150* (Minneapolis: Fortress, 1993), and to Artur Weiser, *The Psalms: A Commentary* (Philadelphia: Westminster, 1962). On "living waters," see C. G. Jung, *Symbols of Transformation*, 2nd ed. (Princeton: Princeton University Press, 1956), and Raymond E. Brown, *The Gospel According to John*, The Anchor Bible (Garden City, N.Y.: Doubleday, 1985).

On sea literature, Robert Foulke, *The Sea Voyage Narrative* (New York: Twayne, 1997), offers a stimulating overview. Sources of mariners' superstitions include Margaret Baker, *The Folklore of the Sea* (London: David and Charles, 1979); Horace Beck, *Folklore and the Sea* (Mystic, Conn.: Mystic Seaport Museum/Wesleyan University Press, 1973); W. Jeffrey Bolster, *Black Jack: African American Seamen in the Age of Sail* (Cambridge: Harvard University Press, 1997); Christopher Columbus,

The Columbus Log, trans. Robert H. Fuson (Camden, Maine: International Marine, 1987); Hans Jürgen Hansen, ed., *Art and the Seafarer* (New York: Viking, 1968); Ronald Hope, *Poor Jack: The Perilous History of the Merchant Seaman* (London: Chatham, 2001); Don H. Kennedy, *Ship Names: Origins and Usages during Forty-Five Centuries* (Newport News, Va.: Mariners Museum/University Press of Virginia, 1974); Carr Laughton and V. Heddon, *Great Storms* (London: Philip Allan, 1927); Leland P. Lovette, *Naval Customs: Traditions and Usage* (Annapolis, Md.: Naval Institute, 1939); Iona Opie and Moira Tatem, eds., *A Dictionary of Superstitions* (New York: Oxford University Press, 1989); Charles Tyng, *Before the Wind: The Memoir of an American Sea Captain, 1808–1833* (New York: Penguin, 1999); and Lyall Watson, *Heaven's Breath: A Natural History of the Wind* (London: Hodder & Stoughton, 1984). Folklorist Camille Bacon-Smith's quotation on the Internet and disaster myths is in the Week in Review section of the *New York Times*, September 23, 2001.

On Mediterranean weather I consulted Rod Heikell, *Italian Waters Pilot*, 5th ed. (St. Ives, U.K.: Imray, 1998), and his *Mediterranean Sailing* (London: Nautical, 1988).

Theodore Roosevelt's account of a bitter squall is in his article "Sou'-Sou' Southerly," which he apparently wrote soon afterward and submitted for publication without success. After noticing a reference to the piece in Edmund Morris's *The Rise of Theodore Roosevelt*, through the good graces of the Theodore Roosevelt Association, and with Morris's assistance, I acquired a copy of the manuscript. This stirring storm story was finally published, with my introduction, in *Gray's Sporting Journal* 13, no. 3 (fall 1988): 70–75. Stephen Sondheim's "Reduction releases power" is in Frank Rich, "Conversations with Sondheim," *New York Times Magazine*, March 12, 2000.

On recovery and coping self-efficacy, see Charles C. Benight, Erika Swift, Jean Sanger, Anne Smith, and Dan Zepplin, "Coping Self-Efficacy as a Mediator of Distress Following a Natural Disaster," *Journal of Applied Social Psychology* 29 (1999): 2,443–64.

John Leach, *Survival Psychology* (New York: New York University Press, 1994), is the source of the estimates of the proportion of heroes, cowards, and others in disaster, based on the research of J. S. Tyhurst (there is more on this topic in the notes section of chapter 7).

On the James Dean effect, see Ed Diener, Derrick Wirtz, and Shigehiro Oishi, "End Effects of Rated Life Quality: The James Dean Effect," *Psychological Science* 12, no. 2 (March 2001): 124–28.

Chapter 2. The *Elizabeth* and Margaret Fuller

My account of the wreck of the *Elizabeth* and its aftermath is based to a small extent on informed conjecture but largely on the contemporary reports in New York and Philadelphia newspapers in late July 1850. (Many of these stories are collected in *American Transcendental Quarterly*, fall 1975.)

The literature on Margaret Fuller is extensive. Especially helpful are the well-annotated *The Letters of Margaret Fuller*, 6 vols., ed. Robert N. Hudspeth (Ithaca, N.Y.: Cornell University Press, 1994). Hudspeth's introduction to volume 1 provides an excellent profile of Fuller. Volume 6 includes several letters by her and Catherine Hasty quoted here. Also helpful are Bell Gale Chevigny, *The Woman and the Myth: Margaret Fuller's Life and Writings*, 2nd ed. (Boston: Northeastern University Press, 1994); Jeffrey Steele, ed., *The Essential Margaret Fuller* (New Brunswick, N.J.: Rutgers University Press, 1992); Charles Capper, *Margaret Fuller: An American Romantic Life*, vol. 1, *The Private Years* (New York: Oxford University Press, 1992); Faith Chipperfield, *In Quest of Love: The Life and Death of Margaret Fuller* (New York: Coward-McCann, 1957); and Eve Kornfeld, *Margaret Fuller: A Brief Biography with Documents* (Boston: Bedford, 1997).

On her community, see Joel Porte, ed., *Emerson in His Journals* (Cambridge, Mass.: Belknap, 1982); Henry David Thoreau, *Writings*, ed. Bradford Torrey (1905; reprint, New York: AMS, 1968); and Thomas R. Mitchell, *Hawthorne's Margaret Fuller Mystery* (Amherst: University of Massachusetts Press, 1998). Thoreau's ruminations on his search at Fire Island are in his *Cape Cod*, available in numerous editions, including a recent volume in the Library of America series.

Henry Bangs's family history is in Dean Dudley, *History and Genealogy of the Bangs Family in America* (Montrose, Mass.: Dudley, 1896), in census records, and in materials provided by Catherine S. Medich of the New Jersey State Archives, Trenton, N.J., and Lori Morse of the Free Library of Philadelphia. His 1852 voyage is documented in *Maritime Records, Port of Philadelphia* (Harrisburg: Pennsylvania Historical Commission, n.d.), sec. 5, Chronological List of Crews, 1852, 35.

On ship captains, see Richard Henry Dana Jr., *The Seaman's Friend* (Boston: Little, Brown and Loring, 1841); Nicholas Dean, *Snow Squall: The Last American Clipper Ship* (Bath, Maine: Maine Maritime Museum, 2001), where I found Charles E. Ranlett's quotation; and Ronald Hope, *Poor Jack: The Perilous History of the Merchant Seaman* (London: Chatham, 2001).

On navigation, see *The American Coast Pilot* ("Blunt's"), 15th and 16th eds. (New York: Blunt, 1847 and 1850); *American Practical Navigator: An Epitome of Navigation and Nautical Astronomy* (Washington, D.C.: Government Printing Office, 1930), best known as "Bowditch"; John F. Campbell, *History and Bibliography of the New American Practical Navigator and the American Coast Pilot* (Salem: Peabody Museum, 1964); George R. Putnam, *Lighthouses and Lightships of the United States* (Boston: Houghton Mifflin, 1917); *Instructions to Light-Keepers/Lighthouse Vessels* (1902; reprint, Great Lakes Lighthouse Keepers Association, 1989); Douglas Phillips-Birt, *The History of Seamanship* (Garden City, N.Y.: Doubleday, 1971); Charles Lee Lewis, *Matthew Fontaine Maury: The Pathfinder of the Seas* (Annapolis, Md.: Naval Institute, 1927); and Edward Rowe Snow, *The Lighthouses of New England, 1716–1973* (New York: Dodd, Mead, 1973).

On weather, "The sleeping giant" is in William Albert Robinson, *To the Great*

Southern Sea (New York: Harcourt Brace, 1956). William Redfield's description of what turned out to be the *Elizabeth*'s weather is in George W. Blunt, ed., *The Way to Avoid the Centre of Our Violent Gales* (New York: Blunt, 1866). David M. Ludlum tracked the 1850 hurricane in *Early American Hurricanes, 1492–1870* (Boston: American Meteorological Society, 1963). See also Lyall Watson, *Heaven's Breath: A Natural History of the Wind* (London: Hodder and Stoughton, 1984); William G. Van Dorn, *Oceanography and Seamanship*, 2nd ed. (Centreville, Md.: Cornell Maritime, 1993); Michael Carr, "Wind, Waves, and Sailors," www.sailnet.com, March 11, 2001; and Eric Newby, *The Last Grain Race* (1956; reprint, Oakland, Calif.: Lonely Planet, 1999).

The account of Captain Colcord and the *Elizabeth*'s wreck at San Francisco is in Frederick C. Matthews, *American Merchant Ships, 1850–1900* (Salem, Mass.: Marine Research Society, 1930). The story of *Katsura* is based on my knowledge as an expert witness in litigation concerning the accident.

The dangers of the approaches to New York harbor are laid out in Jeannette Edwards Rattray, *Ship Ashore! A Record of Maritime Disasters off Montauk and Eastern Long Island, 1640–1955* (New York: Coward-McCann, 1955), the source of "melted like a lump of sugar"; Edward L. Allen, ed., *Pilot Lore: From Sail to Steam* (New York: United New York and New Jersey Sandy Hook Pilots Benevolent Associations, 1922); Robert Greenhalgh Albion, *The Rise of New York Port, 1815–1860* (New York: Scribner's, 1939), the source of the shipboard mortality rates; Bradley Sheard, *Lost Voyages: Two Centuries of Shipwrecks in the Approaches to New York* (Lanham, Md.: National Book Network, 1997); Edwin G. Burrows and Mike Wallace, *Gotham: A History of New York City to 1895* (New York: Oxford University Press, 1999); and *United States Coast Pilot*, 30th ed., 1998.

On Gerard Manley Hopkins and "The Wreck of the *Deutschland*," see Norman White, *Hopkins: A Literary Biography* (Oxford: Clarendon Press, 1992).

On hypothermia, see John Leach, *Survival Psychology* (New York: New York University Press, 1994), and Frank C. Craighead Jr. and John J. Craighead, *How to Survive on Land and Sea*, 4th ed. (Annapolis, Md.: Naval Institute Press, 1974).

On sleep deprivation, I consulted Leach, *Survival Psychology*; Jonathan Shay, "Ethical Standing for Commander Self-Care: The Need for Sleep," *Parameters*, summer 1998; Samuel Eliot Morison, *The Struggle for Guadalcanal, August 1842–February 1943*, History of United States Naval Operations in World War II, vol. 5 (Boston: Little, Brown, 1954); Gregory Belenky, "Sleep, Sleep Deprivation, and Human Performance in Continuous Operations," *Joint Services Conference on Professional Ethics proceedings*, JSCOPE 97, January 19, 1997; Ellen MacArthur's comments, www.sailthatdream.com/current/whats_on/the_vendee/Kingfisher/000429kingfisher.htm; Claudio Stampi, "Around the World in 891 Naps," *Seahorse*, April 2001; and Jan Horbulewicz, "The Parameters of the Psychological Autonomy of Industrial Trawler Crews," in *Seafarer and Community*, ed. Peter H. Fricke (London: Croom Helm, 1973), 67–84.

Chapter 3. The Yankee Gale

The anonymous writer's story of a trip to Georges Bank is in George H. Procter, *The Fishermen's Memorial and Record Book: Containing a List of Vessels and Their Crews Lost from the Port of Gloucester from the Year 1830 to October 1, 1873* (Gloucester, Mass.: Procter Brothers, 1873). Henry David Thoreau's account of his visit to Cape Cod is in his *Cape Cod*. The old captain's picture of "hard-lined, parchment-looking faces" is in W. H. Bunting, "A Day's Work," *WoodenBoat*, November–December 1997.

On mortality rates, my sources include: (wars) *Historical Statistics of the United States: Colonial Times to 1870* (Washington, D.C.: U.S. Department of Commerce, 1976), 2:1140; (Southport and Boothbay) Francis B. Greene, *History of Boothbay, Southport, and Boothbay Harbor, 1623–1905* (Portland, Maine: Loring, Short, and Harmon, 1906), and data from Barbara Skinner Rumsey, Boothbay Region Historical Society; and (Gloucester) Joseph Garland, *The Fishing Schooners of Gloucester* (Boston: Godine, 1983), and data from Ellen Nelson, Cape Ann Historical Association. The mortality rates calculated in the table are based on the assumption that approximately one-fourth of residents of New England fishing towns were active fishermen. See also Eric W. Sager, *Seafaring Labour: The Merchant Marine of Canada, 1820–1914* (Kingston: McGill-Queen's University Press, 1989), as cited by Nicholas Dean in *Snow Squall: The Last American Clipper Ship* (Bath: Maine Maritime Museum, 2001).

Other sources on towns include William Hutchinson Rowe, *The Maritime History of Maine* (1948; reprint, Gardiner, Maine: Harpswell, 1989); Stephan Thernstrom, *Poverty and Progress: Social Mobility in a Nineteenth-Century City* (Cambridge: Harvard University Press, 1964); and Samuel Eliot Morison, *The Maritime History of Massachusetts* (Boston: Houghton Mifflin, 1921). The characterization of Joshua Slocum by his son Aymar is in Walter Teller, *The Search for Captain Slocum* (New York: Scribner's, 1956).

An excellent source on the Yankee Gale, including meteorological observations, is Edward MacDonald, "The Yankee Gale," *Island Magazine* 38 (fall–winter 1995), 17–25. Professor MacDonald, of the University of Prince Edward Island, kindly provided further information. Numerous accounts of the Yankee Gale and fishing off Prince Edward Island are on the *Island Register* Web site maintained by T. W. Stewart and Dave Hunter, www.islandregister.com/yankeegale.html, and on the *Out of Gloucester* Web site maintained by Roberta Sheedy, www.downtosea.com. Thanks to both Dave Hunter and Roberta Sheedy for their helpful correspondence. Hunter's comments about the natural tendency of islanders to assist those in trouble are from personal correspondence.

Conditions on "the Bay" are described in *Sailing Directions: Gulf and River St. Lawrence*, 4th ed. (Ottawa: Department of Fisheries and Oceans, 1980), and in George H. Hepworth, *Starboard and Port: The Nettie Along Shore* (New York: Harper, 1876). Some Prince Edward Island traditions concerning the storm are in Lucy Maud Montgomery, *The Golden Road* (1913).

Henry Bray's lively account of the storm and the wreck of the *Harvest Home* is in Wesley George Pierce, *Going Fishing: The Story of the Deep-Sea Fishermen of New England* (Camden, Maine: International Marine, 1989 [originally published in 1934 as *Goin' Fishin'*]), and is excerpted with the permission of the Boothbay Region Historical Society.

On weather signs and meteorological "bombs," see Michael William Carr, *Weather Predicting Simplified: How to Read Weather Charts and Satellite Images* (Camden, Maine: International Marine, 1999).

The chilling quotation likening the sea to a mausoleum is by J. L. R. Trask in "The Gloucester of Yesterday and the Gloucester of Tomorrow." *Memorial of the Celebration of the 250th Anniversary of the Incorporation of the Town of Gloucester, Mass., August 1892* (Boston: Mudge, 1901). For effects of emotional deprivation at sea, see Jan Horbulewicz, "The Parameters of the Psychological Autonomy of Industrial Trawler Crews," *Seafarer and Community*, ed. Peter H. Fricke (London: Croom Helm, 1973), 67–83. The Gloucester Fishermen's Wives Memorial is described in the Web site of the Gloucester Fishermen's Wives Association, www.gfwa.org.

The description of "The Atlantic Captain" is in Joseph Conrad, *The Mirror of the Sea* (1924).

The bonds between all sailors at sea are described by Samuel Eliot Morison in *The Liberation of the Philippines: Luzon, Mindanao, the Visayas, 1944–1945*, History of United States Naval Operations in World War II, vol. 13 (Boston: Little, Brown, 1959). Special cases are covered in: (around-the-world racing sailors) Derek Lundy, *Godforsaken Sea* (New York: Anchor, 2000); (submariners) Christopher Drew, *New York Times Week in Review*, August 20, 2000; (soldiers) Leo Tolstoy, *War and Peace*, bk. 10, chaps. 31–32; and (wreck survivors) Stephen Crane, "The Open Boat," in *American Sea Writing: A Literary Anthology*, ed. Peter Neill (New York: Library of America, 2000).

Richard Henry Dana's description of the day of mourning at sea is in his *Two Years before the Mast*, chap. 6, and in Neill, ed., *American Sea Writing*. See also Samuel Schapiro, *Richard Henry Dana, Jr., 1815–1882* (East Lansing: Michigan State University Press, 1961). For burial at sea and related beliefs, see Leland P. Lovelle, *Naval Customs: Traditions and Usage* (Annapolis, Md.: Naval Institute, 1939); Horace Beck, *Folklore and the Sea* (Mystic, Conn.: Mystic Seaport Museum/ Wesleyan University Press, 1973), the source of "The Sailor's Grave"; and Iona Opie and Moira Tatem, eds., *A Dictionary of Superstition* (New York: Oxford University Press, 1989). Margaret Fuller's report of the funeral of Captain Seth Hasty is in volume 6 of her letters, cited at the end of chapter 2. My thanks to Rev. Jon Paulus for telling me about the tradition of grieving the losses of Great Lake ships in song.

On disaster-related stress for individuals and communities, see in general Ellen S. Zinner and Mary Beth Williams, eds., *When a Community Weeps: Case Studies in Group Survivorship* (Philadelphia: Brunner/Mazel, 1998), especially Mary Beth

Williams, Ellen S. Zinner, and Richard R. Ellis, "The Connection between Grief and Trauma: An Overview," 3–17, the source of the quotation about opportunity. See also John Leach, *Survival Psychology* (New York: New York University Press, 1994); Daniella David and Thomas A. Mellman, "Dreams Following Hurricane Andrew," *Dreaming* 7 (1997): 209–14; and Bessel A. Van der Kolk and Rachel Yehuda, "Resilience, Vulnerability, and the Course of Posttraumatic Reactions," *Traumatic Stress: The Effects of Overwhelming Experience on Mind, Body, and Society*, ed. Bessel A. Van der Kolk, Alexander McFarlane, and Lars Weisaeth (New York: Guilford, 1996), 155–81. On attitudes of rescuers, including rituals, see B. Raphael, B. Singh, L. Bradbury, and F. Lambert, "Who Helps the Helpers? The Effects of a Disaster on the Rescue Workers," *Omega* 14, no. 1 (1983–84): 9–20; Lasse Nurmi, "The *Estonia* Disaster: National Interventions, Outcomes, and Personal Impacts," in Zinner and Williams, eds., *When a Community Weeps*; and W. Russell Webster, "Rescuers Can Be Victims, Too," Naval Institute *Proceedings*, December 1995. The terrors of the unknown in the context of the Black Death are in Barbara Tuchman, *The Proud Tower: The Calamitous Fourteenth Century* (New York: Knopf, 1978).

For the controversy concerning the treatment of the yachtsman in *The Perfect Storm*, see the interview with Sebastian Junger in U.S. Naval Institute *Proceedings*, July 2000, and Herb McCormick, "Skipper and His Boat Both Survived the Storm," *New York Times*, August 6, 2000.

Chapter 4. The Escape of the *Calliope*

On the storm, helpful contemporary or near-contemporary sources include the daily reports in the *Times* of London, April 1889; Lewis A. Kimberly, "Samoa and the Hurricane of March 1889," *Naval Actions and History, 1799–1898* (Boston: Military Historical Society of Massachusetts, 1902); and Robert Louis Stevenson, *A Footnote to History: Eight Years of Trouble in Samoa* (1892; reprint, Honolulu: University of Hawaii Press, 1996). The U.S. Navy's official report, *Disaster at Apia, Samoa* (Washington, D.C.: Government Printing Office, 1889), is stiff and defensive. Helpful recent materials include Ernest Andrade, "The Great Samoan Hurricane of 1889," *Naval War College Review* 34 (1981): 73–81; J. A. C. Gray, "The Apia Hurricane of 1889," U.S. Naval Institute *Proceedings* 86 (June 1960): 35–39; and Oliver Warner, "Storm at Samoa," *Mariner's Mirror* 44 (1958): 286–93. The storm was analyzed by navy meteorologist Everett Hayden, "The Samoan Hurricane of March 1889," U.S. Naval Institute *Proceedings* 17 (1891): 283–95. The only book on the subject, Edwin P. Hoyt, *The Typhoon That Stopped a War* (New York: David MacKay, 1968), has excellent maps of the harbor.

On the diplomatic context, see R. P. Gilson, *Samoa, 1830 to 1890: The Politics of a Multi-Cultural Community* (Melbourne: Oxford University Press, 1970), and Paul M. Kennedy, *The Samoan Tangle: A Study in Anglo-German-American Relations, 1878–1900* (New York: Barnes & Noble, 1974).

Concerning naval policy and technology, see George W. Baer, *One Hundred Years of Sea Power: The U.S. Navy, 1890–1990* (Stanford: Stanford University Press, 1994); D. K. Brown, *Warrior to Dreadnought: Warship Development, 1860–1905* (London: Chatham, 1997); D. K. Brown, "Seamanship, Steam, and Steel—HMS *Calliope* at Samoa 15–16 March 1889," *Warship* 48 (October 1988): 30–36; Gerhard Koop, "The Imperial German Navy and the Hurricane at Samoa," *Warship* 48 (October 1988): 36–42; Stephen B. Luce, *Text-Book of Seamanship: The Equipping and Handling of Vessels Under Sail or Steam*, rev. ed. (New York: Van Nostrand, 1884); Alfred T. Mahan, *From Sail to Steam: Recollections of a Naval Life* (New York: Harper, 1907); G. A. Osbon, "Passing of the Steam and Sail Corvette: The Comus and Calliope Classes," *Mariner's Mirror* 49 (1963): 193–208; and Harold and Margaret Sprout, *The Rise of American Naval Power, 1776–1918* (Princeton: Princeton University Press, 1939).

On Robert Louis Stevenson, see Ian Bell, *Robert Louis Stevenson: Dreams of Exile* (Edinburgh: Mainstream, 1992); Hunter Davies, *The Teller of Tales: In Search of Robert Louis Stevenson* (London: Sinclair-Stevenson, 1994); and Gavin Daws, *Dream of Islands: Voyages of Self-Discovery in the South Seas* (New York: W. W. Norton, 1980).

On Henry Coey Kane, see his obituary in the *Times* of London, February 1, 1917, and passing references in Lord William Laird Clowes, ed., *The Royal Navy: A History* (Boston: Little, Brown, 1903), vol. 6.

Banjo Paterson's "The Ballad of the *Calliope*" was first published in the *Antipodean* in 1897 and can be found on the Internet at www.gfwa.org. The legends of the dueling bands are laid out in the *New York Times*'s obituaries for Kimberly (January 29, 1902) and Kane (February 1, 1917).

Chapter 5. The Loss of the *Portland*

The excerpt from President McKinley's Thanksgiving Day proclamation is on the Pilgrim Hall Museum's Web site, www.pilgrimhall.org/thankpro.htm.

On the storm, I relied on newspapers of New York, Boston, and Portland and on an essential recent book by Peter Dow Bachelder and Mason Philip Smith, *Four Short Blasts: The Gale of 1898 and the Loss of the Steamer Portland* (Portland, Maine: Provincial Press, 1998). My thanks to Mason Smith for providing many illustrations. The *Portland* gale story is told in less detail in Thomas Harrison Eames, "The Wreck of the Steamer *Portland*," *New England Quarterly* 13 (June 1940): 191–206; E. B. Rideout, "The Day the Weather Bureau Was Right," in *New England's Disastrous Weather* (Camden, Maine: Yankee Books, 1990), 57–60; and Edward Rowe Snow, *Storms and Shipwrecks of New England* (Boston: Yankee Books, 1943). The startling "unending funeral" quotation is in Sylvester Baxter, "The Great November Storm of 1898," *Scribner's Magazine*, November 1899, 515–24. Linus Shaw's vision of the sinking of the *Portland* is described in Russell W. Knight, "Mr. Shaw 'Sees' *Portland* Sink," *American Neptune* 29 (June 1969): 224–25.

On New England steam, see W. H. Bunting, *Portrait of a Port: Boston, 1852–1914* (Cambridge: Belknap/Harvard University Press, 1971); Edwin L. Dunbaugh, *Night Boat to New England, 1815–1900* (New York: Greenwood, 1972); Roger F. Duncan, *Coastal Maine: A Maritime History* (New York: W. W. Norton, 1992); Edward Chase Kirkland, *Men, Cities, and Transportation: A Study in New England History, 1820–1900* (Cambridge: Harvard University Press, 1948); and Samuel Eliot Morison, *The Story of Mount Desert Island, Maine* (Boston: Little, Brown/Atlantic Monthly Press, 1960). Roberta Sheedy of Gloucester, Web master of the excellent Down to the Sea in Ships Web site, passed along the family memory of her grandmother's sighting of the *Portland* as the steamer passed Thacher Island.

Concerning Portland's African American community, see Herbert Adams, "S.S. *Portland,*" *Portland Monthly Magazine Winterguide,* (December 1998), 10–23; Randolph P. Dominic Jr., "Down from the Balcony: The Abyssinian Congregational Church of Portland, Maine," typescript, 1982, in the Maine Historical Society, Portland, Maine; *Anchor of the Soul* (videotape, Maine Public Television, 1995); Randolph Stakeman, "The Black Population of Maine," *New England Journal of Black Studies* 8 (1989): 17–35 (my thanks to Professor Stakeman of Bowdoin College for sending me the piece); W. Jeffrey Bolster, *Black Jacks: African American Seamen in the Age of Sail* (Cambridge: Harvard University Press, 1997); and Mary Malloy, *African Americans in the Maritime Trades: A Guide to Resources in New England* (Sharon, Mass.: Kendall Whaling Museum, 1990). The Maine Historical Society's African American file contains many helpful clippings and other materials.

A search for coverage of the *Portland* disaster in contemporary African American newspapers was disappointing. Appallingly few copies of historical black publications survive in the Negro Newspapers on Microfilm collection, which I consulted at the Schomburg Center for Research in Black Culture in the New York Public Library. Only the December 3, 1889, issue of the *Wichita Tribune* covered the *Portland* gale, with no mention of the ship's large complement of black crew members.

For cultural responses to disasters, see Rachel Yehuda's and Marilyn Bowman's interviews with Martin L. Korn in *Medscape Mental Health* 6, no. 5 (2001).

Edward Rowe Snow wrote about himself in the 25th and 50th *Anniversary Reports* of the Harvard Class of 1932 (Cambridge: Harvard College, 1957, 1982). I also consulted *Story of a Storyteller* (videotape, Chronicle, 1996), a documentary film about Snow provided to me by the *Chronicle* show at the Boston Channel, Needham, Massachusetts, and printed materials sent by Snow's friend Jeremy D'Entremont, of Coastlore Productions. The Edward Rowe Snow Collection in the Special Collections of Boston University includes considerable material about him and the *Portland.* I have quoted or summarized several documents in that collection: Ethel Campbell's letter concerning her visit to the *Portland* (to the Yankee Network, June 23, 1950); Mrs. Harmon S. Babcock's letter concerning her husband (to Snow, April 11, 1956); J. D. Casey's letter concerning the *Amoco Virginia* storm (to Snow, April 5, 1974); and Mrs. Carrie M. S. Courtney's letter concerning Captain Blanchard's reasons for rushing home (to Snow, undated).

Snow's eccentric collection of artifacts is at the Peabody Essex Museum, Salem, Massachusetts; Daniel Finamore provided me a copy of the accession list. Snow described the wreck as "practically disemboweled" in a column that was reprinted in the New Bedford, Massachusetts, *Standard-Times*, November 29, 1998.

Concerning Hollis Blanchard, see the interview with Captain Craig in the Portland *Daily Eastern Argus*, December 6, 1898, and A. M. Austin, "History and Report," typescript, 1924, in the Maine Historical Society. The latter is the confidential internal history of the Portland Steamship Company and its successor, the Eastern Steamship Lines. I have quoted from Carleton Potter Small's letter in the Snow Collection concerning the Blanchard family's fear of publicity (February 24, 1949). The editorial attacking Blanchard was published in the *New York Times*, December 1, 1898.

On weather forecasting in and around 1898, Mark Monmonier uses the *Portland* storm as an example of U.S. Weather Bureau procedures in "Seeing and Forecasting: How Meteorologists Learned to Map, Predict, and Dramatize Weather," on the *Columbia Earthscape* Web site. See also E. B. Garriott, *Long Range Weather Forecasts* (Washington, D.C.: U.S. Weather Bureau, 1892), where Moore, in an introduction, fumed about "the pseudo scientist"; Gilbert H. Grosvenor, "Our Heralds of Storm and Flood," *Century Magazine*, June 1905, 161–78; Alfred J. Henry, "Amplification of Weather Forecasts" (Washington, D.C.: U.S. Weather Bureau, 1900); and Gustavus A. Weber, *The Weather Bureau: Its History, Activities, and Organization* (New York: Appleton, 1922). The story of Moore's approach to William McKinley is in Hobart E. Stocking, "Nine Day Wonders," *Natural History*, September 1943. For the Galveston hurricane, see Erik Larson, *Isaac's Storm* (New York: Random House, 1999). The inaccurate forecast for the 1938 hurricane is in James Dodson, "The Wind That Shook the World," in *New England's Disastrous Weather* (Camden, Maine: Yankee Books, 1990), 3–33.

The Weather Bureau publication *Monthly Weather Review*, vol. 26, November and December 1898, provides considerable information about the incomplete forecast and the storm's history. Thanks to the Geology Library at Columbia University for saving this valuable publication. The former America's Cup yacht *Magic*'s trying experiences in the coastal storm are described in the *New York Herald*, November 29, 1898.

Concerning weather, Alan Watts referred to the 1979 Fastnet Race storm's "corridors of extremely strong winds" in *The Weather Handbook* (Dobbs Ferry, N.Y.: Sheridan House, 1994), and Joseph M. Sienkiewicz described wind as "like a colander" at a safety-at-sea seminar at the U.S. Naval Academy on March 31, 2001. "Bombs" are briefly described in Michael William Carr, *Weather Predicting Simplified: How to Read Weather Charts and Satellite Images* (Camden, Maine: International Marine, 1999). On hurricane prediction errors, see Hugo du Plessis, "Circles of Uncertainty," *Ocean Navigator*, January–February 2001, 88–90. For other storm disasters, the sinking of the *Estonia* is described in Lasse Nurmi, "The *Estonia* Disaster: National Interventions, Outcomes, and Personal Impacts," Ellen S. Zinner and Mary Beth Williams, eds., *When a Community Weeps: Case Studies in Group Survivorship* (Philadelphia: Brunner/Mazel, 1998).

Concerning the 1979 Fastnet and 1998 Sydney–Hobart storms and Hurricane Mitch, see John Rousmaniere, *Fastnet, Force 10*, rev. ed. (New York: W. W. Norton, 2000); Rob Mundle, *Fatal Storm: The Inside Story of the Tragic Sydney–Hobart Race* (Camden, Maine: International Marine, 1999); and Jim Carrier, *The Ship and the Storm: Hurricane Mitch and the Loss of the Fantome* (Camden, Maine: International Marine, 2000). Admiral Nimitz's order to the U.S. Navy Pacific Fleet may be found on the Naval Historical Center's Web site, www.history.navy.mil.

Chapter 6. *Hamrah* and the Ameses

A number of generous people have told me much about *Hamrah* and her people: Phyllis Ames Cox, the Ames boys' cousin; Rose Matteson Tillinghast, the widow of Charles F. Tillinghast Jr., and their daughter Harriet Tillinghast Goodrich; and Hilary Weed Ware, the daughter of Roger Weed. H. Holton Wood, Donald B. Straus, Virginia Graves, and Jane Fisher provided helpful information about Margaret Ames. Charles Ames granted access to his great-aunt Margaret Ames's papers under perfect working conditions. Others who were helpful include Stanley Livingston Jr., Thomas Hazlehurst, Edwin H. Hastings, Richard E. Mooney, Henry H. Anderson Jr., James Barr Ames, Susan Ayer Ames, Danny D. Smith, and my father and brother, the two James A. Rousmanieres. Clippings and other information were provided by Bronwyn Long in Boulder, Colorado; Barbara Conway of the *Transylvania Times* and the staff of the *Asheville Citizens Times*, both in North Carolina; Chris Larade and Anne Connell at the Beaton Institute, University College of Cape Breton, Sydney, Nova Scotia; Charles A. Campo and Richard Warren at the *Bangor Daily News*, in Maine; Sally Foote of the Castine, Maine, Historical Society; and Frank. L. Foster Jr. of the Machiasport, Maine, Historical Society.

On the elder James Barr Ames, see "Memoir of James Barr Ames," in James Barr Ames, *Lectures on Legal History* (Cambridge: Harvard University Press, 1913), 3–26; Charles W. Eliot, "James Barr Ames," *Harvard Law Review* 23 (1910): 321–24; and Kathleen A. Mahoney, "James Barr Ames," *American National Biography*, 1:415. Charles B. McLane described the "insatiable thirst" of cottagers for land and the Dirigo Island scheme in *Islands of the Mid-Maine Coast: Penobscot and Blue Hill Bays* (Woolwich, Maine: Kennebec River Press, 1982), a volume in his superb series of historical-archaeological surveys of Maine's coast. See also Catherine O'Clair Herson, *Sorrento, A Well-Kept Secret: A Photographic Journal* (Sorrento, Maine: n.p., 1995). The "cemetery" quotation is in Harold F. Wilson, *The Hill Country of Northern New England: Its Social and Economic History, 1790–1930* (New York: Columbia University Press, 1936).

On the strenuous life, see David McCullough's study of Theodore Roosevelt's complex makeup in *Mornings on Horseback* (New York: Simon and Schuster/ Touchstone, 1981). Roosevelt's talk is in his book *The Strenuous Life: Essays and*

Addresses (1900); his famous (and often misquoted) comment about "black care" is in his *Ranching Life and the Hunting Trail* (1888), chap. 5. See H. W. Brands, *TR: The Last Romantic* (New York: Basic Books, 1997). See John Muir, *My First Summer in the Sierra* (1911), in Muir, *Nature Writings* (New York: Library of America, 1997); and Maurice Griffiths, *Magic of the Swatchways* (1932; reprint, London: Conway, 1971).

The quotations from William James are in his essays "What Makes a Life Significant," "The Moral Equivalent of War," and "On a Certain Blindness in Human Beings." The first and third are in his *Talks to Teachers* (New York: W. W. Norton, 1948). "The Moral Equivalent of War" is widely anthologized. His wife's comment about his death is in Linda Simon, *Genuine Reality: A Life of William James* (New York: Harcourt Brace, 1999). Joshua Slocum's relationship with the Roosevelts is in Walter Magnes Teller, *The Search for Captain Slocum* (New York, Scribner's, 1956).

For the concern about "nervous exhaustion" and related worries, see Ben Shephard, *A War of Nerves: Soldiers and Psychiatrists in the Twentieth Century* (Cambridge: Harvard University Press, 2001). For character building, Seton, and the Boy Scouts, see Michael Rosenthal, *The Character Factory: Baden-Powell and the Origins of the Boy Scout Movement* (New York: Pantheon, 1986). Charles W. Eliot's parable of the Gott Island boy is in National Education Association, *Proceedings and Addresses* (1900); his outrage at pickoff moves is noted in Henry James, *Charles W. Eliot* (Boston: Houghton Mifflin, 1930), vol. 2.

Material concerning Margaret Ames is drawn from her obituary for her husband in the *Harvard Class of 1907: Thirtieth Anniversary Report*, and from documents in the Ames family collection, quoted here with the Ames family's permission; I have quoted her letter to Phyllis Ames Cox and James Barr Ames, March 3, 1963, and Richard Ames's letters to her of June 14, 1931, and June 29, 1934. See Ken Gormley, *Archibald Cox: Conscience of a Nation* (Reading, Mass.: Addison-Wesley, 1997). Eleanor Roosevelt's frustration is in Andrew W. German, "*Vireo*: A Boat for Franklin D. Roosevelt," *Log of Mystic Seaport* 53, no. 1 (summer 2001): 27. Alfred F. Loomis described his humbling meeting with the Ames boys in *Ocean Racing* (New York: Morrow, 1936).

For Merryweather Camp and Laura Richards, see Danny D. Smith's part biography, part inventory of the Richards papers, *The Yellow House Papers* (Camden, Maine, 1991), and the highly (and I think unfairly) critical chapter on her in Sam Bass Warner Jr., *Province of Reason* (Cambridge: Belknap/Harvard University Press, 1984). The Milton Academy valedictorian's speech, quoting Kipling, is in *Milton Orange and Blue*, June 1930.

Hamrah's construction details and history came from correspondence with Cora Stevens, granddaughter and great-niece of the builders, and with Ethel and Maureen Radzewicz, whose family owned her during the 1960s. I traced the yacht's ownerships in volumes of *Lloyds Register of American Yachts*.

On the background to the 1935 race, see Erling Tambs, *The Cruise of the Teddy*, Mariner's Library (1933; reprint, London: Rupert Hart-Davis, 1949), and his

"Crossing a Grim Atlantic," *Yachting*, August 1935, 43–45, 101–2. Carl Emil Petersen, of Nesøya, Norway, provided other information about this quixotic character in personal correspondence. Loomis's "soft repose" crack and George Roosevelt's article on crew preparation are in *Yachting*, March 1936 and May 1932. Henry H. Anderson Jr. is my source for Roosevelt's attempting to dissuade Ames from entering the race. Helpful prerace reports include those by William H. Taylor in the *New York Herald Tribune*, June 9, 1935, and the *New Yorker*, June 15, 1935 (the second piece is anonymous but is clearly in Taylor's style); by Joe King in the *New York World-Telegram*, June 3, 1935; by John Rendel in the *New York Times*, June 9, 1935; and (the account from the fishermen's hangout) by Glen Perry in the *New York Sun*, June 8, 1935. Most relevant clippings are collected in the scrapbooks in the New York Yacht Club Library and in a scrapbook kept for the yacht *Vamarie* in the club's archives.

For the 1866 ocean race, see Loomis, *Ocean Racing*, and John Rousmaniere, *The Golden Pastime: A New History of Yachting* (New York: W. W. Norton, 1987). Quotations by Thomas Fleming Day and William Nutting are from those sources and from Eric Devine, *Blow the Man Down* (New York: Doubleday, Doran, 1937); John Stephen Doherty, *The Boats They Sailed In* (New York: W. W. Norton, 1985); and John Parkinson Jr., *Nowhere Is Too Far: The Annals of the Cruising Club of America* (New York: Cruising Club of America, 1960). Joshua Slocum's remarks about religion and the sea are in a letter to Clifton Johnson, April 17, 1903, in the Teller Collection, the Kendall Institute, New Bedford Whaling Museum, #89-2, box 5, #32.

On the New York Yacht Club clubhouse, see John Rousmaniere, *The Clubhouse at Sea* (New York: New York Yacht Club, 2001). The quotation about wealth and yachting, by the yachting journalist J. D. Jerrold Kelley, is in Ed Holm, *Yachting's Golden Age* (New York: Knopf, 1999). The description of the spartan, win-or-else regimen in modern-day boats comes from the Internet newsletter *Grand Prix Sailor*, September 27, 2001. Kenneth Davidson's log entry for July 10, 1935, is in *Stormy Weather*'s log in the Roderick Stephens Jr. Collection, G. W. Blunt White Library, Mystic Seaport Museum. Roosevelt is quoted as being "scared pink" in the *New York Herald Tribune*, July 16, 1935.

My account of the *Hamrah* accident is based largely on Charles F. Tillinghast Jr.'s article, "The *Hamrah*'s Unfortunate Voyage," which originally appeared in the *Providence Journal* and was reprinted in the August 1935 *Yachting*, and on other articles based on interviews with Tillinghast or Roger Weed in the newspapers of Sydney, Nova Scotia; Bangor and Portland, Maine; Boston, Massachusetts; Providence, Rhode Island; and New York.

On rescuers and coping with disaster, see the sources for chapter 3. "Howgozit" briefings are described in W. Russell Webster, "Rescuers Can Be Victims, Too," U.S. Naval Institute *Proceedings*, December 1995.

Information about the surviving *Hamrah* sailors came from their autobiographical notes in *Harvard Class of 1938: Triennial Anniversary Report* (Ware); *Harvard Class of 1934: 25th Anniversary Report, 1959* (Weed); and *Harvard Class of 1935:*

25th Anniversary Report, 1960 (Tillinghast). Aspects of Weed's work in the interservice air-sea rescue operations are described in several volumes of Samuel Eliot Morison, *History of United States Naval Operations in World War II* (Boston: Houghton Mifflin, various dates); Malcolm E. Willoughby, *The U.S. Coast Guard in World War II* (Annapolis, Md.: Naval Institute Press, 1957); and John Brook Penfold, "Bring 'em Back Alive—Navy Style," United States Naval Institute *Proceedings* 71, no. 5 (May 1945): 499–504. Roger Weed's disappearance in 1962 and the discovery of his body were covered by the *Denver Post*, December 7–13, 1962, and June 23–24, 1963.

Tillinghast's lovely quotation opening "The action of those who were left" is in his letter to George Roosevelt, February 11, 1936, in the miscellaneous file, Cruising Club of America Archives, G. W. Blunt White Library, Mystic Seaport Museum. His letters concerning the Battle of Savo Island (to George Matteson, undated) and the typhoon (to his parents, April 3, 1945) have been published, along with his account of the *Hamrah* tragedy and other letters, in Rose Tillinghast, *Damon and Pythias in World War II* (Bloomington, Ind.: First Books Library, 2001).

Richard Ames kindly provided the quoted portion of his eulogy for his father, James Barr Ames. Concerning Margaret Ames, see her book, *For Those New to Sorrow* (1961; reprint, New York: n.p., 1991), which includes Laura Richards's poem, "For Margaret G. Ames." Quoted letters to her (from Laura Richards, June 5, 1936 and May 24, 1937) and from her (to James Barr Ames and Phyllis Ames Cox, March 2, 1963), as well as her essay "Longevity," the notebook in which she collected materials for her book, and family photographs are all in the Ames family collection, and are quoted or reproduced with the family's permission.

Chapter 7. The Wreck of the *Pollux*

This chapter is based on interviews with Henry Strauss, on a videotape of the *Pollux* reunion by Terri Strauss, and on Cassie Brown, *Standing into Danger* (Garden City, N.Y.: Doubleday, 1979).

William James wrote about the San Francisco earthquake in "On Some Mental Effects of the Earthquake," reprinted in William James, *Writings, 1902–1910* (New York: Library of America, 1987). His letter to his brother Henry is quoted in Linda Simon, *Genuine Reality: A Life of William James* (New York: Harcourt Brace, 1998).

The conference on stress among merchant mariners is reported in *Traumatic War Neuroses* (New York: United Seamen's Service, 1943). On the phases of a disaster, see John Leach, *Survival Psychology* (New York: New York University Press, 1994) and J. S. Tyhurst, "Individual Reactions to Community Disaster: The Natural History of Psychiatric Phenomena," *American Journal of Psychiatry* 107 (1951): 764–69. Behavior in the 1917 Nova Scotia gas explosion is described in S. H. Prince, *Catastrophe and Social Change* (New York: Columbia University Press, 1920). See also Ben Shephard, *A War of Nerves: Soldiers and Psychiatrists in the Twentieth Century* (Cambridge: Harvard University Press, 2001).

On cigarette smoking in the military, see Phil Richards and John J. Banigan, *How to Abandon Ship* (1942; reprint, Centreville, Md.: Cornell Maritime, 1988); Stephen E. Ambrose, *D-Day: The Climactic Battle of World War II* (New York: Simon and Schuster/Touchstone, 1994); Jean C. Beckham et al., "Smoking in Vietnam Combat Veterans with Post-Traumatic Stress Disorder," *Journal of Traumatic Stress* 8, no. 3 (1995): 461–72; and "U. C. Irvine Researchers Find Links between Emotions and Smoking Behavior," University of California at Irvine Press Release, April 28, 1999, www.communications.uci.edu/releases.

Chapter 8. Derelicts

Data on derelicts are found in Edgar A. Haine, *Disaster at Sea* (New York: Cornwall, 1983).

Mary Celeste

"J. Habakuk Jephson's Statement" is in Arthur Conan Doyle, *The Captain of the Polestar and Other Tales*, among other anthologies. "The Adventure of the Sussex Vampire" is in *The Case-Book of Sherlock Holmes*. See Martin Booth, *The Doctor and the Detective: A Biography of Sir Arthur Conan Doyle* (New York: St. Martin's, 1997); Matthew E. Bunson, *Encyclopedia Sherlockiana* (New York: Macmillan, 1994); and Richard Lancelyn Green and John Michael Gibson, *A Bibliography of A. Conan Doyle* (Oxford: Clarendon Press, 1983).

The most reliable book concerning the *Mary Celeste* is Charles Edey Fay, *Mary Celeste: The Odyssey of an Abandoned Ship* (Salem, Mass.: Peabody Museum, 1942); Fay's theory of the abandonment differs from mine. MacDonald Hastings, *Mary Celeste: A Centenary Record* (London: Michael Joseph, 1972), offers a good summary of Celesteana. Gershom Bradford presented his waterspout theory in "*Mary Celeste*. No, Not Again!" *American Neptune* 10 (July 1950): 191–202 and (somewhat revised) in *The Secret of Mary Celeste and Other Sea Fare* (Barre, Mass.: Barre, 1966). Less persuasive theories are laid out energetically in Oliver W. Cobb, "The 'Mystery' of the *Mary Celeste*," *Yachting*, February 1940, 33–34, 98, 100; J. G. Lockhart's two books (with radically different theses), *A Great Sea Mystery: The True Story of the Mary Celeste* (London: Philip Allan, 1927) and *The Mary Celeste and Other Strange Tales of the Sea* (London: Rupert Hart-Davis, 1952); and in John Maxwell, *The Mary Celeste* (London: Jonathan Cape, 1979). The seaquake theory is proposed by D. Williams in "The *Mary Celeste*: A Classic Seaquake Encounter!," www.deafwhale.com.

Eyewitness accounts of waterspouts quoted here include John Kostecki, in the CNN "Inside Sailing" Web site, December 28, 2001; Ludde Ingvall, in the online newsletter *Scuttlebutt*, December 28, 2001; Quentin DeGrasse, "I Survived a Waterspout," and David Ludlum, "The Vineyard Waterspout," both in *New England's Disastrous Weather* (Camden, Maine: Yankee Books, 1990); and for the cruising boat on the Chesapeake, Gershom Bradford's article cited above. Wind speed data and photographs from the yacht *Illbruck* were passed on to me by Joe Sienkiewicz of the National Weather Service Marine Prediction Center. On the meteorology of waterspouts, see William J. Kotsch, *Weather for the Mariner*, 2nd ed. (Annapolis: Naval Institute Press, 1977). For Azores weather, see Robert B. Silverman, *Cruising Guide to the Azores*, 2nd ed. (N.p.: n.p., 1985). Water and air temperatures are from NOAA, www.nodc.noaa.gov/dsdt/cwtg, and from newspapers. The quotes concerning the noise of storms are from Lincoln Colcord, *The Drifting Diamond* (New York: Macmillan, 1912) (my thanks to Nick Dean for bringing this quotation to my attention); Dominique Wavre in *Scuttlebutt*, December 11, 2000; and Larry Rosenfeld in *Scuttlebutt*, January 30, 2001.

First Draft

The account of Miles Necas's cruise and disappearance is based on my experience in the crew of *Toscana* and on her log; on correspondence with Kris Beach; and on the U.S. Coast Guard accident report on the incident dated December 2, 1996, which I obtained though a Freedom of Information Act request and which includes a photocopy of Necas's log for June 7–27, 1996 (I have standardized the grammar and spelling in the log). See also Eric C. Hiscock, *Around the World in Wanderer III* (London: Oxford University Press, 1956).

Portions of this section first appeared in *Cruising World*, December 1996, and are reprinted with the permission of the editor.

Chapter 9. "Amazing Graces"

Jonah and Paul's Storms

Among the commentaries on the Book of Jonah that I consulted are Karin Almbladh, *Studies in the Book of Jonah* (Uppsala: Acta Universitatis Upsaliensis, 1986), which includes material on views of the sea in ancient Israel; Anthony R. Ceresko, "Jonah," in *The New Jerome Biblical Commentary*, ed. Raymond E. Brown, Joseph A. Fitzmyer, and Roland E. Murphy (Englewood Cliffs, N.J.: Prentice Hall, 1990); James Limburg, *Jonah: A Commentary* (Louisville: Westminster/John Knox, 1993), the source of the quotation from the Talmud; and Phyllis Trible, "The Book of Jonah: Introduction, Commentary, and Reflections," in *The New Interpreter's Bible*, vol. 7 (Nashville: Abingdon, 1996). Trible writes of her lifelong attachment to the story in her *Rhetorical Criticism: Context, Method, and the Book of Jonah* (Minneapolis: Fortress Press, 1994). For the book's recent interpretation in the broader culture, see Yvonne Sherwood's sometimes eccentric *A Biblical Text and Its Afterlives: The Survival of Jonah in Western Culture* (New York: Cambridge University Press, 2000). My thanks to Rabbi Lawrence Troster and to Leah Ruth Robinson Rousmaniere for their insights. For the Book of Jonah's use in Jewish and Christian liturgy, see S. Y. Agnon, *Days of Awe* (New York: Schocken, 1948), and Thomas M. Bolin, *Freedom beyond Forgiveness: The Book of Jonah Re-examined* (Sheffield, Eng.: Journal for the Study of the Old Testament/Sheffield Academic Press, 1997), the source of the data about early Christian art. On the book's psychological themes, see André Lacocque and Pierre-Emmanuel Lacocque, *The Jonah Complex* (Atlanta: John Knox Press, 1981).

Emotional numbing is discussed in Bessel A. van der Kolk's interview with Martin L. Korn in *Medscape Mental Health* 6, no. 5 (2001).

For Paul's shipwreck, see Richard J. Dillon, "Acts of the Apostles," in *The New Jerome Biblical Commentary*; Joseph A. Fitzmyer, *The Acts of the Apostles*, in The Anchor Bible (New York: Doubleday, 1998); and Jefferson White, *Evidence and Paul's Journeys* (Hilliard, Ohio: Parsagard Press, 2001). *The Interpreter's Dictionary of the Bible* (Nashville: Abingdon, 1962) includes discussions of ships in Paul's time. There is a helpful commentary on the seamanship in Paul's storm by a nineteenth-century shipmaster in Samuel Eliot Morison, "Captain Codman on the Mutiny in Dorchester Church, and the Seamanship of Saint Paul," *American Neptune* 2 (April 1942): 99–106.

John Newton and "Amazing Grace"

The definition of grace is from *The Interpreter's Dictionary of the Bible*. The fullest discussion of "Amazing Grace" as a hymn is in Raymond E. Glover, ed., *The Hymnal 1982 Companion*, vol. 3A (New York: Church Publishing, 1994). For their thoughts on the hymn and its success, I thank Sally Campbell, St. John's Church, Cold Spring Harbor, New York; Gerre Hancock, organist and master of choristers, St. Thomas Church, New York, N.Y.; and David Shuler, organist and director of music, St. Luke in the Fields Church, New York, N.Y.

On hymns and shape-note music see Timothy A. Smith, "Antebellum Hymn Repertory of the Southern Singing School," *Hymn* 41 (April 1990): 18–26, and Michael Stone, "Singing the Sacred Harp," *RootsWorld*, www.rootsworld.com.

On Newton, see John Newton and William Cowper, *Olney Hymns in Three Books* (London: Tegg, 1779); Josiah Bull, *John Newton* (London: Religious Tract Society, 1868), which quotes Newton's diary entries; D. Bruce Hindmarsh, *John Newton and the English Evangelical Tradition* (Oxford: Clarendon Press, 1996); Bernard Martin, *John Newton: A Biography* (London: William Heinemann, 1950); David Douglas, "Amazing Grace: A Journey in Time and Faith," *Hymn* 49 (July 1998): 9–12; and Janet M. Todd, "The Preacher as Prophet: John Newton's Evangelical Hymns" *Hymn* 31 (July 1980): 150–54, 158.

On sea stories as metaphors, see Robert Foulke, *The Sea Voyage Narrative*, Twayne's Studies in Literary Themes and Genres (New York: Twayne, 1997), and Donald Wharton's introduction to *In the Trough of the Sea: Selected American Sea-Deliverance Narratives, 1610–1766* (Westport, Conn.: Greenwood Press, 1979). On the symbolism of shipwrecks, see George P. Landow, *Images of Crisis: Literary Iconology, 1750 to the Present* (London: Routledge and Kegan Paul, 1982).

Chapter 10. The Ulysses Generation in the Southern Ocean

Jonathan Raban's comments are in his interview with Michael Upchurch in *Glimmer Train*, fall 1993. *Heart Light*'s experience in the 1994 Queen's Birthday storm is reported by Diviana Wheeler (under the byline Diviana) in her book *Heart Light: Rescue at Sea* (Auckland: Random House New Zealand, 1995) and in Tony Farrington, *Rescue in the Pacific: A True Story of Disaster and Survival in a Force 12 Storm* (Camden, Maine: International Marine, 1996). On belief systems and survival, see John Leach, *Survival Psychology* (New York: New York University Press, 1994).

On William Albert Robinson, see his *To the Great Southern Sea* (New York: Harcourt Brace, 1956) and *Return to the Sea* (Tuckahoe, N.Y.: John de Graff, 1972). On sailing in the Southern Ocean, see Richard Henry Dana Jr., *Two Years before the Mast*; Joshua Slocum, *Sailing Alone around the World*; Francis Chichester, *Gipsy Moth Circles the World* (1967; reprint, Camden, Maine: International Marine, 2001); Joseph Conrad, *The Mirror of the Sea*; and Derek Lundy, *Godforsaken Sea* (New York: Random House, 1998). The quotation by William H. S. Jones is in Miles Smeeton's *Once Is Enough* (see below). Reports on Southern Ocean conditions in modern racing yachts are from the Internet newsletter *Scuttlebutt*, November 16, 2001 (Grant Dalton and John Kostecki) and November 21, 2001 (Knut Frostad, Mark Christensen); from the online magazine *SailNet*, January 29, 2001 (Bill Biewenga); and from the Team Adventure Web site, www.teamadventure.org, February 23, 24, and 26, 2001 (Cam Lewis).

For the Ulysses generation, see J. R. L. Anderson, *The Ulysses Factor: The Exploring Instinct in Man* (New York: Harcourt Brace Jovanovich, 1970). The Tilman quotation is from his *Mischief in Patagonia*, in H. W. Tilman, *The Eight Sailing/Mountain-Exploration Books* (Seattle: Mountaineers, 1987). George Mallory's long quotation is in "Quotes from Everest," www.mnteverest.net/quote. html. Concerning aging and community, see Craig Lambert, "The Talent for Aging Well," *Harvard Magazine*, March–April 2001. My thanks to my brother Peter for bringing this interesting article to my attention.

On the Smeetons, see Miles Smeeton's books: *Once Is Enough* (1959; reprint, Camden, Maine: International Marine, 2001), about *Tzu Hang*'s two attempts on Cape Horn in 1957; *Because the Horn Is There* (1970; reprint, London: Granada, 1985), on the successful third try; and *The Sea Was Our Village* (Sidney, B.C.: Gray's, 1973), on the purchase of *Tzu Hang* and the couple's other voyages. His collection of children's poems is *Alligator Tales (and Crocodiles Too!)* (Gretna, La.: Pelican, 2001). The sailing directions for Patagonia are quoted in William Albert Robinson, *To the Great Southern Sea*. See also Miles Clark's superb biography of the couple, *High Endeavours: The Extraordinary Life and Adventures of Miles and Beryl Smeeton* (Saskatoon, Sask.: Western Producer Prairie Books, 1991). John Guzzwell told of the first capsize in *Trekka Round the World* (London: Rupert Hart-Davis, 1963) and provided further comments in a telephone conversation and during a delightful sail around Poulsbo Bay, Washington.

Acknowledgments

A COMPLEX PROJECT like this requires many hands and brains. I could not have completed, much less begun, this one without the assistance and encouragement of many friends. Most are acknowledged in the Sources sections, but here I wish to thank a few people who helped me along the remarkable stormy voyage that runs from Jonah to Beryl Smeeton and Miles Necas.

I begin, of course, with Leah Ruth Robinson Rousmaniere, my wife, who often set aside her own writing to help me with mine, including offering insights on the Psalms and tutorials on Hebrew roots. My children—Will and Dana Rousmaniere of Gloucester, and Dana and Marinell Rousmaniere of Roslindale—provided all kinds of assistance and encouragement. My brother Peter, sister Kate, and parents James A. and Jessie Rousmaniere read and helpfully commented on chapters, as did Brewster Righter. My brother Ned was a fountain of valuable information on developments in the area of post-traumatic stress disorder. Dr. Walter Penk, an authority in that field to whom I was introduced by Dale Rousmaniere, gave much time to reviewing a draft and steering me clear of errors. The book's many roots came together to form a single growth during early conversations and correspondence with Alex Barnett, Jon Paulus, Nick Dean, and Dave Switzer, among others. My agent, Timothy Seldes, and editor, Jonathan Eaton (with his colleagues at International Marine), have been nothing but strongly supportive from the start.

INDEX

Numbers in *italic* refer to pages with illustrations, maps, or photographs

A

abandoned ships, 211–14. See also *First Draft*; *Mary Celeste*

Abyssinian Church (Portland, Maine), 112–13

Adler, 89, 94, 96, *97*, *104*

adventuring, amateur, 274–77. *See also* "strenuous life" philosophy

African Americans, and *Portland*, 111–13

"Alastor, or The Spirit of Solitude," (Shelley, Percy Bysshe), 6

Albion, Robert Greenhalgh, 39

Alcott, Bronson, 50

Alice Knowles, 222, 224

amateur sailing and racing, 155, 157–63, 169–72, 264–68

"Amazing Grace" (hymn), 249–52, 259

The American Coast Pilot (Blunt), 40, 43, 55

Ames, Dick: and family, 147–48, 150–51; on *Hamrah*, 152–53, 164, 167–68, *170–71*; memorials to, 180–81; at Merryweather Camp, 148, 150. See also *Hamrah*

Ames, Dorothy Abbott, 147

Ames, Harry: and family, 147, *149*, 150; on *Hamrah*, 164, 167–68, *170–71*; memorials to, 180–81. See also *Hamrah*

Ames, James Barr: buys land in Maine, 138, 139; death of, 146; and physical activity, 140

Ames, James Barr (younger), 147, 148, *149*, 181–82

Ames, Margaret Fuller Glover: concerns about transatlantic race, 156; and family, 147, *149*, 150–51, 152; life after accident, 178–80, 182–87; naming of, 53

Ames, Phyllis. *See* Cox, Phyllis Ames

Ames, Richard (elder), 147, 148, 181

Ames, Richard (grandson), 181–82

Ames, Robert Russell: and family, 147–48; on *Hamrah*, 151–53, 164, 166–67, *170–71*, 181; memorials to, 181. See also *Hamrah*

Amoco Virginia, 121

Apia (Samoa), 91, 92, 93, *97*, *100–101*, 103. See also *Calliope*

Ariel: building of, 5, 10, *11*, 12; map of route, *16*; recovery of, 20; wreck narrative, 1–2, 15–17. *See also* Shelley, Percy Bysshe

An Authentic Narrative of Some Remarkable and Interesting Particulars (Newton), 254, 255–57

B

Baer, George W., 88, 105

"The Ballad of the *Calliope*" (Paterson), 103, 105

Bangs, Capt. Elijah, 34–35

Bangs, Capt. Henry, 28; abandons ship, 47; background of, 34–35; exhaustion of, 55–56; fate of, 58; makes navigational errors, 45–46, 54–56; weather tools not used, 43–44. See also *Elizabeth* (1850)

barometers, 43

Bay of Lerici (Italy), 5–6, 13, *16*

Bay State, *119*, 120, 125, 135

Beach, Dan and Kris, 232. See also *First Draft*

Because the Horn Is There (Smeeton), 276–77

Beck, Horace, 8

Before the Wind (Tyng), 78

beliefs. *See* faith, of mariners; superstitions, and the sea

Bennett, James Gordon, Jr., 157–58

Bermuda Race, 1934, 152–54. *See also* Day, Thomas Fleming

Bible, sea portrayed in, 9, 240–48, 262

Bismark, Otto von, 89

Blanchard, Capt. Hollis, *128*; consults Weather Bureau, 120; departs Boston, 109, 120–21; reputation of, 125–27, 134–36; tries to save ship, 122–25. See also *Portland*

Blunt, Edmund March, 40

Blunt's. See *American Coast Pilot* (Blunt)

Bolivar, 5, *11*

Boothbay/Boothbay Harbor (Maine), 60, 68–69, 73

Boston (Mass.) harbor, *119*

About the Author

JOHN ROUSMANIERE is one of the most respected and widely read boating writers. *Fastnet, Force 10*, his first-person account of one of the worst storms in sailing history, has been continuously in print in three languages for more than twenty years. Rousmaniere, who has sailed more than 35,000 miles, also wrote America's most widely used sailing manual, *The Annapolis Book of Seamanship*, now in its third edition. He has written histories of yachting and the America's Cup, and edited several books, including yacht designer Olin Stephens's highly praised autobiography, *All This and Sailing, Too.*

Besides his thirteen books on maritime history and seamanship, he has written books on the histories of religion, law, business, and education. His articles have appeared in the leading boating magazines as well as in *American Heritage*, the *New York Times*, and other publications. He has appeared on CNN, the Learning Channel, A&E, and other television outlets and has lectured widely on seamanship and storms. He won the Captain Fred E. Lawton Boating Safety Award for outstanding contribution to boating safety through the media.

Rousmaniere has earned postgraduate degrees in divinity from Union Theological Seminary and history from Columbia University. The descendant of a French soldier who fought for America in the American Revolution, he has two grown sons and lives in Stamford, Connecticut, and New York with his wife, mystery writer Leah Ruth Robinson.